Reading Disabilities: A Developmental Language Perspective

Reading Disabilities: A Developmental Language Perspective

■

Edited by

Alan G. Kamhi, Ph.D.
Memphis State University
Memphis, Tennessee

Hugh W. Catts, Ph.D.
University of Kansas
Lawrence, Kansas

ALLYN AND BACON
Boston London Toronto Sydney Tokyo Singapore

A Division of Simon & Schuster, Inc.
160 Gould Street
Needham Heights, MA 02194

Printed in the United States of America

10 9 8 7 6 5 4 3 2 95 94 93 92 91

ISBN 0-316-48252-8

Library of Congress Cataloging in Publication Data
Main entry under title:

Reading disabilities : a developmental language perspective / edited by Alan G. Kamhi, Hugh W. Catts.
p. cm.
Bibliography.
Includes index.
1. Reading disability. 2. Children—United States—Language.
3. Reading—United States—Remedial teaching. I. Kamhi, Alan, G.
1950- . II. Catts, Hugh William, 1949-
LB1050.5.R379 1989
372.4'3—dc19 88-22917
CIP

Contents

CONTRIBUTORS

Benita A. Blachman, Ph.D.
School of Education
Department of Special Education
Syracuse University
Syracuse, New York

Hugh W. Catts, Ph.D.
Department of Speech, Language and Hearing
University of Kansas
Lawrence, Kansas

Frank M. Cirrin, Ph.D.
Department of Speech Pathology and Audiology
Idaho State University
Pocatello, Idaho

Alan G. Kamhi, Ph.D.
Department of Audiology and Speech Pathology
Memphis State University
Memphis, Tennessee

Froma P. Roth, Ph.D.
Department of Hearing and Speech Sciences
University of Maryland
College Park, Maryland

Cheryl M. Scott, Ph.D.
Department of Speech and Language Pathology and Audiology
Oklahoma State University
Stillwater, Oklahoma

Nancy J. Spekman, Ph.D.
Marianne Frostig Center of Educational Therapy
Pasadena, California

Carol E. Westby, Ph.D.
Multicultural Training Program in Communicative Disorders
University of New Mexico
Albuquerque, New Mexico

Dedication

To Beth, Susan, Alison, and Franny

ACKNOWLEDGMENTS

The origins of this book can be traced to a hotel restaurant in Cincinnati, Ohio, about five years ago. The table conversation was at first typical, ranging from a discussion of the relationship between language and cognition to predictions of the Cleveland Indians winning the pennant in our lifetimes. On the table was, among other things, a matchbook. During a lull in the conversation, someone spelled aloud the word on the matchbook: H–a–t–h–a–w–a–y. After a short period of silence, one person said, ''Spell it again,'' while another person uttered ''Hathaway.'' As other words were spelled aloud, it became apparent that there was considerable variability among the four adults in playing this simple auditory memory, spelling game.

Our early ruminations about individual differences in reconstructing words spelled aloud led to a scholarly interest in the relationship between spoken and written language disorders and eventually the writing of this book. This book represents the culmination of five years of research on the speech and language processing abilities of children and adults with reading problems. This research has been accompanied by numerous discussions with colleagues and practitioners and most of all between the two of us. Out of these discussions evolved the developmental language perspective espoused in this book. Although we were warned by several colleagues that books strain the best of friendships, ours survived intact despite a poorly timed sailing trip and the usual disagreements about revisions, terminology, and the color of the book. We mistakenly thought that we had to pick one color for the book.

Several people contributed to the writing of this book, most notably six of our friends and colleagues who wrote chapters. Thank you Cheryl, Froma, Nancy, Benita, Carol, and Frank for meeting all of the deadlines and graciously accepting our suggestions for revisions. It has been a pleasure working with all of you; we hope the feeling has been mutual. Special thanks go to Kathy Fulmer, Daria Mauer, and Stephanie Rash for their help with the references and putting together the final manuscript. The staff at College-Hill Press, particularly Marie Linvill and Randy Stevens, have been very helpful and supportive throughout the writing of this book. We would also like to acknowledge the support we have received from our respective departments at Memphis State University and the University of Kansas.

Acknowledgments are, of course, not complete without recognition of the support of friends and family. We wish to thank those special friends for putting up with a seemingly endless series of questions about the book and the usual mood swings that accompany such a prolonged endeavor. This book benefitted greatly from their suggestions, encouragement, and good cheer.

Families typically contribute little to the contents of books. Other than providing some useful anecdotes about early literacy socialization, ours were no exception. What they do provide, however, is a place to rest a weary mind and a tired body. They allow you to hide behind the newspaper, watch meaningless baseball games, and be grumpy after spending long days being friendly and cheerful. In short, families have us at our worst. Too infrequently thanked, this book is dedicated to them.

Alan G. Kamhi
Hugh W. Catts

Preface

Reading has received more attention than any other aspect of education in the United States and other literate societies. Frequently, schools and teachers are judged by how successful they are in teaching children to read. It has been suggested that the ability to read well is the basis for success in school and later in life (Gibson & Levin, 1975). Success in school is clearly dependent on reading, and even though it is possible to have a successful career without being able to read well, individuals who have difficulty reading are at a distinct disadvantage.

There have been many books written about reading and reading disabilities. *Reading Disabilities: A Developmental Language Perspective* is unique, however, in that most of the contributors are speech–language pathologists whose primary area of expertise is language development and disorders. To understand why language specialists are interested in reading disabilities, one must understand the change that has occurred over the last 20 years in theories of reading and reading disability.

Before the early 1970s, reading was viewed as a visual perceptual process (Hermann, 1959), and reading problems were attributed to deficits in visual-perceptual processes. One notable exception was Helmer Myklebust who began emphasizing the auditory bases of learning disorders in the early 1950s. His well-known book *Auditory Disorders in Children: A Manual for Differential Diagnosis* was published in 1954. Thirteen years later, Myklebust teamed with Doris Johnson to write their seminal book on learning disabilities, in which they discussed the relationship between oral and written language disorders and noted that children with reading disabilities often had spoken language deficits.

Johnson and Myklebust's work laid the foundation for the now widely accepted view that reading problems reflect limitations in language, not general cognitive limitations or limitations of visual perception. This view was espoused in the early 1970s by Mattingly (1972), Lerner (1972), and Shankweiler and Liberman (1972). Evidence supporting language-based theories of reading has accumulated rapidly in the last 15 years. Among the contributors to the research base have been Liberman, Perfetti, Shankweiler, Stanovich, and Vellutino. Lower-level phonological correlates of reading as well as higher-level syntactic and semantic correlates have been studied in this work (Liberman & Shankweiler, 1985; Perfetti, 1985; Stanovich, 1985, 1986; Vellutino, 1979; also see Jorm & Share, 1983, and Wagner & Torgesen, 1987), and this research is discussed in several chapters of this book.

The change from visually based theories of reading disabilities to language-based theories opened the door for language specialists to become interested in reading problems. Speech-language pathologists have become increasingly more involved in the identification, assessment, and treatment of individuals with reading problems. The contribution a language specialist can make in serving individuals with reading disabilities is gradually becoming recognized by parents, teachers, reading specialists, special educators, and psychologists. This recognition has led to an increase in the collaborative efforts between these professionals and speech-language pathologists.

These collaborative efforts have been encouraged and supported by writings and presentations from well-known language specialists. Almost 15 years ago, Norma Rees (1974) and Joel Stark (1975) wrote about the role of the speech-language pathologist in reading disabilities. More recently, several books have successfully bridged the gap between language and reading disabilities, including Wallach and Butler's (1984) book on language-learning disabilities, Simon's (1985a, b) two volumes on classroom skills and success, Carrow-Woolfolk and Lynch's (1982) text on children's language disorders, and Snowling's (1985) volume on written language problems in children. Professional organizations, such as the National Joint Committee on Learning Disabilities, Council for Exceptional Children, the Orton Dyslexia Society, and the American Speech-Language-Hearing Association have also played an important role in making interdisciplinary efforts a reality. These organizations have published position statements advocating cooperative efforts among the various professions. In addition, the scholarly publications supported by these associations have disseminated considerable information about language and reading and the benefits of collaborative efforts.

Wallach and Butler's book on language-learning disabilities is particularly noteworthy. This book represented the first comprehensive attempt to integrate research on language development and disorders with research on learning and reading disabilities. Like the present book, contributors were all language specialists. In fact, two of the contributors to the present book also wrote chapters in Wallach and Butler's book. Although written by language specialists, many from the field of speech-language pathology, Wallach and Butler's book bridged the gap across disciplines. Their book provided an important link for professionals involved in serving children and adolescents with language-based learning disorders. The present book attempts to make this link even stronger by focusing more closely on the relationship between language and reading disorders.

It is now generally taken for granted that reading is a language-based skill. The interesting questions concern the exact nature of the relationships between the processes that underlie spoken and written language. This book represents our attempt to pull together a large body of theoretical, experimental, and clinical literature concerned with language and reading disorders. Since we began investigating the relationship between spoken and written language development and disorders, we have become increasingly struck by the different ways research on language and reading has been interpreted by theorists and practitioners. The gamut runs from an emphasis on phonological processing skills and their associated cognitive processes to higher-level language, text processes, and metacognitive abilities.

Because oral language and reading are not simple constructs, simplistic answers to questions about the relationship between the two are precluded. For example, there are five general domains of language knowledge: syntax, morphology, semantics, phonology, and pragmatics (see Chapter 1). A variety of cognitive resources are involved in acquiring and using each of these different kinds of language knowledge. In addition, different representational systems might be involved in storing these rules. Reading is also not easily reduced to one measure or knowledge domain. Word recognition, for example, involves different cognitive processes and language knowledge than text comprehension. The relationship between spoken and written language is made even more complex when one attempts to account for the changes that occur in language and reading skills throughout development.

In this book, we make it clear that it is not enough to recognize that reading is a language-based ability or that reading problems reflect limitations in language. To develop appropriate assessment plans and effective teaching and remedial procedures, it is necessary to develop an appreciation for the specific relationships that exist between spoken and written language components and how these relationships change throughout development. Although considerably more research is needed to specify the exact nature of these developmental relationships, it is possible to draw some general conclusions from current research. For example, the relationship between spoken and written language is dynamic and reciprocal. In other words, the relationship changes throughout the developmental period and the direction of causality can go both ways; from spoken language to reading and from reading to spoken language. Another conclusion is that phonological processing abilities account for the majority of individual variation in early reading performance, whereas other kinds of language, conceptual, and metacognitive knowledge/processes account for a greater portion of reading ability in more proficient readers.

These two conclusions are consistent with the developmental language perspective of reading disabilities taken in this book. The gist of this perspective is that reading is a language-based skill. Reading requires sophisticated linguistic and metalinguistic knowledge as well as a full range of cognitive and metacognitive processes. This perspective is consistent with the view presented in Chapter 2 which suggests that a large group of children with reading disabilities are best characterized as having a developmental language impairment. The manifestations of this impairment change throughout development. For example, during the preschool years, it may be manifested in difficulty learning spoken language, whereas during the early school years, it may be manifested in difficulty learning to read. During adolescence and adulthood, the impairment may be manifested in writing and spelling problems, poor verbal short-term memory, and expressive language problems. In Chapter 3, we suggest that the language impairment is initially caused by a basic processing limitation that disrupts the acquisition and use of spoken and written language. Reciprocal causation factors contribute further to the specific manifestations of the language impairment.

We have attempted to maintain a developmental language perspective in each of the individual chapters. Some chapters, however, lend themselves better to this perspective than others. The heterogeneity of the population, terminologic issues, service delivery concerns, and the overwhelming complexity of language and underlying cognitive processes sometimes obscure the common thread that links the individual chapters of the book. That common thread is language. All of the chapters consider aspects of spoken and written language development and disorders.

This book consists of 11 chapters. The first three chapters lay the theoretical foundation for the rest of the book. Chapter 1 provides an in-depth comparison of the processes and knowledge involved in spoken and written language. A basic theme of this chapter is that reading is not a simple derivative of spoken language. Although spoken and written language have much in common, there are also fundamental differences between the two. For example, spoken and written language converge in the vocabulary, syntactic, script, story, and world knowledge both share. Important differences, however, exist in the biological and social bases of spoken language development and the explicit phonological awareness required to become a proficient reader. The development of reading is also reviewed in this chapter.

In Chapters 2 and 3, the characteristics of individuals with reading problems and the possible causes of such problems are presented. It is generally recognized that the population of individuals with reading problems is heterogeneous with respect to the severity of the reading disability, the presence of associated deficits (e.g., intellectual, emotional, and attentional), and cognitive-linguistic abilities. Chapter 2 begins with a discussion of terminological and definitional issues. The educationally-based term *reading disability* is used in most chapters of the book because it is the one most widely used by researchers and practitioners. At the end of this section, we present our view that many children with reading disabilities are best characterized as having a developmental language impairment. In the next part of the chapter, the subtyping literature is reviewed. Subtyping studies are one approach to impose some order on the heterogeneous population of individuals with reading problems.

In Chapter 3, the heterogeneity issue is addressed by considering the factors that contribute to individual differences in reading ability. These factors include visual perception, phonological processing, higher-level language knowledge, memory, metacognitive abilities, and motivational states. The interaction, or reciprocal causation effects, between various factors is emphasized. One of the principal claims made in this chapter is that reading disabilities are best described as a language-based disorder, but are best explained by a basic processing limitation. Several possibilities about the nature of this processing limitation are discussed in this chapter and in Chapter 4.

Chapters 4 and 5 focus on the relationship between phonological processing abilities and reading. In Chapter 4, literature is reviewed demonstrating the strong link between phonological processing deficits and reading disabilities. This literature provides overwhelming evidence that disabled readers have deficits in encoding, retrieving, and using phonologically based memory codes. After reiterating the importance of phonological awareness for learning to read, Benita Blachman, in Chapter 5, describes procedures to assess and train phonological awareness.

Chapters 6 and 7 are devoted to higher-level language and metacognitive processes. In Chapter 6, Froma Roth and Nancy Spekman examine the relationship between higher-level spoken language abilities and reading performance. They review relevant literature in semantics, syntax, and discourse. In Chapter 7, Carol Westby discusses how schema knowledge and metacognitive processing function in comprehending narrative and expository text. Westby provides information to aid practitioners in assessing and facilitating higher-level comprehension processes.

In Chapters 8 and 9, Cheryl Scott focuses on writing development and disorders. Most research and theory about written language development and disorders has focused on reading at the expense of writing. This is somewhat analogous to describing how children come to understand oral language, but not how they learn to produce it. In Chapter 8, Scott describes the various components involved in writing and then provides a comprehensive discussion of the development of writing. Chapter 9 focuses on the problem writer and procedures to assess and improve writing abilities in students of various ages and skill levels.

Chapter 10 offers a small dose of reality. In the best of all possible worlds, individuals with reading problems would receive the best treatment possible from professionals most qualified to serve them. In reality, however, there are many barriers that limit and sometimes prevent the realization of this goal. These barriers include economic and political constraints, eligibility regulations, professional territoriality, and a reluctance to adopt innovative service delivery models. In Chapter 10, Frank Cirrin provides a detailed review of the problems in providing optimal services. Knowledge of the constraints on optimal service delivery is a necessary first step toward the best-of-all-possible-worlds ideal. In recognition of the difficulty in attaining such an ideal, Cirrin offers some specific suggestions to provide optimal services in the face of existing constraints on such services.

In Chapter 11, we return to some of the major themes of the book. We reiterate and further defend our characterization of reading disabilities as a developmental language impairment. In doing so, we discuss the factors that may contribute to individual differences in spoken and written language abilities.

REFERENCES

Carrow-Woolfolk, E., and Lynch, J. (1982). *An integrative approach to language disorders in children*. New York: Grune & Stratton.

Gibson, E., and Levin, H. (1975). *The psychology of reading*. Cambridge, MA: MIT Press.

Hermann, K. (1959). *Reading disability*. Copenhagen: Munksgaard.

Johnson, D., and Myklebust, H. (1967). *Learning disabilities: Educational principles and practices*. New York: Grune & Stratton.

Jorm, A., and Share, D. (1983). Phonological recoding and reading acquisition. *Applied Psycholinguistics, 4*, 103–147.

Lerner, J. (1972). Reading disability as a language disorder. *Acta Symbolica, 3*, 39–45.

Liberman, I., and Shankweiler, D. (1985). Phonology and the problems of learning to read and write. *Remedial and Special Education, 6*, 8–17.

Mattingly, I. (1972). Reading, the linguistic process, and linguistic awareness. In J. Kavanagh and I. Mattingly (Eds.), *Language by ear and by eye*, 133–147. Cambridge, MA: MIT Press.

Myklebust, H. (1954). *Auditory disorders in children: A manual for differential diagnosis*. New York: Grune & Stratton.

Perfetti, C. (1985). *Reading ability*. New York: Oxford University Press.

Rees, N. (1974). The speech pathologist and the reading process. *ASHA, 16,* 255–258.

Shankweiler, D., and Liberman, I. (1972). Misreading: A search for causes. In J. Kavanaugh and I. Mattingly (Eds.), *Language by ear and by eye,* 293–317. Cambridge, MA: MIT Press.

Simon, C. (1985a). *Communication skills and classroom success: Assessment of language-learning disabled students.* San Diego, CA: College-Hill Press.

Simon, C. (1985b). *Communication skills and classroom success: Therapy methodologies for language-learning disabled students.* San Diego, CA: College-Hill Press.

Snowling, M. (1985). *Children's written language difficulties.* Windsor, Berkshire: Nfer-Nelson.

Stanovich, K. (1985). Explaining the variance in reading ability in terms of psychological processes. What have we learned? *Annals of Dyslexia, 35,* 67–96.

Stanovich, K. (1986). Matthew effects in reading: Some consequences of individual differences in the acquisition of literacy. *Reading Research Quarterly, 21,* 360–406.

Stark, J. (1975). Reading failure: A language-based problem. *ASHA, 17,* 832–834.

Vellutino, F. (1979). *Dyslexia: Theory and research.* Cambridge, MA: MIT Press.

Wagner, R., and Torgesen, J. (1987). The nature of phonological processing and its causal role in the acquisition of reading skills. *Psychological Review, 101,* 192–212.

Wallach, G., and Butler, K. (1984). *Language learning disabilities in school-age children.* Baltimore: Williams & Wilkins.

1

Language and Reading: Convergences, Divergences, and Development

Alan G. Kamhi
& Hugh W. Catts

Much has been written recently about the linguistic bases of reading (Catts & Kamhi, 1986; Liberman, 1983; Perfetti, 1985; Stanovich, 1986; Vellutino, 1979). It is now generally acknowledged that reading shares many of the same processes and sources of knowledge involved in talking and understanding. In reading this literature, however, it is possible to get the erroneous impression that reading is a simple derivative of spoken language; that is, if one can talk, one can read. This is not the case at all, as will become clear in this chapter. Although spoken language and reading have much in common in terms of the knowledge and processes they tap, there are also fundamental, nontrivial differences between the two. Knowledge of the similarities and differences between spoken language and reading is critical for understanding how children learn to read and why some children have difficulty learning to read.

The chapter begins with a definition of language and reading. This is followed by an in-depth comparison of the processes and knowledge involved in processing spoken and written language. Other differences between spoken and written language are then discussed. The chapter concludes with the presentation of a stage model of reading development.

Defining Language

Current definitions of language are broad based and highly integrative. An example of such a definition was endorsed by the American Speech-Language-Hearing Association several years ago (ASHA, 1983, p. 44).

> Language is a complex and dynamic system of conventional symbols that is used in various modes for thought and communication. Contemporary views of human language hold that: (a) language evolves within specific historical, social, and cultural contexts; (b) language, as rule governed behavior, is described by at least five parameters—phonologic, morphologic, syntactic, semantic, and pragmatic; (c) language learning and use are determined by the interaction of biological, cognitive, psychosocial, and environmental factors; and (d) effective use of language for communication requires a broad understanding of human interaction including such associated factors as nonverbal cues, motivation, and sociocultural roles.

As reflected in the definition, it is generally agreed that there are five parameters of language. These parameters are described briefly below.

Phonology

Phonology is the aspect of language concerned with the rules that govern the distribution and sequencing of speech sounds. It includes a description of what the sounds are and their component features (phonetics) as well as the distributional rules that govern how the sounds can be used in various word positions and the sequence rules that describe which sounds may be combined. For example, the /ʒ/ sound that occurs in the word *measure* is never used to begin an English word. Distributional rules are different in different languages. In French, for example, the /ʒ/ sound can occur in the word-initial position, as in *je* and *jouer.* An example of a sequence rule in English would be that /r/ can follow /t/ or /d/ in an initial consonant cluster (e.g., *truck, draw*), but /l/ cannot.

Semantics

Semantics is the aspect of language that governs the meaning of words and word combinations. Sometimes semantics is divided into lexical and relational semantics. *Lexical semantics* involves the meaning conveyed by individual words. Words have both intensional and extensional meanings. Intensional meanings refer to the defining characteristics or criterial features of a word. A dog is a dog because it has four legs, barks, and licks people's faces. The extension of a word is the set of objects, entities, or events to which a word might apply in the world. The set of all real or imaginary dogs that fit the intensional criteria becomes the extension of the entity *dog*.

Relational semantics refers to the relationships that exist between words. For example, in the sentence *The Panda bear is eating bamboo*, the word *bear* not only has a lexical meaning, but it also is the agent engaged in the activity of eating. *Bamboo* is referred to as the "patient" (Chafe, 1970) because its state is being changed by the action of the verb. Words are thus seen as expressing abstract relational meanings in addition to their lexical meanings.

MORPHOLOGY

In addition to the content words that refer to objects, entities, and events, there is a group of words and inflections that convey subtle meaning and serve specific grammatical and pragmatic functions. These words have been referred to as *grammatical morphemes*. Grammatical morphemes modulate meaning. Consider the sentences *Elmore is playing tennis*, *Elmore plays tennis*, *Elmore played tennis*, and *Elmore has played tennis*. The major elements of meaning are similar in each of these sentences. The first sentence describes an action currently in progress, whereas the next sentence depicts a habitual occurrence. The last two sentences describe actions that have taken place sometime in the past. What differentiates these sentences are the grammatical morphemes (inflections and auxiliary forms) that change the tense and aspect (e.g., durative or perfective) of the sentences.

SYNTAX

Syntax refers to the rule system that governs how words are combined into larger meaningful units of phrases, clauses, and sentences. Syntactic rules specify word order, sentence organization, and the relationships between words, word classes, and sentence constituents, such as noun phrases and verb phrases. Knowledge of syntax enables an individual to make judgments of well-formedness or grammaticality. For example, all mature English speakers would judge the sentence *The boy hit the ball* as well formed and grammatical. In contrast, the sentence *Hit the boy ball the* would be judged as ungrammatical. It should be apparent that knowledge of syntax plays an important role in understanding language.

Pragmatics

Pragmatics concerns the use of language in context. Language does not occur in a vacuum. It is used to serve a variety of communication functions, such as declaring, greeting, requesting information, and answering questions. Communicative intentions are best achieved by being sensitive to the listener's communicative needs and nonlinguistic context. Speakers must take into account what the listener knows and does not know about a topic. Pragmatics thus encompasses rules of conversation or discourse. Speakers must learn how to initiate conversations, take turns, maintain and change topics, and provide the appropriate amount of information in a clear manner. It has become evident recently that different kinds of discourse contexts involve different sets of rules (Lund & Duchan, 1988). The most frequent kinds of discourse children encounter are conversational, classroom, narrative, and event discourse.

Defining Reading

There are two basic components involved in reading: word recognition (decoding) and comprehension. Definitions of reading can be divided according to whether the decoding or comprehension aspects of reading are emphasized. Reading defined as decoding ability is the skill of transforming printed words into spoken words. Although this definition is a narrow one, its advantage is that it delineates a restricted set of processes to be examined (Perfetti, 1986). The broader definition is that reading is thinking guided by print. Reading ability defined in this way is associated with skill in comprehending texts. Although this is the more accepted definition of reading among researchers and practitioners, Perfetti (1985) has pointed out both practical and theoretical problems with this broad definition.

The basic problem is that with a broad definition of reading, a theory of reading necessarily becomes a theory of inferencing, a theory of schemata, and a theory of learning. Crowder (1982), who is one of the few psychologists to advocate a decoding definition of reading, made the following analogy between the ''psychology of reading'' and the ''psychology of braille.'' The psychology of braille does not include such topics as inferences and schema application. These abilities involve broad-based cognitive-linguistic processes. Crowder argued that it was superfluous to make the study of these higher-level processes part of the study of braille. The study of braille is necessarily restricted to the decoding process, or how a reader decodes braille into language. By analogy, the study of reading should also be restricted to the decoding process. Instead, the psychology of reading has, in effect, become the study of thinking guided by print.

Perfetti goes on to make the point that there may be two levels of literacy, one for each definition. Basic literacy conforms to the narrow definition, whereas intelligent literacy conforms to the broad definition. The decoding definition is thus more applicable to children learning to read, whereas the thinking definition is more applicable to older children and adults who learn from text.

Models of Oral and Written Language Comprehension

In a book about language and reading, an understanding of the similarities and differences between oral and written language is crucial. The sections that follow compare the specific processes and knowledge involved in comprehending oral and written language. First, however, a brief overview of models of language and reading is necessary.

Models of oral and written language comprehension have often been divided into three general classes: bottom-up, top-down, and interactive. Bottom-up models view oral and written language comprehension as a step-by-step process that begins with the initial detection of an auditory or visual stimulus. The initial input goes through a series of stages in which it is "chunked" in progressively larger and more meaningful units. Top-down models, in contrast, emphasize the importance of scripts, schemata, and inferences that allow one to make hypotheses and predictions about the information being processed. Familiarity with the content, structure, and function of the different kinds of oral and written discourse enables the listener and reader to be less dependent on low-level perceptual information to construct meanings.

Reliance on top-down versus bottom-up processes varies with the material being processed and the skill of the reader. Bottom-up processes are presumed to be necessary when reading isolated, decontextualized words, whereas top-down processes facilitate not only word recognition but also discourse-level comprehension. Top-down processes are especially important when reading partially illegible material, such as cursive writing. The model of oral and written language comprehension depicted in Figure 1-1 includes both bottom-up and top-down components.

Many current theorists of language and reading (Butler, 1984; Duchan, 1983; Perfetti, 1985; Rumelhart, 1977; Stanovich, 1985) have

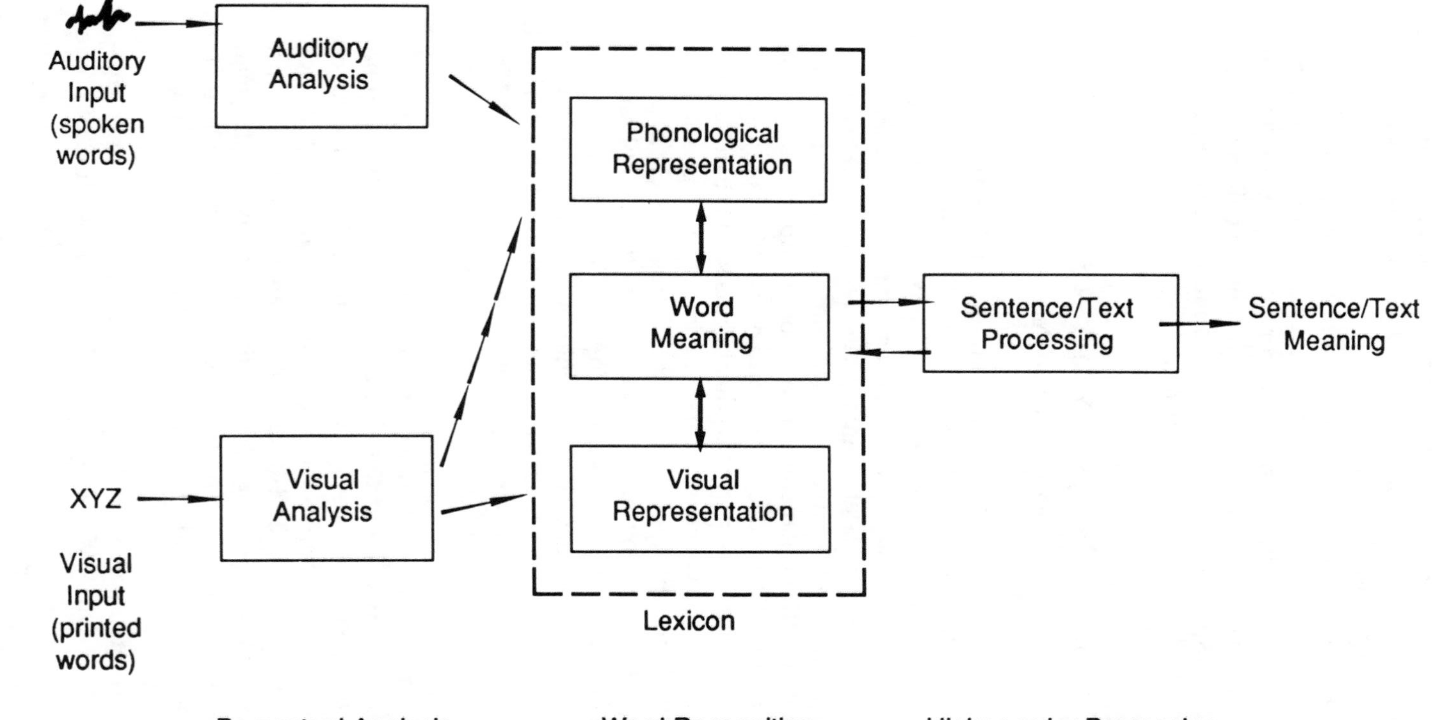

FIGURE 1-1. A model of spoken and written language comprehension. From Catts, H.W., and Kamhi, A.G. (1986). The linguistic basis of reading disorders: Implications for the speech-language pathologist. *Language, Speech, and Hearing Services in Schools, 17,* p. 31. Copyright 1986 by the American Speech-Language-Hearing Association. Reprinted by permission.

advocated interactive models in which both bottom-up and top-down processes contribute to reading and language comprehension. An interactive model of reading comprehension, for example, would acknowledge that individuals must have proficient word recognition skills as well as higher-level linguistic and conceptual knowledge in order to be good readers. Whereas bottom-up and top-down models emphasize sequential processing, interactive models allow for parallel or simultaneous processing to occur. Although more complex than serial processing models, parallel processing models better reflect the types of processing that occur in complex tasks such as reading. Computer simulations are usually used to test the adequacy of parallel processing models.

Just and Carpenter (1987), for example, have developed a simulation parallel processing model called READER. READER progresses through a sentence one word at a time, operating on several levels in parallel. These levels include a lexical level, semantic and syntactic level, referential level, and text-schema level. (The knowledge associated with each of these levels will be described later in this chapter.) The processing of each word proceeds as far as possible at all levels before moving on to the next word. McClelland (1986) described another parallel processing model, called PABLO. For this model, the levels include visual features, letters, words, syntax, and semantics. A detailed review of parallel processing models of reading is beyond the scope of this chapter. For our purposes, it is sufficient to note that simplistic serial processing models, whether bottom-up or top-down, cannot adequately capture the complex interactions that occur within and between different processing levels.

COMPARING ORAL AND WRITTEN LANGUAGE COMPREHENSION

We have found that the model depicted in Figure 1-1 provides a useful framework for comparing the processes and knowledge involved in comprehending spoken and written language. This model, though unique, shares components with other processing models (Cutting & Pisoni, 1978; Thomson, 1984). Although the components of the model will be discussed in a linear, bottom-up fashion, the model should be viewed as an interactive one that allows for parallel processing within and between levels.

PERCEPTUAL ANALYSES

The input to the perceptual analyses is speech or print. In order for this input to be recognized, it must be detected and analyzed. The sensory mechanisms involved in the detection of speech and print are distinctive; the ear is used to detect speech and the eye is used to detect print. Sensory deficits involving hearing or vision place a child at risk for spoken and written language problems. Children born deaf cannot detect the speech signal through the auditory modality and, as a result, have considerable difficulty developing intelligible speech. Individuals who are blind cannot detect print through the visual modality. Braille, which relies on the tactile modality, is one way to bypass the visual deficit. An intact auditory system provides the blind another avenue to access text material by way of tape recordings.

Once the input has been detected, the segmental and suprasegmental features of spoken and written words are analyzed. In speech the processes underlying phonetic discrimination and phonemic identification are involved. *Phonetic discrimination* refers to the ability to hear (detect) the difference between two sounds that differ phonetically and acoustically. For example, the initial *t* in the word *tap* is phonetically different from the final *t* in the word *bat*. Phonetic differences that do not affect meaning are often referred to as *allophonic variations*. If the *t* sounds in the words above were changed to *k* sounds, this would change the meaning of the words. *Tap* would become *cap*, and *bat* would become *back*. The phonetic differences between /t/ and /k/ are thus also phonemic differences because they change the meaning of the word. The task for the young child learning language is to determine which differences between sounds make a difference in meaning.

The language a child is learning determines which phonetic differences are phonemic. In Japanese, for example, the differences between /r/ and /l/ are allophonic. In English, however, the phonetic differences between /r/ and /l/ make a difference in meaning. In French the front rounded vowel /y/ is phonemically different from the back rounded /u/. An American who does not make this distinction will not be able to differentiate between the words *tout* (all) and *tu* (you). These examples are meant to illustrate that learning phonemic categories requires knowledge of the language being learned. The acquisition of phonological knowledge about language necessarily involves higher-level conceptual processes. Low-level perceptual processes, such as detection and discrimination, do not lead to knowledge about phonemic categories. In light of these points, it is important to note that in most listening situations, individuals seldom have to make distinctions between minimal phoneme pairs (e.g., *p/b* in the words *pin* and *bin*) that are common stimuli on tests of discrimination. In many instances, lexical and higher-level language knowledge often eliminate the need for phonemic-level identification.

In reading, just as with speech, discrimination and identification processes might be involved. In reading, *discrimination* refers to the ability to see (detect) the visual differences between letters. *Identification* requires knowledge of the correspondences between letters and phonemes. For example, the child who confuses the letters *b* and *d* in words such as *bad* and *dad* is often said to have a visual discrimination problem. It is more likely, however, that the child can perceive the visual differences between the letters *b* and *d* but has not learned that the letter *b* is associated with the phoneme /b/ and the letter *d* is associated with the phoneme /d/. In other words, the child has not learned the phoneme-letter correspondences for these two sounds.

To illustrate the difference between a low-level visual discrimination ability and a higher-level conceptual (identification) ability, consider the following analogy. One of the first author's colleagues has two young boys, ages 7 and 10. I see these children about once a year. Although I know that one of the boys is named Michael and the other Joshua, each year I forget which name goes with which child. Although the boys look alike in that they both have dark hair and are obvious siblings, they are easily differentiated. The 10 year old, for example, is much bigger than the 7 year old. The difficulty I have associating each child with his own name is clearly not caused by a visual discrimination problem. I have no difficulty differentiating the bigger child from the smaller one. My problem is associating a particular characteristic or set of characteristics with a name. This is similar to the problem children have associating the features of a particular phoneme with a letter.

These examples are meant to illustrate that discriminating between speech sounds or letters is not particularly difficult. With respect to language, the difficulty is learning which phonetic differences make a difference in meaning. With respect to reading, the difficulty is learning which sounds are associated with which letters. In both cases, what often appear to be discrimination problems are in fact higher-level language-based conceptual problems.

WORD RECOGNITION PROCESSES

Reading and spoken language begin to share similar knowledge domains and processes in the word recognition stage. Until this point, the processing of print and speech involves different sensory and perceptual processes. In the word recognition stage, the features identified in the previous perceptual stage are used to access the mental lexicon. The words heard or seen must activate or be associated with previously stored concepts in the individual's mental lexicon. These stored concepts in the mental lexicon represent one's vocabulary. Importantly, the content and structure of the mental lexicon is essentially the same for reading and oral language. The content of the lexicon includes information about the word's phonological or visual form as well as information about the word's meaning and how the word relates to other words. Just and Carpenter (1987, p. 62) provided an example of what kind of conceptual information would appear in the mental lexicon for the word *pencil*.

> It refers to an instrument used for writing or drawing; it is a manmade physical object, usually cylindrical in shape; and it functions by leaving a trail of graphite along a writing surface. . . . A pencil is one of a class of writing instruments and a close relative of the *pen*, *eraser*, and *sharpener*.

The mental lexicon also includes syntactic and semantic information that indicates part of speech (e.g., noun, verb, or adjective) and possible syntactic and semantic roles. For example, the syntactic information about *pencil* might indicate that it is a noun that functions semantically as an instrument (''She wrote the letter with a pencil'') or as a patient (''Peggy bought a pencil'').

The structure of the mental lexicon has received considerable research attention during the past 20 years. Network models (see Figure 1-2) consisting of nodes corresponding to concepts and features have been a popular way to depict the structure of the lexicon (Collins & Loftus, 1975; Collins & Quillian, 1969). Early network models were hierarchical in nature, with the ordering in the hierarchy defined by set inclusion relations. For example, higher-order concepts such as *animal* included lower-order concepts such as *bird* and *sparrow*. More recent network models have been referred to as *heterarchical*, reflecting concepts from ill-structured domains (see Figure 1-3) (Just & Carpenter, 1987). Although theorists might differ in their portrayal of the content and structure of the mental lexicon, they generally agree that the mental lexicon is the same for language and reading. The way in which word meanings are accessed can differ, however, in spoken language and reading.

In processing speech, word meaning is accessed through a word's phonological representation. The output of the perceptual analysis is a representation of a word's acoustic and phonetic features. These acoustic-phonetic representations of speech input are used by the listener to activate or instantiate a word's phonological representation in the lexicon. This may involve the listener attempting to match acoustic-phonetic representations with phonological representations. Phonological representations are directly linked to a word's meaning because this information is stored together for each word in the mental lexicon.

Phonological representations stored in the mental lexicon can take one of several forms. Words may be represented in clusters (e.g., ''it's a''

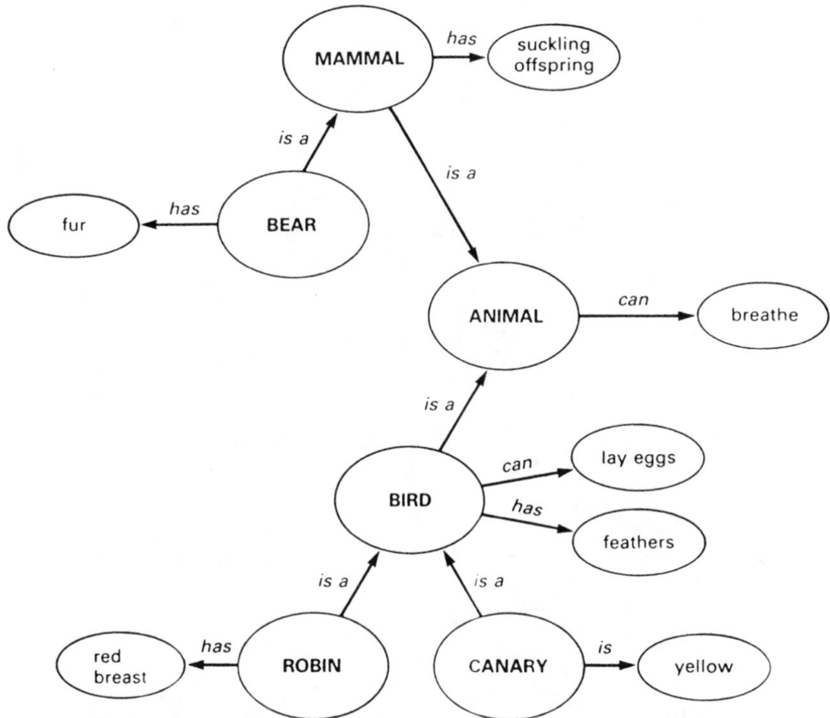

FIGURE 1-2. A depiction of the hierarchial relations among the concepts of *animal, bird, robin,* and the like in semantic memory. Concepts are linked to their superordinates with *is a* relations. Properties of the concept are linked by relations such as *has, is,* and *can*. From Just, M., and Carpenter, P. (1987). *The psychology of reading and language comprehension*, p. 66. Boston: Allyn and Bacon. Copyright 1987 by Allyn and Bacon, Inc. Reprinted by permission.

as "itsa"; "did you know" as [dɪdʒəno]) or as individual words without discrete syllable or phonemic information. Alternatively, phonological representations might contain syllablic and phonemic segments. Although the nature of phonological representations can differ, it is unlikely that preliterate children represent speech as discrete phonemic segments. Most children are not aware until age five or six that speech consists of discrete sounds (Fox & Routh, 1975; Liberman, Shankweiler, Fischer, & Carter, 1974; Tunmer & Bowey, 1984).

In contrast to speech, in which there is only one way to access a word's meaning, in reading there are two ways: indirectly, by way of a phonological representation, or directly, by way of a visual representation (see Figure 1-1). Use of a visual representation to access the lexicon

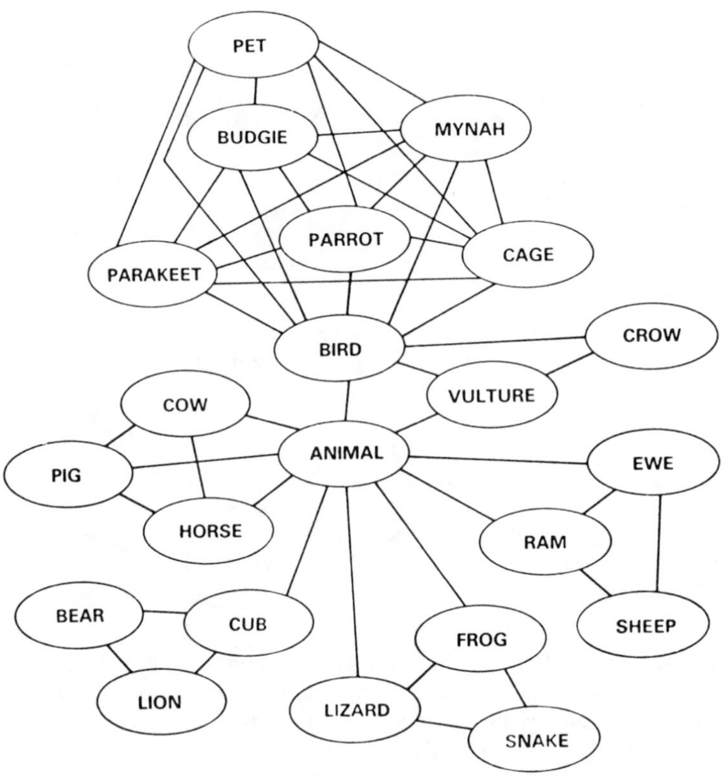

FIGURE 1-3. A depiction of a heterarchial network. (The labels on the links have been deleted.) From Just, M. and Carpenter, P. (1987). *The psychology of reading and language comprehension*, p. 67. Boston: Allyn and Bacon. Copyright 1987 by Allyn and Bacon, Inc. Reprinted by permission.

is variously referred to as the direct, visual, look-and-say, or whole-word approach. In accessing the lexicon in this way, the reader locates the word in the lexicon whose visual representation contains the same segmental and/or holistic features as those identified in the previous perceptual analysis stage. In other words, a match is made between the perceived visual configuration and a visual representation that is part of the mental lexicon for the particular word.

In alphabetic languages, such as English, word meaning can also be accessed through a phonological representation (Baron, 1977).

Referred to as the *indirect* or *phonetic* approach, the reader uses knowledge of phoneme-grapheme correspondence rules to recode the visually perceived letters into their corresponding phonemes. Individual phonemes are then blended together to form a phonological sequence that is matched to a similar sequence in the lexicon. The phonetic approach is particularly important in the development of reading. The ability to decode printed words phonetically allows children to read words they know but have never seen in print. Reading by the phonetic approach also causes the child to attend to the letter sequences within words. The knowledge gained about letter sequence makes the child's visual representations more precise (Barron, 1981).

Reading by the phonetic route is thus similar to speech recognition in that a word is recognized by way of its phonological representation. There is one important difference, however, in using phonological representations to access meaning in comprehending spoken and written language. In order to successfully use the phonetic route in reading, one must have explicit awareness of the phonological structure of words; specifically, the knowledge that words consist of discrete phonemic segments (Treiman & Baron, 1981). These segments are not readily apparent to young children because the sound segments of speech are blended together in the acoustic signal. For example, the word *cat* is one acoustic event; its sound segments do not correspond exactly to its three written symbols. Although preschool children might show some phonological awareness, several years of explicit instruction and practice is usually required for a child to become efficient in using the phonetic approach.

Discourse-Level Comprehension Processes

Up to this point, we have considered the processes involved in recognizing words. Oral and written language, however, consists of longer discourse units, such as sentences, conversations, paragraphs, and texts. In order to understand these kinds of discourse-level units, listeners and readers rely on their previously stored knowledge about language and the world. Basic reasoning abilities, such as drawing analogies and making inferences, as well as metacognitive abilities, such as comprehension monitoring, also play an important role in understanding spoken and written language. In the sections to follow, we consider the roles that higher-level language, cognitive, and metacognitive knowledge play in processing discourse-level information.

Syntactic and Morphologic Knowledge

A variety of syntactic cues are used by listeners and readers in comprehending speech and text. These cues include word order, grammatical morphemes, and function words such as relative pronouns, conjunctions, and modals. Listeners and readers often use syntactic cues to figure out the meaning of unknown words. Grammatical morphemes, for example, provide information about word classes. Adverbs are signaled by the inflections *-ly* and *-y,* whereas adjectives are marked by the suffixes *-able* and *-al*. Verbs are signaled by the inflections *-ed, -ing,* and *-en*. Nouns are marked by definite and indefinite articles, plural and possessive markers, and suffixes such as *-ment* and *-ness*. The reason why readers are able to make any sense at all out of a sentence like ''Twas brillig and the slithy toves did gyre and gimble in the wabe'' is that inflections (*y* and *s*) and syntactic markers (*the* and *did*) provide cues about grammatical form class.

SEMANTIC KNOWLEDGE

Semantic knowledge includes information about the roles played by various participants in a state or action and the circumstances surrounding these states and actions. Semantic information is often represented in terms of predicates, arguments, and circumstances that correspond to actions, roles, and the time and place when the action or state occurs (Van Dijk & Kintsch, 1983). Consider the sentence *Alison gave the doll to Franny yesterday.* The predicate *give* has three arguments: agent (Alison), object or patient (doll), and beneficiary (Franny). The circumstance is that the action took place yesterday.

WORLD KNOWLEDGE

World knowledge is sometimes considered a part of semantic knowledge. Some theorists, however, find it useful to distinguish between knowledge that is specific to language and knowledge that is more general in nature. Just and Carpenter (1987) questioned why the sentence *Jake ate the sausage with relish* is ambiguous, while *Jake ate the ice cream with relish* is not. They answered that one knows that relish is not normally eaten with ice cream. Such information is not specific to language; instead, it reflects general knowledge about the tastes of foods to assign with *relish*.

World knowledge can be divided into knowledge of specific content domains and knowledge of interpersonal relations. Specific content domains would include academic subjects such as history, geography, mathematics, and English literature; procedural knowledge such as how to fix a car, tie a shoelace, and play tennis; and scriptlike knowledge of familiar events. Interpersonal knowledge involves such things as knowledge of human needs, motivations, attitudes, emotions, values, human behavior, personality traits, and relationships. It should be evident how these kinds of world knowledge play an important role in processing spoken and written language.

Referential Knowledge

An important aspect of spoken and written language comprehension is determining the referent of the utterance or text. For example, a sentence such as *He flew to Tunis* has only one syntactic and semantic representation, but can have many different referents (Just & Carpenter, 1987). One can envision a person flying on a jet or a propeller-driven plane, or being self-propelled a la Superman. It is also possible to have two different phrases that have the same referent. *The morning star* and *the evening star* both refer to the planet Venus.

In processing discourse-level units of speech and text, listeners and readers construct an initial referential representation and then modify this representation based on the information provided in subsequent sentences. Individuals must recognize instances that refer to the same referent (i.e., coreference) and distinguish these instances from references to new entities (Just & Carpenter, 1987). It is generally acknowledged that the determination of coreference is based on (1) language-based cues, such as word meanings, syntax, and anaphoric devices; and (2) knowledge-based cues that evoke the individual's knowledge of the content domain (Just & Carpenter, 1987).

The linguistic information provided by pronouns about gender, number, and case are examples of cues that indicate the referent of an expression. Other language cues for coreference include the use of the definite article *the* instead of the indefinite *a*. The definite article generally indicates that the referent of the phrase has already been mentioned or is easily inferred. Synonyms are also useful devices to refer to the same entity.

The referential level of processing is especially important in recalling larger amounts of spoken and written discourse. Listeners and readers generally remember the gist of what was said or written rather than the particular words or structures used to express the content. A study by Bransford, Barclay, and Franks (1972) is often cited in support of this point. In this study, subjects were presented with sentence pairs such as *The frog sat on a log* and *The fish swam under the log*. Many subjects later reported that they had read the sentence *The fish swam under the frog*. This sentence was, of course, inferred from the first two sentences. Just and Carpenter added that the reason subjects thought they had read this sentence was that it accurately described the referential situation they had mentally represented. One would expect the same sort of inference if the sentences were presented orally. Findings such as these suggest that memory for spoken and written discourse is based to a large extent on the nature of the referential representation constructed.

Script Knowledge

In order to understand larger units of spoken and written discourse, one must not only make sense of each sentence, but also determine the relation of a particular sentence to other portions of the discourse. One must also construct an interpretation of the discourse that integrates information about participants, objects, and events described in the discourse. Perfetti (1985) referred to this process as *text modeling*. An individual's world knowledge, as mentioned earlier, plays an important role in constructing such interpretations. World knowledge is supplemented, however, by specific knowledge about event content and structure.

The main theory of the organization of content knowledge grew out of attempts (e.g., Schank & Abelson, 1977) to explain comprehension of narrative texts involving familiar events such as a birthday party or going to a restaurant. The knowledge that represents a familiar event is a particular type of schema called a *script*. Scripts can be thought of as generalized event representations or structures. Scripts contain slots for the components of an event, such as the main actions, participants, goals, and typical position of each action. Scripts make it easier to process familiar events by providing individuals with a coherent structure into which they can insert new information. Scripts also allow individuals to add necessary information that might be omitted in spoken or written discourse. For example, familiarity with a restaurant script allows listeners and readers to anticipate some mention of the menu. If no mention of the menu is made, but information about the kind of restaurant is given (e.g., Italian), one can infer the contents of the menu.

Story-Schema Knowledge

There has been considerable interest in recent years about children's knowledge of story structure (Mandler & Johnson, 1977; Stein & Glenn, 1979). Stories are an important genre for all societies. Stories also represent a type of discourse that is common in both oral and written language. Some discourse types, such as conversation, are particular to spoken language, whereas others, such as poetry and novels, are particular to written language.

The structure of stories is thought to follow some sort of story schema or story grammar. A story schema can be viewed as a mental framework that contains slots for each story component, such as a setting, goal, obstacle, and resolution. Story grammars represent a slightly different characterization of the knowledge of story structures. Story grammars specify the hierarchical relations among the components more directly than a story schema (Mandler & Johnson, 1977; Stein & Glenn, 1979). Story grammars attempt to specify the structural organization of stories in the same way that syntactic grammars specify the structural organization of sentences (Just & Carpenter, 1987, p. 231). The main structural components of a story are a setting and an episode. The setting introduces the characters and the context of the story. Episodes can be further divided into an initiating event, internal response, attempt, consequence, and reaction. Knowledge of the structure and function of stories, like knowledge of scripts, can facilitate comprehension of spoken and written language (Just & Carpenter, 1987; Perfetti, 1985).

Making Inferences

Inferencing is involved at several different levels in the processing of spoken and written discourse. Inferencing is required when there is no explicit indication in written or spoken discourse about how the sentences or clauses are related. At the referential level, for example, one might have to infer that two different expressions are referring to the same entity. At the discourse level, one might have to infer how a fact fits into a particular script or story grammar slot. Inferences can pertain to any aspect of meaning, including space, time, causality, and logic. Inferences are based on knowledge of the world, of scripts/schemata, and of the information that has already been processed.

Two main types of inferences have been identified (Just & Carpenter, 1987): backward and forward inferences. *Backward inferences* are variously referred to as bridging assumptions (Clark & Clark, 1977), integrative inferences, or connective inferences. Consider the sentences *He walked into the classroom* and *The chalk was gone.* In these sentences, there is no previous mention or antecedent for *the chalk*. In order to make sense of these sentences, one must infer that the classroom should have chalk in it. More specifically, the inference (or *implicature*) *The room referred to by* a room *once had chalk in it* must be added to the representation of the two sentences actually spoken or written.

Forward inferencing embellishes or elaborates the representation of the currently spoken or read text. For example, given the sentence *The two year old was eating ice cream*, a forward inference might be that the child's face was smeared with ice cream.

METACOGNITIVE ABILITIES

Metacognition refers to one's knowledge and control of one's cognitive system (Brown, 1987). Metacognitive abilities have been associated with several aspects of reading, including establishing the purpose for reading, identifying important ideas, activating prior knowledge, evaluating the text for clarity, compensating for failures to understand, and assessing one's level of comprehension (Brown, 1987). Brown added that it is not clear whether all or just certain components of these activities are metacognitive. The use of strategies to facilitate comprehension and comprehension monitoring are discussed briefly below.

The use of strategies to facilitate reading comprehension has been well documented (Brown & Campione, 1984; Markman, 1977). There are several different kinds of strategies an individual might use to facilitate comprehension, such as taking notes, underlining selected sentences in the text, or verbal rehearsal. To effectively implement these strategies, an individual must not only be aware of them, but also know something about their potential effects on learning. Although much of the interest in strategy use has focused on reading comprehension, the ability to implement strategies should also aid oral language comprehension.

The ability to monitor comprehension plays an important role in both oral and written language comprehension (Dollaghan & Kaston, 1986; Markman, 1977). When faced with a word, sentence, paragraph, or other text element that is not understood, it is necessary to do something to aid understanding, such as ask for clarification or reread the text in question. Individuals who are adept at monitoring their comprehension are more proficient processors of oral and written language. A more complete discussion of the relationship between metacognitive knowledge and reading appears in Chapter 3.

DIFFERENCES BETWEEN ORAL AND WRITTEN LANGUAGE

Delineating the similarities and differences in the processes and knowledge involved in oral and written language comprehension only begins to capture the complex relationship that exists between language and reading. Consider, for example, the following question posed by Gleitman and Rozin (1977, p. 2): Why is the more general and complex task of learning to speak and understand less difficult and less variable than what appears to be a trivial derivative of this (i.e., learning to read and write)? These authors proceed to point out two major differences between learning to talk and learning to read. We add a third important difference.

The first major difference is that learning to read requires explicit knowledge of the phonological aspects of speech. To become an efficient reader, one must learn the various correspondences between phonemes and letters. The knowledge that words consist of discrete phonemes is crucial for constructing phoneme-grapheme correspondence rules. Oral language comprehension also requires analysis of utterances into smaller phonological units. But the analysis of the speech stream by the listener is carried out below the level of consciousness by evolutionarily old and highly adapted auditory perceptual processes (Lieberman, 1973). The human perceptual system is thus biologically adapted to process speech. In contrast, the human visual system is not biologically adapted to process written text. This introduces the second major difference between learning to talk and learning to read: Reading is a comparatively new and arbitrary human ability for which specific biological adaptations do not yet exist.

A third important difference is that almost all humans are reared in environments in which spoken language is the principal means of communication. Thus, not only are we biologically endowed to learn language, but we are socialized to use language to communicate. This is not true for reading. More than 40 percent of the world's adult population cannot read or write at all, and an additional 25 percent do not have sufficient mastery of a writing system for it to be of significant practical use (Stubbs, 1980, cited in Perara, 1984). The principal reason for this high rate of illiteracy is that individuals are raised in environments in which reading has little cultural value.

In a recent book, *Children's Writing and Reading: Analysing Classroom Language,* Perara (1984) discussed additional differences between spoken and written language. An understanding of these differences helps to further explain why reading is not a simple derivative of spoken language. The differences discussed in the next section, however, in no way diminish the linguistic bases of reading and reading disorders.

In order to emphasize the contrasts between written and spoken language, Perara compared prototypical speech (conversation) to prototypical written language (literature or informative prose). She acknowledged, however, that there is a full range of spoken and written discourse types. Certain discourse types have some characteristics of written language and vice versa. For example, speeches and lectures can be planned much like writing, radio talk lacks a visual dimension and contextual support, and tape recordings are durable.

Physical Differences

Whereas speech consists of temporally ordered sounds, writing consists of marks made on a surface (e.g., paper) in a two-dimensional space. As such, writing is relatively durable; it can be read and reread.

Speech, unless it is recorded, is ephemeral. It has no existence independent of the speaker. The durability of writing gives the reader control over how fast or slow to read. Certain texts can be savored, whereas others can be skimmed. The listener, in contrast, is tied to the fleeting speech of the speaker. Missed words or sentences will be lost if clarification is not requested.

Perara (1984, p. 161) noted that readers often have the benefit of a whole range of visual cues, such as running headlines, different-size type, color, and summaries or abstracts. In addition, a device such as the footnote allows the writer to provide additional information without interrupting the main thread of the text. Such devices allow the reader to decide the level at which he or she will read. The listener, in contrast, is completely dependent on the speaker's selection of material. Note, however, that the listener could choose not to listen to the speaker's message.

SITUATIONAL DIFFERENCES

The most frequent type of spoken language is face-to-face communication. Conversations are often interactive exchanges between two or more individuals. Questions are followed by answers, requests by responses, and statements by acknowledgments. When a listener does not understand something, a clarification is requested. Careful planning is not the rule in conversational discourse. When speakers pause too long before talking, they will usually be interrupted. Despite this time pressure to speak, misunderstandings are infrequent; when they occur, they are easily resolved by repeating or rephrasing the message. Nonverbal communication acts, such as gestures, facial expressions, and body postures, also help to clarify messages. Speakers and listeners also share the same nonlinguistic setting. People and objects that are visible can be referred to by pronouns rather than by noun phrases (even without prior reference). Also, many adverbials and prepositions can be expressed by *here, there,* and *like this.*

In constrast to spoken language, writing and reading are often individual endeavors. The writer receives no prompting about what to write and no immediate feedback on the clarity of the writing. But the writer is generally under less severe time constraints and can thus take more time and search for the best way to express a message. The writer can also correct and revise a text until a final copy is produced. Such care and precision is necessary in writing because there are no contextual and nonverbal cues to aid comprehension. The written text thus has to bear the whole burden of communication, which is one reason why writing is usually more precise than talking.

Functional Differences

One of the earliest needs to generate a writing system was to retain accurate records of property, commercial transactions, and legal judgments. A Chinese proverb holds that "The palest ink is better than the best memory." Writing has enabled the knowledge of centuries to accumulate, thus allowing each new generation to build on the ideas, discoveries, and inventions of the generation or generations before. Many academic subjects, such as history, geography, the physical sciences, and social sciences, owe their very existence to writing (Perara, 1984, p. 164). Another function not served by speech is labeling. Although speech is used to label objects in a referential sense, written labels serve more of an information function. Consider such labels as street names; signposts; nameplates on theaters, offices, and public buildings; brand labels; and danger warnings. Written language can also serve a variety of communicative functions, such as relating stories, events, and experiences; sharing information; and making requests. Finally, a specialized function of writing is found in literature. Societies have oral literatures, but oral literatures are restricted to a few types, such as ballads, epic poetry, drama, folk stories, and myths. Essays, novels, diaries, and memoirs are some of the genres that are particular to writing.

Perara has suggested that the most basic uses of writing involve the recording of facts, ideas, and information. In contrast, although speech also has an informative function, Perara has argued that an equally important function of speech is the role it plays in establishing and maintaining human relationships. She has noted that a large part of everyday speech with friends, acquaintances, and other individuals serves social-interpersonal functions rather than intellectual ones.

One advantage writing has over speech, according to Perara (1984, p. 165), is that it allows ideas to be explored at leisure and in private. Writing can thus become a means of extending and clarifying one's thinking and ideas. Often in conversation when a controversial topic is raised, there is a tendency for opinions to polarize. Someone who tries to take both sides of a issue might be pressed to select one particular view. In writing, however, one can take time to develop a line of thought, to weigh opposing arguments, to notice errors in reasoning, and to develop new lines of thinking.

Form Differences

The most obvious difference in form is that speech consists of sounds whereas written language consists of letters. As indicated earlier, this would not be so much a problem if speech sounds (i.e., phonemes) stood in one-to-one correspondence with written letters. Form differences between spoken and written language are not limited to the discrete segments (i.e., phonemes and letters) that make up speech and text. Spoken and written language also differ in how they represent suprasegmental, paralinguistic, and prosodic features. *Paralinguistic features* include pitch and timbre differences that distinguish male and female voices; general voice quality, such as breathiness, hoarseness, or nasality; and the general manner of how an utterance is produced, such as shouted, whispered, or spoken. Perara has pointed out that these features do not usually affect the actual meaning of an utterance; however, they may reflect the speaker's attitude about what is being said.

Prosodic features include intonation, stress, and rhythm. Perara presented four functions of prosodic features: (1) to enable the communicative intent of an utterance to differ from its grammatical form (e.g., *He's lost it* versus *He's lost it?*), (2) to group words into information units, (3) to place emphasis, and (4) to convey the speaker's attitude. These functions differ in the extent to which they can be reflected in writing. Whereas punctuation effectively changes the communicative intent of an utterance, it is not so effective in signaling which words belong together in information units. Italics, underlining, and the use of capital letters are some ways to distribute emphasis throughout a written utterance. But heavy use of these devices in formal writing is usually discouraged. Expressing attitudes in writing is clearly difficult. Perara (1984, p. 178) provided an example of how much attitudinal information is conveyed by prosodic features in the following quote of a journalist who listened to one of the Watergate tapes:

> Once you hear the tapes, and the tone in which he [Nixon] uttered the comments which previously have only been available in a neutral transcript, any last shred of doubt about his guilt must disappear.

Perara goes on to consider the extent to which the writing system represents the segmental and suprasegmental aspects of speech. Among other things, she pointed out that graphemes represent the "citation" (well-spoken) form of words rather than the degraded productions that often occur in fast speech (e.g., compare "did you know" to [dɪdʒəno]). Punctuation can signal the grammatical function of a sentence and mark some prosodic boundaries. The writer, however, has no conventional way to express voice quality, volume, rate of speech, rhythm, and intonational patterns.

DIFFERENCES IN GRAMMATICAL STRUCTURE

Samples of spoken language uncover relatively high frequencies of cordination, repetition, and rephrasing. Perara suggested that conversational samples are low in lexical density and high in redundancy. By this she meant that lexical items are spaced out, separated by grammatical words, and that a high number of total words is used to convey a relatively small amount of information. Written language, in contrast, is high in lexical density and low in redundancy. This results from the use of grammatical structures that decrease redundancy and increase lexical density.

Perara has suggested that in conversation it is more common to provide small amounts of information at a time. Most written language, by contrast, is more dense lexically as well as propositionally. Conversations, because of their interactive nature, are generally less coherent than writing. Speakers are free to change the subject at almost any point in a conversation. Topics need not be related in any logical way. In writing, however, an overall theme is necessary. Topic changes must be justified and explicitly made. Writing also has prescribed rules for organizing content. These rules cover the use of topic sentences, paragraph structure, and introductory and concluding statements.

BASIC FACTORS IN READING AND LANGUAGE DEVELOPMENT

It should be clear that although there is considerable overlap in the processes involved in spoken and written language, there are also many important differences between the two. These differences explain to a large extent why learning to read is not a simple derivative of learning to talk and to understand. In the definition of language given earlier in this chapter, it was stated that language learning and use are determined by the interaction of biological, cognitive, psychosocial, and environmental factors. Learning to read is also determined by the interaction of these four factors. However, the relative importance or weight of these factors for learning to read is not the same as it is for learning spoken language. Before reviewing the actual stages of reading development, we first consider the role that these factors play in reading and language development.

Biological factors are crucial in learning spoken and written language. As indicated earlier, however, one important difference between learning to talk and learning to read is that the analysis of the speech stream is carried out below the level of consciousness by evolutionary old and highly adapted auditory processes. In contrast, the human visual system is not biologically adapted to process written text. By itself, this difference does not necessarily make learning to read more difficult than learning to talk; it does suggest, however, that learning to read requires more attentional resources than does learning to talk.

Environmental factors play different but equally important roles in learning spoken and written language. As noted previously, almost all humans are reared in environments in which spoken language is the principal means of communication. Thus, not only are we biologically endowed to learn language, but we are also socialized to use language to communicate. It is extremely rare, for example, to find a child who did not develop language because of the absence of environmental input. The case of Genie (Curtiss, 1977) is an example of one of the few documented cases of such a child. As indicated earlier, about 40 percent of the world's adult population cannot read. In most cases, illiteracy is caused by environmental factors. Individuals reared in societies in which reading ability is not of cultural value will probably have little exposure to print and no formal instruction in reading.

Because the biological and social bases of reading are not as strong as they are for spoken language, psychosocial factors, such as motivational and attentional states, often play a more important role in learning to read than in learning to talk. Unless a child has a severe emotional disorder, such as autism, language learning will be relatively unaffected by motivational and attentional states. This is not the case in learning to read because reading requires a considerable amount of motivational and attentional resources. Reading difficulties in individuals with motivational and attentional problems have been well documented (Hallahan, Kauffman, & Lloyd, 1985).

Cognitive factors play a fundamental role in learning spoken and written language because spoken and written language are essentially cognitive achievements. Both rely on basic cognitive processes to encode, store, and retrieve information. In addition, the same store of linguistic and conceptual knowledge is tapped by readers as by speakers and listeners. Metacognitive abilities, however, play a more important role in learning to read than in learning to talk and understand. This is because children cannot reflect on their cognitive systems until they are approximately four years of age (Hakes, 1982). Thus, children cannot use metacognitive strategies to facilitate much of langage acquisition. Later developing aspects of language, such as reading, can be facilitated by such strategies.

STAGES OF READING DEVELOPMENT

In order to make sense out of the developmental changes that occur in children's oral and written language abilities, theorists and practitioners have found it useful to identify distinct developmental stages. For example, Roger Brown's (1973) five stages of language development based on *mean length of utterance* (MLU) are well known to students in child language. Stage models of development, however, tend to oversimplify development and obscure individual differences. Another problem with stage models is the way in which stages are differentiated. Quantitative criteria such as MLU make it easy to distinguish between stages, but they also risk not capturing important qualitative changes in development (Johnston & Kamhi, 1984). Attempting to reflect qualitative or structural changes is also problematic, however. One of the criticisms of Piaget's stages of cognitive development is that children perform at different stage levels for different tasks.

In spite of these concerns, stage models can capture basic developmental changes in ability and thus provide a framework for understanding the individual differences that exist between children. The stage model of reading presented below was developed by Jeanne Chall (1983) and is one of the most frequently cited models in the literature. Chall (1983, p. 10) cautions that her stage model should be viewed as a theory that needs to be confirmed or disconfirmed. She based her theory on several assumptions and hypotheses. Among the most important were the following:

1. Stages of reading development resemble stages of cognitive and language development. Reading stages have a definite structure and differ from one another in qualitative ways, generally following a hierarchical progression.
2. Individuals progress through the stages by interacting with their environment—home, school, community, and culture.
3. The existence of successive stages means that readers do different things with printed matter at each successive stage, although the term *reading* is commonly used for all of the stages.
4. Successive stages are characterized by a gradual improvement in the ability to read language that is more complex, more technical, and more abstract.
5. The reader's response to the text becomes more inferential, more critical, and more constructive.

Chall identified six stages of reading, beginning with Stage 0, the prereading stage. These stages are discussed below.

STAGE 0: PREREADING (BIRTH TO 5 TO 6 YEARS)

Until recently, the prereading stage has received little attention. However, it covers a greater period of time and encompasses more developmental changes than any of the other stages (Chall, 1983). From birth until the beginning of formal education (age five or six in the United States), children growing up in literate cultures accumulate knowledge about letters, words, and books. The term "literacy socialization" has been used to refer to the social and cultural aspects of learning to read. Literacy socialization focuses on the role of the environment in fostering the child's awareness of the purposes and conventions of print. During the prereading stage, children also learn a lot about language. Knowledge acquired about language is of two general types: (1) primary linguistic knowledge necessary to understand and produce well-formed utterances, and (2) metalinguistic knowledge that involves the awareness that language consists of discrete phonemes, words, phrases, and sentences. Of particular importance for learning to read is the awareness that words consist of discrete phoneme-sized units. The knowledge children acquire about literacy and language during the prereading period is discussed below.

LITERACY SOCIALIZATION

Van Kleeck and Schuele (1987) discussed three specific areas of literacy socialization: (1) literacy artifacts, (2) literacy events, and (3) types of knowledge children gain from literacy experiences. Most children growing up in middle-and upper-class homes are surrounded by literacy artifacts from the time of birth. Characters from nursey rhymes decorate walls, sheets and crib borders often have pictures and writing, alphabet blocks and books might be on the shelf, and T-shirts often have slogans or city names printed on them. In addition to the child's own possessions, homes are filled with such items as books, newspapers, magazines, mail, pens, crayons, and note pads.

More important than literacy artifacts are the literacy events children participate in and observe and the knowledge they acquire from these events. The most instructionally organized literacy event is reading stories to children. There is now considerable research that demonstrates the important role that reading activities play in literacy socialization (Heath, 1982; Snow & Goldfield, 1983). Heath, for example, found that there were three kinds of information children learn to talk about during book-reading routines: (1) *what* explanations, (2) *reason* explanations, and (3) *affective* explanations. Learning to respond to these kinds of questions prepares children for the types of questions they will encounter from teachers throughout elementary school. Not surprisingly, Heath found that children who had the most success learning to read in school came from an environment in which reading routines and written language were a dominant aspect of their daily lives.

The first author's older daughter, Alison, is an excellent example how early experience with print and stories influences later reading performance. My wife, who has a degree in comparative literature, and I are almost always reading. Like many bright children of overeducated parents, Alison began "reading" *Peter Rabbit* from memory when she was about two years old. This story had been read to Alison so many times that she had memorized the text that went along with each picture. She was also able to read nursery rhymes in the same fashion. To strangers who didn't know better, it appeared that Alison was actually reading.

My younger daughter, Franny, had even more exposure to print activities because of her older sister. Before Franny could walk, she would lie on the floor next to her five-year-old sister and draw on blank computer paper while Alison wrote stories. Now almost two years old, a nightly ritual is Franny sitting on my lap "reading" one of her books while I read the newspaper.

Preschoolers obviously learn a great deal about literacy before they actually learn how to read. It is not uncommon for children to enter kindergarten with the ability to recite the alphabet, recognize letters, use a typewriter or a computer, write their name and a few other words, and sight read a dozen or more written words. Children who begin school with such extensive knowledge about literacy have a considerable advantage in learning to read over children who come from environments in which literacy socialization is not a dominant aspect of their lives.

Linguistic Knowledge and Metalinguistic Awareness

During the prereading stage, children acquire considerable knowledge about language. This knowledge enables them to be fairly competent communicators by the time they enter school. By five years of age, children can express abstract conceptual notions involving temporal, spatial, and causal relations. These notions are often expressed in complex sentence structures that include multiple embeddings of subordinate, relative, and infinitive clauses. By five years of age, children also have considerable knowledge of familiar scripts and story structure.

As discussed earlier in this chapter, knowledge of syntactic, semantic, and discourse-level structures contributes to reading performance. More predictive of early reading performance, however, is a child's phonological awareness; that is, the ability to reflect on and make judgments about the discrete phonological properties of words (Bradley & Bryant, 1985; Mann & Liberman, 1984; Wagner & Torgesen, 1987).

Although phonological awareness is a late-developing skill for most children (Hakes, 1982), children as young as two years old begin to show some appreciation of the sound system. This awareness is seen in children's spontaneous speech repairs, rhyming behaviors, and nonsense sound play. One of our favorite examples of early phonological awareness comes from the first author's daughter, Alison, who at around age two put a plastic letter *T* in a cup and said "Look Daddy, I'm pouring tea." It is also not uncommon for preschool children to exhibit a specific awareness of sound-symbol associations. Van Kleeck and Schuele (1987) provided the following examples from three-year-old children: "/b/ is the sound for *bark* and *bar*, the 'buh' sound; "I know /d/ words—*daddy, dog*"; "There's an /s/ in the Safeway sign"; and "Tell me a food that starts with a—" (pp. 28–29).

Given the importance of the prereading stage for early reading success, it is somewhat curious that this stage is referred to as Stage 0 by theorists such as Chall. The 0 implies that not much happens. Yet, in fact, so much learning takes place during the prereading stage that it would probably be useful to divide this stage into a series of substages that would better reflect the different kinds of learning that take place during this period. Frith (1985), for example, proposed a logographic or whole-word stage to mark the end of the prereading stage and a transition to Chall's Stage 1. The logographic stage is characterized by the acquisition of about 20 sight words. Children in this stage are, for the most part, insensitive to letter order and phoneme-grapheme correspondences. They pay particular attention to the first letter in words and word shape.

STAGE 1: INITIAL READING OR DECODING (5 TO 7 YEARS)

This stage is marked by the learning of phoneme-grapheme correspondence rules. Frith (1985) referred to this stage as the phonetic or alphabetic stage. Chall noted that by the end of this stage, children have gained the insight about the nature of the spelling system. It is generally acknowledged that constructing associations between letters and phonemes is the fundamental task facing the beginning reader (Blachman, 1984; Mann, 1984). Two significant problems face all speakers of English. First, phonemes are abstract linguistic concepts rather than physically real entities, and as such do not correspond to discrete and invariant sounds. As a result of coarticulation, the sound segments of speech blend together in running, conversational speech. Recall the example of the word *cat* cited earlier in this chapter. The word *cat* is one acoustic event with no detectable sound segments that correspond exactly to its three written symbols. Perhaps a better example is the phrase *did you know,* which in normal conversational speech is pronounced [dɪdʒəno]. A child who was told that the letter *y* corresponds to the "ya" sound would have difficulty constructing an association between this sound and letter because there is no "ya" sound in this sentence.

A second related problem facing the beginning reader of English is that acoustic-phonetic characteristics of phonemes differ as a function of the phonetic context in which they occur. For example, the aspirated /t/ in the word *top* is different acoustically and phonetically than the unaspirated /t/ in *stop* and the unreleased /t/ in *pot*. In other words, each phoneme has several different phonetic variations. The abstract nature of phonemic categories and the phonetic variations of phonemes make the task of constructing phoneme-grapheme correspondence rules a formidable one.

A third problem facing beginning readers is the irregularities of the orthography. There are 251 different spellings for the 44 sounds of English (Horn, 1926). Consider, for example, all of the different orthographies associated with the vowel sound /i/—ie, e, ei, i, y, ea, ee—or the consonant /f/—f, ff, gh, ph. Children also have to learn that there are different ways to depict each letter. Each grapheme has an upper- and lowercase form, script and print form, and a typewritten form. Some graphemes (e.g., *a*) might have four or five different forms.

STAGE 2: UNGLUING FROM PRINT (7 TO 9 YEARS)

Stage 2 is a consolidation of what was learned in Stage 1. Children in this stage learn how to use their decoding skills, the redundancies of the language, and their knowledge of scripts and story structure to derive meaning more easily and fluently from text. The gradual automatization of decoding skills frees the child from the print and allows her or him to devote more attentional resources to focus on meaning. This stage corresponds to Frith's orthographic stage, in which the child directly recognizes words on the basis of orthographic patterns. By the end of this stage, the child has formed a substantial sight vocabulary based on the orthographic structure (e.g., spelling) of words.

STAGE 3: READING TO LEARN (9 TO 14 YEARS)

Stage 3 marks the beginning of the long course of reading to learn. It is at this stage that decoding skills have become fully automatized, thus freeing up attentional resources to focus on text comprehension and learning. Prior to this stage, reading skill has been equated with decoding skill. This stage fits the traditional concept of the difference between primary and later schooling. In the primary grades children learn to read, whereas in the higher grades they read to learn. In traditional schools children in the fourth grade begin to study the so-called subject areas, such as history, geography, and science. Such content subjects are purposely not introduced until children have presumably become relatively proficient readers (i.e., decoders). The reading in Stage 3, according to Chall, is primarily for facts, concepts, or how to do things. Chall divides Stage 3 into two phases. In the initial phase, children (age 9–11) can read serious material of adult length but cannot read most adult popular literature. During the second phase (junior high level), preadolescents are able to read most popular magazines, popular adult fiction, *Reader's Digest*, and newspapers. Literary fiction and news magazines, such as *Newsweek* and *Time*, are still beyond the reading abilities of children at this stage.

STAGES 4 AND 5: MULTIPLE VIEWPOINTS (14 TO 18 YEARS)/ CONSTRUCTION AND RECONSTRUCTION (18 AND ABOVE)

It is probably more appropriate to consider the final two stages as stages of cognitive development rather than reading development. As adolescents become capable of more abstract levels of thought, the information they are able to learn from reading increases. Chall has noted that the essential characteristic of Stage 4 is that the reader can now deal with more than one point of view, whereas the essential characteristic of Stage 5 is that reading is viewed as constructive; that is, the reader constructs knowledge using basic reasoning processes, such as analysis, synthesis, and judgment. Not coincidentally, the ability to consider alternative solutions to problems, an aspect of hypothetical-deductive reasoning, is one of the hallmarks of the formal operational period that marks adolescent thought (Piaget, 1954). A true understanding of how individuals become more critical and thoughtful readers requires a comprehensive inquiry into cognitive development during the adolescent period. For a recent review of adolescent cognitive development, see Kamhi and Lee (1988).

SUMMARY

We began Chapter 1 with the comment that the recent emphasis on the linguistic bases of reading sometimes has led to the erroneous conclusion that reading is a simple derivative of spoken language. The major theme of this chapter is that despite the commonalities between spoken and written language, there are fundamental, nontrivial differences between the two. The convergence between spoken and written language is most evident in the vocabulary both share. Readers and listeners also rely on common sources of syntactic, script, story, and world knowledge. The most fundamental differences between oral and spoken language involve the perceptual and social bases of spoken language development and the explicit phonological awareness required to become a proficient reader. These differences explain to a large extent why learning to read is not a simple derivative of spoken language as well as why some children have difficulty learning to read.

REFERENCES

ASHA Committe on Language. (June 1983). Definition of language. *ASHA, 25,* 44.

Baron, J. (1977). Mechanisms for pronouncing printed words: Use and acquisition. In D. LaBerge and S. Samuels (Eds.), *Basic processes in reading: Perception and comprehension,* 175–216. Hillsdale, NJ: Erlbaum.

Barron, R. (1981). Development of visual word recognition: A review. In G. Mackinnon and T. Waller (Eds.), *Readıng research: Advances in theory and practice, 1,* 119–158. New York: Academic Press.

Blachman, B. (1984). Language analysis skills and early reading acquisition. In G. Wallach and K. Butler (Eds.), *Lnaguage learning disabilities in school-age children,* 271–287. Baltimore: Williams and Wilkins.

Bradley, L., and Bryant, P. (1985). *Rhyme and reason in reading and spelling.* Ann Arbor, MI: University of Michigan Press.

Bransford, J., Barclay, J., and Franks, J. (1972). Sentence memory: A constructive versus interpretive approach. *Cognitive Psychology, 3,* 193–209.

Brown, A. (1987). Metacognition, executive control, self-regulation and other more mysterious mechanisms. In F. Weinert and R. Kluwe (Eds.), *Metacognition, motivation, and understanding,* 65–116. Hillsdale, NJ: Erlbaum.

Brown, R. (1973). *A first language.* Cambridge, MA: Harvard University Press.

Brown, A., and Campione, J. (1984). Three faces of transfer: Implications for early competence, individual differences, and instruction. In M. Lamb, A. Brown, and B. Rogoff (Eds.), *Advances in developmental psychology, 3,* 143–193. Hillsdale, NJ: Erlbaum.

Butler, K. (1984). Language processing: Halfway up the down staircase. In G. Wallach and K. Butler (Eds.), *Language learning disabilities in school-age children,* 60–81. Baltimore: Williams and Wilkins.

Catts, H., and Kamhi, A. (1986). The linguistic basis of reading disorders: Implications for the speech-language pathologist. *Language, Speech, and Hearing Services in Schools, 17,* 329–341.

Chafe, W. (1970). *Meaning and the structure of language.* Chicago: The University of Chicago Press.

Chall, J. (1983). *Stages of reading development*. New York: McGraw-Hill.

Clark, H., and Clark, E. (1977). *Psychology and language*. New York: Harcourt Brace Jovanovich.

Collins, A., and Loftus, E. (1975). A spreading activation theory of semantic processing. *Psychological Review, 82*, 407–428.

Collins, A., and Quillian, M. (1969). Retrieval time from semantic memory. *Journal of Verbal Learning and Verbal Behavior, 8*, 240–248.

Crowder, R. (1982). *The psychology of reading*. New York: Oxford University Press.

Curtiss, S. (1977). *Genie: A psycholinguistic study of a modern-day 'Wild Child'*. New York: Academic Press.

Cutting, J., and Pisoni, D. (1978). An information-processing approach to speech perception. In J. Kavanagh and W. Strange (Eds.), *Speech and language in the laboratory, school, and clinic*, 38–71. Cambridge, MA: MIT Press.

Dollaghan, C., and Kaston, N. (1986). A comprehension monitoring program for language impaired children. *Journal of Speech and Hearing Disorders, 51*, 264–271.

Duchan, J. (1983). Language processing and geodesic domes. In T. Gallagher and C. Prutting (Eds.), *Pragmatic assessment and intervention issues in language*, 83–100. San Diego: College-Hill Press.

Fox, B., and Routh, D. (1975). Analyzing spoken language into words, syllables, and phonemes: A developmental study. *Journal of Psycholinguistic Research, 4*, 331–342.

Frith, U. (1985). Beneath the surface of developmental dyslexia. In K. Patterson, J. Marshall, and M. Coltheart (Eds.), *Surface dyslexia: Neuropsychological and cognitive studies of phonological reading*, 301–333. Hillsdale, NJ: Earlbaum.

Gleitman, L., and Rozin, P. (1977). The structure and acquisition of reading, 1: Relations between orthographies and the structure of language. In A. Reber and D. Scarborough (Eds.), *Toward a psychology of reading*, 1–53. The proceedings of the CUNY conferences. New York: Wiley.

Gough, P. (1984). Word recognition. In R. Barr, M. Kamil, and P. Rosenthal (Eds.), *Handbook of reading research*, 225–255. New York: Longman.

Hakes, D. (1982). The development of metalinguistic abilities: What develops? In S. Kuczaj (Eds.), *Language, cognition, and culture*, 163–210. Hillsdale, NJ: Erlbaum.

Hallahan, D., Kauffman, J., and Lloyd, J. (1985). *Introduction to learning disabilities*, (2nd Ed.). Englewood Cliffs, NJ: Prentice-Hall.

Heath, S. B. (1982). What no bedtime story means: Narrative skills at home and at school. *Language in Society, 11*, 49–76.

Horn, E. (1926). *A basic writing vocabulary*. University of Iowa Monographs in Education, No. 4. Iowa City: University of Iowa Press.

Johnston, J., and Kamhi, A. (1984). The same can be less: Syntactic and semantic aspects of the utterances of language impaired children. *Merrill-Palmer Quarterly, 30*, 65–86.

Just, M., and Carpenter, P. (1987). *The psychology of reading and language comprehension*. Boston: Allyn and Bacon, Inc.

Kamhi, A., and Lee, R. (1988). Cognitive development in older children. In M. Nippold (Ed.) *Later language development: Ages nine through nineteen,* 127–159. San Diego: College-Hill Press.

Lerner, J. (1986). *Learning disabilities: Theories, diagnosis, and teaching strategies,* (4th Ed.). Boston: Houghton Mifflin.

Liberman, I. (1983). A language-oriented view of reading and its disabilities. In H. Myklebust (Ed.), *Progress in learning disabilities,* 81–101. New York: Grune and Stratton.

Liberman, I., Shankweiler, D., Fischer, F., and Carter, B. (1974). Explicit syllable and phoneme segmentation in young children. *Journal of Experimental Child Psychology, 18,* 201–212.

Lieberman, P. (1973). On the evolution of language: A unified view. *Cognition, 2,* 59–94.

Lund, N., and Duchan, J. (1988). *Assessing children's language in naturalistic contexts,* (2nd Ed.). Englewood Cliffs, NJ: Prentice-Hall.

Mandler, J., and Johnson, N. (1977). Remembrance of things parsed: Story structure and recall. *Cognitive Psychology, 9,* 111–151.

Mann, V. (1984). Longitudinal prediction and prevention of reading difficulty. *Annals of Dyslexia, 34,* 117–137.

Mann, V., and Liberman, I. (1984). Phonological awareness and verbal short-term memory. *Journal of Learning Disabilities, 17,* 592–599.

Markman, E. (1977). Realizing that you don't understand. *Child Development, 45,* 986–992.

McClelland, J. (1986). The programmable blackboard model of reading. In J. McClelland and D. Rumelhart (Eds.), *Parallel distributed processes: Psychological and biological models, 2,* 122–170. Cambridge, MA: MIT Press.

Perara, K. (1984). *Children's writing and reading: Analysing classroom language.* Oxford: Blackwell.

Perfetti, C. (1985). *Reading ability.* New York: Oxford University Press.

Perfetti, C. (1986). Cognitive and linguistic components of reading ability. In B. Foorman and A. Siegel (Eds.), *Acquisition of reading skills,* 1–41. Hillsdale, NJ: Erlbaum.

Piaget, J. (1954). *The construction of reality in the child.* New York: Basic Books.

Pisoni, D. (1978). Speech perception. In W. Estes (Ed.), *Handbook of learning and cognitive processes, 6,* 171–203. Hillsdale, NJ: Erlbaum.

Rumelhart, D. (1977). Toward an interactive model of reading. In S. Dornic and P. Rabbit (Eds.), *Attention and performance VI,* 183–221. Hillsdale, NJ: Erlbaum.

Schank, R., and Abelson, R. (1977). *Scripts, plans, goals, and understanding: An inquiry into human knowledge structures.* Hillsdale, NJ: Erlbaum.

Schuberth, R., and Eimas, P. (1977). Effects of context on the classification of words and nonwords. *Journal of Experimental Psychology: Human Perception and Performance, 3,* 27–36.

Snow, C., and Goldfield, B. (1983). Turn the page please: Situation-specific language acquisition. *Journal of Child Language, 10,* 551–569.

Stanovich, K. (1980). Toward an interactive-compensatory model of individual differences in the development of reading fluency. *Reading Research Quarterly, 16,* 32–71.

Stanovich, K. (1985). Explaining the variance in reading ability in terms of psychological processes: What have we learned? *Annals of Dyslexia, 35,* 67–96.

Stanovich, K. (1986). Matthew effects in reading: Some consequences of individual differences in the acquisition of literacy. *Reading Research Quarterly, 21,* 360–406.

Stanovich, K., and West, R. (1983). The generalizability of context effects on word recognition: A reconsideration of the roles of parafoveal priming and sentence context. *Memory and Cognition, 11,* 49–58.

Stein, N., and Glenn, C. (1979). An analysis of story comprehension in elementary school children. In R. Freedle (Ed.), *New directions in discourse processing,* 53–120. Norwood, NJ: Ablex.

Thomson, M. (1984). *Developmental dyslexia: Its nature, assessment, and remediation.* Baltimore: Edward Arnold.

Treiman, R., and Baron, J. (1981). Segmental analysis ability: Development and relation to reading ability. In G. Mackinnon and T. Waller (Eds.), *Reading research: Advances in theory and practice, 3,* 159–198. New York: Academic Press.

Tulving, E., and Gold, C. (1963). Stimulus information and contextual information as determinants of tachistoscopic recognition of words. *Journal of Experimental Psychology, 66,* 319–327.

Tunmer, W., and Bowey, J. (1984). Metalinguistic awareness and reading acquisition. In W. Tunmer, C. Pratt, and M. Herriman (Eds.), *Metalinguistic awareness in children: Theory, research, and implications,* 144–169. New York: Springer-Verlag.

Van Dijk, T., and Kintsch, W. (1983). *Strategies of discourse comprehension.* Cambridge, MA: MIT Press.

Van Kleeck, A., and Schuele, C. (1987). Precursors to literacy: Normal development. *Topics in Language Disorders, 7,* 13–31.

Vellutino, F. (1979). *Dyslexia: Theory and Research.* Cambridge, MA: MIT Press.

Wagner, R., and Torgesen, J. (1987). The nature of phonological processing and its causal role in the acquisition of reading skills. *Psychological Review, 101,* 192–212.

Wallach, G., and Butler, K. (1984). *Language learning disabilities in school-age children.* Baltimore: Williams and Wilkins.

2

Reading Disabilities: Terminology, Definitions, and Subtyping Issues

Alan G. Kamhi
& Hugh W. Catts

In a recent report, Stedman and Kaestle (1987) estimated that 20 percent of the adult population, or about 35 million people, have difficulties with simple reading tasks such as following directions on a medicine bottle or reading product labels, traffic signs, and street signs. Liberman (1987) does not find this number surprising because it is not uncommon to find that 20 percent of the children in early grades are labeled learning disabled. Although many of these children are not truly learning disabled, most have been identified because of problems learning to read. The population of children who experience reading problems is a heterogeneous one with respect to the severity of the reading disability, the presence of associated deficits (e.g., intellectual, attentional, and social); and basic perceptual, conceptual, and linguistic processing abilities.

In the first part of this chapter, we attempt to make some sense of the different ways children with reading problems have been defined. In this section, we suggest that a large group of individuals with reading disabilities are best characterized as having a developmental language impairment. In the second part of the chapter, we consider the ways in which children with reading problems have been classified and subtyped.

Terminology

Many different terms have been used to label individuals who demonstrate reading problems. Some of the more frequently used terms are specific reading disability, reading disability, dyslexia, and developmental dyslexia. The term *disability* is often used interchangeably with *disorder, impairment,* and in England, *retardation*. More general terms, such as *learning disabled,* and *poor reader,* are also used to describe children with reading disabilities. The term *language learning disabled* has been used in recent years by many speech-language pathologists to describe school-age children who have spoken and written language deficits.

Of all the terms used to describe children with reading disabilities, the term *dyslexia* has been the most confusing and the most misunderstood. Etymologically, dyslexia means difficulty with words. Historically, dyslexia was originally used in the late nineteenth century to describe the ''word blindness'' associated with speech difficulty or aphasia caused by injuries to the left hemisphere (cf. Thomson, 1984). Orton (1937) was the first to describe a childhood reading disability as *developmental alexia,* in which an individual had particular difficulty learning to read with no evidence of accompanying physical, mental, or emotional abnormalities. Orton (1937) is more often cited, however, for the importance he placed on letter reversals and word confusions in the diagnosis of dyslexia. Even today, many people still think that a child who reads *was* for *saw* is dyslexic. Research, however, has demonstrated that reversal errors have little diagnostic significance (see Perfetti, 1985, and Chapter 3). Despite the confusion surrounding the term, it is still used by many researchers and practitioners to describe specific reading disabled individuals. Several different definitions of dyslexia will be considered in the next section.

Other terms used to label children with reading deficits have problems of their own. The term *learning disability,* for example, is generally agreed to be too broad a label because of the heterogeneity of the groups of children encompassed by the label (Ceci & Baker, 1987). The label *language learning disability,* despite its emphasis on language is also problematic. This term is currently used by many speech-language pathologists to describe learning and reading disabled children. Some reading theorists have also embraced this label (Ceci & Baker, 1987). Use of the term has served to emphasize the language bases of reading disabilities for speech-language pathologists. As such, the term has played an important role in getting speech-language pathologists involved in serving children with reading problems. For the most part, however, use of the term has been restricted to professionals in speech-language pathology.

There are several problems with the term that make its use problematic. First, there is no body of research involving language learning disabled children. Researchers study reading disabled or dyslexic students. Second, there are no federal and few state or local guidelines for serving language learning disabled children. Third, and most importantly, there are no clear criteria to differentiate reading disabled children with and without language learning disorders. If a reading disability is viewed as a language-based disorder, then all children with reading problems have a language learning disorder. If the term is ever to become truly useful, it needs to be clearly defined. A possible definition is offered in the next section of the chapter.

Throughout this chapter, the terms *reading disabled* and dyslexia will be used interchangeably. Despite the confusion and misconceptions surrounding the term *dyslexia,* it remains a popular term among a small group of researchers and practitioners in the United States. Indeed, it is all but impossible to discuss definitional issues and research on reading disabilities without encountering the term. Whenever possible, however, we have attempted to use the educationally based term *reading disabled* throughout the book because this term is the one currently used by most theorists and practitioners. Although the definition of this term is no more clear cut than definitions of dyslexia, there are fewer misconceptions associated with this label.

DEFINING READING DISABILITY

The way in which children with reading impairments are defined has both theoretical and educational implications. The validity of research on children with reading disabilities depends in large part on the criteria used to select the subjects for study. One reason for some of the confusion in the reading literature (see Stanovich, 1986) is that researchers have used varying criteria to select reading disabled subjects. The principal educational implications of defining a reading disability concern identifying the population of disabled readers who are eligible for remedial services. Definitions are thus not trivial matters for scholars to debate.

The population of reading disabled individuals that has received the most attention in the literature are often described as having a specific reading disability or what has often been referred to as dyslexia. Defining what constitutes a specific reading disability or dyslexia, however, has proved to be no easy task (Hynd & Cohen, 1983). The definitional problem can be attributed to the fact that so many individuals from different professions (e.g., medicine, education, psychology, and speech pathology) have taken an interest in these children. These individuals invariably have different orientations and theoretical biases that influence how they define this group of poor readers. Because much of the literature concerning definitions of this population refers to these individuals as dyslexic, we will use the term *dyslexia* rather than *specific reading disability*. The reader who prefers the term *specific reading disability* might wish to substitute this term for dyslexia in the next few pages.

One can begin by distinguishing among definitions of dyslexia according to how broad-based and discriminating they are. The most broad-based and least discriminating definition is that dyslexia is simply "difficulty in reading" (Kolb & Whinshaw, 1980). The International Reading Association lists a similar definition as a third and presumably least preferable choice:

> 3. Dyslexia is a popular term for any difficulty in reading of any intensity and from any cause(s). *Note*: Dyslexia in this sense is a term which describes a symptom, not a disease. (Harris and Hodges, 1981, p. 95)

Most theorists and practitioners agree that the term *dyslexia* should not be used to characterize the whole population of individuals who experience reading difficulty. Rather, the term should be used to identify a subgroup of individuals with reading disabilities.

There are basically two ways to make definitions more explicit: by exclusion or by inclusion. Exclusionary definitions exclude children from the dyslexic category on the basis of associated factors that might contribute to poor reading. These factors include low intelligence, poor instruction, sensory deficits, brain damage, severe emotional disturbance, and sociocultural factors. The three definitions cited below all have exclusionary components.

> A dyslexic is a child who is normal or above at least in nonverbal IQ, two years behind in reading achievement, and with a reading disability that is not explainable primarily by social, economic, motivation, or emotional factors. (Perfetti, 1985, p. 180)

> Specific developmental dyslexia is a disorder manifested by difficulty in learning to read, despite conventional instruction, adequate intelligence, and sociocultural opportunity. It is dependent upon fundamental cognitive disabilities which are frequently of constitutional origin. (World Federation of Neurology, cited in Thomson, 1984, p. 10)

> Dyslexia is a medical term for incomplete alexia; partial but severe inability to read; historically (but less common in current use), word

blindness. *Note*: Dyslexia in this sense applies to persons who ordinarily have adequate vision, hearing, intelligence, and general language functioning. Dyslexia is a rare but definable and diagnosable form of primary reading retardation with some form of central nervous system dysfunction. It is not attributable to environmental causes or other handicapping conditions. (International Reading Association, Harris & Hodges, 1981)

There are several problems with exclusionary definitions. For example, an exclusionary definition does not define the presence of symptoms that have been found to be consistently associated with the disorder. Such definitions usually define the deficit in reading in terms of a discrepancy between measures of reading ability and mental age, chronological age, or grade level. There are problems, however, in the use of discrepancy formulas to identify dyslexic children or any learning disabled child. In fact, the Council for Learning Disabilities has recently written a position paper recommending that the use of discrepancy formulas to identify learning disabilities should be phased out (see *Journal of Learning Disabilities*, 1987, p. 349). Some of the problems with discrepancy criteria are noted below.

Discrepancy formulas based on IQ fail to consider the overlap between some of the IQ subtests and reading tests (e.g., vocabulary and comprehension measures). Indeed, the correlation between intelligence tests and reading performance is about .5 in the early elementary grades and rises to as high as .75 in adults (Stanovich, Cunningham, & Feeman, 1984). Another problem with discrepancy formulas concerns the reading tests used to identify an impairment. Reading tests are not uniform in the aspects of reading they measure. Some may measure only decoding skills or comprehension; others may include measures of spelling, writing, and oral reading. Some tests are timed, whereas others are untimed (Rudel, 1985). Rudel, for example, found that a sample of 50 subjects referred for reading difficulty had a mean discrepancy of 23.9 months between mental age and reading age using the Gray Oral Reading Test, a timed test. In contrast, these same children had a mean discrepancy of only 8.6 months using the Wide Range Achievement Test, which tests the reading of single words and is not timed.

There are other problems with exclusionary definitions. For example, by excluding from the dyslexic category all children with IQs below 85 or 90, one is saying that only children who have average intelligence can possibly be dyslexic. But as Thomson (1984) has pointed out, dyslexia can affect individuals across all levels of intelligence, whether a genetic or environmental cause is also involved. Thomson also takes issue with the exclusion of brain-damaged individuals. He notes that many theories and definitions mention that dyslexia is presumed to be due to central nervous system dysfunction. It is a moot point, therefore, about "when a constitutional difference in the central nervous system becomes different from definitive tissue damage or where gross handicaps shade into more circumscribed behavioral effects" (Thomson, 1984, p. 11).

As indicated earlier, one of the major problems with exclusionary definitions is that they say more about what dyslexia is not than what it is. Little information is provided about the specific behaviors exhibited by dyslexic individuals. Inclusionary definitions, by contrast, delimit the specific abilities and disabilities that characterize dyslexic individuals. In other words, such definitions stress positive rather than negative factors. Proponents of an inclusionary approach include Rutter (1978), who has advocated studying all children with severe reading problems in order to evaluate the contributions of associated factors, and Rudel (1985) who attempted in her research to delineate the specific language and motor correlates of dyslexia. An example of an inclusionary definition is provided by Thomson:

> Dyslexia is experienced by children of adequate intelligence, as a general language deficit which is a specific manifestation of a wider limitation in processing all forms of information in short-term memory, be they visually or auditorally presented. This wider limitation exhibits itself in tasks requiring the heaviest use and access to short-term memory, such as reading, but particularly spelling. (Wheeler & Watkins, 1979; cited in Thomson, 1984, p. 12)

There are several other factors that distinguish definitions of dyslexia, including the degree of severity, attribution of cause, and most important for our interest, how dyslexia is viewed relative to a general language impairment. The more explicit definitions of dyslexia generally specify that the reading problem is a severe one. This specification provides a means to distinguish between the larger group of children who have some problems learning to read and those who have a severe reading disability. A severe reading problem is usually defined as at least two years below the child's expected reading age (Rutter, 1978) or nonverbal IQ (Perfetti, 1985). In addition to the problems with discrepancy criteria discussed above, one problem with severity criteria such as these concerns the relationship between severity and age. A two-year reading delay in a 7-year-old is more severe than a two-year delay in a 12-year-old. It is thus more difficult for a younger child to be diagnosed as having a severe reading problem than an older child.

Definitions of dyslexia can also be distinguished by whether or not they attribute a cause for the reading problem. For example, the definition proposed by Critchley and Critchley (1978) indicates that the disorder is cognitive in nature and usually genetically determined. As mentioned earlier, some definitions specify that the disorder is the direct result of central nervous system dysfunction. Specific processing deficiencies that underlie the reading problem might also be mentioned, as in Wheeler and Watkins' definition quoted earlier. The most noteworthy aspect of the definition proposed by Wheeler and Watkins, however, is that it defines dyslexia as a general language deficit.

DYSLEXIA AS A DEVELOPMENTAL LANGUAGE IMPAIRMENT

The definition proposed by Wheeler and Watkins is consistent with our view that dyslexia is best characterized as a developmental language impairment. Research reviewed throughout this book demonstrates that dyslexia is more than a reading failure; it is a language problem that begins early in life and continues throughout childhood, adolescence, and into adulthood. The manifestation of the impairment, however, changes with age. During the preschool years, the impairment is manifested in difficulty learning spoken language. Research indicates that dyslexic children may be delayed in producing their first words and phrases, have morphologic and syntactic deficits, and exhibit phonological processing deficits (Aram & Nation, 1980; Ingram, Mason, & Blackburn, 1970; Chapter 4 of this volume). On entering school, dyslexic children experience significant difficulties acquiring word recognition and spelling skills (Thomson, 1984). Deficits in spoken language abilities might also be evident (see Chapter 6). During the later school years, dyslexic children encounter comprehension problems (e.g., difficulty reading to learn) as well as continued problems in writing, spelling, and oral reading. Research reviewed in Chapters 6 and 7 indicates that these children often have deficits in semantic, syntactic, and discourse aspects of spoken language. As adults, dyslexic individuals will continue to experience problems in spoken and written language (Johnson & Blalock, 1987).

The recognition that there exists a large group of individuals whose reading problems are a manifestation of a developmental language impairment is consistent with the view that there are qualitative differences between individuals with reading problems. Unlike conceptions of dyslexia discussed earlier in the chapter, severity of the reading problem, a quantitative distinction, is not a criterion for the disorder. In fact, it is possible to be characterized as dyslexic and not have a severe reading problem. Many individuals who exhibit characteristics of dyslexia learn to read, but continue to have problems in other aspects of oral and written language. Conversely, children who have a severe reading problem might not be dyslexic. They might simply have a reading problem that does not reflect a developmental language impairment. It is also possible to have a problem learning to talk or understand without being dyslexic. Not all children who experience early oral language learning difficulties go on to experience lifelong problems in oral and written language (Aram & Nation, 1980).

We are not alone in the recognition that there is a large group of individuals whose reading problems reflect a developmental language impairment. Orton (1937), a pioneer in the field of dyslexia, acknowledged the relationship between oral and written language disorders 50 years ago. More recently, Chasty (1985), Vellutino (1979), Thomson (1984), and Rudel (1985) have proposed language-based definitions of dyslexia. Chasty, for example, stated that "to think of dyslexia only in terms of reading failure is grossly to oversimplify the complexity of the language development process" (p. 14). He goes on to state that dyslexia is a failure in a developmental communication system and can be defined as an

> organizing difficulty which is usually congenital, but occasionally acquired; which affects physical skill development in laterality, information processing in short-term memory and perception, and so causes significant interference in the development of language in the individual. By language we mean talk, reading, spelling, writing, number, and essay writing. Central to this concept of dyslexia is the idea of a developmental language disorder. (p. 23)

The term *dyslexia* has been used throughout this section to refer to the children whose reading problems reflect a developmental language impairment. The term *specific reading disabled* is sometimes used to refer to these children. A problem with this term, however, is that it places emphasis on written language deficits rather than the more general language deficits associated with the disorder. The most appropriate label for these children may be *language-learning disabled*. This label captures the essence of the disorder, namely, that it is first and foremost a language disorder rather than just a reading disorder. As indicated earlier in this chapter, however, this term does not have wide appeal in disciplines other than speech-language pathology, and it has not been well defined. Perhaps the definition suggested here might eliminate some of the problems with the present use of the term.

CLASSIFYING READING DISABLED CHILDREN

The lack of agreement about how best to label and define reading disabilities is reflected in the problems researchers have had in classifying and subtyping individuals with reading disabilities. Defining the population of reading disabled individuals to be classified is a necessary first step in any subtype study. Classification obviously differs according to the population sampled. To illustrate this point, Morris, Blashfield, and Satz (1986) give the example of a study in which 70 percent of the children have significant expressive language problems. The classification of this sample would be very different than that of a sample in which only 40 percent of the children had expressive language problems. Or consider how a definition that excludes children with intellectual and neurological problems would lead to the selection of a very different sample of reading disabled children than a definition that includes these children.

Given the diverse theoretical assumptions of researchers and the variety of measurement batteries used, it is probably unrealistic to expect that a reliable and valid classification system for reading disabled children could ever be developed. Nevertheless, there is clear value in attempting to delineate reliable subgroups of individuals with reading disabilities. As will become clear in this chapter, the subtyping research has provided important information about the relationships among linguistic, cognitive, and reading skills. This research also has important implications for differential diagnosis of reading disabilities and remediation plans (Lyon, 1985). Thus, although it is probably unreasonable to expect that researchers and practitioners will agree on a subtyping system, it is reasonable to attempt to differentiate among the reading disabled population according to a limited number of factors and abilities. In this way, what one calls a subtype is not as important as how the population of reading disabled individuals varies in the ability or factor in question. In the sections to follow, we will consider subtypes based on (1) causal factors and associated abilities, (2) the nature of reading disability and errors exhibited, (3) combinations of (1) and (2), and (4) language abilities.

Subtypes Based on Causal Factors and Associated Abilities

One of the first studies to classify children based on associated factors was conducted by Kinsbourne and Warrington (1963). In this study, children were divided into two groups based on verbal-performance IQ discrepancies on the WISC or WAIS. Group 1, the "language retarded group," included six children who had at least a 20-point discrepancy in favor of the performance scale. As might be expected, these children performed poorly on measures of language expression and comprehension. Group 2, termed the "Gerstmann group," included seven children who had at least a 20-point discrepancy in favor of the verbal scale. These children also demonstrated finger agnosias, significant retardation in right-left orientation, arithmetic, and drawing.

Somewhat consistent with these groups, Johnson and Myklebust (1967) differentiated between auditory dyslexia and visual dyslexia. Children with auditory dyslexia were said to experience difficulty remembering and sequencing auditory symbols, whereas children with visual dyslexia confused letters and words that looked the same.

The Isle of Wight Studies

The Isle of Wight studies (Berger, Yule, & Rutter, 1975; Rutter, Tizard, & Whitmore, 1970) involved approximately 4,500 children between the ages of 9 and 14 years of age. The overall purpose of these studies was to examine the characteristics of children whose reading performance was two standard deviations below their predicted reading age. Two groups of children with reading deficits were identified on the basis of IQ. "Backward readers" were defined as having reading and WISC scores at least 30 months below chronological age (mean IQ = 80). Children with "specific reading retardation" had IQ scores within normal limits (mean IQ = 102). As indicated in an earlier section, Rutter was interested in understanding the relationship between associated factors (e.g., intelligence) and reading performance.

Other than the differences in IQ, the backward readers exhibited delayed development in other areas, such as walking, fine-motor skills, and speech and language. These children showed more overt neurologial features and organic dysfunctions (e.g., 11 percent had cerebral palsy). The children also were more likely to come from large families and disadvantaged homes. The specific reading retardates, in contrast, only showed delays in speech and language. There was also a higher proportion of boys (76 percent) than in the backward readers (54 percent). The group of specific reading retardates seems to fit well with the group of children identified by exclusionary definitions of dyslexia and reading disability.

Mattis and Colleagues

The use of IQ to distinguish among reading subgroups represents an a priori, theoretically motivated division. Another approach to subgrouping is to administer measures of neuropsychological processing and classify individuals based on identifiable performance patterns. Mattis and his colleagues (Mattis, French, & Rapin, 1975) were among the first investigators to take this approach. The sample tested included 113 children between 11 and 12 years of age. The children were initially divided into three groups based on reading ability and existence of brain damage: a brain-damaged normal reader group, a brain-damaged dyslexic group, and a non-brain-damaged dyslexic group. The first group was included to be able to exclude neurological deficiencies not associated with dyslexia. All children had verbal or performance IQs of at least 80 and showed no evidence of severe emotional disturbance. Dyslexia was defined as reading two or more grade levels below age on the WRAT.

The three subgroups identified by Mattis et al. were distinguished by their language, articulation/graphomotor, and perceptual abilities. The group of children with a language disorder (39 percent) had anomia plus one additional impairment of language functioning involving comprehension as measured by the Token Test, imitative speech, or speech-sound discrimination.

The group of children with articulatory and graphomotor problems (37 percent) were said to have speech articulation deficiencies without an apparent language deficit. However, articulation was measured by performance on the ITPA Sound Blending subtest, not a traditional test of articulation. Performance on a sound-blending task may be as much a measure of working memory and phonological awareness as it is a measure of articulation ability.

The group of children with visual-spatial perceptual disorders (16 percent) had verbal IQ scores more than 10 points above performance IQ, a lower percentile score on the Raven's Coloured Progressive Matrices than performance IQ, and performance below the borderline level on the Benton Test of Visual Retention.

With respect to the comparison between brain-damaged and non-brain-damaged dyslexic groups, there were differences in the number of children in the three subgroups. However, there were no differences between the brain-damaged and non-brain-damaged children within the same subgroup. These findings suggest that the most similar characteristics among children with reading disabilities are behavioral rather than neurological. The findings also suggest that any one of several independent clusters of higher cortical deficiencies, whatever their etiology, is sufficient to result in reading problems.

Statistical Classification Studies

Petrauskas and Rourke (1979) were among the first researchers to use cluster analyses to classify children with reading disabilities. The sample of children consisted of 133 children with reading disabilities and 27 normal readers. The children were all 7 or 8 years old. A battery of 20 neuropsychological measures was selected that tapped tactile, sequencing, motor, visual-spatial, auditory-verbal, and abstract conceptual abilities. Three reliable profiles emerged, with 74 poor readers and

5 normal readers having high loadings on the factors. Type 1 contained the largest number of subjects (40). These children were most impaired on measures of verbal fluency and sentence memory. They also exhibited the largest verbal-performance IQ discrepancy on the WISC. Petrauskas and Rourke have suggested that this type is similar to the language disorder group described by Mattis et al. (1975). Type 2 contained 26 subjects. This subgroup was characterized by poor finger localization, verbal fluency, sentence memory, and immediate visual-spatial memory. Type 3 contained 13 subjects and was characterized by very poor scores on the picture-matching concept formation task, plus poor verbal fluency, sentence memory, and immediate visual-spatial memory. This subgroup is most similar to the articulation and graphomotor subgroup in the Mattis et al. (1975) study.

The findings from this study led Petrauskas and Rourke (p. 34) to conclude that deficiencies in language skills are involved in a large proportion of reading difficulties, whereas deficiencies in other skills (e.g., visual perceptual abilities) are related to reading deficits, but to a lesser and more variable extent. This is exemplified by children in the two most reliable types (1 and 2) who have poor language abilities and age-appropriate visual-perceptual skills.

Fisk and Rourke (1979) performed similar analyses on 264 older children with reading disabilities. The children all performed below the 30th percentile on the reading, spelling, and math subtests of the WRAT. From the total sample, three subsamples were composed, based on 2-year age intervals: 9–10 years, 11–12 years, and 13–14 years. There were 100 subjects in the first two subsamples and 64 in the third one. Twenty-one measures similar to the ones used by Petrauskas and Rourke (1979) were employed.

Two patterns of deficits were found in all three age groups and one type common to the two older age groups. The first pattern (Subtype A) was similar to Type 2 described by Petrauskas and Rourke (1979). The 52 children in this subtype had marked finger localization problems, poor auditory-verbal processing, and above average performance on visual perceptual tasks. The second pattern, which included 51 children, was similar to Type 1 in the companion study. These children had clear deficiencies in language processes and well-developed visual-spatial and eye-hand coordination skills. The third pattern contained 39 children in the two older groups. The most distinguishable aspect of this subgroup was poor performance in fingertip number-writing perception. These children also had moderate difficulty in sound-symbol matching tasks, mild impairment in general store of information, and intact visual-perceptual abilities.

The subtypes of older children thus are quite similar to those identified for younger children. The dominant pattern in the identified subtypes is poor performance on a variety of tests tapping language abilities coupled with above-average performance on visual perceptual tasks.

In a recent cluster analysis study, Morris, Blashfield, and Satz (1986) classified a sample of 222 children that contained 80 children with reading disabilities. The study was part of the Florida Longitudinal Project that began in 1970. Neuropsychological, family, academic, and behavioral data were obtained over a nine-year period. All of the children were administered a battery of 13 measures of neuropsychological skills in kindergarten, the end of second grade, and the end of fifth grade. Factor analysis of this battery (Fletcher & Satz, 1980) revealed three factors across the different age groups. Because of the limited variance accounted for by the third factor, only those tasks that loaded highly on the first two factors were retained. These two factors were verbal/conceptual (PPVT, naming, similarities, and dichotic listening) and sensorimotor/perceptual (Recognition-Discrimination Test, Embedded Figures, Test of Visual-Motor Integration, and Auditory-Visual Integration Test).

Children were initially clustered into two groups reflecting a basic division between good and poor readers. These groups were then further divided into three groups of poor readers (Types A, B, and C) and two groups of good readers (Types D and E). Type A children initially showed deficient verbal skills and below-average levels of visual-perceptual motor skills. Verbal skills remained significantly deficient across time, whereas perceptual motor skills became significantly above average. In addition, these children exhibited poor academic achievement and were rated by teachers as being more active and emotionally reactive than their peers. The parents of these children all fell in the average category, except for fathers' achievement level, which was below average.

Type B children showed increasing deficits in performance, especially in verbal-conceptual skills, as they became older. Verbal abilities were at average levels in kindergarten but became significantly delayed as the children got older. These children and their parents had below-average achievement scores, but the families were average in SES and education. These children also had "more than average" problems on neurological and birth history ratings (p. 378).

Type C children and their families were below average on all tests and ratings. Morris et al. referred to this group as the "slow" cluster group and noted that these children would not be included in classification studies that exclude children from lower SES backgrounds. They further noted that many of these children probably had IQs below 90. These children showed a strong relationship between their abilities and achievement levels in that both were below average. This group also showed improvement in all of their abilities as they got older. However, they showed a "mildly increasing deficit relative to the population norms, suggesting that they had a slightly slower rate of ability development" (p. 386).

Spreen and Haaf (1986) were the first researchers to examine the persistence of subtypes into adulthood. The three subtypes first noted by Mattis et al. (1975) (i.e., visuo-perceptual, linguistic, and articulo-graphomotor) were identified in two separate cluster analyses of 8- to 12-year old children with learning disabilities. In addition to these three subtypes, a minimally impaired and a severely impaired subtype were noted. Spreen and Haaf questioned whether the same clusters would appear in the population of subjects after a 15-year interval. The analysis included some subjects who were not part of the original sample and an adult control group who were considered average learners in childhood. Cluster analyses readily distinguished the average learners from the learning disabled group on measures of reading and cognition. In terms of subtype changes from childhood to adulthood, the reading disabled subjects who displayed a visual-spatial deficit in childhood continued to show this impairment. Reading and math problems also persisted into adult age. The subjects who showed linguistic impairment early in life appeared in overall low-performance adult clusters, suggesting a poor long-term outcome. The extent of the language deficit is thus an important predictor of long-term outcome.

Summary of Subtypes Based on Causal Factors and Associated Abilities

A consistent finding in the subtype studies reviewed in this section is the prevalence of language deficits in the majority of children who demonstrate reading problems. Visual-perceptual deficits, in contrast, were only present in a small proportion of subjects. Moreover, the proportion of reading disabled children exhibiting language deficits would no doubt increase if more measures of phonological processing, higher-level discourse, figurative language, and metalinguistic skills were also obtained.

Subtypes Based on the Nature of the Reading Disability

Marshall (1984) has argued that classifications based on associated symptomotology, such as the ones just presented, do not represent systematic analyses of reading impairment because they fail to specify the precise nature of the reading disorder that the children demonstrate. Marshall adds that such taxonomies fail to establish whether the associated deficits are necessary or sufficient conditions for reading impairments and, as a result, are severely limited in the theoretical insight they provide and therapeutic measures they may suggest (p. 46).

There are two general approaches that have been used to classify reading disabled individuals on the basis of their reading performance. The first approach is to identify subgroups based on clinical inferences. This approach involves distinguishing subgroups according to some measure of reading performance, such as whether the reader uses a direct (whole-word) or indirect (phonetic) route to decode words. Marshall and Boder's work is most representative of this approach. The second approach, as in the previous section, is to use multivariate statistical classification techniques (e.g., Q-factor analysis) to identify subgroups of reading disability based on patterns of reading performance. Representative studies reflecting each of these approaches are considered below.

THE CLINICAL INFERENTIAL APPROACH

DEEP, PHONOLOGICAL, AND SURFACE DYSLEXIA. One of the earliest attempts to classify reading disabled individuals using a clinical inferential approach involved individuals with acquired dyslexia (Coltheart, Patterson, & Marshall, 1980; Marshall & Newcombe, 1973; Patterson, Marshall, & Coltheart 1985). Acquired dyslexia is defined as the occurrence of reading deficits in previously literate adults who have suffered neurological damage (Patterson, 1981). As indicated in the previous chapter, there are two main reading routes: a direct whole-word approach and an indirect phonetic approach. Based on these approaches and the types of errors made, three syndromes of acquired dyslexia have been identified: deep, phonological, and surface.

Individuals with deep and phonological dyslexia have considerable difficulty using the phonological route for reading. They have difficulty accessing meaning using a phonological code and, as one would expect, perform poorly when asked to read nonsense words. Individuals with deep dyslexia, unlike those with phonological dyslexia, often make semantic errors. A semantic error involves substituting a word from the same conceptual domain (e.g., *car/automobile, student/teacher, apple/tomato*). Other symptoms include visual errors (confusing visually similar words), morphological errors (adding suffixes or prefixes), and a greater facility understanding content words as opposed to function words (Thomson, 1984, p. 59). In contrast, individuals with phonological dyslexia do not make semantic errors and do not have difficulty with function words. They also make visual errors, but not as many as those with deep dyslexia.

Individuals with surface dyslexia rely mostly on the phonetic route. Sight vocabulary is thought to be impaired. These individuals have difficulty accessing meaning. Thomson notes that they are generally not sensitive to semantic aspects of words, but are affected by characteristics of the orthographic representation, such as word length and regularity of spelling.

There have been several attempts to draw parallels between syndromes of acquired dyslexia and subtypes of developmental dyslexia. For example, Marshall (1984) questioned whether developmental disorders of reading could be partitioned into the syndromes of acquired dyslexia that have been identified in the literature. Marshall added three categories—attentional, direct, and visual dyslexia—to the three just discussed. Marshall then reviewed the evidence in support of developmental parallels for each of the six syndromes. He found little evidence for developmental patterns of attentional, visual, or deep dyslexia. The strongest evidence was found for a parallel between surface and developmental dyslexia (Coltheart, Masterson, Byng, Prior, & Riddoch, 1983; Holmes, 1978). Holmes, for example, argued that the context-sensitive nature of English orthography was the main problem for children in acquiring a sight vocabulary. She found that many children with reading disabilities experienced considerable difficulty reading words that contained complex consonant clusters, silent consonants, and applying the *e* rule (*wage*/*wag*, *quite*/*quit*).

Marshall (1984) found some evidence for the existence of a developmental phonological dyslexia. Temple and Marshall (1983) reported on a 17-year-old girl who had considerable difficulty reading nonsense words compared to real words. Her responses to nonsense words were typically real words that were visually similar to the stimulus word. Marshall (1984) noted that this developmental case is very similar to the case of acquired phonological dyslexia reported by Patterson (1982).

There is also some evidence for children exhibiting direct dyslexia. In direct dyslexia, the individual shows excellent ability to read aloud both nonsense and real words, but there is little comprehension of what has been read. The term *hyperlexia* has been used to describe children whose ability to read aloud is dramatically better than their comprehension and also better than their oral language abilities. The existence of hyperlexic children has been well documented (e.g., Healy, 1982; Silberberg & Silberberg, 1967). Because of their severe oral language deficits, however, hyperlexic children resemble individuals with acquired direct dyslexia only in their reading abilities. In other words, hyperlexic individuals have very different cognitive and linguistic abilities than individuals with direct dyslexia. This is just one of several problems with comparing syndromes of acquired dyslexia with developmental dyslexia.

Another problem is that researchers do not all draw the same parallels between acquired and developmental dyslexia. Jorm (1979), for example, argued that developmental dyslexia is most similar to deep dyslexia because individuals with developmental dyslexia have difficulty reading nonsense words, greater difficulty with content words than function words, and a tendency to make visual errors. Thus, individuals with developmental dyslexia, like those with deep dyslexia, have difficulty using the phonetic route for reading.

The most serious problem in drawing parallels between acquired and developmental dyslexia concerns the developmental variability in normal and disabled children's reading performance. For example, normal children also use two basic approaches to reading and make the same kinds of errors that children with reading disabilities exhibit (Perfetti, 1985). One would not label a young first-grade nonreader a "deep dyslexic" because of difficulty reading nonsense words. Patterns of individual differences in word recognition approaches (whole-word versus phonetic) have also been found to be similar in dyslexic and good readers (Treiman & Hirsh-Pasek, 1985). In addition, a well-known aspect of learning to read is that the types of reading errors children make change as a function of age (e.g., Thomson, 1984). This means that the same child would demonstrate different dyslexic syndromes as the nature of reading errors changes with age.

In sum, we agree with Thomson's (p. 61) comment that the description of acquired dyslexia has been useful in drawing attention to the components of the reading process, but the kinds of classification systems used are not readily applicable to children with reading problems.

DYSPHONETIC, DYSEIDETIC, AND ALEXIA SUBGROUPS. At about the same time Marshall began to describe acquired dyslexias, Elena Boder (1971, 1973) described three subgroups of developmental dyslexia based on reading and spelling abilities: dysphonetic dyslexia, dyseidetic dyslexia, and alexia. The dysphonetic subgroup reflects a primary deficit in phonetic-based skills. Children in this group have difficulty constructing sound-letter correspondence rules. They rely heavily on global, whole-word strategies to read. The dyseidetic group's principal deficit is in the ability to perceive whole words. These children can read phonetically but treat most words as if they were being read for the first time. The alexic group has a deficit in both phonetic and whole-word skills. This group is obviously the most severely handicapped.

Support for the existence of the three subgroups came from a study involving 107 children diagnosed as dyslexic (Boder, 1971, 1973). All of the children had IQ scores within normal limits on the Stanford-Binet, had no known neurological damage, and were at least two years below grade level in reading on the Wide Range Achievement Test. The sample contained 92 boys and 15 girls. Of the 107 children in the study, Boder found that 100 exhibited one of the three reading-spelling patterns. Reading and spelling were strongly related so that each was mutually predictive. Of the 100 children, the majority (67) were classified as dysphonetic, 10 were classified as dyseidetic, and 23 were alexic. Boder noted that there was some difficulty in differentiating young dyseidetic children from young alexic children. These children were often not differentiable during early grades. After considerable remedial instruction (seven years in some cases), the dyseidetic children's ability to develop word analysis skills became evident.

Boder's classification system is similar to that of Marshall in that it also relies on error types and deficits in word recognition routes. Some of the problems with Marshall's subgroups thus also apply to Boder's proposed subgroups. For example, the error patterns identified by Boder also occur in young normal children learning to read. Also, because the error patterns occur at different stages in normal reading development, dysphonetic and dyseidetic subjects may actually have similar underlying deficits but be at different stages in reading development. There is, in fact, evidence to suggest that dysphonetic and dyseidetic subjects do not vary in their ability to recall letters presented auditorily and visually (Van de Bos, 1982; cited in Perfetti, 1985). Speech perception abilities in the two groups have also been found to be similar (Godfrey, Syrdal-Lasky, Millay, & Knox, 1981). Perfetti suggests that it might be that the only differences between dysphonetic and dyseidetic subjects is in spelling abilities, for it is the pattern of spelling that is used to determine the subclassification.

Decoding versus Comprehension Problems

Perhaps the most obvious way to categorize reading ability is to distinguish between decoding problems and comprehension problems. Although this subtyping scheme appears straightforward, it is not possible to isolate the independent effects of comprehension abilities until decoding skills have become automatized sometime during the third or fourth grade. Consistent with this point, Satz, Taylor, Friel, and Fletcher (1978), identified one group of disabled readers in grades one and two who had significant word recognition problems. A second group of children with reading disabilities were identified in the fifth grade. Up until this time, these children read normally and had no apparent decoding problems. These two groups of poor readers are somewhat consistent with the distinction Chall (1983) made between learning to read and reading to learn. Note, however, that some of the older children's reading problems might stem from inefficient decoding skills. Reading problems might not have been detected earlier because the texts were simple and thus did not require efficient, rapid decoding skills. Metacognitive deficiences might also play an important role in these older children's reading problems.

RATE DISABLED VERSUS ACCURACY DISABLED READERS

Another subtyping scheme that considers decoding and comprehension skills has been suggested by Lovett (1984, 1987). Lovett distinguished between an accuracy disabled group and a rate disabled group, based on the model of reading proposed by LaBerge and Samuels (1974). The accuracy disabled group evidences significant problems in decoding accuracy, whereas the rate disabled group evidences a marked deficit in reading rate despite grade appropriate decoding accuracy. To be classified as accuracy disabled, a child has to score at least one and a half years below grade-level expectations on at least four of five different measures of word recognition. To be classified as rate disabled, a child has to score close to, at, or above grade level on four or more measures of word recognition and at least a year and a half below grade level on four of five measures of reading speed (e.g., Durell Oral Reading, Gilmore Oral Reading, and Test of Rapid Reading Responses).

Lovett (1987) has found evidence that these subtypes demonstrate distinct patterns of reading and language performance and respond in different ways to standard remediation approaches. In the 1987 study, she administered 17 tests of oral and written language to 32 accuracy disabled, 32 rate disabled, and 32 normal readers. Subjects were matched for age, sex, and IQ. Children ranged in age from 8 to 13 years (M = 10.9). The oral language tests focused on lexical knowledge, as reflected by naming tasks and the PPVT, and syntactic and morphologic knowledge, as measured by the Berry-Talbot Language Test (Berry, 1977) and the grammatic closure subtest on the ITPA. The written language battery included standardized and experimental measures of single-word recognition, decoding in context, reading rate, reading comprehension, sound-symbol processing, and related academic skills.

The data essentially confirmed the distinctiveness of the three samples of children. The accuracy disabled children produced more errors, read more slowly, and showed poorer comprehension than the rate disabled and normal children. The errors these children made in reading pseudowords suggested that, at a mean age of 11 years, they still fail to remember basic phoneme-letter correspondences. With respect to language abilities, the accuracy disabled sample demonstrated deficiencies in morphological and syntactic knowledge compared to rate disabled and normal peers. The accuracy disabled readers were also significantly slower than the rate disabled children in naming of serial-letter arrays and analyzing individual speech sounds. Regarding this sample, Lovett (1987, p. 257) concluded:

> These data suggest that accuracy disabled children suffer a multidimensional language impairment coupled with specific sound analysis difficulties and a seeming inability to automatize or consolidate single letter identities and/or names.

The reading abilities of the rate disabled sample were more selectively impaired. There were no differences between these children and the normal readers in their identification of regular and exception words, suggesting that both groups were equally adept in using phonological recoding and word-specific (direct access) routes to comprehension. Although these groups were equivalent in accuracy measures, the rate disabled subjects exhibited significant impairments in word recognition speed in addition to those already documented in reading rate for connected text. The rate disabled readers took particularly long identifying infrequently used words. Lovett suggested that the slow word recognition times of the rate disabled children had an adverse effect on their ability to read connected text. Although these children are accurate in recognizing words in isolation, they do not do so well identifying words in context. Lovett argues that the depressed word recognition speeds of the rate disabled readers interfere with their ability to process words in connected text. She speculates that the children become functionally overloaded by the demands of processing large units of text.

With respect to oral language abilities, the rate disabled readers and the normal readers were identical with one exception. The rate disabled subjects were slower in accessing and providing names for single- and multiple-element visual arrays. Importantly, slow naming times were not apparent on auditory or associative naming measures, indicating that the rate disability could not be attributed to a general word retrieval or lexical access deficit. The rate deficit thus appears to be specific to language in its visual form.

The Statistical Classification Approach

Doehring and Hoshko (1977) were the first researchers to use cluster analyses to classify poor readers based on measures of reading performance. Two samples of children with reading problems were administered tasks that evaluated visual matching, auditory matching, oral reading, and visual scanning abilities. The first sample (n = 34, age range = 8–17) met "the usual criteria of reading disabilities," whereas the second sample (n = 31, age range = 8–12) had a primary diagnosis of learning disability (21 children), childhood aphasia (5 children), and mental retardation (5 children). Three different profiles of reading skill deficits were found. Children with the Type O profile (oral reading problems) were poorest at oral word, phrase, and sentence reading, and near normal in silent reading. Children with Type A profile (intermodal association problems) had difficulty rapidly matching spoken and printed letters, words, and syllables. Those with Type S profile (sequential relation problems) were particularly poor in visual and auditory-visual matching of words and syllables as compared to letters. Type A and Type S profiles were also found in the sample of children with mixed problems, along with Type V (visual perception problems) for a small number of children who were poor in rapid visual matching. Five children could not be classified.

The identification of a subgroup of reading disabled children that only have oral reading problems represents an important finding. Previous attempts to classify children with reading problems had not considered that some children would only have difficulty reading aloud. Children with Type A profiles might be similar to the rate disabled readers identified by Lovett.

Summary of Subtypes Based on Nature of Reading Disabilities

There are a variety of ways to subgroup reading disabilities based on the nature of the reading disability. Marshall and Newcombe (1973) and Boder (1973) subdivided individuals with reading disability based on error patterns and reading route. A problem with this approach was that the same error patterns identified in disabled readers are also found in normal readers. Another problem was that error patterns and reading route change with development in both normal and disabled readers. The research also indicated that disabled readers were not more likely to use one reading route (e.g., whole-word) than good readers (Treiman & Hirsh-Pasek, 1985). Lovett (1984, 1987) provided evidence that rate disabled and accuracy disabled subgroups show distinct patterns of reading and language performance, and also respond in different ways to standard remediation approaches. This classification appears to have some utility in subdividing reading disabled children. The major contribution of a cluster analysis of reading measures was the identification of a subgroup of children whose primary problem was in reading aloud (Doehring & Hoshko, 1977).

SUBTYPES BASED ON READING AND NONREADING SKILLS

The classification systems reviewed thus far have been based either on associated symptomotology or on reading performance. In this section, we discuss in some detail a study by Doehring and his colleagues (Doehring, Trites, Patel, & Fiedorowicz, 1981) in which subgroups of reading disabilities were proposed based on patterns of reading performance, language abilities, and associated factors.

Doehring et al. administered a battery of reading, language, and neuropsychological tests to a sample of 88 subjects with reading disabilities. The majority of subjects were delayed by at least two years in some aspect of standardized reading achievement and were within the normal range of intelligence. Children with associated deficits were not included. The majority of the subjects were between 8 and 14 years old. Nine of the subjects were older than 14 years; three subjects were older than 20. The average age of the 88 subjects was 12 years, 3 months, which corresponded to an expected grade level of 6.75.

READING SUBTYPES

Classification of the subjects according to reading skill deficits revealed three profiles that closely resembled those found in an earlier study (Doehring & Hoshko, 1977): Type O—Oral Reading Deficit, Type A—Association Deficit, and Type S—Sequential Deficit. Forty subjects had loadings of .40 and above for Type O, 22 subjects loaded highly on Type A, and 17 subjects loaded highest on Type S. Sixteen subjects were not classified into any of the types.

LANGUAGE PATTERNS

Doehring et al. looked next at the interactive patterns of language deficits. Unlike previous researchers, Doehring et al. recognized that different types of language deficits might be involved in different types of reading disabilities. Specifically, they anticipated that reading disabilities were more likely to interact with lower-level (i.e., below the level of single words) than with higher-level language skills. The battery of language tests consisted of 11 tests that measured phonological processing (e.g., phoneme segmentation and blending), short-term verbal memory, serial naming, and morphological, semantic, and syntactic knowledge and usage. To assess expressive language, a short language sample (at least 15 utterances) was analyzed using Lee's (1974) Developmental Sentence Scoring procedure. A total of 22 language measures were obtained from the 11 tests administered.

The 22 language measures were administered to 10 normally achieving children at each grade level from kindergarten through grade six, for a total of 70 children. The normative sample had no hearing or uncorrected visual problems, used English as their first language, and showed adequate (i.e., not too high or low) school achievement. Scores increased from the lower to higher grades on all language measures with the exception of serial naming of numbers, which had a very early ceiling.

Doehring et al. first analyzed the average performance of the entire sample of 88 disabled readers on the 22 language measures. In general, the subjects were as impaired in language skills as they were in reading skills. They performed poorest on the morphophonemic and expressive language (DSS) measures, scoring at about the level of normal first graders. They were about five years below grade level in phoneme deletion (elison task), serial naming of months, and the most advanced part of the Token Test. They were three to four years below grade level on the three other phonological processing tasks: naming days, repeating unrelated words, and repeating randomized words in sentences. Performance on the remaining tests was approximately two to three years below grade level.

The pattern of language performance indicated that the disabled readers had the most difficulty at low levels of language involving phonological and morphological knowledge. Note, however, that the subjects' extremely poor performance on the measure of expressive syntax is not consistent with this pattern. The disabled readers had the least difficulty on tasks measuring higher levels of semantic knowledge. These findings are thus generally consistent with the large body of literature demonstrating a strong relationship between phonological processing and reading performance (see Chapter 4).

Reading and Language Patterns

Doehring et al. next considered the average language test scores of the subjects relative to their reading classification. The language test profiles did not show different patterns of deficit as Doehring et al. expected they would. In fact, the only discrepancy was that Type A and Type S subjects had lower DSS scores than Type O subjects. Other than this, the three reading types showed the same general pattern of a more severe impairment in phonemic-level abilities than in higher-level language abilities. Q-factor analyses of the language tests alone and of the combined reading and language tests revealed a complex relationship between language and reading disabilities. The Type O reading deficit was asssociated with two different types of language deficits (short-term verbal memory and word retrieval deficit), whereas a single pattern of language deficit (poor serial naming) was associated with the other two types of reading disabilities.

NEUROPSYCHOLOGICAL PATTERNS

In addition to the battery of reading and language tests, each subject was administered a battery of six to eight neuropsychological tests developed by the second author (Trites, 1977, cited in Doehring et al., 1981). The behaviors tested by this battery included attention, perception, memory, intellectual ability, language ability, concept formation, sensory and motor skills, personality, and achievement. The majority of verbal measures on the battery were verbal subtests from the WISC or the WAIS, and many of the visual measures were performance subtests of these tests. There were 7 measures of verbal ability, 13 measures of visual skill, 7 measures of tactile skill, and 10 measures of motor and tactile skill.

In general, the sample of 88 reading disabled subjects performed above the average expected for clinical referrals (Doehring et al., 1981, p. 154). On the WISC, the group average was slightly below normal for all but one of the verbal subtests (similarities) and slightly above normal for all but one of the performance subtests (coding). Only performance on the digit span fell below one standard deviation of normal. Lateralization tasks revealed no indication of cerebral dysfunction. The subjects performed above average on all of the tactile measures except bilateral finger agnosia.

Performance on the neuropsychological battery was considered next in terms of the reading deficit subtypes. The Type O subjects tended to be the least impaired; their WISC scores were comparable or superior to those of the other types. Concept formation ability was particularly good for nonverbal stimuli. Type A was the most impaired group. WISC scores were lower than those of the other types. Auditory attention memory span was short and verbal concept formation skills were below average. The predominant deficit of Type S subjects was spatial in nature. Performance on the Raven Progressive Matrices, Right-Left Discrimination, and tactual performance tests was poor in comparison with the other types.

The study by Doehring et al. might be considered the ultimate classification study. It is difficult to conceive of a study in which subjects would be administered a larger battery of tests that evaluated reading, language, and cognitive abilities. The findings suggest that it was perhaps naive to think that clear patterns of reading, language, and cognitive performance would characterize a population of subjects with reading disabilities. Particularly noteworthy, given our language perspective, was the finding that language deficiencies were characteristic of all three subgroups of reading disability. Recall that many studies (e.g, Petrauskas and Rourke, 1979) have found that language deficiencies are characteristic of only certain subgroups of the population of individuals with reading disabilities. These studies, however, have not included measures of phonological processing. Instead, measures of higher-level syntactic and semantic proficiency were used. But, as Doehring et al. have shown, disabled readers perform most like normal readers on most higher-level language measures.

In short, if one defines language as including knowledge of phonological components in addition to higher-level syntactic, semantic, and discourse knowledge, then language deficits become a defining characteristic of a reading disability. That is, it is not possible to have a reading disability without a deficit in some aspect of phonological, syntactic, semantic, or discourse processing. This view of reading disability will be elaborated in the next chapter.

Subtypes Based on Language Abilities

The subtyping studies reviewed above involved grouping children according to their reading or associated processing abilities. Whereas some of these subtyping schemes identified children with language deficits as the largest subgroup, divisions of this subgroup were less common. A subtyping scheme based specifically on spoken language abilities was recently suggested by Donahue (1986). She proposed the presence of at least three subtypes of language disorders in children with reading disabilities. The first group are children who have a preschool language impairment. These children, often labeled "language impaired/disordered," are generally seen by a speech-language pathologist during the preschool years. Most of these children have subsequent problems learning to read (Aram & Nation, 1980; Korngold, Menyuk, Liebergott, & Chesnick, 1988), and often become relabeled as "learning/reading disabled."

The second group of children are not identified until they enter school and have problems learning to read. Donahue has suggested that if these children have oral language problems, they are too subtle to be detected during the preschool years. Poor performance on measures of phonological processing is evident, however, during the preschool years. Although these children generally have age-appropriate spoken-language abilities when they enter school, spoken language deficiencies become more noticeable with the increased importance of classroom and narrative discourse abilities (see Chapters 6 and 7).

Donahue's characterization of the third group of children is somewhat sketchy. The existence of this group is based on the important role that reading plays in the continued development of many language skills. Children in this group have age-appropriate oral language skills, but have difficulty learning to read for other reasons (e.g., attentional, motivational, or instructional factors). The reading problem results in the child having less exposure to new vocabulary and sophisticated syntactic structures. Reciprocal causation factors such as these have an important influence on the relationship between spoken and written language. These factors are discussed further in the next chapter.

The Relationship Between Spoken and Written Language Disorders

It is relatively easy to distinguish between young school-age children who have noticeable spoken language deficits and those who do not. The more interesting question underlying a language-based subtyping scheme concerns the relationship between spoken and written language disorders. If spoken and written language abilities are directly correlated or are linked to a common third variable, one would expect that severe spoken language deficits would be associated with a severe reading problem. This does not appear to be the case, however. In two recent studies, we compared the reading and phonological processing abilities of two groups of six to eight year-old children matched for nonverbal intelligence. The first group had documented spoken language deficits and were receiving speech-language therapy. The second group had no history of spoken language deficits and were enrolled in reading resource rooms (Kamhi & Catts, 1986; Kamhi, Catts, Mauer, Apel, & Gentry, 1988). In both studies, we found essentially no differences in reading and phonological processing abilities between the two groups. The reading abilities of the two groups were at least one year below expected grade level. These findings suggest that although spoken language problems are strongly linked to reading problems, the causal relationship between spoken and written language problems is not straightforward. In the next chapter, we will suggest that it is not the spoken-language deficit that causes the reading problem, but an underlying processing limitation(s) that affects both spoken and written language development.

Another reason that spoken and written language abilities might not be directly correlated is because different aspects of language (e.g., speech development) develop somewhat independently of other aspects (e.g., syntax and semantics). Evidence for the independence of speech and language development can be found in a recent longitudinal study of speech-delayed children by Shriberg and Kwiatkowski (1988). In this study, Shriberg and Kwiatkowski found that speech-delayed children without associated cognitive or language impairments did not tend to have later academic problems. Speech-only-delayed children represented a relatively small portion, 20–25 percent, of the population of speech-delayed children. The remaining 75–80 percent of children with speech delays who had cognitive or language deficits tended to have subsequent academic problems.

Some other aspects of language also might develop independently. For example, expressive language deficits have been shown to characterize some groups of reading disabled children, but not others (Doehring et al., 1981). Examples of expressive language deficits include reduced syntactic-semantic complexity and frequent errors in the use of grammatical morphemes. In contrast, differences in receptive language abilities have not been associated with distinct subgroups (Doehring et al., 1981; Lovett, 1987). In short, although deficits in spoken and written language tend to co-occur, certain aspects of spoken language, particularly expressive speech and language, seem to develop independently of other aspects of spoken language and reading.

Summary and Critique of Classification of Children with Reading Disabilities

In the introduction to this section on classification, we noted that it was probably unrealistic to expect that a reliable and valid classification system for reading disabled children could ever be developed. A review of selected subtyping studies, such as the one just completed, can sometimes leave even the most discerning reader in a confused state. What is to be learned from these subtyping studies other than there are numerous ways to divide a heterogeneous population? How does one decide which of the subtypes are valid and which are not?

The subtyping research has provided considerable information about the reading, language, and associated abilities of individuals with reading disabilities. The knowledge gained about the heterogeneity of individuals with reading problems has helped to develop inclusionary definitions of reading disabilities and has contributed considerably to the understanding of causal correlates of reading disabilities. Despite these contributions, some theorists (Kavale & Forness, 1987) feel that the subtyping research should be evaluated in terms of its primary purpose of classifying reading disabled individuals into subtypes.

Kavale and Forness (1987) have written an excellent critical analysis of subtyping studies. Among the many points they make is that there is a strong association between the measures used in a subtype study and the resulting subgroups. In other words, a researcher who uses visual-spatial and linguistic measures is likely to find evidence of a linguistic and visual-spatial subgroup. Kavale and Forness also point out some problems with cluster analysis, the statistical technique used in many of the subtype studies. They note that multivariate data sets do not automatically qualify for cluster analysis. Clustering tendency in the data needs to be tested first to determine the extent to which groups of homogeneous members exist in the data. Failure to perform such testing may lead to spurious results because clustering methods produce groupings from any data set, or as Kavale and Forness wrote: "garbage in, clusters out" (p. 377). Good empirically based classification systems may be parsimonious and have structural integrity, but may not be useful because of their limited educational relevance.

In light of these points, clinicians and educators need to be somewhat wary of the proliferation of subtyping schemes and classification systems. In particular, it is important to remember that subgroups are not completely homogeneous with respect to reading, language, or associated abilities. Subgroups account for only a portion of the variance that exist among individuals with reading disabilities. Deciding which subtyping system to use depends in part on whether an individual is using subtypes to address theoretically motivated research questions or make clinical/educational decisions concerning service delivery and intervention planning. For example, the use of exclusionary criteria to distinguish reading disabled subtypes allows a researcher to address the relationship between associated factors and reading performance. Subtypes based on reading and language abilities, in contrast, tend to provide some direction for intervention programming.

SUMMARY

In this chapter, we have considered the ways in which children with reading disabilities have been labeled, defined, and subtyped. We suggested that many individuals with reading disabilities are best characterized as having a developmental language impairment whose manifestations change with age. This view is supported by the subtyping literature in which children with language deficits were generally identified as the largest subgroup. It is also supported by research discussed throughout this book that documents the different kinds of language deficits demonstrated by children with reading disabilities. The characterization of a reading disability as a developmental language impairment thus places the emphasis where it belongs—on language.

REFERENCES

Aram, D., and Nation, J. (1980). Preschool language disorders and subsequent language and academic difficulties. *Journal of Communication Disorders, 13,* 229–241.

Berger, M., Yule, W., and Rutter, M. (1975). Attainment and adjustment in two geographical areas: II. The prevalence of specific reading retardation. *British Journal of Psychiatry, 126,* 510–519.

Berry, M. (1977). *The Berry-Talbot developmental guide to comprehension of grammar.* Rockford, IL: M. Berry.

Boder, E. (1971). Developmental dyslexia: A diagnostic screening procedure based on three characteristic patterns of reading and spelling. In B. Bateman (Ed.), *Learning disorders, 4.* Seattle: Special Child Publications.

Boder, E. (1973). Developmental dyslexia: A diagnostic approach based on three atypical reading-spelling patterns. *Developmental Medicine and Child Neurology, 15,* 663–687.

Byrne, B. (1981). Deficient syntactic control in poor readers: Is a weak phonetic memory code responsible? *Applied Psycholinguistics, 3,* 201–212.

Ceci, S., and Baker, S. (1987). Commentary: How shall we conceptualize the language problems of learning disabled children? In S. Ceci (Ed.), *Handbook of cognitive, social, and neuropsychological aspects of learning disabilities, 2,* 103–115. Hillsdale, NJ: Erlbaum.

Chall, J. (1983). *Stages of reading development.* New York: McGraw-Hill.

Chasty, H. (1985). What is dyslexia? A developmental language perspective. In M. Snowling (Ed.), *Children's written language difficulties: Assessment and management,* 11–28. Windsor, Berkshire: NFER-Nelson Publishing Co.

Coltheart, M., Masterson, J., Byng, S., Prior, M., and Riddoch, J., (1983). Surface dyslexia. *Quarterly Journal of Experimental Psychology, 35,* A, 469–495.

Coltheart, M., Patterson, K., and Marshall, J. (Eds.) (1980). *Deep dyslexia.* London: Routledge and Kegan Paul.

Critchley, M., and Critchley, E. (1978). *Dyslexia defined.* London: Heinemann.

Doehring, D., and Hoshko, I. (1977). Classification of reading problems by the Q-technique of factor analysis. *Cortex, 13,* 281–294.

Doehring, D., Trites, R., Patel, P., and Fiedorowicz, C. (1981). *Reading disabilities: The interaction of reading, language, and neuropsychological deficits.* New York: Academic Press.

Donahue, M. (1986). Linguistic and communicative development in learning disabled children. In S. Ceci (Ed.), *Handbook of cognitive, social, and neuropsychological aspects of learning disabilities, 1,* 263–291. Hillsdale, NJ: Erlbaum.

Fisk, I., and Rourke, B. (1979). Identification of subtypes of learning-disabled children at three age levels: A neuropsychological multivariate approach. *Journal of Clinical Neuropsychology, 1,* 289–310.

Fletcher, J., and Satz, P. (1980). Developmental changes in the neuropsychological correlates of reading achievement: A six year longitudinal follow-up. *Journal of Clinical Neuropsychology, 2,* 23–37.

Godfrey, J., Syrdal-Lasky, A., Millay, K., and Knox, C. (1981). Performance of dyslexic children on speech perception tests. *Journal of Experimental Child Psychology, 32,* 401–424.

Harris, T., and Hodges, R. (1981). *A dictionary of reading and related terms.* Newark: International Reading Association.

Healy, J. (1982). The enigma of hyperlexia. *Reading Research Quarterly, 17,* 319–338.

Holmes, J. (1978). Regression and reading breakdown. In A. Caramazza and E. Zurif (Eds.), *Language acquisition and language breakdown.* Baltimore: Johns Hopkins University Press.

Hynd, G., and Cohen, M. (1983). *Dyslexia: Neuropsychological theory, research, and clinical differentiation.* New York: Grune and Stratton.

Ingram, T.T.S., Mason, M., and Blackburn, I. (1970). A retrospective study of 82 children with reading disabilities. *Developmental Medical Child Neurology, 12,* 271–281.

Johnson, D., and Myklebust, H. (1967). *Learning disabilities: Educational principles and practices.* New York: Grune and Stratton.

Johnson, D., and Blalock, J. (1987). *Adults with learning disabilities: Clinical studies.* New York: Grune and Stratton.

Jorm, A. (1979). The cognitive and neurological basis of developmental dyslexia: A theoretical framework and review. *Cognition, 7,* 19–33.

Kamhi, A., and Catts, H. (1986). Toward an understanding of developmental language and reading disorders. *Journal of Speech and Hearing Disorders, 51,* 337-347.

Kamhi, A., Catts, H., Mauer, D., Apel, K., and Gentry, B. (1988). Phonological and spatial processing abilities in language and reading impaired children. *Journal of Speech and Hearing Disorders, 53,* 316–327.

Kavale, K., and Forness, S. (1987). The far side of heterogeneity: A critical analysis of empirical subtyping research in learning disabilities. *Journal of Learning Disabilities, 20,* 374–383.

Kinsbourne, M., and Warrington, E. (1963). Developmental factors in reading and writing backwardness. *British Journal of Psychology, 54,* 145–156.

Kolb, D., and Whinshaw, I. (1980). *Fundamentals of human neuropsychology.* San Francisco: W. H. Freeman and Co.

Korngold, B., Menyuk, P., Liebergott, J., and Chesnick, M. (1988). Early oral language as predictors of reading performance in first and second grade. Paper presented at the Symposium on Research in Child Language Disorders, Madison, WI.

LaBerge, D., and Samuels, S. (1974). Toward a theory of automatic information processing in reading. *Cognitive Psyhology, 6,* 293–323.

Lee, L. (1974). *Developmental sentence analysis.* Evanston, IL: Northwestern University Press.

Liberman, I. (1987). Language and literacy: The obligation of the schools of education. *Bulletin of the Orton Dyslexic Society.*

Lovett, M. (1984). A developmental perspective on reading dysfunction: Accuracy and rate criteria in the subtyping of dyslexic children. *Brain and Language, 22,* 67–91.

Lovett, M. (1987). A developmental approach to reading disability: Accuracy and speed criteria of normal and deficient reading skill. *Child Development, 58,* 234–260.

Lyon, R. (1985). Identification and remediation of learning disability subtypes: Preliminary findings. *Learning Disabilities Focus, 1,* 21–35.

Lyon, R., and Watson, B. (1981). Empirically derived subgroups of learning disabled readers: Diagnostic characteristics. *Journal of Learning Disabilities, 14,* 256–261.

Marshall, J. (1984). Toward a rational taxonomy of the developmental dyslexias. In R. Malatesha and H. Whitaker (Eds.), *Dyslexia: A global issue, 45–58.* The Hague: Martinus Nighoff.

Marshall, J., and Newcombe, F. (1973). Patterns of paralexia: A psycholinguistic approach. *Journal of Psycholinguistic Research, 2,* 175–200.

Mattis, S., French, J., and Rapin, I. (1975). Dyslexia in children and young adults: Three independent neuropsychological syndromes. *Developmental Medicine and Child Neurology, 17,* 150–163.

Maxwell, S., and Wallach, G. (1984). The language-learning disabilities connection: Symptoms of early language disability change over time. In G. Wallach and K. Butler, (Eds.), *Language learning disabilities in school-age children, 35–60.* Baltimore: Williams and Wilkins.

Morris, R., Blashfield, R., and Satz, P. (1986). Developmental classification of reading-disabled children. *Journal of Clinical and Experimental Neuropsychology, 8,* 371–392.

Orton, S. (1937). *Reading, writing, and speech problems in children.* New York: Norton.

Patterson, K. (1981). Neuropsychological approaches to the study of reading. *British Journal of Psychology, 72,* 151–174.

Patterson, K. (1982). The relationship between reading and phonological coding: Further neuropsychological observations. In A. Ellis (Ed.), *Normality and pathology in cognitive functions, 74–98.* London: Academic Press.

Patterson, K., Marshall, J., and Coltheart, M. (Eds.)(1985). *Surface dyslexia: Neuropsychological and cognitive studies of phonological reading.* Hillsdale, NJ: Erlbaum.

Perfetti, C. (1985). *Reading ability.* New York: Oxford University Press.

Petrauskas, R., and Rourke, B. (1979). Identification of subtypes of retarded readers: A neuropsychological multivariate approach. *Journal of Clinical Neuropsychology, 1,* 17–37.

Rudel, R. (1985). The definition of dyslexia: Language and motor deficits. In F. Duffy and N. Geschwind (Eds.), *Dyslexia: A neuroscientific approach to clinical evaluation, 33–54.* Boston: Little, Brown.

Rutter, M. (1978). Prevalence and types of dyslexia. In A. Benton and D. Pearl (Eds.), *Dyslexia: An appraisal of current knowledge,* 145–167. New York and London: Oxford University Press.

Rutter, M., Tizard, J., and Whitmore, K. (1970). *Education, health, and behavior.* London: Longman.

Satz, P., Taylor, H., Friel, J., and Fletcher, J. (1978). Some developmental and predictive precursors of reading disabilities: A six-year follow-up. In A. Benton and D. Pearl (Eds.), *Dyslexia: An appraisal of current knowledge,* 313–348. New York: Oxford University Press.

Shriberg, L., and Kwiatkowski, J. (1988). A follow-up study of children with phonologic disorders of unknown origin. *Journal of Speech and Hearing Disorders, 53,* 144–156.

Silberberg, N., and Silberberg, M. (1967). Hyperlexia: Specific word recognition skills in young children. *Exceptional Children, 34,* 41–42.

Spreen, O., and Haaf, R. (1986). Empirically derived learning disability subtypes: A replication attempt and longitudinal patterns over 15 years. *Journal of Learning Disabilities, 19,* 170–181.

Stanovich, K. (1986). Toward an interactive compensatory model of individual differences in the development of reading fluency. *Reading Research Quarterly, 16,* 32–71.

Stanovich, K., Cunningham, A., and Freeman, D. (1984). Relation between early reading acquisition and word decoding with and without context: A longitudinal study of first-grade children. *Journal of Educational Psychology, 76,* 668–677.

Stedman, L., and Kaestle, C. (1987). Literacy and reading performance in the United States from 1880 to the present. *Reading Research Quarterly, 22,* 8–46.

Temple, C., and Marshall, J. (1983). A case study of developmental phonological dyslexia. *British Journal of Psychology, 74,* 517–533.

Thomson, M. (1984). *Developmental dyslexia: Its nature, assessment, and remediation.* London: Edward Arnold.

Treiman, R., and Hirsh-Pasek, K. (1985). Are there qualitative differences in reading behavior between dyslexics and normal readers? *Memory & Cognition, 13,* 357–364.

Vellutino, F. (1979). *Dyslexia: Theory and research.* Cambridge, MA: MIT Press.

Wheeler, T., and Watkins, E. (1979). A review of symptomology. *Dyslexia Review, 2,* 1, 12–16.

Yule, W., Rutter, M., Berger, M., and Thomson, J. (1974). Over and under achievement in reading: Distribution in the general population. *British Journal of Educational Psychology, 44,* 1, 1–12.

3

Causes and Consequences of Reading Disabilities

Alan G. Kamhi

A common theme in Chapter 2 was the heterogeneity of the population of individuals with reading disabilities. Heterogeneity has contributed to the problems in defining and labeling children and adults who have reading disabilities. Attempts to identify homogeneous subgroups of individuals with reading disabilities represent one way to deal with the heterogeneity problem. Another way to approach the heterogeneity issue is to study the factors that contribute to individual differences in reading ability. It is not an exaggeration to say that good readers and poor readers have been compared on just about every perceptual, cognitive, and linguistic task that has ever been devised (Stanovich, 1986a). As Stanovich (p. 361) aptly noted, group performance differences have been found on a large number of these tasks. The problem is thus not a lack of empirical evidence, but rather difficulty in deciding how to interpret the evidence.

Stanovich (1986a) discussed several problems with the existing evidence. First, for many years researchers failed to recognize that performance on any single task was the result of many different information processing operations. The failure to appreciate the specific cognitive demands of a task made it common for researchers to observe a performance difference between a group of good readers and a group of poor readers on a particular task and then conclude that the ability presumed to be tapped by the task was responsible for the reading disability. For example, a difference between good readers and poor readers on a perceptual task was interpreted to mean that a visual processing deficit was the key to reading failure. Such a finding, however, should mark the beginning of a careful task analysis to uncover the specific cognitive locus of the difference (Stanovich, 1986a, p. 362).

A second, more serious problem with the existing evidence involves causation. Because most studies have employed correlational designs, it is often difficult to determine the direction of causality. After a performance difference has been found between good readers and poor readers and the specific process deficit has been identified, the researcher still must address the question of whether the performance difference (1) causes variation in reading performance, (2) is itself caused by differences in reading performance, or (3) is related to a third underlying variable. It is also possible for a specific deficit to cause variation in reading performance and, in turn, be affected by poor reading performance.

A third problem is the possibility that causal relationships between reading and cognitive factors change with development. As Stanovich (1986a, p. 362) pointed out, individual differences in a particular cognitive ability may be a causal determinant early in development but have no further effects on reading later in development. Related to the developmental issue are the changes that occur in measures of reading performance. Young children who are poor readers have difficulty in word recognition processes. Measures of letter and word identification/attack skills capture these reading deficiencies. Older children with reading problems eventually develop accurate word recognition skills, although they might be slower in implementing these skills (Lovett, 1987). Deficient reading performance is thus going to be best captured by measures of oral reading and reading comprehension. Measures of word recognition speed would also be appropriate; such measures, however, generally are not used in the educational settings.

A final concern involves the population of children on which most of this evidence has been collected. This population is the one defined by exlusionary criteria discussed in Chapter 2. This subgroup of individuals with reading disabilities evidences significant reading difficulty despite average or above average intelligence; intact (or corrected) sensory functions; and no apparent neurological, emotional, or social disorders. These individuals also have had adequate exposure to reading instruction and are not "encumbered by sociocultural differences" (Vellutino, 1979). Studying individual differences in this particular group of individuals with reading disabilities will thus not reveal the nature of the relationship between reading and associated factors, such as intelligence, neurological functions, and emotional behavior.

Despite the problems in interpreting aforementioned individual differences in cognitive processes and reading performance, the evidence does converge on a general set of conclusions. The following sections discuss the various deficits that have been proposed to account for reading failure. The deficits that contribute most to word recognition problems and early reading failure will be reviewed first. These include visual perceptual deficits, phonological processing deficits, higher-level language deficits, and memory deficiences. The deficits that contribute most to text-comprehension difficulties and later reading failure will be considered next. These include deficits in higher-level language processes, metacognitive abilities, and motivational states. The final part of the chapter discusses the influence of reciprocal causation factors, the assumption of specificity, and how best to describe and explain a reading disability.

Factors that Influence Word Recognition

Consistent with other theorists (Perfetti, 1985; Stanovich, 1985, 1986a; Torgesen, 1985; Vellutino, 1979), we believe that the specific cognitive processes that underlie word recognition processes explain the majority of variance in early reading performance. The relationship between reading comprehension and word recognition skills is quite strong, particularly in children first learning to read. Stanovich, Cunningham, and Feeman (1984) found that across a wide variety of studies involving children in grades one through six, the correlations between word recognition speed/accuracy and reading comprehension ranged from .50 to .80. The relationship is apparent even at the earliest stages of reading (Groff, 1978), which suggests that it is unlikely that word recognition skill is an incidental correlate of the reading experience of good readers. Evidence also comes from longitudinal and training studies. Lesgold and Resnick (1982), using a longitudinal design, found that increased word recognition speed leads to improved reading comprehension rather than the reverse. Lovett, Ransby, and Barron (1988) found that training oral and written language comprehension skills did not improve reading performance. The children did, however, benefit from remediation that targeted decoding skills. In the sections to follow, we consider the factors that contribute to word recognition skill.

Visual Perceptual Processing Skills

For many years, visual perceptual deficits were thought to be the principal cause of word recognition and early reading problems (Herman, 1959; Orton, 1925). This view was strongly influenced by clinical observations of letter reversals in children with reading problems. There are two kinds of reversals. In one, the letters of a word are interchanged (e.g., was/saw and nip/pin). In the other case, a letter is read as a mirror-image reversal (e.g., d/b, p/q). As indicated in Chapter 2, reversal errors have become synonymous with the term *dyslexia*.

There are several problems in using reversal errors to support a perceptual basis to word recognition difficulties. First, both kinds of reversal errors are also made by normally developing beginning readers. Indeed, good readers have been found to make the same proportion of reversal errors as poor readers (Holmes & Peper, 1977). Second, reversal errors account for only 25 percent of misread letters among low-ability readers (Liberman, Shankweiler, Orlando, Harris, and Berti, 1971). Third, reversed orientation errors are quite variable across and within low-ability readers. Finally, researchers (Vellutino, Steger, & Kandel, 1972) have shown that when reversal errors do occur, they usually are not the result of visual perceptual problems. In the Vellutino et al. study, when poor readers were asked to copy words that they reversed in reading (e.g., ''was''), they had no difficulty doing so. These findings led Vellutino (1979) to conclude that reversal errors are more likely due to problems in associating verbal labels with visual symbols than to spatial confusions. In other words, reversal errors reflect a higher-level language problem rather than a low-level visual discrimination problem.

Reversal errors represent only one source of evidence in support of the perceptual deficit view. Other visual tasks (e.g., masking tasks, fusion paradigms, and detection tasks) have been used to study different aspects of visual perception such as visual segmentation, encoding, feature extraction, and visual persistence. The bulk of the evidence (Stanovich, 1986a; or Vellutino & Scanlon, 1982, for a review) supports a minimal or nonexistent relationship between visual processing abilities and reading ability. However, as Stanovich (1986a, p. 71) has argued, the issue should not be decided by simply adding up the number of studies on either side. Stanovich invoked Calfee's (1977) concept of a ''clean'' psychological test that involves being sure that the tasks employed isolate the process in question to eliminate possible contamination of other cognitive processes. Unfortunately, much of the literature on visual processes is confounded by verbal short-term memory and familiarity factors. When these factors are experimentally controlled, the literature becomes more clear: The more an experiment specifically isolates a visual process, the smaller the performance difference between good readers and poor readers (Vellutino, 1979).

Vellutino et al. (1972), for example, found that poor readers (grades two through eight) performed as well as good readers recalling words that were presented tachistoscopically. The exception involved words that taxed the upper limit of poor readers' short-term memory span. The poor readers did not perform as well as the normal readers in pronouncing and spelling the words. These findings were replicated in a later study by Vellutino, Smith, Steger, and Kaman (1975). Vellutino and Scanlon (1982, p. 200) argue that the noteworthy aspect in these studies is that many of the words were visually similar to other English words (e.g., was/saw, loin/lion, calm/clam), yet the poor readers actually had less difficulty copying the words than the good readers, although they named them incorrectly.

Several studies have shown that good readers use linguistic codes for visual storage more effectively than poor readers (Swanson, 1978; Huba, Vellutino, & Scanlon, cited in Vellutino & Scanlon, 1982). Swanson, for example, presented subjects with a serial memory task using geometric shapes. Prior to the experiment, half of the subjects received either discrimination training or labeling training. Using words to label geometric shapes is an example of using linguistic codes to store visual information. Contrary to what the visual-deficit view would predict, good and poor readers who received the discrimination training did not differ on the serial memory task. In other words, the two groups were apparently similar in their visual-perceptual abilities. Differences favoring the normal group were found, however, in the groups who received the naming training.

Results from visual training studies also fail to support the visual deficit view. As Stanovich (1986a, p. 71) wrote, "It is generally accepted that visual perception training programs have been ineffective in promoting reading acquisition." Taken together, it should be apparent that visual perceptual processes play a minimal role in explaining individual variation in early reading performance and, therefore, play a minimal causal role in early reading failure.

MEMORY PROCESSES

The complexity and diversity of memory processes preclude simple conclusions about the relationship between reading and memory. Memory processes are involved not only in word recognition, but also in higher-level comprehension processes. Torgesen (1985) has provided a useful framework for understanding memory processes. He has suggested that at least three factors influence these processes: (1) basic processing operations and capacities, (2) the richness and relevance of the knowledge base, and (3) control strategies. Each of these factors will be discussed.

BASIC PROCESSING DEFICIENCIES

There are essentially two basic processes involved in memory: encoding and retrieval. Encoding refers to the "process of translating sensory input into a representational form that can be stored in memory'' (Torgesen, 1985, p. 350). Retrieval refers to the operations involved in accessing information from long-term memory. A large body of literature has shown that poor readers have difficulty encoding and retrieving information that is coded phonologically (Bradley & Bryant, 1985; Juel, Griffith, & Gough, 1986; Liberman, 1987; Mann, 1986; Perfetti, 1986; Share, Jorm, Maclean, & Matthews, 1984; Stanovich, 1986a; Torgesen, 1985; Wagner & Torgesen, 1987). The difficulty poor readers have in encoding phonological information have been attributed either to difficulty in forming accurate representations of phonological information (Vellutino, Harding, Phillips, & Steger, 1975) or low-level perceptual deficits (Tallal, 1980). Poor readers have also been shown to be slower than good readers in retrieving phonological information from long-term memory (Miles & Ellis, 1981; Perfetti & Lesgold, 1979; Torgesen & Houck, 1980; Wolf, 1986). Retrieval deficiencies can be caused by inefficient encoding processes or by a deficit in the retrieval mechanism itself.

Because the ability to process (encode and retrieve) phonological information plays such an important role in learning to read, the next chapter in this book is devoted entirely to this subject. A question that is addressed in Chapter 4, and at other points in the present chapter, is whether poor readers' memory deficiencies are limited to processing phonological information.

Knowledge Deficiencies

The extent of the current knowledge base plays a very important role in one's ability to encode and retrieve information. Incoming information that can be integrated with existing knowledge is more easily remembered than information that cannot be related to existing knowledge (Anderson, 1986). The poor performance of poor readers on some memory tasks is due in part to the limitations in their knowledge base (Perfetti, 1985; Torgesen, 1985). Reading difficulties, in turn, limit the development of the knowledge base and thus contribute to the memory problems experienced by poor readers (Stanovich, 1986a). This is an example of reciprocal causation, which will be discussed in a later section.

Control Strategy Deficiencies

Inefficient use of control strategies is another source of differences between good readers and poor readers. *Control strategies* are mental operations that are consciously organized to facilitate performance on a specific task. The notion in this case is that poor readers are less likely to use active, planful strategies that facilitate memory performance. Rehearsal, elaboration (thinking of verbal or visual associations), and clustering or chunking information are some examples of such strategies. The use of strategic problem-solving behaviors has been studied extensively in children with reading disabilities. These studies are reviewed in the subsequent section on metacognitive processes.

Shankweiler and Crain (1987) have suggested that a deficiency in the efficient management of the control mechanism of working memory might contribute to a reading disability. Working memory is viewed as having processing functions as well as storage functions (Perfetti & Lesgold, 1979). Shankweiler and Crain assign "executive" status to the processing component of working memory, and view this component as a control mechanism that is capable of integrating phonological, syntactic, and semantic information. The control mechanism transfers phonologically analyzed material out of the buffer and pushes it upward throughout the higher-level parsers, thus freeing the buffer for succeeding material. According to Shankweiler and Crain (p. 150), it is this transfer of information that is constrained by word recognition abilities. The control mechanism component in working memory thus functions to regulate the flow of information between the phonological buffer and higher-level parsers. Shankweiler and Crain suggest that poor readers have difficulty managing or regulating the flow of information. When information passes through the buffer too fast, some information will be lost; if it is too slow, integration will be impaired.

There is little doubt that children with reading disabilities have memory problems. The literature reviewed here and in the next chapter indicates that poor readers may have difficulties encoding phonological information in short-term memory, retrieving phonologically coded information from long-term memory, using strategies to facilitate memory performance, and efficiently regulating the flow of information in working memory. These memory deficiencies have unfortunate consequences for all aspects of reading performance.

Higher-level Language Contributions to Word Recognition

Attributing reading failure to phonological processing deficits or visual perceptual deficits provides bottom-up explanations for reading failure. However, several researchers, most notably Goodman (1967, 1976) and Smith (1971), have proposed that top-down processing models provide more accurate explanations of reading performance. Smith (1971), for example, has argued that good readers are more proficient in making hypotheses and predictions of upcoming words based on their knowledge of syntactic and semantic rules. With regard to reading failure, Smith (1971, p. 221) has written that "the more difficulty a reader has with reading, the more he relies on the visual information. . . . The cause of the difficulty is inability to make full use of syntactic and semantic redundancy of nonvisual sources of information."

There is little doubt that higher-level language processes influence reading performance. Questions have been raised, however, about whether these processes influence word recognition abilities or just text-level comprehension skills, and how much of the variation in reading performance is accounted for by higher-level language abilities. The use of syntactic and semantic cues to facilitate reading is usually referred to as *context effects*. An example of a context effect is for a word to be recognized more rapidly when it occurs in a sentence or discourse context than when it is presented in isolation.

Context effects on reading have received considerable research attention and caused much confusion for teachers and reading specialists. One reason for this confusion, as Stanovich (1986a, p. 366) has pointed out, is that researchers often fail to distinguish between the use of context to facilitate word recognition and the use of context to facilitate text comprehension. As will become clear, the effects of context on word recognition and text comprehension differ for good readers and poor readers. Another reason for confusion is the different terminology used to discuss the effects of higher-level language knowledge on reading. Whereas many practitioners talk about targeting general language and problem-solving skills, researchers talk about context effects. Practitioners interested in finding research support for their intervention efforts with respect to higher-level language knowledge might not be aware that the vast literature on context effects is relevant to their endeavors as well.

Perfetti and his colleagues have conducted extensive studies of the role of context in word recognition (Hogaboam & Perfetti, 1978; Perfetti, Finger, & Hogaboam, 1978; Perfetti & Hogaboam, 1975; Perfetti & Roth, 1981). In all of these experiments, a comparison was made between word recognition in a discourse context and word recognition in isolation. In the Perfetti et al. 1978 study, for example, subjects were required to predict an upcoming word and identify the word immediately after they made their prediction. High-ability readers were more accurate in predicting the exact word (32 percent compared to 23 percent for the low-ability readers). However, high-ability readers showed a gain of 50 milliseconds in identifying a word after a correct prediction, whereas low-ability readers showed a gain of 180 milliseconds. Thus, the effect of a successful prediction was larger for the low-ability reader.

In another study, Perfetti and Roth (1981) found that the word recognition skills of fourth grade high-ability readers operated most efficiently without context. The low-ability readers, all of whom had slower word recognition processes, were more dependent on context. Word recognition speed was faster when a word was predictable from context than when the word was not predictable.

Perfetti (1985, p. 144) summarized the results of these studies: "Both low-ability readers and high-ability readers name words faster in context than in isolation. This is true whether the context is read or heard by the subject and whether the context is a long story or merely pairs of sentences." Further, the word identification latencies of the low-ability readers were actually more affected by context than were those of the high-ability readers. Thus, low-ability readers were helped more by context than were high-ability readers. Perfetti's basic conclusion from this series of studies is that the context effect depends on an individual's word-identification speed, or what might be termed *decoding efficiency*. High-ability readers and low-ability readers with the same word identification time should therefore show the same context effect. Perfetti and Roth (1981) found this to be the case. In short, context effects are greater for slower word rates, whether these slow rates occur in high-ability or low-ability readers.

Stanovich (1986a) reviewed other research that has investigated context effects using different research paradigms. His conclusion is similar to Perfetti's: "The research consistently indicates that not only do the poorer readers in these studies use context, but they often show somewhat larger contextual effects than do the better readers" (p. 366). In light of the evidence against context effects on word recognition processes, Stanovich appropriately noted that it might seem difficult to understand how the claim that poor readers are less reliant on context gained popularity and credibility. He has offered several explanations for why this might have happened.

The first explanation concerns the possible confusion about context effects on word recognition processes versus context effects on text-level comprehension processes. Because good readers are more likely to use context to facilitate text-level comprehension, there might have been a tendency to overgeneralize this relationship to word recognition processes.

A second explanation concerns the confusion surrounding information processing concepts. Theorists, such as Goodman and Smith, who propose top-down models of reading, have defended the position that skilled readers rely less on visual cues in reading. As noted above, Smith (1971) has contended that good readers formulate hypotheses about upcoming words based on the linguistic redundancy in sentences and, as a result, only need to perceive a few visual features in a particular word. But recent eye-tracking studies (Just & Carpenter, 1980; Zola, 1984) have found that fluent readers sample the full visual array rather completely, even when they are reading predictable words. Their more efficient word recognition processes, however, allow them to do this sampling more quickly than poor readers. More efficient word recognition skills, as Perfetti and Stanovich have argued, lead to less reliance on contextual information.

Although Smith and Goodman's explanation of top-down influences proved to be inaccurate because of their incorrect interpretation of context effects, they did inspire the insight that readers need to allocate attentional resources to comprehension processes rather than to word recognition processes in order to become fluent readers. Recall Chall's Stage 3 of reading development (see Chapter 1) when the word recognition processes become automatized, allowing the reader to begin to read to learn. The key factor, however, in freeing up attentional resources is not greater use of higher-level language processes (context cues), but the automatization of word recognition processes.

A third explanation concerns the ubiquity of contextual facilitation. Context effects are easily documented because they occur readily in all readers. It is perhaps easy to imagine how the observation of context effects in good readers led to the conclusion that poor readers were not very proficient in using context cues. However, unlike other skills that are highly variable, such as phonological processing skills, the variability in the ability to use context to facilitate word recognition is so low that it is unlikely that it is a major determinant of individual differences in reading performance. As Stanovich (1986a) wrote, "the very ubiquity of contextual facilitation. . .is precisely the thing that prevents it from being a cause of individual differences" (p. 369).

The view that poor readers do not use contextual cues as efficiently as good readers is thus not accurate. The research has clearly shown that it is word recognition efficiency that determines the extent to which a reader uses contextual information. Because poor readers have deficient word recognition skills, they are more reliant on contextual cues. These data support an interactive-compensatory model of reading, advocated by both Perfetti and Stanovich. A key aspect of this model is the notion that when the bottom-up decoding processes involved in word recognition are deficient, the individual compensates by relying more heavily on other processes and knowledge sources, such as contextual information.

Factors that Influence Text Comprehension

Although the largest amount of variation in reading comprehension is explained by individual differences in word recognition skills, processes independent of word recognition skill also influence reading comprehension, especially at more advanced levels of reading acquisition. The independence of word recognition and text-level comprehension problems was clearly demonstrated in a study by Satz, Taylor, Friel, and Fletcher (1978), discussed in Chapter 2. Recall that this study identified two distinct groups of children with reading disabilities. The group identified in grades one and two had significant word recognition problems, whereas the group of children identified in the fifth grade was thought to have a general comprehension or metacognitive deficit. These two groups seemed consistent with Chall's (1983) distinction between learning to read and reading to learn. Children who experience early reading difficulties have difficulty learning to read, whereas children who experience later reading difficulties have difficulty reading to learn.

In this section, the factors that influence text comprehension and children's ability to read to learn are discussed. Although the factors that influence early reading failure also affect later reading performance, there are a number of cognitive and linguistic processes that play an important role in comprehension performance. These include vocabulary knowledge, semantic and syntactic knowledge, schema knowledge, and metacognitive processes. Affective and motivational states may also have an important influence on reading performance.

VOCABULARY KNOWLEDGE

Knowledge of word meanings is a crucial aspect of understanding text. Comprehension of larger text units begins with the construction of simple propositions from individual words. Some theorists (Perfetti, 1985; Vellutino & Scanlon, 1982) include vocabulary under the more general heading of semantic encoding processes. Individual differences in knowledge of word meanings are an obvious correlate of reading performance. This is borne out by research showing that the correlation between vocabulary and reading ability is high throughout development (Anderson & Freebody, 1979; Stanovich, Cunningham, & Feeman, 1984). As Perfetti (1985) pointed out, however, good readers not only know more word meanings than poor readers, but they also have more elaborated semantic representations of word meanings. To support this contention, Perfetti cited a study by Curtis (1980) who found that high-vocabulary subjects had greater breadth as well as depth of vocabulary. Depth was reflected in the ability to give an acceptable synonym or definition. Breadth was reflected in the ability to provide some association with or partial definition for unfamiliar words.

The relationship between comprehension and vocabulary knowledge was further demonstrated in an experiment by Beck, Perfetti, and

McKeown (1982). Texts consisting of well-known and unfamiliar words were presented to fourth grade students. When 9 percent of the words were unfamiliar, recall of the semantic (propositional) content of the text was only 19 percent. Subjects who were taught the meanings of the novel words were able to recall about 27 percent of the semantic context units.

Although vocabulary knowledge clearly has an impact on text comprehension, the causal relationship between vocabulary deficiencies and reading failure is not straightforward. An explanation of general reading disability based on vocabulary differences would imply that differences between poor readers and good readers would not exist in texts that contain known words. Perfetti (1985) has shown, however, that differences between good readers and poor readers are found on such texts. He attributes these differences to a slower general rate of symbol activation and retrieval. In other words, even familiar words are recognized more slowly by poor readers.

It should be apparent that vocabulary is involved in a reciprocal causal relationship with reading performance (Stanovich, 1986a). Deficient word recognition processes lead to a slower growth in vocabulary, which in turn contributes to reading failure. During the preschool years, children learn most of their vocabulary from verbal interactions. Beginning about the third grade, however, reading becomes the major determinant of vocabulary growth (Nagy & Anderson, 1984). Thus, the more a child reads, the better his or her vocabulary will become. Good readers who enjoy reading are more likely to read than poor readers. More will be said about reciprocal causation effects in a later section.

SYNTACTIC KNOWLEDGE

Knowledge of the grammatical rules that govern how words and phrases can be combined and ordered is crucial for constructing accurate interpretations of text. Syntactic knowledge also includes an understanding of grammatical morphemes (e.g., inflections and auxiliary forms) and the various function words (e.g., conjunctions, pronouns, and modals) that modulate meanings and intentions. Much of the research that has looked at the influence of syntactic knowledge on reading has focused on the facilitating effects such knowledge has on word recognition processes. This research was discussed in the previous section on context effects. Recall that it was argued that higher-level language knowledge was used by both good readers and poor readers to aid reading performance. There was, in fact, some evidence that poor readers are sometimes more dependent on higher-level language cues than good readers.

Although there is evidence that poor readers rely heavily on higher-level language knowledge to aid word recognition, several studies have shown that poor readers have deficiencies in their syntactic knowledge. For example, Fry, Johnson, and Muehl (1970) summarized the results of two dissertations by Fry (1967) and Schulte (1967) that compared language samples of good and poor second-grade readers. In addition to larger speaking vocabularies and greater verbal fluency, the good readers used more complex, complete sentences and more transformations than poor readers.

There is also evidence that poor readers have deficient listening comprehension skills (Berger, 1978; Chall, 1983; Curtis, 1980; Goldsmith, 1977; Stanovich, Cunningham, & Feeman, 1984). The relationship between listening comprehension and reading is strongly affected by an individual's level of reading ability. Curtis (1980), for example, found that reading and listening comprehension were not significantly correlated in the second grade. By the third grade, however, the correlation was .66, and by the fifth grade, .74. In another study, Goldsmith (1977) found that poor readers between 9 and 12 years old were less proficient than normal readers in processing relative clauses on both reading and listening comprehension tasks. Studies by Berger (1978) and Smiley, Oakley, Worthen, Campione, and Brown (1977) have also reported equally poor reading and listening comprehension abilities in older school-age children (i.e., fifth and seventh graders).

In addition to deficient listening comprehension skills, poor readers have been found to have deficient knowledge of inflectional morphology. Brittain (1970), for example, reported a significant correlation between a composite measure of reading and performance on a test of morphological generalization modeled after Berko's (1958) "wug" study. Vellutino and Scanlon (1982) also cited evidence that performance on a test of morphology administered in kindergarten was predictive of reading performance in the first grade.

Taken together, the research indicates that there is a positive relationship between measures of syntactic knowledge and reading performance in more mature readers. The data, however, are only correlational in nature. It is unclear, for example, how much of an adverse effect the syntactic deficit has on reading. Even theorists, such as Vellutino and Scanlon, who find the relationship between syntactic and reading deficits suggestive of a causal relationship, admit that the syntactic deficiencies might be secondary manifestations of problems in other aspects of language, such as lexical development or phonological processing. These points suggest that it is important to look beyond the superficial positive relationship between higher-level language abilities and reading to the underlying cognitive and metacognitive processes that might explain this relationship. I will return to these issues at the end of the chapter.

SCHEMA KNOWLEDGE

As indicated in Chapter 1 of this book, a person's comprehension of a text is based in part on what he or she knows about the world. The basic assumption with respect to reading is that high-ability readers have more relevant knowledge than low-ability readers. As Perfetti noted (1985, p. 75), "This conclusion must be correct. The more one knows about everything, the more one will be able to read anything." Perfetti does not find this a particularly useful explanation for general reading ability because reading ability then becomes indistinguishable from general intellectual ability. Not surprisingly, the correlations between measures of intelligence, especially verbal intelligence, and reading ability are in the moderate to high range (Perfetti, 1985).

Differences in the amount of knowledge one has about a particular subject matter will have an obvious impact on one's ability to comprehend a specific text. The more knowledge a person has about a particular subject matter, the easier it will be for that person to understand a text on that subject. Consider the example of a physician who has excellent comprehension of an anatomy and physiology text, but has difficulty understanding a text about judicial procedures. A lawyer, on the other hand, would have little trouble understanding the judicial text, but would have considerable difficulty with the anatomy text. A high-ability reader thus might be viewed as someone who has a large number of useful schemata that facilitate comprehension of a large number of texts, whereas a low-ability reader would be viewed as someone who has only a limited number of useful schemata. As before, this is not a very useful concept of reading ability. In this case, the problem is that one is accounting only for differences in understanding specific texts, not for differences in general reading ability.

Perfetti has proposed two ways that schema theory might be applied to general reading ability: (1) deficiencies in schema selection, and (2) deficiencies in schema flexibility. Schema selection refers to the ability to activate or select the right schema or schemata for a particular text. Perhaps poor readers are more likely to activate the wrong schemata when reading. Although there is no relevant research that addresses this question, Perfetti has suggested that it is difficult to see how schema selection could be a serious problem. Texts, he has argued, are usually not so "perverse" as to invite the activation of the wrong schema.

Schema flexibility is a variation of the schema selection problem in that it refers to the difficulty one might have accommodating schematic knowledge to specific text information or the inability to apply a different schema when necessary. Another example of schema inflexibility is the reader who uses too much of a top-down strategy in his or her comprehension and as a result has difficulty incorporating information that deviates from the activated schema. Schema flexibility may be related to metacognitive processes, which are discussed in the next section.

There should be little doubt that schema knowledge and the application of this knowledge play an important role in reading comprehension, especially in more mature readers. Individual differences in schema knowledge and application probably do not account for much of the variability in reading performance in young readers. As is the case with vocabulary, however, good readers will acquire more knowledge through reading than poor readers, and this larger knowledge base will be reflected in a better understanding of a greater number of texts.

Metacognitive Processes

Up to this point we have considered the effect of deficiencies in specific abilities on reading performance. Attributing reading failure to a deficit in a specific ability is consistent with definitions of reading and learning disabilities that include the assumption that the disability is caused by a specific deficit in one or more of the cognitive processes involved in learning. A problem with this assumption, as we saw in the review of memory research, is that poor performance can be caused by a failure to efficiently apply a particular ability. It is necessary, therefore, to make a distinction between ability and performance (Torgesen, 1977). Factors that influence performance independent of ability include metacognitive processes and affective and motivational states.

Perfetti (1985) has suggested that there are at least three different sorts of metacognitive abilities that might have an impact on reading performance: (1) awareness of strategies to apply to text comprehension, (2) awareness of the different kinds of text structure, and (3) awareness of comprehension problems. There are several different kinds of strategies an individual might use to facilitate comprehension, such as taking notes, underlining selected sentences in the text, or verbal rehearsal. In order to effectively implement these strategies, an individual must not only be aware of them, but also know something about their potential effects on learning. By awareness of structural levels, Perfetti is referring to the differences that exist in the importance of text material. Important text material should receive more processing resources than less important material. Studies (e.g., Smiley et al., 1977) have shown, however, that both good readers and poor readers are more likely to recall more important than unimportant information. The third metacognitive ability is comprehension monitoring. Selected literature dealing with strategy use and comprehension monitoring is reviewed below.

Strategy Use

Torgesen (1977) has made an excellent case for how the inability to use efficient strategies can contribute to learning and reading problems. He begins by noting that the learning that takes place during preschool has been viewed as "incidental learning" because it occurs as a natural consequence of normal interaction with the environment. In school, however, the child must learn information so that it may be recalled at some later time. This type of learning requires attention-demanding control processes and is therefore facilitated by the use of efficient strategies for studying and remembering information. Controlled attentional learning begins to become an important measure of achievement level at around the third or fourth grade. It is no coincidence that this is also the point at which children begin to read to learn and around the time when a "new" group of reading disabled children is identified. These children with reading disabilities have had little difficulty learning to decode. They are being identified at the time when reading measures are sensitive to how well they read to learn.

Problems in reading to learn can stem from deficits in the higher-level language and schema knowledge already discussed or from deficiencies in metacognitive processes. Deficits in poor readers' use of metamemory strategies, an aspect of metacognition, have been well documented in the literature. For example, Torgesen and Goldman (1977) asked second grade children with reading disabilities to recall the sequences in which a group of pictures were presented after a 15-second delay. During the delay period, the children were observed for evidence of the use of rehearsal, such as lip movement or whispering. The poor readers were found to recall fewer pictures and rehearse less than the control group. When the two groups were encouraged to rehearse, the differences disappeared. Other studies (Haines & Torgesen, 1979; Tarver, Hallahan, Kauffman, & Ball, 1976) have also found that young poor readers do not label and rehearse as much as good readers.

Differences in older poor readers' use of memory enhancing strategies have also been found. In another study by Torgesen (1977), fourth grade poor readers were found to use inefficient strategies on two different kinds of memory tasks. One task examined study behaviors after the children prepared to recall 24 pictures of common objects that could be grouped into four conceptual categories. Differences in recall and study behavior were found. The good readers moved the pictures around more, verbalized the picture names more often, exhibited less off-task behavior, and more often grouped the pictures into conceptual categories. As before, brief training in the use of categorization as a mnemonic strategy eliminated the group differences in recall. The other task involved studying a horizontal array of pictures to be recalled in order from left to right. The good readers again showed more verbalization and engaged in more chunking and rehearsal during a study period.

In a related study, Torgesen, Bowen, and Ivey (1978) found greater differences in recall between good and poor readers when digit sequences were presented and studied for 10 seconds than when similar digits were presented at 1-second intervals. The simultaneous presentation of the digits allowed for greater opportunity for the children to develop their own study strategies. The results from these studies indicate that the performance difference between good readers and poor readers is greater on tasks that provide opportunities for strategy use. This conclusion has been supported by subsequent studies in which performance deficits between good readers and poor readers are reduced on tasks that preclude the use of strategies (Cermak, Goldberg, Cermak, & Drake, 1980; Cohen, 1982).

The results from this series of studies led Torgesen (1980, p. 367) to the general conclusion that poor readers often fail to use efficient task strategies spontaneously. The use of efficient task strategies requires an active adaptation to tasks. Torgesen cited a study by Wong (1979) that provides additional evidence that poor readers process information less actively than good readers. In the study, Wong examined the extent to which second and sixth grade good and poor readers engaged in active construction processes in a listening comprehension task. Previous research (Paris & Lindauer, 1976) had demonstrated that older normal children could recall sentences if given a retrieval cue that was implied by the sentence. For example, *shovel* is a retrieval cue for the sentence *The workman dug a hole in the ground*. Such cues did not aid younger children's ability to recall sentences. Wong found a significant group by condition interaction. The poor readers showed the same recall performance with the explicitly cued sentences, but they performed more poorly than the good readers when the sentences were not cued. In a follow-up experiment, Wong showed that, when prompted, poor readers could use the inference processes that were required to generate implied consequences.

The research on strategy use is quite uniform in finding that poor readers do not perform as well as good readers on tasks that provide opportunities for strategy use. It is possible that inefficient strategy use explains the difficulty poor readers experience in applying their knowledge. Thus, deficiencies in the application of schema knowledge, for example, might stem from the inability to recognize which strategies might help activate a particular schema (Perfetti, 1985, p. 78).

Comprehension Monitoring

To read to learn, children not only must use certain strategies to facilitate recall of important information, but also must be able to monitor their own comprehension. When faced with a word, sentence, or text that they do not understand, they need to do something to aid their understanding, such as reread the text in question or ask their teacher. Studies have shown that young children are not very good at monitoring their comprehension in this way (Capelli & Markman, 1985; Flavell, Speer, Green, & August, 1981; Markman, 1979). Children with reading and learning disabilities are particularly prone to have difficulty monitoring comprehension (Brown & Campione, 1984).

The ability to monitor one's comprehension depends in part on how well an individual can construct meaning. Comprehension and comprehension monitoring are closely related processes that depend on each other for optimal functioning (Capelli & Markman, 1985). To understand something as well as possible, it is necessary to continuously monitor the comprehension process. Thus, the better one's comprehension skills, the more likely one is to be a good monitor (Capelli & Markman, 1985; Markman, 1981).

The relationship between comprehension and comprehension monitoring skills reflects the active, constructive processes involved in constructing meanings. As individuals read, they integrate new information into an initial interpretation. This interpretation becomes elaborated and revised as the reader acquires new information. This kind of constructive, inferential process can provide information about how well some information is understood (Capelli & Markman, 1985, Chapter 1). Several studies (Paris & Lindauer, 1976) have shown that young normal readers are less able to use this kind of constructive, inferential comprehension than adults. However, researchers (Palincsar & Brown, 1984) have found that it is possible to train school-age children to generate and evaluate inferences as they read. Improvement in comprehension monitoring led to an increased ability to detect inconsistencies in texts.

Brown and her colleagues (Brown & Campione, 1984; Palincsar & Brown, 1984) conducted a series of studies in which they attempted to improve comprehension monitoring abilities in poor readers. Subjects were seventh grade disadvantaged students who were decoding at grade level but were experiencing two- to three-year delays in reading comprehension. Four areas were targeted: summarizing (self-review), questioning, clarifying, and predicting. Level of reading performance improved dramatically after 20 sessions. There was no drop in performance for up to an eight-week period. Brown's research indicates that deficient comprehension monitoring skills might play an important role in explaining comprehension difficulties in older children with reading disabilities.

Although deficiencies in metacognitive processes, such as strategy use and comprehension monitoring, play an obvious role in contributing to reading problems in older children, deficiencies in these processes may also be caused by the reading problem. The research has shown quite clearly that poor readers have no difficulty learning to implement efficient task strategies and comprehension monitoring procedures (Torgesen, 1980). In some cases deficient metacognitive processes may derive from motivational factors. These factors are discussed below.

Motivational Factors

In recent years, there has been increasing interest in the effects of children's repeated academic failure on subsequent performance. The notion of learned helplessness theory (Abramson, Garber, & Seligman, 1980) and research on attribution theory (Weiner, 1980) have been useful in understanding the relationship of motivational factors and reading failure. Learned helplessness refers to the perception of being helpless to control events. Attribution theory refers to an individual's expectation of an event's outcome, feelings about an experience, and motivation toward future experiences (Winograd & Niquette, 1988).

Winograd and Niquette (1988, pp. 131-132) described several ways in which learned helplessness contributes to reading problems. First, children who experience learned helplessness might fail to use appropriate skills and strategies because they have difficulty perceiving the relationship between their efforts and task outcomes. Second, these children often attribute reading difficulties to low ability, an attribution that leads to a lack of persistence and motivation and low self-esteem. Third, helpless children often develop considerable negative feelings about reading. Beliefs and attributions such as these lead children to become easily frustrated or to give up very quickly in the face of difficulty (Licht & Kistner, 1986). It is, of course, not unreasonable for children with reading disabilities to hold lower expectations about their reading abilities. Such beliefs often reflect reality.

Although the consequences of learned helplessness, negative attribution, and motivational deficits seem obvious, Licht and Kistner (1986, p. 227) make the important point that all children do not respond the same way to repeated failure. Some children, they note, are able to maintain confidence in their abilities by blaming the teacher for their difficulty. Others respond in a more adaptive manner by attributing their difficulties to insufficient effort. Licht and Kistner proceed to consider the factors that may contribute to differences in the way in which children respond to academic failures.

The most obvious variable is frequency. Those children who experience failure most frequently would be expected to show greater motivational deficits. Although there is some support for this prediction (Black, 1974; Kistner & Licht, 1984), it is not the only factor. There are some children who fail frequently who are confident they will eventually succeed, just as there are some highly successful children who lack confidence in their abilities (Licht & Dweck, 1983). A number of classroom or family variables may also contribute to how children respond to failure. For example, some children may receive praise for effort, whereas others will receive praise only if their answer is completely correct (Licht & Kistner, 1986, p. 229).

Developmental factors also influence individual differences in children's response to failure. In contrast to adults, children in the early school years tend to view intellectual ability as a direct reflection of effort. "In other words, the more you try, the more you will learn, and the more intelligent you will become" (Licht & Kistner, 1986, p. 230). Consistent with this belief, young children often view successes achieved with considerable effort as an indication of higher ability than successes achieved with little effort (Kun, 1977). By about 7 years of age, children begin to realize that they must perform better than their peers to be considered high in ability (Nicholls, 1978, 1980). Most 7-year-olds, however, still believe that effort can change ability. It is not until age 10 that the majority of children begin to view intelligence as something that constrains ability (Nicholls, 1978). Nicholls suggested that the concept of intelligence as a fixed capacity might not be fully developed until age 13 or later. The implication of this developmental information is that children who experience repeated academic failures will not attribute these failures to low ability until they are at least 10 years old. Prior to this time, ability is changeable and is tied closely to effort. In support of this conclusion, studies (Licht & Kistner, 1986) have shown that older children (e.g., sixth graders) show a greater likelihood of decreased performance levels following failure than younger children (e.g., second graders).

Although the research shows that older children are more

vulnerable to motivational factors, young children who experience repeated difficulty reading might be less motivated to read because of the negative feelings associated with reading. Such children might not develop a poor self image until age 10 or so, but the negative attitudes associated with repeated reading difficulty inevitably make reading less enjoyable, which, in turn, leads to less interest and time spent in reading activities.

RECIPROCAL CAUSATION FACTORS

The effects of reciprocal causation factors have been noted in several of the previous sections. Because reading depends on a large number of cognitive processes and is subject to the influence of motivational and instructional factors, many factors can contribute to reading failure. Although certain deficits account for a larger proportion of individual differences in reading than do other deficits, a true understanding of reading disabilities must consider the complex interactions that occur over time between the cognitive processes that underlie reading performance and the motivational states that sustain performance.

Stanovich (1986a) described two basic kinds of reciprocal relationships: those that are developmentally limited and those that are operative throughout reading development. Stanovich suggests that the relationship between phonological awareness and reading seems to be developmentally limited. As discussed earlier and in the next chapter, individual differences in phonological awareness have been causally linked to variations in early reading ability. Success in early reading leads, in turn, to better phonological awareness. However, because children move quickly into stages where direct visual access predominates, variation in phonological awareness can no longer be the primary causal determinant of differences in reading ability. There will thus be a point when the facilitation of phonological awareness by reading becomes less important because the level of phonological awareness is no longer influencing reading ability (Stanovich, 1986a, p. 379). Hence, the characterization of the relationship between phonological awareness and reading as developmentally limited.

More powerful reciprocal relationships are those that operate throughout reading development. Differences in basic processing abilities (e.g., rate of access to phonological-coded information in memory), motivation, vocabulary, higher-level language knowledge, and metacognitive processes may be involved in long-term reciprocal relationships with reading. The reciprocal relationship between vocabulary and reading was mentioned briefly in an earlier section.

Reading, it was argued, is a major determinant of vocabulary growth. Increased vocabulary leads, in turn, to more efficient reading. The volume of reading experience thus becomes a critical variable in determining individual differences in reading ability. Not surprisingly, several studies (e.g., Allington, 1984; Biemiller, 1977) have found differences in the amount of reading by good readers and poor readers. Allington (1984), for example, reported that average skilled readers read approximately three times as many words as average less-skilled readers. Nagy and Anderson (1984) have estimated that average middle school children might read 1,000,000 words a year in school compared to only 100,000 words for the least motivated students. Voracious readers might read as many as 50,000,000 words during a year. Differences in the volume of reading among readers might even be greater when reading done outside school is considered.

The differences in reading volume between motivated and unmotivated students lead to a "rich-get-richer" and "poor-get-poorer" (Matthew effects) phenomenon. As Stanovich (1986a, p. 381) has noted,

> the very children who are reading well and who have good vocabularies will read more, learn more word meanings, and hence read even better. Children with inadequate vocabularies—who read slowly and without enjoyment—read less, and as a result have slower development of vocabulary knowledge, which inhibits further growth in reading ability.

The reciprocal effects can also be found between higher-level language abilities and reading. The assumption typically has been that deficiencies in language knowledge contribute to reading difficulty. However, several investigators (e.g., Mann, 1986; Perfetti, 1985) have shown that the ability to comprehend more complex syntactic structures is in part the result of reading experience. In a similar vein, Torgesen (1985) has posited that some of the memory performance differences between good and poor readers might be the indirect result of the reading problem. The increased knowledge base of the good readers, which accounts in part for enhanced memory performance, is often a consequence of greater reading experiences.

Reciprocal causation effects are clearly involved in explaining the motivational differences that are associated with variability in reading ability. As indicated in the previous section, repeated experiences of reading failure will usually lead to reduced enjoyment and motivation to read. Metacognitive processes, such as strategy use and the ability to monitor comprehension, may also be affected by reading difficulties. Recall that poor readers do not perform as well as good readers on measures of strategy use and comprehension monitoring.

It should be clear from these examples how certain differences between good and poor readers might be a consequence of the reading disability as well as a cause that sustains or, in many cases, exacerbates the extent of the disability. The phenomenon of reciprocal causation has important implications for the assumption of specificity that pervades the reading disability literature. This assumption is considered below.

The Assumption of Specificity

The assumption of specificity underlies all exclusionary definitions of reading disability. Recall that in such definitions reading disability is defined as a marked difficulty in learning to read in the absence of intellectual, emotional, physical, and environmental deficiencies. One of the crucial aspects of this definition has been the idea of "essentially normal intelligence." The media-popularized view of reading disability has typically turned "essentially normal intelligence" into "brighter-than-average" (Stanovich, 1986b). This portrayal of children with reading disabilities is unfortunately grossly inaccurate. For one, most reading disabled children perform below 100 on measures of intelligence. Stanovich (1986b), in a review of relevant studies, found that learning disabled subjects consistently have lower IQ scores than matched, controlled groups. IQs generally were in the low 90s. A more accurate statement about intelligence, therefore, is that intelligence is somewhat below normal for children with learning disabilities. Note that the relatively low IQs reflect the fact that several IQ subtests (e.g., vocabulary, coding, information, and digit span) correlate quite highly with measures of reading.

A second problem for the specificity assumption relates to the effects of reciprocal causation. For the disorder to remain specific to reading and not affect other aspects of language and academic performance, there could be no reciprocal causation. For this to occur, a child would have to remain relatively immune to the negative effects that reading failure has on other areas of performance. Indeed, few children manage to fully avoid the consequences of reading failure on language, cognitive, and academic performances.

A third problem with the specificity assumption is that researchers have uncovered differences between reading disabled and normal readers on a wide variety of cognitive tasks. In fact, there have been so many cognitive differences uncovered that it seems more appropriate to characterize people with reading disabilities as suffering from a general cognitive impairment rather than a specific reading disability.

Although the evidence appears to be overwhelmingly against the specificity assumption, Stanovich (1986a) has suggested three ways to escape the paradox that threatens to undermine the notion of specificity in dyslexia: (1) subject selection, (2) subtypes, and (3) a developmental hypothesis. The subjects used in most studies, Stanovich notes, come from schools that do not identify children with reading disabilities in accord with the basic definition of dyslexia. The result is that a sizeable proportion of the school-labeled subjects are low-ability readers with mild IQ deficits. These children are not characteristic of the dyslexic individual who has a severe reading disability in the presence of normal cognitive functioning.

A second way out of the paradox involves the notion of subtypes. If there are distinct subtypes of reading disabled children, each with a distinct single-factor deficit, the results of a study involving several subtypes will mistakenly indicate multiple deficits. Unfortunately, the subtyping literature is often contradictory and confusing (see Chapter 2). Although there is unequivocal evidence for distinct subtypes, there is no agreed-on taxonomy of subtypes among theorists and practitioners. Despite these problems, Stanovich suggests that the use of subtype notions along with a conservative definition of reading disability "might establish a firmer empirical foundation for the assumption of specificity" (p. 388).

Stanovich's third alternative is the most interesting one theoretically and the most promising for escaping the paradox. Stanovich proposes a developmental version of the specificity hypothesis. More specifically, he suggests that there is developmental change in the cognitive specificity of the deficits displayed by children with reading disabilities. During the early school years, performance is characterized by a high degree of specificity. Stanovich speculates that the best candidate for the critically deficient process is phonological awareness. As the child gets older, changes in specificity occur as a consequence of the individual differences in reading acquisition and the reciprocal relationships that exist among reading, other cognitive skills, language, metacognitive processes, and motivational factors. In other words, by the time a child is in the fourth grade or so, the disability is not specific to reading.

Although the specificity of the reading disability decreases with age, it may never be specific to reading even in beginning readers. As pointed out in Chapter 2, there is a large subgroup of reading disabled individuals whose reading disability is but one of several manifestations of a developmental language impairment. Other young poor readers might show associated symptomatology, such as low intelligence, or have deficiencies in other language and learning activities.

It should be apparent from the points raised in this section that there are several problems with the specificity assumption.

DESCRIBING AND EXPLAINING READING DISABILITIES

In our quest to understand reading disabilities, we must ultimately face the question of what is the best way to describe and explain these disabilities. The characterization of reading disabilities as a language-based disorder seems quite appropriate at a descriptive level. The notion of a language-based disorder seems to capture the essence of the reading disability. Reading is a language-based skill, and therefore a reading disability is a language-based disorder.

A potential problem with describing a reading disability as a language-based disorder is that this description sometimes leads to the incorrect assumption that there is a distinct subgroup of children who have language-based reading disorders. The claim, however, is that all problems in learning to read are language based. Those who argue for the existence of a distinct group of children with language-based reading disorders must be able to differentiate these children from those who demonstrate non-language-based reading disorders. At first glance this might appear easy to do. Language-based reading disorders would encompass all children who have phonological processing deficits, higher-level language deficiencies, and vocabulary deficits. Non-language-based disorders would include children whose reading problem could be attributed solely to visual deficits, attentional or motivational factors, and perhaps certain cognitive and metacognitive deficiencies. A problem with these distinctions, however, is that they ignore the reciprocal interactions that occur between the so-called language factors and nonlanguage factors. Even if the initial cause of reading failure can be attributed solely to a nonlanguage factor, such as a visual-perceptual deficit, subsequent reading failure will influence the development of phonological awareness, vocabulary, oral language comprehension, memory performance, and so forth.

Although a reading disorder can be described accurately as a language-based problem, this does not necessarily mean that it is best explained as a language disorder. An oft-cited language-based explanation of a reading disability is that deficiencies in language knowledge cause the reading problem (Vellutino, 1979). Shankweiler and Crain (1987) referred to this as the structural lag hypothesis. The basic notion is that reading demands more linguistic knowledge than some beginning readers have. A child who is delayed in learning spoken language would be particularly vulnerable for reading problems because the child would not have the necessary language knowledge required to learn to read.

Shankweiler and Crain (1987) considered two versions of the structural lag hypothesis: a syntactic lag hypothesis and a phonological lag hypothesis. The syntactic lag hypothesis involves delays in the acquisition of syntactic structures. For example, a child learning to read might not have acquired the syntactic rules needed to understand passive sentences or restrictive relative clauses. Without this knowledge, such a child would probably have difficulty understanding texts with passives and restrictive clauses. However, a syntactic deficit cannot explain why poor readers have problems in lower levels of language processing, such as phonologic analysis and orthographic decoding (Shankweiler & Crain, 1987, p. 147).

The phonological lag hypothesis posits a delay in the acquisition of some aspect of phonological knowledge, such as the awareness that words consist of discrete phonemes. The relationship between phonological awareness and early reading performance has been well documented (Stanovich, 1986a, and Chapter 4 of this book). But a deficit in phonological awareness does not explain why poor readers perform poorly on verbal short-term memory tasks and other measures of phonological processing. In other words, the question of what causes the phonological awareness problem has not been answered.

The most critical problem with the structural lag hypothesis, however, is that it merely describes areas of deficient knowledge; it does not explain the initial cause of these knowledge deficiencies. An analogy with a specific language impairment will help to clarify this point. One would not think of asking whether a specific language impairment was a language-based disorder or attempt to explain a language disorder as a delay in the acquisition of language knowledge. This is a descriptive characterization, not an explanatory one. To explain a specific language impairment, it is necessary to look for specific processing deficits (see Johnston, 1987, for a review). By analogy, a reading disability, which is a language-based disorder, cannot be explained as a language disorder. One must search for the specific processing limitations that underlie the reading disability.

Several possibilities were suggested in this chapter about the nature of these processing limitations. Some of these are discussed further in subsequent chapters. These limitations include (1) difficulty forming accurate representations of phonological information in long-term memory (Vellutino, Harding, Phillips, & Steger, 1975), (2) slow rate of access to verbal information stored in long-term memory (Miles & Ellis, 1981; Perfetti, 1985), (3) low-level perceptual deficits (Tallal, 1980), (4) inefficient regulation of information in working memory

(Shankweiler & Crain, 1987), and (5) difficulty constructing narrative and discourse schemata (Perfetti, 1985; Stanovich, 1986a). Although there is research support for all of these possibilities, the evidence presented in this chapter and in Chapter 4 suggests that the first two limitations are more likely sources of the initial reading disability than the latter three. Future research is needed to further support this claim.

Additional research is also needed to determine the specificity of the processing limitation. It is clearly not specific to content or knowledge domains, such as reading, because it affects spoken as well as written language. Problems with the specificity assumption were pointed out in the previous section. The processing limitation might be specific to phonological information, or it could affect the processing of all linguistic information. The alternative is that the processing limitation is not specific to phonological or linguistic information, but rather to input that places similar demands on the processing system. Support for this claim would involve showing that disabled readers perform poorly on certain nonlinguistic tasks. The tasks most likely to cause problems are those that involve rapid sequential processing of discrete information. There currently is not much evidence to support this claim (Stanovich, 1986a), but we (Kamhi, Catts, Mauer, Apel, & Gentry, 1988) recently found evidence that reading disabled children performed below age level on two mental imagery tasks. Although these tasks did not involve rapid sequential processing, our findings suggest that the processing limitation might not be limited to phonological or linguistic information.

SUMMARY

Chapter 3 has considered the various deficits that have been proposed to account for reading failure. The first part of the chapter reviewed deficits that contribute most to word recognition problems and early reading failure. These included visual-perceptual deficits, deficiencies in memory processes, and higher-level language deficits. Also discussed were the deficits that contribute most to text-comprehension difficulties and later reading failure. These included deficits in higher-level language knowledge, metacognitive abilities, and motivational states. The final part of the chapter considered reciprocal causation factors, followed by a discussion of the specificity assumption and whether or not a reading disability is best viewed as a cognitive or language disorder. It was argued that reading disabilities are best described as a language-based disorder but best explained as a processing limitation. Several suggestions about the nature of this processing limitation were provided.

REFERENCES

Abramson, L., Garber, J., and Seligman, M. (1980). Learned helplessness in humans: An attributional analysis. In J. Garber and M. Seligman (Eds.), *Human helplessness: Theory and applications*, 146–187. New York: Academic Press.

Allington, R. (1984). Content coverage and contextual reading in reading groups. *Journal of Reading Behavior, 16*, 85–96.

Anderson, J. (1986). *Cognitive psychology and its implications.* New York: W. H. Freeman and Co.

Anderson, R., and Freebody, P. (1979). *Vocabulary knowledge.* (Tech. Rep. No. 136). Urbana-Champaign: University of Illinois, Center for the Study of Reading.

Beck, I., Perfetti, C., and McKeown, M. (1982). Effects of long-term vocabulary instruction on lexical access and reading comprehension. *Journal of Educational Psychology, 74*, 506–521.

Berger, N. (1978). Why can't John read? Perhaps he's not a good listener. *Journal of Learning Disabilities, 11*, 31–36.

Berko, J. (1958). The child's learning of English morphology. *Word, 14*, 150–177.

Biemiller, A. (1977). Relationships between oral reading rates for letters, words, and simple text in the development of reading achievement. *Reading Research Quarterly, 13*, 223–253.

Black, W. (1974). Self-concept as related to achievement and age in learning-disabled children. *Child Development, 45*, 1137–1140.

Bradley, L., and Bryant, P. (1985). *Rhyme and reason in reading and spelling.* International Academy for Research in Learning Disabilities Monograph Series, No. 1. Ann Arbor, MI: University of Michigan Press.

Brady, S., Shankweiler, D., and Mann, V. (1983). Speech perception and memory coding in relation to reading ability. *Journal of Experimental Psychology, 35*, 345–367.

Brittain, M. (1970). Inflectional performance and early reading achievement. *Reading Research Quarterly, 6*, 34–48.

Brown, A., and Campione, J. (1984). Three faces of transfer: Implications for early competence, individual differences, and instruction. In M. Lamb, A. Brown, and B. Rogoff (Eds.), *Advances in developmental psychology, 3*, 143–192. Hillsdale, NJ: Erlbaum.

Calfee, R. (1977). Assessment of independent reading skills: Basic research and practical applications. In A. Reber and D. Scarborough (Eds.), *Towards a psychology of reading*, 289–325. Hillside, NJ: Erlbaum.

Capelli, C., and Markman, E. (1985). Improving comprehension monitoring through training in hypothesis-testing. Paper presented at the Annual Meeting of the Society for Research in Child Development, Toronto.

Cermak, L., Goldberg, J., Cermak, S., and Drake, C. (1980). The short-term memory ability of children with learning disabilities. *Journal of Learning Disabilities, 13*, 20–24.

Chall, J. (1983). *Stages of reading development.* New York: McGraw-Hill.

Cohen, R. (1982). Individual differences in short-term memory. *International Review of Research in Mental Retardation, 11*, 43–77.

Chomsky, N. (1965). *Aspects of a theory of syntax.* Cambridge, MA: MIT Press.

Curtis, M. (1980). Development of components of reading skill. *Journal of Educational Psychology, 72,* 656–669.

Flavell, J., Speer, J., Green, F., and August, D. (1981). The development of comprehension monitoring and knowledge about communication. *Monographs of the Society for Research in Child Development, 46* (Serial No. 191).

Fry, M., Johnson, C., and Muehl, S. (1970). Oral language production in relation to reading achievement among select second graders. In D. Bakker and P. Satz (Eds.), *Specific reading disability: Advances in theory and method,* 203–245. Rotterdam: University Press.

Goldsmith, S. (1977). Reading disability: Some support for a psycholinguistic base. Paper presented at the Boston University Conference on Language Development, Boston.

Goodman, K. (1967). Reading: A psycholinguistic guessing game. *Journal of the Reading Specialist, 6,* 126–135.

Goodman, K. (1976). Reading: A psycholinguistic guessing game. In H. Singer and R. Ruddell (Eds.), *Theoretical models and processes of reading,* 497–508. Newark, DE: International Reading Association.

Groff, P. (1978). Should children learn to read words? *Reading World, 17,* 256–264.

Haines, D., and Torgesen, J. (1979). The effects of incentives on rehearsal and short-term memory in children with reading problems. *Learning Disability Quarterly, 2,* 48–55.

Herman, K. (1959). *Reading disability.* Copenhagen: Munksgaard.

Hogaboam, T., and Perfetti, C. (1978). Reading skill and the role of verbal experience in decoding. *Journal of Educational Psychology, 70,* 717–729.

Holmes, D., and Peper, R. (1977). An evaluation of the use of spelling error in the diagnosis of reading disabilities. *Child Development, 48,* 1708–1711.

Johnston, J. (1987). The language disordered child. In N. Lass, L. McReynolds, J. Northern, and D. Yoder (Eds.), *Handbook of speech-pathology and audiology,* 2nd Ed., 173–205. Philadelphia: B. C. Decker.

Juel, C., Griffith, P., and Gough, P. (1986). Acquisition of literacy: A longitudinal study of children in first and second grade. *Journal of Educational Psychology, 78,* 243–255.

Just, M., and Carpenter, P. (1980). A theory of reading: From eye fixations to comprehension. *Psychological Review, 87,* 329–354.

Kamhi, A., Catts, H., Mauer, D., Apel, K., and Gentry, B. (1988). Phonological and spatial processing abilities in language and reading impaired children. *Journal of Hearing and Speech Disorders, 53,* xxx–xxx.

Kistner, J., and Licht, B. (1984). Cognitive-motivational factors affecting academic persistence of learning disabled children. Paper presented at the Meeting of the Association for Children and Adults with Learning Disabilities, New Orleans.

Kun, A. (1977). Development of the magnitude—covariation and compensation schemata in ability and effort attributions of performance. *Child Development, 48,* 862–873.

Lesgold, A., and Resnick, L. (1982). How reading disabilities develop:

Perspectives from a longitudinal study. In J. Das, R. Mulcahy, and A. Wall (Eds.), *Theory and research in learning disability,* 155–187. New York: Plenum.

Liberman, I. (1987). *Language and literacy: The obligation of the schools of education.* Bulletin of the Orton Dyslexic Society.

Liberman, I., Shankweiler, D., Orlando, C., Harris, K., and Berti, F. (1971). Letter confusion and reversals of sequence in the beginning reader: Implications for Orton's theory of developmental dyslexia. *Cortex, 7,* 127–142.

Licht, B., and Dweck, C. (1983). Sex differences in achievement orientations: Consequences or academic choices and attainments. In M. Marland (Eds.), *Sex differentiation and schools,* 72–97. London: Heinemann.

Licht, B., and Kistner, J. (1986). Motivational problems of learning-disabled children: Individual differences and their implications for treatment. In J. Torgesen and B. Wong (Eds.), *Psychological and educational perspectives on learning disabilities,* 225–257. New York: Academic Press.

Lovett, M. (1987). A developmental approach to reading disability: Accuracy and speed criteria of normal and deficient reading skill. *Child Development, 58,* 234–260.

Lovett, M., Ransby, M., and Barron, R. (1988). Treatment, subtype, and word type effects in dyslexic children's response to remediation. *Brain and* Language, *29,* 328–349.

Mann, V. (1986). Why some children encounter reading problems: The contribution of difficulties with language processing and phonological sophistication to early reading disability. In J. Torgesen and B. Wong (Eds.), *Psychological and educational perspectives on learning disabilities,* 133–161. New York: Academic Press.

Markman, E. (1979). Realizing that you don't understand: Elementary school children's awareness of inconsistencies. *Child Development, 50,* 643–655.

Markman, E. (1981). Comprehension monitoring. In W. Dickson (Ed.), *Children's oral communication skills,* 143–179. New York: Academic Press.

Mattingly, I. (1972). Reading, the linguistic process, and linguistic awareness. In J. Kavanagh and I. Mattingly (Eds.), *Language by ear and by eye,* 133–147. Cambridge, MS: MIT Press.

Miles, T., and Ellis, N. (1981). A lexical encoding deficiency I and II. Experimental evidence and classical observations. In G. Pavlidis and T. Miles (Eds.), *Dyslexia research and its application to education,* 53–89. Chichester: Wiley.

Nagy, W., and Anderson, R. (1984). How many words are there in printed school English? *Reading Research Quarterly, 19,* 304–330.

Nicholls, J. (1978). The development of the concepts of effort and ability, perception of academic attainment and the understanding that difficult tasks require more ability. *Child Devleopment, 49,* 800–814.

Nicholls, J. (1980). The development of the concept of difficulty. *Merrill-Palmer Quarterly, 26,* 271–281.

Orton, S. (1925). "Word-blindness" in school children. *Archives of Neurology and Psychiatry, 14,* 581–615.

Palincsar, A., and Brown, A. (1984). Reciprocal teaching of comprehension-fostering and comprehension-monitoring activities. *Cognition and Instruction, 1,* 117–175.

Paris, S., and Lindauer, B. (1976). The role of interference in children's comprehension and memory for sentences. *Cognitive Psychology, 8,* 217–227.

Perfetti, C. (1985). *Reading ability.* New York: Oxford University Press.

Perfetti, C. (1986). Cognitive and linguistic components of reading ability. In B. Forman and A. Siegel (Eds.), *Acquisition of reading skills,* 1–41. Hillsdale, NJ: Erlbaum.

Perfetti, C., Finger, E., and Hogaboam, T. (1978). Sources of vocalization latency differences between skilled and less skilled young readers. *Journal of Educational Psychology, 70,* 730–739.

Perfetti, C., and Hogaboam, T. (1975). The relationship between single word decoding and reading comprehension skill. *Journal of Educational Psychology, 67,* 461–469.

Perfetti, C., and Lesgold, A. (1979). Coding and comprehension in skilled reading and implications for reading instruction. In L. Resnick and P. Weaver (Eds.), *Theory and practice of early reading, 1,* 60–84. Hillsdale, NJ: Erlbaum.

Perfetti, C., and Roth, S. (1981). Some of the interactive processes in reading and their role in reading skills. In A. Lesgold and C. Perfetti (Eds.), *Interactive processes in reading,* 269–297. Hillsdale, NJ: Erlbaum.

Pisoni, D. (1978). Speech perception. In W. Estes (Ed.), *Handbook of learning and cognitive processes, 6,* 171–203. Hillsdale, NJ: Erlbaum.

Rutter, M. (1978). Prevalence and types of dyslexia. In A. Benton and D. Pearl (Eds.), *Dyslexia: An appraisal of current knowledge,* 134–169. New York and London: Oxford University Press.

Satz, P., Taylor, H., Friel, J., and Fletcher, J. (1978). Some developmental and predictive precursors of reading disabilities: A six-year follow-up. In A. Benton and D. Pearl (Eds.), *Dyslexia: An appraisal of current knowledge,* 313–348. New York: Oxford University Press.

Shankweiler, D., and Crain, S. (1987). Language mechanisms and reading disorder: A modular approach. In P. Bertelson (Ed.), *The onset of literacy: Cognitive processes in reading acquisition,* 139–169. Amsterdam: Elsevier.

Share, D., Jorm, A., Maclean, R., and Matthews, R. (1984). Sources of individual differences in reading acquisition. *Journal of Educational Psychology, 76,* 1309–1324.

Smiley, S., Oakley, D., Worthen, D., Campione, J., and Brown, A. (1977). Recall of thematically relevant material by adolescent good and poor readers as a function of written and oral presentation. *Journal of Educational Psychology, 69,* 881–887.

Smith, F. (1971). *Understanding reading: A psycholinguistic analysis of reading and learning to read.* New York: Holt, Reinhart, and Winston.

Stanovich, K. (1985). Explaining the variance in reading ability in terms of psychological processes: What have we learned? *Annals of Dyslexia, 35,* 67–96.

Stanovich, K. (1986a). Matthew effects in reading: Some consequences of individual differences in the acquisition of literacy. *Reading Research Quarterly, 21,* 360–406.

Stanovich, K. (1986b). Cognitive processes and the reading problems of learning-disabled children: Evaluating the assumption of specificity. In J. Torgesen and B. Wong (Eds.), *Psychological and educational perspectives on learning disabilities*, 87–131. New York: Academic Press.

Stanovich, K. (1988). Science and learning disabilities. *Journal of Learning Disabilities, 21,* 210–215.

Stanovich, K., Cunningham, A., and Feeman, D. (1984). Relation between early reading acquisition and word decoding with and without context: A longitudinal study of first-grade children. *Journal of Educational Psychology, 76,* 668–677.

Swanson, L. (1978). Verbal encoding effects on the visual short-term memory of learning-disabled and normal readers. *Journal of Educational Psychology, 70,* 539–544.

Tallal, P. (1980). Auditory temporal perception, phonics, and reading disabilities in children. *Brain and Language, 9,* 182–198.

Tarver, S., Hallahan, D., Kauffman, J., and Ball, D. (1976). Verbal rehearsal and selective attention in children with learning disabilities: A developmental lag. *Journal of Experimental Child Psychology, 22,* 375–385.

Torgesen, J. (1977). The role of nonspecific factors in the task performance of learning disabled children: A theoretical assessment. *Journal of Learning Disabilities, 10,* 24–34.

Torgesen, J. (1980). Conceptual and educational implications of the use of efficient task strategies by learning disabled children. *Journal of Learning Disabilities, 13,* 364–371.

Torgesen, J. (1985). Memory processes in reading disordered children. *Journal of Learning Disabilities, 18,* 350–357.

Torgesen, J., Bowen, C., and Ivey, C. (1978). Task structure vs. modality of presentation: A study of the current validity of visual-aural digit span test. *Journal of Educational Psychology, 70,* 451–456.

Torgesen, J., and Goldman, T. (1977). Rehearsal and short-term memory in reading disabled children. *Child Development, 48,* 56–60.

Torgesen, J., and Houck, D. (1980). Processing deficiencies of learning disabled children who perform poorly on the digit span test. *Journal of Educational Psychology, 72,* 141–160.

Vellutino, F. (1979). *Dyslexia: Theory and research.* Cambridge, MA: MIT Press.

Vellutino, F., Harding, C., Phillips, F., and Steger, J. (1975). Differential transfer in poor and normal readers. *Journal of Genetic Psychology, 126,* 3–18.

Vellutino, F., and Scanlon, D. (1982). Verbal processing in poor and normal readers. In C. Brainerd and M. Pressley (Eds.), *Verbal processes in children.* New York: Springer-Verlag.

Vellutino, F., Smith, H., Steger, J., and Kaman, M. (1975). Reading disability: Age differences and the perceptual deficit hypothesis. *Child Development, 46,* 487–493.

Vellutino, F., Steger, J., and Kandel, G. (1972). Reading disability: An investigation of the perceptual deficit hypothesis. *Cortex, 8,* 106–118.

Vogel, S. (1974). Syntactic abilities in normal and dyslexic children. *Journal of Learning Disabilities, 7,* 103–109.

Wagner, R., and Torgesen, J. (1987). The nature of phonological processing and its causal role in the acquisition of reading skills. *Psychological Bulletin, 101,* 192–212.

Weiner, B. (1980). The role of affect in rational (attributional) approaches to human motivation. *Educational Researchers, 9,* 4–11.

Winograd, P., and Niquette, G. (1988). Assessing learned helplessness in poor readers. *Topics in Language Disorders, 8,* 38–55.

Wolf, M. (1986). Rapid alternating stimulus naming in the developmental dyslexias. *Brain and Language, 27,* 360–379.

Zola, D. (1984). Redundancy and word perception during reading. *Perception & Psychoacoustics, 36,* 277–284.

4

Phonological Processing Deficits and Reading Disabilities

Hugh W. Catts

During the last 10 to 15 years, significant advances have been made in the area of developmental reading disabilities. Prominent among these advances is research that demonstrates that deficits in phonological processing are related to reading failure in a large number of otherwise normally developing children (Frith, 1981; Liberman & Shankweiler, 1985; Stanovich, 1986a; Wagner & Torgesen, 1987). Phonological processing refers to various linguistic operations that make use of information about the speech sound (i.e., phonological) structure of the language. The ability to perform these linguistic operations appears to be somewhat independent of general cognitive ability, but highly related to reading development (Stanovich, 1986b). Deficits in phonological processing are argued to underlie the difficulties some children have in developing and using written language (Jorm & Share, 1983). These deficits have been linked to problems in word recognition, oral reading, and reading comprehension. This chapter reviews research concerning phonological processing and reading disabilities and discusses the interrelationships among various aspects of phonological processing. Also addressed is the influence of phonological processing deficits on specific aspects of the development of reading ability.

Attention will be directed primarily at research concerning speech sound processing in children with specific reading disabilities as defined in Chapter 2. Numerous investigations, however, have also examined the processing of phonological information in children with less severe reading deficits (Brady, Shankweiler, & Mann, 1983; Treiman & Baron, 1981; Wolf, 1984). In this research, children have usually been selected from the normal classroom and have been divided into good readers and poor readers. Because this work (Perfetti, 1985; Stanovich, 1986a) has generally revealed quantitative rather than qualitative differences between poor readers and specific reading disabled children, it is relevant to this discussion.

Research in the area of phonological processing and its relationship to reading achievement has examined various aspects of language processing. These have included (1) the encoding of phonological information in long-term memory, (2) the retrieval of phonological information from long-term memory, (3) the use of speech sound information in working memory, (4) the explicit awareness of the phonological structure of the language, and (5) the production of speech sound sequences. Research in each of these five areas will be considered below.

ENCODING OF PHONOLOGICAL INFORMATION

In the acquisition of oral language, individuals learn the names or arbitrary speech sound sequences associated with objects, actions, and events in the world about them. This requires perceptually analyzing the speech signal, deriving the phonological structure of words, and storing the phonological representations or names of these words in long-term or semantic memory. The translation of sensory input into a representational form is often referred to as *encoding* (Jorm & Share, 1983; Torgesen, 1985).

Research suggests that children with reading disabilities may have difficulty in the process of encoding phonological information in memory (i.e., learning the names of words). For example, Vellutino and his colleagues (Vellutino, Harding, Phillips, & Steger, 1975; Vellutino, Steger, Harding, & Phillips, 1975; Vellutino, Steger, & Pruzek, 1973) conducted a series of investigations involving paired-associate learning of verbal and nonverbal information in normal and reading disabled (RD) children. In one study (Vellutino, Steger, et al., 1975), subjects were taught to pair visual stimuli (novel pictured objects) with verbal auditory (spoken nonsense words) or nonverbal auditory responses (cough or hiss). After training, subjects were presented with the visual stimuli and the appropriate responses were requested. RD children were found to have significantly more difficulty than normal readers in learning to associate spoken nonsense words with the visual stimuli. The RD and normal subjects, however, performed in a comparable manner when learning to pair nonverbal responses (e.g., hiss) with the pictured objects. Similar results have been observed by others using paired-associate learning of verbal and nonverbal stimuli (Done & Miles, 1978; Gascon & Goodglass, 1978; Otto, 1961). Vellutino, Steger, et al. concluded on the basis of their results that RD children do not have a general deficit in associating information in memory. Rather, they may have a specific problem in developing phonological memory codes that can be used to form associations in memory.

Others have examined the relationship between phonological encoding and reading disabilities by having subjects repeat real and/or nonsense words. For example, Snowling, Goulandris, Bowlby, and Howell (1985) had dyslexic, age matched, and reading matched control children repeat high and low frequency real words and nonsense words. They found that high frequency words were repeated equally well by all three groups. However, dyslexic subjects performed more poorly than age matched controls in the repetition of low frequency words and more poorly than both groups in the repetition of nonsense words. Snowling et al. concluded that dyslexic children have a specific deficit in identifying the phonological segments in new, unfamiliar words, and, as a result, have difficulty repeating these words. This conclusion is supported further by Kamhi, Catts, Mauer, Apel, and Gentry (1988), who found that RD children made significantly more errors than good readers in the repetition of single monosyllabic nonsense words, three-item monosyllabic nonsense word strings, and multisyllabic nonsense words.

The difficulties RD children have in encoding phonological information are often assumed to be the result of problems in auditory perception. It is frequently concluded from clinical observations that RD children have problems in auditory discrimination. That is, these children are thought to have perceptual difficulties that prevent them from detecting the acoustic distinctions in the speech signal. Whereas there is some limited support for low-level perceptual deficits in poor readers (McCrosky & Kidder, 1980; Tallal, 1980; Zurif & Carson, 1970), the difficulties many of these children have in encoding phonological information may be more linguistic in nature. In fact, many RD children may be able to detect and discriminate the acoustic/phonetic cues that underlie speech perception, but be unable to utilize this information to derive the phonological structure of spoken words accurately or automatically. Several recent studies illustrate the difficulties poor readers have in the perception of speech.

Brady, Shankweiler, and Mann (1983) investigated good and poor readers' perception of speech (monosyllabic real words) and nonspeech (environmental sounds) stimuli. Stimuli were presented in a quiet and noise masked condition. The poor readers made significantly more errors than good readers in identifying the speech stimuli in noise. No group differences were observed in the other conditions. On the basis of these results, Brady et al. concluded that poor readers did not have a general auditory perceptual deficit, but rather a problem that was specific to the perception of speech. This deficit was argued to limit poor readers' identification of the phonetic content of spoken words, particularly in unfavorable listening conditions. In another study, Godfrey, Syrdal-Lasky, Millay, and Knox (1981) examined dyslexic children's identification and discrimination of synthesized stop consonant vowel series. Their results showed that the dyslexic subjects' speech perception abilities were not grossly abnormal. However, dyslexics were less consistent in their linguistic classification of auditory cues. Godfrey et al. suggested that inconsistency in phonetic classification might result in the formation of inadequate phonological memory codes.

Further investigations are needed to better understand the difficulties RD children may have in the perception of speech. This work will need to consider poor readers' speech perception in highly structured and controlled stimulus conditions (see Blumstein & Stevens, 1980; Kewley-Port, Pisoni, & Studdert-Kennedy, 1983), as well as in situations more akin to everyday speech perception. Research also should examine further the perception of nonspeech stimuli in order to rule out a general auditory perceptual dysfunction in RD children. However, to accomplish this, nonspeech measures will need to have more similar task and perceptual demands (Watson & Foyle, 1985) to that of the speech measures than has been the case in the past. As noted above, nonspeech measures have often involved simply identifying familiar environmental sounds. In addition, future investigations will need to more fully consider possible individual differences in RD children's speech and nonspeech perceptual abilities.

RETRIEVAL OF PHONOLOGICAL INFORMATION

Clinical observations have often revealed word finding problems in the speech of RD children (Johnson & Myklebust, 1967). The characteristics of these word finding problems include the substitution of a related word for an intended word, the use of descriptive definitions (e.g., "you can cut with it") or gestures, and the overuse of imprecise words and phrases (e.g., "stuff" and "you know"). The word finding difficulties observed clinically in RD children have also been borne out in research. For example, Denckla and Rudel (1976a) administered the Oldfield-Wingfield Picture Naming Test to dyslexic, nondyslexic learning disabled (LD) and normal achieving children. Dyslexic children were slower and made more errors in this naming task than nondyslexic LD and normal subjects. Numerous other investigators have also found RD children (and related groups, such as language impaired children) to perform less accurately and/or more slowly than normal children on confrontation picture naming tasks (Catts, 1986; Fried-Oken, 1984; German, 1979, 1982; Leonard, Nippold, Kail, & Hale, 1983; Kamhi et al., 1988; Katz, 1986; Rubin & Liberman, 1983; Wolf, 1982).

Word finding problems have been explained generally in terms of deficits in memory storage or retrieval processes (Kail & Leonard, 1986; Katz, 1986; Wiig and Semel, 1984). According to the storage deficit hypothesis, children have naming difficulties because some words are not represented in their vocabulary or the representations of these words are not fully elaborated. Both semantic and phonological factors may play a role in storage limitations. That is, children could be slow to learn the semantic features that characterize a word and distinguish it from other words, or children could have problems in establishing a phonological representation for the word. Attempts have often been made to control storage factors by equating reading groups on a general test of receptive vocabulary (Denckla & Rudel, 1976a; German, 1979; Wolf, 1982) or by providing a comprehension measure of the specific items employed in the naming task (Katz, 1986). Equating reading groups on receptive vocabulary measures, however, by no means assures they will be comparable in expressive lexical knowledge. Children may have a similar understanding of a given word, but differ considerably in how they use the word in their expressive language.

The storage deficit hypothesis is supported by research showing that poor readers have particular difficulty in recalling low frequency words (Denckla & Rudel, 1976a; German, 1979; Katz, 1986). Low frequency or uncommon words should be especially difficult to recall for children who have problems storing the semantic aspects of new words in their lexicon. Poor readers may also have deficits storing the phonological aspects of new words. Katz (1986), for example, found that RD children had difficulty recalling words with phonologically long names and that their naming errors were often phonologically related to intended words. On the basis of these results, he concluded that poor readers may often have difficulty developing phonological representations and that this makes it particularly difficult to recall many multisyllabic words. In other words, he suggests that a phonological encoding problem, such as that discussed in the first section of this chapter, contributes to the naming problems of many RD children.

Whereas some evidence supports a storage deficit hypothesis for word finding problems, a large number of investigations suggest some of these problems are the result of retrieval difficulties. According to the retrieval deficit hypothesis, problems in accessing phonological representations from memory are responsible for slowed or inaccurate naming in RD children. Wolf (1982), for example, observed that poor readers often had difficulty recalling the names of common objects on the Boston Naming Test. In this study, normal readers demonstrated the typical effects of word frequency on naming, whereas poor readers were found to have difficulty in naming both common and uncommon words. Because common words should have adequate representations in memory, difficulty in recalling these words suggests breakdowns in the retrieval process.

Numerous other studies have also reported that RD children demonstrate word finding problems when recalling common names. In one of the earliest studies to address naming deficits and reading disability, Denckla (1972) found that dyslexics often were slow and inaccurate in naming colors. In a follow-up investigation, Denckla and Rudel (1976b) examined what they termed "rapid automatized naming" in poor readers. They compared dyslexic, nondyslexic LD and normal children on tasks requiring the rapid naming of a repeated series of five familiar letters, digits, colors, or objects. They observed that the dyslexic subjects performed significantly slower in these naming tasks than nondyslexic LD children who, in turn, were slower than normal subjects.

More recently, Blachman (1984) examined rapid automatized naming in relation to reading achievement among 34 kindergarten and 34 first grade children. Reading ability was assessed in kindergarten children primarily by measuring letter identification and grapheme-phoneme correspondence knowledge. In first grade children, word identification and word attack skills were tested. Subjects were also administered tests of phonological processing that included the rapid naming of colors, objects, or letters. Results indicated that rapid naming of colors was a good predictor of literacy skills in kindergarten, whereas the rapid naming of letters was strongly correlated with reading in first grade. Blachman (1984, p. 619) concluded that " the ability to automatize a recently learned set of verbal labels (colors in kindergarten and letters in first grade) is related to the ability to learn a new set of labels (letters in kindergarten and words in first grade)."

The most extensive investigation of rapid naming and its relationship to reading ability was conducted by Wolf and her colleagues (Wolf, 1984, 1986; Wolf, Bally, & Morris, 1985). In a longitudinal study, they examined 115 children with varying reading abilities at the end of kindergarten and then again at the end of first and second grades.

Children were administered three continuous naming tasks (digits, colors, and objects) and two alternating naming tasks involving the naming of alternating patterns of letters and digits or letters, digits and colors. According to Wolf (1986), the alternating naming tasks not only require low-level retrieval abilities, but also necessitate the use of some high-level cognitive skills; for example, controlled attention to the alternating pattern of stimuli (e.g., ABAB, ABCABC). Reading ability was examined using word recognition, oral reading, and reading comprehension tasks.

The results of this investigation showed that rapid naming tasks were good predictors of reading across a wide range of abilities. Children who performed poorly on these tasks (especially the alternating stimulus tasks) in kindergarten generally had significant reading difficulties at the end of second grade. Rapid naming of letters and rapid naming of digits were more strongly related to reading across grades than naming tasks involving colors or objects. Furthermore, rapid naming of letters or digits was more highly correlated with oral reading and word recognition than with reading comprehension tasks. The alternating stimulus tasks were the ones most strongly correlated with reading comprehension. Wolf et al. (1985) explained these relationships by proposing that the rapid naming of letters or digits and word identification and oral reading all involve automatic retrieval of overlearned symbolic information. On the other hand, rapid naming of alternating stimuli and reading comprehension tasks involve both low-level automatic skills and high-level attention demanding processes.

The studies of rapid naming of familiar stimuli and reading achievement cited above each employed continuous lists of items to be named. Recently, Stanovich (1981, 1985) challenged the validity of continuous list naming tasks as measures of retrieval processes. He argued that performance on the continuous naming task may be influenced as much by various sequential-response, scanning, and motor-production strategies as by retrieval processes. He further suggested that a discrete trial procedure that measures reaction time to name a single stimulus may be a more valid measure of the ability to retrieve phonological memory codes. Employing such a discrete trial procedure, Stanovich (1981) found no significant differences between skilled and less skilled first grade readers in naming colors, digits, letters, or pictures. Significant group differences, however, were observed in naming familiar printed words. Perfetti, Finger, and Hogaboam (1978) have reported similar results in discrete trial naming tasks with skilled and less skilled third grade readers.

These results seem to demonstrate that the strength of the relationship between the retrieval of phonological information and reading ability may not be as strong as some have suggested. However, as

Stanovich (1981) has pointed out, these findings are specific to skilled and less skilled readers within the normal classroom. Differences in retrieval abilities have been observed in discrete trial naming tasks when children with more extreme differences in reading ability have been employed. For example, Lorsbach and Gray (1985) found significant differences between specific reading disabled and normal children in the speed in which they named letters and digits in a discrete trial naming paradigm.

Reading group differences in name retrieval have also been observed in studies that have employed a different type of discrete trial naming paradigm; that is, Posner and Mitchell's (1967) letter matching paradigm. In this paradigm, subjects are required to judge whether letter pairs are the same or different. These letter pairs are either physically identical (e.g., AA), identical in name (e.g., A a), or different (e.g., AB, Ab). Although no overt naming response is required, subjects must access phonological codes to make name identity judgments. Therefore, a slower speed to make name identity decisions is suggestive of less proficiency in retrieving phonological information. Ellis and Miles (1978) employed this letter matching technique with dyslexic and normal children. As predicted, dyslexic subjects were significantly slower than control subjects in name identity judgments but not in making physical identity decisions. Ellis (1981) has reported similar results using a modified version of the letter matching technique with normal and dyslexic children. In addition, Jackson and McClelland (1979) and Jackson (1980) have extended these findings to adult readers. Using the letter matching procedure, they found that college age skilled readers were quicker than less skilled readers at accessing the names of letters as well as novel characters whose names they had just been taught. Again, no group differences were found in reaction times involving physical identity.

Taken together, these various results present a strong case for a relationship between naming and reading ability. The strength of this relationship depends on the specific stimuli, technique, and subjects employed. Nevertheless, the slower and less accurate a child is in naming, the more likely he or she is to have reading difficulties. In many cases, deficits in the storage of phonological or semantic information probably underlie these word finding deficits. However, in some instances, naming problems seem to be specific to breakdowns in retrieval processes.

The Use of Phonological Codes in Working Memory

One of the most consistent findings in the investigation of RD children is that they perform poorly on tasks involving the storage of verbal information in short-term memory, or what more recently has been referred to as working memory (Jorm, 1979, 1983; Torgesen, 1985). This work indicates that compared to good readers, poor readers have deficits in the short-term recall of digits (Miles, 1983; Cohen & Netley, 1981), letters (Shankweiler, Liberman, Mark, Fowler, & Fischer, 1979), words (Byrne & Shea, 1979; Vellutino & Scanlon, 1982), and sentences (Mann, Liberman, & Shankweiler, 1980). This difficulty is observed whether the stimuli are presented in a visual or auditory mode (Shankweiler et al., 1979). These memory deficits are, however, confined to tasks involving verbal material. Research has typically failed to find differences between good and poor readers when the stimuli to be remembered cannot easily be coded in a verbal manner (Brady, 1986; Holmes & McKeever, 1979; Katz, Shankweiler, & Liberman, 1981; Liberman, Mann, Shankweiler, & Werfelman, 1982).

The working memory problems of poor readers have been explained in terms of both deficits in the use of active memorization strategies and deficiencies in basic phonological processing (Torgesen, 1985; Stanovich, 1986a). Several studies suggest that poor readers are less likely than good readers to employ mnemonic strategies to facilitate short-term recall. For example, Torgesen and Goldman (1977) have observed that good readers more often employed verbal rehearsal spontaneously in recall tasks than did poor readers. Research also indicates that poor readers often differ from good readers in the retention of the earliest items in a serial recall task (Bauer, 1979; Cohen & Netley, 1978; Tarver, Hallahan, Kauffman, & Ball, 1976). Because the use of memorization strategies has the greatest effect on retention of early items, this reported difference in primacy effects also seems to suggest that poor readers do not employ verbal rehearsal or other mnemonic strategies as effectively as good readers.

Cohen and Netley (1981) have demonstrated that RD children's deficits in working memory may go beyond inefficient use of mnemonic strategies. They compared RD children to normal controls on a serial running memory task. In this task, subjects were presented with lists of digits that varied in length from 16 to 26 items and in rate from 2.3 to 13.2 digits per second. Upon completion of each list, subjects were required to repeat the final three digits in the correct serial order. The variable length of the lists, together with rapid rates of presentation, made it virtually impossible for the children to effectively employ verbal rehearsal. The results showed that in such a task, RD children continue to demonstrate poorer recall performance than normal subjects (also see Torgesen & Houck, 1980). Cohen & Netley concluded that the RD children's decrement in performance on these tasks is due to a phonological processing deficit involving the reduced ability to code a serial speech sound pattern in working memory.

There are several ways to represent information in working memory.

These include using mental images or various types of linguistic codes, such as semantically or propositionally based ones or phonologically based codes. Research suggests that phonological codes are the most efficient for storing verbal information (Baddeley & Hitch, 1974; Conrad, 1964). This appears to be the case even when the sensory input is visual in nature (Conrad, 1964). Cohen and Netley (1981) as well as other investigations have suggested that it is the use of the phonological code in working memory that is particularly problematic for poor readers.

Byrne and Shea (1979) examined the use of memory codes in good and poor beginning readers. Subjects listened to a continuous list of words and were required to indicate whether each word had occurred earlier in the list. Some words in the list were semantically related to items presented earlier (e.g., *city* and *town*), whereas others were phonetically related (e.g., *home* and *comb*). False positive responses (saying that a word had occurred before, when it had not) were taken as indications of how words were coded in memory. That is, if words were coded in terms of their phonetic features, false positives should occur most often on phonetically related words. Their results showed that good readers made both semantically and phonetically related false positives, indicating that they encoded both phonetic and semantic features in memory. Poor readers, on the other hand, made many meaning based errors but almost no phonetically based errors. Byrne and Shea concluded that "the phonetic code, which occupies a unique place in memory in most people, does not carry its usual load in young poor readers" (p. 337).

Other investigators have also used phonetic confusability as an index for examining differences in phonological coding in good and poor readers. For example, Shankweiler et al. (1979) employed a task originally developed by Conrad (1964) in which subjects were required to recall sequences of five letters. Half of the letter sequences contained phonetically confusable items (drawn from the set BCDGPTVZ) and the other half phonetically nonconfusable letters (drawn from the set HKLQRSWY). Whereas good readers recalled significantly more nonconfusable letters than poor readers, this advantage was virtually eliminated in the case of phonetically confusable letters. The results were the same whether the letters were presented in a visual or auditory mode. Shankweiler et al. concluded that the poor readers were less affected by phonetic confusability because of their inability to access or form high quality phonological representations in working memory. The findings from this study have been replicated in subsequent studies in which phonetically confusable and nonconfusable words and sentences were used (Brady et al., 1983; Mann et al., 1980).

Not all studies, however, are in agreement with Shankweiler et al. (1979). For example, several studies have failed to uncover reduced phonetic confusability effects in poor readers (Bisanz, Das, & Mancini, 1984; Hall, Ewing, Tinzmann, & Wilson, 1981; Hall, Wilson, Humphreys, Tinzmann, and Bowyer, 1983; Johnston, 1982). Some have argued that group differences in phonetic confusability effects arise more from experimental design flaws than from memory coding differences in good and poor readers (Hall et al., 1983). Johnston (1982), on the other hand, has suggested that the lack of consistency among studies may be due to differences in the age of subjects. The poor readers in the above studies were generally older than those employed by Shankweiler et al. (1979). Regardless of the conclusions to be drawn from studies of phonetic confusability, the bulk of the evidence continues to suggest that RD children have deficits in coding phonological information in working memory.

The deficits RD children have in using phonological codes in working memory may be related to their problems in the retrieval of speech sound codes from long-term memory (Baddeley, 1979; Lorsbach & Gray, 1985; Spring & Capps, 1974; Spring & Perry, 1983; Torgesen & Houck, 1980). According to Baddeley (1979), to hold a string of familiar items such as digits, letters, or words in working memory, the individual must activate or retrieve the phonological codes for these stimuli from long-term lexical storage. Baddeley and others (e.g., Lorsbach & Gray, 1985) argued that because RD children retrieve phonological codes from long-term memory at a slower rate than good readers, they perform more poorly in tasks requiring the short-term retention of verbal information. In other words, slowed retrieval is thought to delay the storage of items in working memory and thus take up processing time that could be used for verbal rehearsal or other higher-level processes.

PHONOLOGICAL AWARENESS

In the early stages of language acquisition, children focus their attention predominantly on the content and use of language. Little attention is given to the speech sound structure of language. However, with development, children gradually come to appreciate this structure. For example, they become explicitly aware that speech is composed of individual words and that words may rhyme or share segments with other words. They also come to realize that words are divisible into syllabic and phonemic units. This explicit knowledge about the sound structure of the language is referred to as *phonological awareness* (Hakes, 1982).

A large body of literature has documented that phonological awareness is related to reading ability (Blachman, 1984; Wagner & Torgesen, 1987). Studies have shown that RD children perform more poorly than normal readers on tasks measuring speech sound awareness. Fox and Routh (1980), for example, examined the phonemic analysis skills of first grade children with average, mildly depressed, and severely depressed reading ability. In the experimental task, children were required to "say just a little bit" of spoken syllables. The severely reading disabled children were found to be unable to divide syllables into phonemes, whereas children with mildly depressed or average reading ability were quite capable in this task.

Bradley and Bryant (1978) found that children with reading disabilities were strikingly insensitive to rhyme and alliteration. In their study, they compared a group of RD children to a group of younger normal children matched for reading ability. Subjects participated in a task in which they had to choose the odd member from a list of spoken words, such as *lot, cot, hat, pot*. Even though the RD children were, on the average, 3½ years older than the normal control subjects, they performed significantly worse on this task than did normal readers.

More recently, Katz (1986) showed that RD third grade children were less aware of word length than normal readers. Subjects were required to determine if the names of pictured objects had a similar number of syllables or not. Names were generally one or three syllables in length. A posttest naming task was employed to rule out group differences in naming ability. The results showed that even when RD children knew the names of objects, they were less able than normal readers to make judgments about the length of these names.

Other investigations have examined speech sound awareness in children whose reading abilities vary across the continuum. The results of this work have consistently supported a strong positive relationship between children's awareness of the phonological structure of words and their reading ability (Blachman & James, 1985; Helfgott, 1976; Liberman, Shankweiler, Fischer, & Carter, 1974; Mann & Liberman, 1984; Sawyer, 1987; Share, Jorm, Maclean, & Matthews, 1984; Treiman & Baron, 1981; Tunmer & Nesdale, 1985; Zifcak, 1981). This relationship has been demonstrated across a wide range of subject ages (Calfee, Lindamood, & Lindamood, 1973), languages (Cossu, Shankweiler, Liberman, Katz, & Tola, 1988; Lundberg, Olofsson, & Wall, 1980; Lundberg, Frost, & Peterson, 1987, cited in Lundberg, 1987) and experimental tasks (Stanovich, Cunningham, & Cramer, 1984).

The relationship between phonological awareness and reading ability appears to be one in which causation is bidirectional (Ehri, 1979; Perfetti, Beck, & Hughes, 1981; Stanovich, 1986b). That is, phonological awareness may be both an antecedent of reading development and a consequence of reading experience. In support of the latter, research (Read, Zhang, Nie, & Ding, 1986) has shown that some aspects of phonological awareness do not seem to be the natural result of maturation but rather the consequence of learning an alphabetic orthography. Without this instruction, individuals may gain only minimal explicit awareness of phonemic units. For example, Morais, Cary, Alegria, & Bertelson (1979) investigated the ability of illiterate adults from a farm community in Portugal to add, delete, and reverse the phonemes of real and nonsense words. The illiterate subjects were found to perform significantly more poorly in these tasks than control subjects from the same area who had received some reading instruction as an adult. Morais, Bertelson, Cary, and Alegria (1986) have recently replicated their findings in another study involving literate and illiterate Portuguese subjects. Although they again found minimal phoneme segmentation abilities among illiterate subjects, they did observe that these subjects had acquired some abilities in syllable segmentation and rhyme awareness. Liberman, Rubin, Duques, and Carlisle (1985) and Read and Ruyter (1985) have also reported limited phonological awareness among illiterate subjects in the United States. Liberman et al. (1985) found that adults attending a literacy class performed no better than first grade children on a phoneme segmentation task.

The above studies might be criticized because they employed individuals who were illiterate in adulthood and therefore, perhaps, were atypical subjects. However, similar findings have been reported by Read et al. (1986) in literate adults. These investigators examined the ability to add or delete phonemes from spoken syllables in two groups of Chinese adults. Subjects in one group were competent users of the traditional logographic writing system. In this system, there is only a minimal relationship between orthographic characters and the phonological composition of the words they represent (Taylor, 1981). Subjects in a second group were also competent in the traditional system but had learned a supplemental alphabetic system (i.e., pinyin) during their elementary education. Results indicated that the subjects who had once learned an alphabetic system had more advanced skills in phoneme segmentation than those who only knew the traditional logographic system. These results thus suggest that it is not just any reading instruction that promotes phonological awareness, but instruction involving a phonologically based writing system.

Although specific reading experience has been shown to increase phonological awareness, there is also good reason to believe that some aspects of speech sound awareness develop independent of reading instruction and have a significant effect on reading ability. One of the studies cited above provides support for this relationship. Recall that Bradley and Bryant (1978) found that young normal children performed better on tasks of phonological awareness than did older RD children. Because it is unlikely that the normal children had as much experience with written language (being on the average 3½ years younger) as the RD children, reading experience itself could not account for group differences in sensitivity to rhyme and alliteration. Rather, as the authors concluded, RD children's problems in reading were at least in part the consequence of their difficulties in phonological awareness.

Some investigations have attempted to reduce the confounding effects of reading instruction by examining phonological awareness in children before formal written language instruction has begun (Helfgott, 1976; Lundberg, Olofsson, & Wall, 1980; Mann & Liberman, 1984; Stanovich, Cunningham, & Cramer, 1984). These investigators assessed kindergarten children's awareness of rhyme, syllables, or phonemes and compared this awareness to reading ability in first grade. The results of these studies have consistently shown that early sound awareness is a good predictor of later literacy. One problem in interpreting this work, however, is that these studies generally did not control the effects of informal literacy instruction by parents and siblings. It is quite possible that early informal instruction in reading may have influenced both phonological awareness and later reading ability.

Bradley and Bryant (1983) attempted to control the effects of informal literacy instruction by selecting only those four- to five-year-old preschoolers who demonstrated no reading ability at all (e.g., those who could not read any words on the Schonell reading test). They found that the rhyme and alliteration awareness of these subjects at age four to five years was significantly correlated with their reading ability three years later. More recently, Lundberg, Frost, and Petersen (1987, cited in Lundberg, 1987) measured phonological awareness in Danish kindergarten children and compared this awareness to their reading ability in first grade. In Denmark it is traditional to withhold both formal and informal reading instruction until children enter first grade at the age of seven years. Thus, the authors argued that the phonological awareness of the kindergarten children was relatively unaffected by literacy instruction. Results indicated that the kindergarten children had acquired awareness of rhyme and syllables but minimal knowledge of phonemes. The extent of this awareness, particularly awareness of phonemes, was moderately related to reading development in first grade. A bit disconcerting, however, was the finding that reading in first grade was also moderately related to letter knowledge in kindergarten. This may indicate that some kindergarten children are learning something about literacy (at least letter names) and that this knowledge is influencing their phonological awareness and later reading ability.

In an attempt to clarify further the relationship between phonological awareness and reading, investigators have experimentally manipulated speech sound awareness in training studies (Ball & Blachman, 1987; Bradley & Bryant, 1983; Fox & Routh, 1976; Lundberg 1987; Olofsson & Lundberg, 1983; Rosner, 1971; Treiman & Baron, 1983). Blachman (this volume) discusses these studies in more detail. Briefly, however, this research has shown that the awareness of the speech sound structure of the language can be explicitly taught and that this knowledge has a positive effect on the development of literacy. Thus, the theoretical implication of these findings is that reading ability is, in part, the result of phonological awareness.

In summary, a large number of studies now indicate that phonological awareness is related to reading ability and that this relationship is reciprocal in nature. Children appear to acquire some aspects of speech sound awareness as part of their maturation of cognitive-linguistic abilities. For most children this includes awareness of rhyme, alliteration, and the syllabic structure of words. Variability in this awareness appears to be causally related to reading ability. That is, children with limited awareness of these aspects of language often experience difficulties in learning to read, whereas those with a high degree of sound awareness often excel at reading. Awareness of phonological segments, on the other hand, is significantly influenced by reading experience or instruction. Children who successfully learn an alphabetic writing system become explicitly aware of phoneme-sized units and can perform a wide variety of tasks that require the segmentation and/or manipulation of these units. Individuals, however, who are illiterate or who are raised in a culture that does not employ an alphabetic orthography may have very limited explicit awareness of phonemes.

Production of Phonological Sequences

A final area of phonological processing that has been empirically linked to reading ability is speech production/articulation. Clinical observations have revealed that RD children often display difficulties in producing speech sound sequences (Blalock, 1982; Chasty, 1986; Johnson & Myklebust, 1967; Klein, 1986; Miles, 1974). These difficulties, however, are generally acknowledged to be limited to the production of complex phonological sequences, like those found in some multisyllabic words (Harris-Schmidt & Noell, 1983).

Catts (1986) recently examined the speech production deficits of a group of RD children. Twenty RD adolescent subjects were compared to 20 normal readers on three speech production tasks. These tasks included the naming of pictured objects with phonologically complex names (e.g., *ambulance, thermometer*), the repetition of phonologically complex words (e.g., *specific, aluminum*), and the repetition of phonologically complex phrases (e.g., *brown and blue plaid pants, the priest blessed the bread*). The RD subjects were observed to make significantly more speech production errors in each of the tasks than did the normal subjects. An examination of the errors revealed that in the naming or repetition of multisyllabic words, RD subjects' errors were generally word-specific substitutions or omissions of sound segments. Often these errors did not appear to be conditioned by the phonetic context in which they occurred. Catts suggested that such an error pattern may be a reflection of RD children's difficulties in encoding phonological information in memory. That is, encoding deficits, such as those discussed earlier in this chapter, may have prevented the RD subjects from representing the phonological detail needed to accurately produce some of the stimulus words in this study. Such a conclusion is consistent with Snowling (1981), who also found deficits in RD children's production of multisyllabic words. She argued that RD children have deficiencies in determining the nature and order of the phonemes in words and that this makes it difficult for them to accurately produce many less familiar multisyllabic words.

Whereas some of the speech production errors of RD children may be the result of phonological encoding deficits, others appear to result from difficulties in outputting phonological information. Catts (1986) offered such an explanation to account for the problems many of the RD children had in the phrase repetition task. In this task, the individual stimulus words were generally common monosyllabic words that were likely to have been represented accurately by subjects. However, because of the phonetic similarity between the stimulus words in the phrases, errors were expected to arise in speech planning or articulation. The finding that RD subjects made significantly more errors in this task than normal subjects thus suggests that RD subjects may have problems planning/articulating speech sound segments.

More recently, Catts (1987) investigated the speech production abilities of dyslexic and normal college students. Subjects rapidly repeated a series of phonologically complex and less complex phrases. The complex phrases were two or three syllables in length and contained similar phonetic segments or consonant clusters in similar syllabic positions (e.g., *she sews, bright blue beam*). The less complex phrases had approximately the same number of segments as the complex items, but contained less phonetic similarity across syllables (e.g., *he sews, dark blue hat*). The phrases were produced by the experimenter in a fixed quasi-random order. Subjects were instructed to repeat each phrase once at a normal rate to assure they had correctly encoded the phrase and then produce the phrase repeatedly as fast as they could while trying not to make any errors. The average phrase duration and total number of errors during the first 10 repetitions of each phrase were taken as an index of proficiency of speech output (Smith, Hillenbrand, Wasowicz, & Preston, 1986).

Results showed that the dyslexic subjects repeated both the complex and less complex phrases at a significantly slower rate than did the normal subjects. Dyslexic subjects were also observed to make significantly more errors in the production of the complex phrases than did the normal controls. As expected, few errors occurred in the production of the less complex phrases. It was concluded that dyslexics are less proficient than normal individuals in outputting speech sound sequences.

A further examination of the data suggested that the dyslexics' problems in speech production arise at least in part from difficulties during the planning stage. It was observed that almost all of the dyslexics' errors were "slips of the tongue" involving the anticipation or perseveration of sound segments (e.g., *blight blue beam* for *bright blue beam*). Whereas errors such as these might occasionally result from difficulties in the actual articulation of speech, most are thought to arise during the planning stage of speech production (Bock, 1982; Dell, 1986; Shattuck-Hufnagel, 1983). In speech planning, abstract lexical units are converted into a serial order of phonological segments. During this conversion, errors may occur and result in segments being misordered or misproduced. The observation that dyslexics made significantly more of these errors than normal subjects suggests that they are less proficient in this planning process. That is, dyslexics may be slower and less accurate than normal individuals in converting lexical information into a sequential sound based code.

In summary, clinical observations and research indicate that many RD individuals have difficulties in producing speech sound sequences. These difficulties appear to be the result of deficits in encoding phonological information as well as problems in planning and, perhaps, articulating phonologically complex sound sequences.

INTERRELATIONSHIPS

In various sections of this chapter, it was suggested that deficits/abilities in one area of phonological processing may be related to deficits/abilities in other areas. For example, it was argued that deficiencies in encoding phonological information may, in part, underlie problems in the retrieval of this information and in the production of speech sound sequences. The nature of the interrelationships between various aspects of phonological processing has been considered by other researchers as well (Jorm & Share, 1983; Wagner et al., 1987; Wagner & Torgesen, 1987). Jorm and Share (1983), for example, proposed that individual differences in the various aspects of phonological processing result, to a large degree, from children's varying ability to code phonological information in long-term memory. They argued that the efficiency with which information is represented in memory significantly influences the speed at which this information can be retrieved. Following Baddeley's (1979) model of working memory, they further proposed that the speed of retrieval of phonological information, in turn, influences how automatically and accurately this information can be coded in working memory. In addition, Jorm and Share have suggested that phonological awareness is also directly related to phonological encoding. Specifically, they have argued that efficient storage of phonological information leads to increased explicit awareness of this information.

More recently, Wagner and his colleagues (Wagner et al., 1987; Wagner & Torgesen, 1987) have proposed a theoretical framework from which to evaluate possible interrelationships. They offered five alternative models concerning the underlying nature of phonological processing. These include: (1) a *general ability model,* which proposes that the various aspects of phonological processing are part of a single latent phonological ability, (2) a *specific ability model,* which states that each of the aspects of phonological processing represent distinct cognitive-linguistic abilities, (3) an *awareness versus use model,* which proposes that the awareness of the phonological structure of the language is independent from retrieving and coding phonological information in memory, (4) an *awareness/coding versus retrieval model,* which states that phonological awareness and coding in working memory represent one latent phonological ability and retrieval represents another, and (5) an *awareness/retrieval versus coding model,* which proposes that phonological awareness and retrieval represent one latent ability and phonological coding in working memory represents another. As stated, this theoretical framework does not include phonological encoding and the production of phonological sequences. These aspects of phonological processing, however, could be easily incorporated into this framework.

Although various theoretical models have been proposed to account for the relationship between different aspects of phonological processing, only limited empirical evidence is available to evaluate these models. Research in phonological processing has, for the most part, been directed toward only one aspect of this processing at a time. As a result, work in any one area of phonological processing has progressed in relative isolation from that in other areas. A small number of studies, however, have examined multiple aspects of phonological processing in relationship to reading ability, as well as to each other (Blachman, 1984; Lorsbach & Gray, 1985; Mann & Liberman, 1984; Torgesen & Houck, 1980; Wagner et al., 1987). A number of studies have shown, for example, that speed of retrieval of phonological information is significantly related to the ability to use phonological codes in working memory (Lorsbach & Gray, 1985; Spring, 1976; Spring & Capps, 1974; Spring & Perry, 1983; Torgesen & Houck, 1980). This work indicates that children who are slow to retrieve phonological information from memory do poorly in the short-term retention of this information. Others have reported a relationship between encoding of phonological information and the use of this information in working memory. Specifically, Done and Miles (1978) found a significant correlation ($r = .64$) between a measure of digit span and a measure of verbal-visual paired-associate learning in normal and dyslexic adolescents.

Other investigations have also examined phonological awareness in relation to the retrieval of phonological information and/or the use of phonological codes in working memory. Blachman (1984), for instance, investigated rapid naming of colors, objects or letters, syllable segmentation, and rhyming ability in kindergarten and first grade children. Whereas measures of rapid naming and phonological awareness were related to reading ability, 12 of the 13 possible correlations between naming speed and phonological awareness were found to be nonsignificant. Thus, Blachman concluded that these two measures of phonological processing were tapping somewhat different aspects of linguistic processing.

In another study, Mann and Liberman (1984) found a small but significant correlation between syllable segmentation (e.g., phonological awareness) and memory of word strings (e.g., phonological coding in working memory). Wagner and Torgesen (1987) performed a further analysis on these data and showed that even though syllable segmentation and memory span were somewhat related, they contributed separately to predicting reading ability.

Taken together, the above research appears to support the awareness versus use model. That is, measures of encoding phonological information, retrieving phonological information, and using phonological codes in working memory seem to be interrelated and somewhat distinct from measures of phonological awareness. Recently, however, Wagner et al. (1987) have provided data that suggest that measures of phonological awareness are, in fact, related to some aspects of phonological processing and not to others. In the most extensive study of the interrelationships between measures of phonological processing, they tested 111 kindergarten children on 12 phonological processing tasks. These measures fell into three different categories: those involving (1) phonological awareness, (2) rapid retrieval of phonological information, and (3) phonological coding in working memory. Factor analysis indicated that measures of phonological awareness and phonological coding in memory were interrelated and somewhat distinct from those involving phonological retrieval. Thus, these data seem to support the awareness/coding versus retrieval model.

Wagner et al. (1987) explained the observed relationship between phonological awareness and coding by noting that tests of sound awareness typically involve auditory presentation of speech stimuli that must be held and/or manipulated in working memory. Thus, a deficit in phonological coding in working memory could result in difficulties in phonological awareness tasks. Although factor analysis differentiated phonological awareness/coding from phonological retrieval, these factors were found to be moderately correlated (with IQ partialled out). Wagner et al. argued that this suggests that whereas these factors may represent two latent phonological abilities, they may also share some general processes or funds of knowledge.

Clearly, continued investigation will be necessary to delineate the interrelationships between the various aspects of phonological processing. As in the case of Wagner et al. (1987), this work will need to consider multiple measures of phonological processing in large groups of children. In addition, these interrelationships need to be examined in children who differ in age and reading ability.

EFFECTS OF PHONOLOGICAL PROCESSING ON SPECIFIC ASPECTS OF READING

In Chapter 1 it was argued that reading could be divided into the processes of word recognition and comprehension. This section addresses specific relationships between abilities/deficits in phonological processing and those in word recognition and comprehension. For the most part, this discussion rests on theoretical rather than empirical ground. With few exceptions (Treiman & Baron, 1983) research has yet to isolate the effects of phonological processing on specific aspects of written language development.

In order to consider adequately the effects of phonological processing deficits on word recognition, it is first necessary to review briefly the cognitive-linguistic processes involved in recognizing printed words.

Recall that word recognition entails accessing lexical information stored in memory. Traditionally, it has been argued that there are two approaches for this lexical access (Baron, 1977). In one approach, words are recognized directly on the basis of their visual/orthographic characteristics. In this, the whole word or sight word approach, a match is made between the word's overall shape and/or letter pattern and a similar visual representation in memory. In alphabetic languages, a second approach for lexical access is available. In this, the phonetic approach, the reader employs knowledge of grapheme-phoneme correspondence to recode letters and/or letter groups into phonemes. These phonemes are blended together to form sound sequences that are then matched with phonological representations in the lexicon. More recently it has been proposed that the reader can also decode words phonetically by the use of analogies (Glushko, 1979). In this approach, a new word such as *nade* is read by retrieving the pronunciation of an analogous word such as *made*.

The phonetic route plays a particularly important role in the early stages of reading development. Specifically, this approach allows children to recognize words that are part of their oral vocabulary but that have never been encountered in print. Proficiency in the use of this approach thus can free children from the need for direct instruction and allow them to build independently a sight vocabulary. Another important aspect of the phonetic route is that its use draws children's attention to the specific letter patterns of words. As a result, children's visual representations of words become more elaborate, and words become easier to identify directly by the sight word approach.

Deficits in phonological processing could present difficulties for the development and use of both the phonetic and whole word approaches to word recognition. In the case of the phonetic route, children need to learn that the alphabetic system represents the phonemic segments in words. This requires that children have enough explicit knowledge of the phonological structure of the language to understand that words can be segmented into phonemic units. Without this awareness, children are faced with the task of learning to associate letters with sound segments they cannot fully appreciate. The relationship between a word's spelling and its pronunciation may appear arbitrary to children with poor phonological awareness. As a result, these children are slow to break the alphabetic code and learn the correspondence between graphemes and the phonemes they represent.

Phonological processing abilities may not only influence the acquisition of grapheme-phoneme correspondence knowledge, but may have a significant effect on the application of this knowledge in decoding words. In reading by way of the phonetic approach, the reader sequentially converts letters or letter groups into phonemes. This involves retrieving the phonemes that correspond to letters and placing these sound segments in working memory where they can be stored momentarily and then blended together to form words. The use of analogies to decode words phonetically also involves the retrieval of speech sound information and the brief storage of this information. Thus, the ability to retrieve phonological information and/or the use of phonological codes in working memory is critical to the decoding process.

Children with deficits in phonological processing no doubt will show significant problems in using the phonetic approach for word recognition. Their slow retrieval of speech sound codes and the poor quality of these memory codes will make it particularly difficult to store and blend phonemic units in working memory. In addition, reading by the phonetic route may be less efficient because these children are often poor at word closure. Most normal readers need only decode a portion of many multisyllabic words before they can accurately recognize them. Their knowledge of the sound patterns of the language and the saliency of these sound patterns in their lexicon allows many normal children to identify a word such as *principal* after only decoding the first two syllables. Children with phonological processing deficits, however, may lack this salient awareness and, as a result, need to decode each word completely before they can identify it. Even then they often struggle, continuously trying to blend together the sounds in the word without recognizing the lexical item they are approximating.

Phonological processing abilities can further be linked with proficiency in the development and use of the whole word approach for word recognition. In this approach the reader relies on the association between a word's shape and letter configuration and its meaning and pronunciation. On encountering a printed word, the reader must rapidly retrieve the word's semantic and phonological codes and place this information in working memory. In oral reading, phonological codes are further converted into overt speech.

Because the whole word route relies heavily on learning to associate printed words with phonological patterns (i.e., paired-associate learning), RD children with deficits in encoding phonological information in memory will experience difficulties in using this approach efficiently. Encoding deficits, however, should only affect the acquisition of those sight words that are not part of the child's oral vocabulary. In such cases, the child not only must learn an association, but must develop a new phonological representation. Research has shown that poor readers often have difficulty forming new phonological memory codes (e.g., Vellutino, Steger, et al., 1975).

The paired-associate learning necessary for sight word reading can also be disrupted indirectly by phonological processing deficits. As discussed above, the successful use of the phonetic route in decoding words results in the elaboration of orthographic representations that can be used subsequently for direct visual recognition of these words. Conversely, Jorm and Share (1983) pointed out that every failure to decode an unfamiliar word is a learning trial missed for the whole word approach. Thus, difficulties in phonological processing that interfere with the use of the phonetic approach also will slow the acquisition of a sight word vocabulary.

Although many children with phonological processing deficits may have problems in developing a sight vocabulary, they will eventually learn to recognize many words by way of the sight word approach. However, because RD children often also have deficits in retrieving phonological information, they will usually be slow and occasionally inaccurate in accessing the phonological codes or pronunciations of words in their sight vocabulary. This can be noted particularly in their oral reading. Even after years of instruction and practice, the oral reading of many RD individuals is slow and laborious.

Phonological processing deficits can affect oral reading in other ways as well. Recently, Catts (1987) reported that the difficulties dyslexics have in repeating some multisyllabic words is also evident in their oral reading. He noted that on encountering a printed multisyllabic word, adult dyslexics occasionally demonstrated several attempts at pronouncing the word before saying it correctly. Whereas poor decoding skills may account in part for these difficulties, subjects often reported that they knew the word but still could not pronounce it correctly. For example, one subject who was attempting to read the word *memorandum* produced the following:

memo   mendemrandum   menerandum
("I'm not pronouncing that right")
mendemrandum [and then quietly to himself]
randum   memorandum

Examples such as this may be indicative of problems in speech planning rather than difficulties in word recognition. That is, on occasion poor readers may correctly access a lexical item but have difficulty in formulating and/or executing the output plan for its articulation. Of course, the effects of this problem, no doubt, are compounded by poor readers' inability to rapidly access grapheme-phoneme correspondences to supplement their production of the word.

The influence of speech planning on oral reading may go beyond difficulty reading multisyllabic words. In fact, speech planning deficits may account in part for some of the pauses, hesitations, or false starts that are frequently observed in the oral reading of RD individuals. Future investigations will need to examine more closely the role of speech planning in oral reading.

Phonological processing deficits can also interfere with reading comprehension. As noted above, these deficits often result in slowed or inaccurate word recognition. Perfetti (1985) has recently argued that the efficiency of word recognition indirectly affects efficiency of comprehension. Working within an information processing framework, he proposed that the reader has a finite amount of processing capacity available for reading. Processing resources used in lexical access thus take away from resources that can be allocated to the higher-level processes of propositional encoding and text modeling. Under most circumstances, this is not a problem for skilled readers because word recognition is so automatic. As a result, a large proportion of their processing resources can be devoted to comprehending the text. However, for less skilled readers (e.g., those with phonological processing deficits), an inordinate amount of processing resources must be allocated to recognizing words. Consequently, limited resources may be available for reading comprehension.

The ability to use phonological codes in working memory also has been linked to reading comprehension. Recently, Mann, Shankweiler, and Smith (1984) examined the relationship between phonological coding in STM and sentence comprehension. They compared good and poor readers' ability to repeat and comprehend spoken sentences containing embedded relative clauses, such as, *The dog that the sheep chased stood on the turtle.* Because sentences like this violate the minimal distance principle, they place heavy demands on verbal memory. Poor readers were found to make significantly more errors than good readers in both repeating test sentences and acting out the meaning of these sentences. Mann et al. concluded that difficulties in representing speech sound information in working memory was responsible at least in part for these group differences. They argued that because of inefficient phonological coding, poor readers often fail to remember some of the words of a sentence and therefore are unable to recover fully the syntactic structure. Mann et al. acknowledged, however, that poor readers may also have a specific deficit in the acquisition of syntactic knowledge that may be independent of poor phonological coding (see Byrne, 1981).

Although the above research involved the comprehension of spoken sentences, the results are also relevant to the comprehension of printed text. In order to extract meaning from written sentences or text, the reader often must remember words occurring earlier in sentences until subsequent words can be decoded. Therefore, difficulties in representing phonological information in working memory could disrupt reading comprehension (Shankweiler & Crain, 1987). Of course, in written language processing, the reader is free to review earlier portions of the text if memory fails. However, this requires the utilization of processing resources that otherwise might be used for comprehension itself.

SUMMARY

This chapter has examined the relationship between specific reading disabilities and deficits in processing speech sound information. It was argued that RD children often have deficits in encoding, retrieving, and using phonological memory codes. Poor readers also have been observed to have difficulties in the production of phonological sequences and in the explicit awareness of the speech sound structure of the language. These various deficits in phonological processing appear to be interrelated, but the exact nature of these interrelationships is yet to be determined. It is unclear whether RD children have a unitary phonological processing deficit that manifests itself in different forms or whether several distinct phonological processing limitations are involved in reading disabilities. Finally, it was proposed that phonological processing deficits are causally related to difficulties in specific subskills of reading. However, it was noted that limited research is available to evaluate proposed relationships. Future investigations will need to examine specifically how phonological processing abilities may be related to the acquisition of written language skills. Research will also need to consider the possibility that some aspects of phonological processing may in part be a consequence rather than an antecedent of reading ability.

REFERENCES

Baddeley, A. (1979). Working memory and reading. In P. Kolers, M. Wrolstad, and H. Bouma (Eds.), *Processing of visible language.* New York: Plenum Publishing Corp.

Baddeley, A., and Hitch, G. (1974). Working memory. In G. Bower (Ed.), *The psychology of learning and motivation*, 47–90. New York: Academic Press.

Ball, E., and Blachman, B. (1987). *A reading readiness program with an emphasis on phoneme segmentation.* Paper presented at the Annual Conference of the Orton Dyslexia Society, San Francisco.

Baron J., (1977). Mechanisms for pronouncing printed words: Use and application. In D. Laberge and S. Samuels (Eds.), *Basic processes in reading: Perception and comprehension*, 175–216. Hillsdale, NJ: Erlbaum.

Bauer, R. (1979). Memory, acquisition, and category clustering in learning-disabled children. *Journal of Experimental Child Psychology, 27,* 365–383.

Bisanz, G., Das, J., and Mancini, G. (1984). Children's memory for phonemically confusable and nonconfusable letters: Changes with age and reading ability. *Child Development, 55,* 1845–1854.

Blachman, B. (1984). Relationship of rapid naming ability and language analysis skills to kindergarten and first-grade reading achievement. *Journal of Educational Psychology, 76,* 610–622.

Blachman, B., and James, S. (1985). Metalinguistic abilities and reading achievement in first grade children. In J. Niles and R. Lalik (Eds.)., *Issues in literacy: A research perspective. Thirty-fourth Yearbook of the National Reading Conference.* Rochester, NY: National Reading Conference.

Blalock, J. (1982). Persistent auditory language deficits in adults with learning disabilities. *Journal of Learning Disabilities, 15,* 604–609.

Blumstein, S., and Stevens, K.(1980). Perceptual invariance and onset spectra for stop consonants in different vowel environments. *Journal of the Acoustic Society of America, 67,* 648–662.

Bock, J. (1982). Toward a cognitive psychology of syntax: Information processing contributions to sentence formation. *Psychological Review, 89,* 1–47.

Bradley, L., and Bryant, P. (1978). Difficulties in auditory organization as a possible cause of reading backwardness. *Nature, 271,* 746–747.

Bradley, L., and Bryant, P. (1983). Categorizing sounds and learning to read: A causal connection. *Nature, 301,* 419–421.

Brady, S. (1986). Short-term memory, phonological processing, and reading ability. *Annals of Dyslexia, 36,* 138–153.

Brady, S., Shankweiler, D., and Mann, V. (1983). Speech perception and memory coding in relation to reading ability. *Journal of Experimental Psychology, 35,* 345–367.

Byrne, B., and Shea, P. (1979). Semantic and phonetic memory codes in beginning readers. *Memory and Cognition, 7,* 333–338.

Calfee, R., Lindamood, P., and Lindamood, C. (1973). Acoustic-phonetic skills and reading: Kindergarten through twelfth grade. *Journal of Educational Psychology, 64,* 293–298.

Catts, H. (1986). Speech production/phonological deficits in reading disordered children. *Journal of Learning Disabilities, 19,* 504–508.

Catts, H. (1987). *Can't read, can't spell, can't talk so good either.* Paper presented at the Annual Conference of American Speech-Language-Hearing Association, New Orleans.

Chasty, H. (1986). What is dyslexia? A developmental language perspective. In M. Snowling (Ed.) *Children's written language difficulties: Assessment and management.* Windsor, Bershire: Nfer-Nelson.

Cohen, R., and Netley, C. (1978). Cognitive deficits, learning disabilities, and WISC verbal-performance consistency. *Developmental Psychology, 14,* 624–634.

Cohen, R., and Netley, C. (1981). Short-term memory deficits in reading disabled children, in the absence of opportunity for rehearsal strategies. *Intelligence, 5,* 69–76.

Conrad, R. (1964). Acoustic confusions in immediate memory. *British Journal of Psychology, 5,* 75–84.

Cossu, G., Shankweiler, D., Liberman, I., Katz, L., and Tola, G. (1988). Awareness of phonological segments and reading ability in Italian children. *Applied Psycholinguistics, 9,* 1-16.

Dell, C. (1986). A spreading activation theory of retrieval and sentence production. *Psychological Review, 93,* 283-321.

Denckla, M., (1972). Color-naming deficits in dyslexic boys. *Cortex, 8,* 164–176.

Denckla, M., and Rudel, R. (1976a). Naming of pictured objects by dyslexic and other learning disabled children. *Brain and Language, 3,* 1–15.

Denckla, M., and Rudel, R. (1976b). Rapid 'automatized' naming (R.A.N.): Dyslexia differentiated from other learning disabilities. *Neuropsychologia, 14,* 471–479.

Done, D., and Miles, T. (1978). Learning, memory, and dyslexia. In M. Gruneberg, P. Morris, and R. Sykes (Eds.), *Practical aspects of memory.* London: Academic Press.

Ehri, L. (1979). Linguistic insight: Threshold of reading acquisition. In T. Walker and G. Mackinnon (Eds.), *Reading research: Advances in research and theory,* 63–114. New York: Academic Press.

Ellis, N. (1981). Visual and name coding in dyslexic children. *Psychological Research, 43,* 201–218.

Ellis, N., and Miles, T. (1978). Visual information processing in dyslexic children. In M. Gruneberg, P. Morris, and R. Sykes (Eds.), *Practical aspects of memory.* London: Academic Press.

Fox, B., and Routh, D. (1976). Phonemic analysis and synthesis as word attack skills. *Journal of Educational Psychology, 68,* 70–74.

Fox, B., and Routh, D. (1980). Phonemic analysis and severe reading disability. *Journal of Psycholinguistic Research, 9,* 115–119.

Fried-Oken, M. (1984). *The development of naming skills in normal and language deficit children.* Unpublished doctoral dissertation. Boston University, Boston.

Frith, U. (1981). Experimental approaches to developmental dyslexia: An introduction. *Psychological Research, 43,* 97–109.

Gascon, G., and Goodglass, H. (1978). Reading retardation and information content of stimuli in paired associate learning. *Cortex, 6,* 417–429.

German, D. (1979). Word-finding skills in children with learning disabilities. *Journal of Learning Disabilities, 12,* 176–181.

German, D. (1982). Word-finding substitutions in children with learning disabilities. *Language, Speech, and Hearing Services in Schools, 13,* 223–230.

Glushko, R. (1979). The organization and activation of orthographic knowledge in reading aloud. *Journal of Experimental Psychology: Human Perception and Performance, 5,* 674–691.

Godfrey, J., Syrdal-Lasky, A., Millay, K., and Knox, C. (1981). Performance of dyslexic children on speech perception tests. *Journal of Experimental Child Psychology, 32,* 401–424.

Hakes, D. (1982). The development of metalinguistic abilities: What develops? In S. Kuczaj (Ed.), *Language, cognition, and culture,* 163–210. Hillsdale, NJ: Erlbaum.

Hall, H., Ewing, A., Tinzmann, M., and Wilson, K. (1981). Phonetic coding in dyslexics and normal readers. *Bulletin of Psychonomic Society, 17,* 177–178.

Hall, J., Wilson, K., Humphreys, M., Tinzmann, M., and Bowyer, P. (1983). Phonemic-similiarity effects in good vs. poor readers. *Memory and Cognition, 11,* 520–527.

Harris-Schmidt, G., and Noell, E. (1983). In C. Wren (Ed.), *Language learning disabilities: Diagnosis and remediation.* Rockville, MD: Aspen.

Helfgott, J. (1976). Phonemic segmentation and blending skills of kindergarten children: Implication for beginning reading acquisition. *Comtemporary Educational Psychology, 1,* 157–169.

Holmes, D., and McKeever, W. (1979). Material-specific serial memory deficit in adolescent dyslexics. *Cortex, 15,* 51–62.

Jackson, M. (1980). Further evidence for a relationship between memory access and reading ability. *Journal of Verbal Learning and Verbal Behavior, 19,* 683–694.

Jackson, M., and McClelland, J. (1979). Processing determinants of reading speed. *Journal of Experimental Psychology: General, 108,* 151–181.

Johnson, D., and Myklebust, H. (1967). *Learning disabilities: Educational principles and practices.* New York: Grune and Stratton.

Johnston, R. (1982). Phonological coding in dyslexic readers. *British Journal of Psychology, 73,* 455–460.

Jorm, A. (1979). The cognitive and neurological basis of developmental dyslexia: A theoretical framework and review. *Cognition, 7,* 19–33.

Jorm, A. (1983). Specific reading retardation and working memory: A review. *British Journal of Psychology, 74,* 311–342.

Jorm, A., and Share, D. (1983). Phonological recoding and reading acquisition. *Applied Psycholinguistics, 4,* 103–147.

Kail, R., and Leonard, L. (1986). *Word-finding abilities in language impaired children.* ASHA Monograph, *25,* 1–36. Rockville, MD: ASHA.

Kamhi, A., Catts, H., Mauer, D., Apel, K., and Gentry, B. (1988). Phonological and spatial processing abilities in language and reading impaired children. *Journal of Hearing and Speech Disorders, 53,* 316–327.

Katz, R. (1986). Phonological deficiencies in children with reading disability: Evidence from an object-naming task. *Cognition, 22,* 225–257.

Katz, R., Shankweiler, D., and Liberman, I. (1981). Memory for item order and phonetic recoding in the beginning reader. *Journal of Experimental Psychology, 32,* 474–484.

Kewley-Port, D., Pisoni, D., and Studdert-Kennedy, M. (1983). Perception of static and dynamic cues to place of articulation in initial stop consonants. *Journal of the Acoustic Society of America, 73,* 1779–1753.

Klein, H. (1986). The assessment of some persisting language difficulties in the learning disabled. In M. Snowling (Ed.), *Children's written language difficulties: Assessment and management.* Windsor, Bershire: Nfer-Nelson.

Leonard, L., Nippold, M., Kail, R., and Hale, C. (1983). Picture naming in language impaired children. *Journal of Speech and Hearing Research, 26,* 609–615.

Liberman, I., Shankweiler, D., Fischer, F., and Carter, B. (1974). Reading and the awareness of linguistic segments. *Journal of Experimental Child Psychology, 18,* 201-212.

Liberman, I., Mann, V., Shankweiler, D., and Werfelman, M. (1982). Children's memory for recurring linguistic and non-linguistic material in relation to reading ability. *Cortex, 18,* 367-375.

Liberman, I., Rubin, H., Duques, S., and Carlisle, J. (1985). Linguistic abilities and spelling proficiency in kindergartners and adult poor spellers. In J. Kavangh and D. Gray (Eds.), *Biobehavioral measures of dyslexia.* Parkton, MD: York Press, Inc.

Liberman, I., and Shankweiler, D. (1985). Phonology and the problems of learning to read and write. *Remedial and Special Education, 6,* 8-17.

Lorsbach, T., and Gray, J. (1985). The relationship between processing rate and memory span in learning disabled children. Paper presented at the annual meeting of the American Educational Research Association, Chicago.

Lundberg, I. (1987). Phonological awareness facilitates reading and spelling acquisition. In *Intimacy with Language,* 56-63. Baltimore, MD: The Orton Dyslexic Society.

Lundberg, I., Olofsson, A., and Wall, S. (1980). Reading and spelling skills in the first school years, predicted from phonemic awareness skills in kindergarten. *Scandinavian Journal of Psychology, 21,* 59-173.

Mann, V., and Liberman, I. (1984). Phonological awareness and verbal short-term memory. *Journal of Learning Disabilities, 17,* 592-599.

Mann, V., Liberman, I., and Shankweiler, D. (1980). Children's memory for sentences and word strings in relation to reading ability. *Memory and Cognition, 8,* 329-335.

Mann, V., Shankweiler, D., and Smith, S. (1984). The association between comprehension of spoken sentences and early reading ability: The role of phonetic representation. *Journal of Child Language, II,* 627-643.

McCrosky, R., and Kidder, H. (1980). Auditory fusion among learning disabled, reading disabled, and normal children. *Journal of Learning Disabilities, 13,* 69-76.

Miles, T. (1974). *Understanding dyslexia.* London: Priory Press.

Miles, T. (1983). *Dyslexia.* Springfield, IL: Charles C. Thomas Publishers.

Morais, J., Bertelson, P., Cary, L., and Alegria, J. (1986). Literacy training and speech segmentation. *Cognition, 24,* 45-64.

Morais, J., Cary, L., Alegria, J., and Bertelson, P. (1979). Does awareness of speech as a sequence of phones arise spontaneously? *Cognition,* 1979, *7,* 323-331.

Olofsson, A., and Lundberg, I. (1983). Can phonemic awareness be trained in kindergarten? *Scandinavian Journal of Psychology, 24,* 35-44.

Otto, W. (1961). The acquisition and retention of paired associates by good, average, and poor readers. *Journal of Educational Psychology, 52,* 241-248.

Perfetti, C. (1985). *Reading ability.* New York: Oxford University Press.

Perfetti, C., Beck, I., and Hughes, C. (1981). Phonemic knowledge and learning to read. Paper presented at the Meeting of the Society for Research in Child Development. Boston, MA.

Perfetti, C., Finger, E., and Hogaboam, T. (1978). Sources of vocalization latency differences between skilled and less skilled young readers. *Journal of Educational Psychology, 70,* 730–739.

Posner, M., and Mitchell, R. (1967). Chronometric analysis of classification. *Psychological Review, 74,* 392–409.

Read, C., and Ruyter, L. (1985). Reading and spelling skills in adults of low literacy. *Remedial and Special Education, 6,* 43–52.

Read, C., Zhang, Y., Nie, H., and Ding, B. (1986). The ability to manipulate speech sounds depends on knowing alphabetic writing. *Cognition, 24,* 31–44.

Rosner, J. (1971). *Phonic analysis training and beginning reading skills.* Pittsburgh: University of Pittsburgh Learning Research and Development Center Publication Series, No. 9.

Rubin, H., and Liberman, I. (1983). Exploring the oral and written language errors made by language disabled children. *Annals of Dyslexia, 33,* 111–120.

Sawyer, D. (1987). Auditory segmenting ability in identification of children who are "at risk" for reading acquisition. Paper presented at the Annual Conference of the Orton Dyslexia Society, San Francisco, CA.

Shankweiler, D., and Crain, S. (1987). Language mechanisms and reading disorders: A modular approach. In P. Bertelson (Ed.), *The onset of literacy.* Cambridge, MA: MIT Press.

Shankweiler, D., Liberman, I., Mark, L., Fowler, C., and Fischer, F. (1979). The speech code and learning to read. *Journal of Experimental Psychology: Human Learning and Memory, 5,* 531–545.

Share, D., Jorm, A., Maclean, R., and Matthews, R. (1984). Sources of individual differences in reading acquisition. *Journal of Educational Psychology, 76,* 1309–1324.

Shattuck-Hufnagel, S. (1983). Sublexical units and suprasegmental structure in speech production planning. In P. MacNeilage (Ed.), *The production of speech,* 109–136. New York: Springer-Verlag.

Smith, B., Hillenbrand, J., Wasowicz, J., and Preston, J. (1986). Durational characteristics of vocal and subvocal speech: Implications concerning phonological organization and articulatory difficulty. *Journal of Phonetics, 14,* 265–281.

Snowling, M. (1981). Phonemic deficits in developmental dyslexia. *Psychological Research, 43,* 219–234.

Snowling, M., Goulandris, N., Bowlby, M., and Howell, P. (1985). Segmentation and speech perception in relation to reading skill: A developmental analysis. *Journal of Experimental Child Psychology, 41,* 489–507.

Spring, C. (1976). Encoding speed and memory span in dyslexic children. *Journal of Special Education, 10,* 35–40.

Spring, C., and Capps, C. (1974). Encoding speed, rehearsal, and probed recall of dyslexic boys. *Journal of Educational Psychology, 66,* 780–786.

Spring, C., and Perry, L. (1983). Naming speed and serial recall in poor and adequate readers. *Contemporary Educational Psychology, 8,* 141–145.

Stanovich, K. (1981). Relationship between word decoding speed, general name-retrieval ability, and reading progress in first grade children. *Journal of Educational Psychology, 73,* 809–815.

Stanovich, K. (1985). Explaining the variance in reading ability in terms of psychological processes: What have we learned? *Annals of Dyslexia, 35,* 67–96.

Stanovich, K. (1986a). Cognitive processes and the reading problems of learning disabled children: Evaluating the assumption of specificity. In J. Torgesen and B. Wong (Eds.), *Psychological and educational perspectives on learning disabilities,* 87–131. New York: Academic Press.

Stanovich, K. (1986b). Matthew effects in reading: Some consequences of individual differences in the acquisition of literacy. *Research Reading Quarterly, 21,* 360–406.

Stanovich, K., Cunningham, A., and Cramer, B. (1984). Assessing phonological awareness in kindergarten children: Issues of task comparability. *Journal of Experimental Child Psychology, 38,* 175–190.

Tallal, P. (1980). Auditory temporal perception, phonics, and reading disabilities in children. *Brain and Language, 9,* 182–198.

Tarver, S., Hallahan, D., Kauffman, J., and Ball, D. (1976). Verbal rehearsal and selective attention in children with learning disabilities: A developmental lag. *Journal of Experimental Child Psychology, 22,* 375–385.

Taylor, I. (1981). Writing systems and reading. In G. Mackinnon and T. Waller (Eds.), *Reading Research Advances in Theory and Practice.* New York: Academic Press.

Torgesen, J. (1985). Memory processes in reading disordered children. *Journal of Learning Disabilities, 18,* 350–357.

Torgesen, J., and Goldman, T. (1977). Verbal rehearsal and short-term memory in reading disabled children. *Child Development, 48,* 56–60.

Torgesen, J. and Houck, D. (1980). Processing deficiencies of learning-disabled children who perform poorly on the digit span test. *Journal of Educational Psychology, 72,* 141–160.

Treiman, R., and Baron, J. (1981). Segmental analysis ability: Development and relation to reading ability. In G. Mackinnon and T. Waller (Eds.), *Reading research: Advances in theory and practice, 3,* 159–198. New York: Academic Press.

Treiman, R., and Baron, J. (1983). Phonemic-analysis training helps children benefit from spelling-sound rules. *Memory and Cognition, 11,* 382–389.

Tunmer, W., and Nesdale, A. (1985). Phonemic segmentation skill and beginning reading. *Journal of Educational Psychology, 77,* 417–427.

Vellutino, F., Harding, C., Phillips, F., and Steger, J. (1975). Differential transfer in poor and normal readers. *Journal of Genetic Psychology, 126,* 3–18.

Vellutino, F., and Scanlon, D. (1982). Verbal processing in poor and normal readers. In C. Brainerd and M. Pressley (Eds.), *Verbal processes in children.* New York: Springer-Verlag.

Vellutino, F., Steger, J., Harding, C., and Phillips, F. (1975). Verbal vs. nonverbal paired-associate learning in poor and normal readers. *Neuropsychologia, 15,* 75–82.

Vellutino, F., Steger, J., and Pruzek, R. (1973). Inter- versus intrasensory deficit in pair-associate learning in poor and normal readers. *Canadian Journal of Behavioral Science, 5,* 111–123.

Wagner, R., Balthazor, M., Harley, S., Morgan, S., Rashotte, C., Shanner, R., Simmons, K., and Stage, S. (1987). The nature of prereaders' phonological processing abilities. *Cognitive Development, 2,* 355–373.

Wagner, R., and Torgesen, J. (1987). The nature of phonological processing and its causal role in the acquisition of reading skills. *Psychological Bulletin, 101,* 192–212.

Watson, C., and Foyle, D. (1985). Central factors in discrimination and identification of complex sounds. *Journal of the Acoustic Society of America, 78,* 375–380.

Wiig, E., and Semel, E. (1984). *Language assessment and intervention for the learning disabled.* Columbus, OH: Merrill.

Wolf, M. (1982). The word-retrieval process and reading in children and aphasics. In K. Nelson (Ed.), *Children's language, 3,* 437–493. New York: Gardner Press.

Wolf, M. (1984). Naming, reading, and the dyslexias: A longitudinal overview. *Annals of Dyslexia, 34,* 87–136.

Wolf, M. (1986). Rapid alternating stimulus naming in developmental dyslexias. *Brain and Language, 27,* 360–379.

Wolf, M., Bally, H., and Morris, R. (1985). Automaticity, retrieval processes, and reading: A longitudinal study in average and impaired readers. *Child Development, 57,* 988–1000.

Zifcak, M. (1981). Phonological awareness and reading acquisition. *Contemporary Educational Psychology, 6,* 117–126.

Zurif, E., and Carson, G. (1970). Dyslexia in relation to cerebral dominance and temporal analysis. *Neuropsychologia, 8,* 351–361.

5

Phonological Awareness and Word Recognition: Assessment and Intervention

Benita A. Blachman

During the last 20 years, considerable progress has been made in understanding the relationship between reading and language (Liberman, 1971, 1983; Perfetti, 1985; Vellutino, 1979). Perhaps the most productive area of inquiry concerns relationships between reading and language-related skills in the phonological domain (Liberman & Shankweiler, 1985). Researchers have investigated a variety of phonological processing deficits in an attempt to locate the source of the difficulty experienced by many poor readers (Catts, this volume; Wagner, 1986; Wagner & Torgesen, 1987). Problems in the retrieval of phonological information (demonstrated by word-finding errors and by slowness on rapid naming tasks) may, for example, interfere with the development of automatized word recognition (Blachman, 1984b; Denckla & Rudel, 1976). Difficulty with phonetic recoding in working memory (Brady, 1986; Shankweiler, Liberman, Mark, Fowler, & Fischer, 1979) may create processing limitations in short-term memory that contribute to poor sentence comprehension (Crain & Shankweiler, in press; Liberman & Shankweiler, 1985).

Another potential source of difficulty for the poor reader is in the area of phonological awareness. Phonological awareness refers to the awareness of, and ability to manipulate, the phonological segments in words—specifically, the phonemes represented in an alphabetic orthography. Originally referred to as linguistic awareness (Mattingly, 1972), this is the area of phonological processing that has received the most attention and about which we have the greatest consensus. Researchers have consistently demonstrated a relationship between phonological awareness and reading success (for reviews see Blachman, 1984a; Wagner, 1986; Wagner & Torgesen, 1987; and Williams, 1986). This relationship exists regardless of the task used to measure phonological awareness, such as sound counting, sound deletion (say *sun* without the /s/), sound manipulation (reversing phonemes), and sound categorization (categorizing words by beginning, end, or middle sounds). In addition, recent evidence suggests that training in phonological awareness has a positive impact on reading achievement (Ball & Blachman, in press; Bradley & Bryant, 1983, 1985; Williams, 1979a, 1980). This chapter focuses on the importance of phonological awareness in reading acquisition and the effects on reading of training in phonological awareness. Clinical suggestions for teaching and assessment will also be discussed.

IMPORTANCE OF PHONOLOGICAL AWARENESS

In order to understand the nature of the problems children face as beginning readers, we must first consider the requirements of the particular writing system that we are asking children to read. In an alphabetic writing system, such as English, the basic task facing the beginning reader is to construct a link between the signs of print and the sounds of speech (Liberman, 1971). To construct this link, the reader must become aware that speech can be segmented into the sublexical units, or phonemes, that are more or less represented by an alphabetic script. However, we now know that all would-be readers do not demonstrate equal ability to access these phonemic segments.

Understanding the complex relationship among the phonemes in the speech stream has helped to shed light on the difficulty some children and adults have with phoneme segmentation. Because the individual phonemes in a word (such as *bag*) are coarticulated during speech production (the consonants are folded into the vowel), we hear only a single acoustic unit—the syllable (A. Liberman, Cooper, Shankweiler, & Studdert-Kennedy, 1967; Liberman, 1971). Thus, when we pronounce a word such as *bag*, we are actually transmitting information about each segment simultaneously. In contrast, when we write the word *bag*, each letter is produced in isolation in a fixed sequence. In order to understand why the written word *bag* has three segments, the beginning reader must become aware of the three segments in the spoken utterance. It is this awareness that many young children and older disabled readers lack (Blachman, 1983, 1984a; Bruce, 1964; Byrne & Ledez, 1983; Fox & Routh, 1975, 1980; Liberman, 1973; Liberman, Shankweiler, Fischer, & Carter, 1974; Morais, Bertelson, Cary, & Alegria, 1986; Morais, Cary, Alegria, & Bertelson, 1979; Read & Ruyter, 1985).

Considerable evidence is now available that children who lack phonological awareness are among those most likely to become poor readers. It has been demonstrated in numerous longitudinal studies that performance on tasks measuring phonological awareness in kindergarten or first grade are powerful predictors of reading achievement (Blachman & James, 1986; Bradley & Bryant, 1983, 1985; Juel, Griffith, & Gough, 1986; Lundberg, Olofsson, & Wall, 1980; Mann, 1984; Mann & Liberman, 1984; Share, Jorm, Maclean, & Matthews, 1984; Stanovich, Cunningham, & Cramer, 1984; Tornéus, 1984). (It is also likely that learning to read facilitates the development of phonological awareness. See Catts, this volume, for a discussion of this issue.) Without phonological awareness, the systematic relationships between letters and sounds are likely to be difficult to grasp. Problems in phonological awareness may be reflected in a child's inability to "break the code," resulting in poor word recognition and spelling strategies.

The cumulative consequences of early problems in phonological awareness have been described in detail by Stanovich (1986). He has suggested that "it is apparently important that the prerequisite phonological awareness and skill at spelling-to-sound mapping be in place *early* in the child's development, because their absence can initiate a causal chain of escalating negative side effects" (p. 364). Stanovich pointed out, for example, that the difficulty experienced in breaking the code means that the poorer reader in the low reading group does not have the opportunity to read as many words per reading lesson as readers in higher groups and is less likely to read at home. Materials are often too difficult, and early reading experiences are unrewarding. The result is that poor readers practice less and are slow to develop automatic word recognition strategies. Without the necessary automaticity, the poor reader is forced to use valuable cognitive resources for word recognition, reducing the resources available for comprehension. Comprehension suffers; the poor reader accumulates negative experiences with reading-related activities and continues to read less than the good reader. Because reading itself fosters the development of factors important in reading comprehension, such as vocabulary and increased general knowledge, less involvement in and reduced exposure to reading exacerbate the individual differences between good and poor readers. Based on his extensive review, Stanovich (1986, p. 393) hypothesizes the following:

> If there is a specific cause of reading disability at all, it resides in the area of phonological awareness. Slow development in this area delays early code-breaking progress and initiates the cascade of interacting achievement failures and motivational problems.

One of the earliest component skills of breaking the code is understanding that speech can be segmented into the phonemic units represented in an alphabetic orthography (Liberman, Shankweiler, Blachman, Camp, & Werfelman, 1980; Williams, 1986). It seems logical to ask if training in this skill has an effect on early reading achievement. This question will be considered next.

TRAINING PHONOLOGICAL AWARENESS

In the first group of studies to be reviewed, the focus was on children who were already learning to read (Rosner, 1971; Wallach & Wallach, 1976; Williams, 1979a, 1980). In the second group of more recent studies, researchers have focused on training phonological awareness in prereading children in kindergarten or preschool classes (Ball & Blachman, in press; Bradley, 1987; Bradley & Bryant, 1983, 1985; Content, Kolinsky, Morais, & Bertelson, 1986; Fox & Routh, 1984; Hohn & Ehri, 1984; Lundberg, 1987; Olofsson & Lundberg, 1983, 1985; Treiman & Baron, 1983).

TRAINING BEGINNING READERS

Some preliminary support for the effect on reading of training in phoneme awareness was provided by a small study (Rosner, 1971) using a version of Rosner's Perceptual Skills Curriculum (Rosner, 1973). A small (n = 8) experimental group of first graders received 3 1/2 months of training in phoneme deletion (e.g., "Say /sun/, now say it again without the /s/"). These children were matched on IQ and pretreatment auditory analysis scores to a no-treatment control group. Both groups were also receiving classroom reading instruction. After training, the experimental group had higher scores on the Auditory Analysis Test and were able to read significantly more words from the instructional material and more transfer words not included in training than were the no-treatment control group.

Another first-grade study demonstrated the effectiveness of a tutorial program that emphasized phoneme analysis and synthesis with low-readiness children (Wallach & Wallach, 1976). In addition to the regular classroom reading instruction, the children were tutored by minority mothers who used a program that focused on recognition of beginning sounds, sound-symbol relationships, recognition and manipulation of sounds in all positions of the word, and direct instruction in blending phonetically regular consonant-vowel-consonant (CVC) words. In the final stages of the program, children moved into regular classroom reading materials. On posttreatment reading tests, these children performed significantly better than the controls.

The effectiveness of teaching phoneme analysis and blending was also demonstrated with older (ages 7 to 12) learning disabled children (Williams, 1979a, 1980). For 20 minutes a day, 3 to 4 times per week for 6 months, teachers used a prepared program (The ABD's of Reading) to supplement the classroom reading program. Children were taught to analyze words into syllables and into phonemes, and they were taught to blend two-phoneme and then three-phoneme CVC units. Wooden squares were used to represent first the syllable and then the phonemes. This was followed by teaching sound-symbol correspondences and placing letter symbols on the wooden squares. Children were also taught to read and spell CVC combinations, more complex combinations (e.g., CCVCC), and two-syllable words with these patterns. Posttest results based on data from 60 experimental and 42 control subjects indicated that the experimental subjects performed significantly better than control subjects on knowledge of letter-sound correspondences, on phoneme analysis and phoneme blending tasks, and on decoding of CVC trigrams. A subgroup of experimental (n = 28) and control (n = 28) children completed two additional tests to measure transfer of skills. On these additional measures, the experimental group outperformed the control group on the ability to decode CVC nonsense and real word combinations (half of the items had been used in training, and the other half were new combinations).

These studies (Wallach & Wallach, 1976; Williams, 1979a, 1980) suggest that supplementing traditional classsroom reading programs with training in phoneme analysis and blending, letter-sound correspondences, and decoding of CVC patterns results in better word recognition than traditional classroom reading programs used alone. However, because these studies evaluated many program components, it is not possible to isolate the effect on reading of training in phonological awareness. It is also possible that the treatment results reflect the increased time that the experimental subjects spent on reading-related activites, rather than the particular content of those activities.

In several recent studies attempts have been made to measure more specifically the effect on reading of training in phoneme awareness. In order to do this, researchers have focused their attention on younger children who have not yet been taught to read.

TRAINING PREREADERS

LABORATORY SIMULATIONS

Treiman and Baron (1983) were able to demonstrate in two experiments involving prereaders in preschool and kindergarten that phonemic analysis (consisting of phoneme-segmentation training in Experiment 1 and segmentation and blending training in Experiment 2) helped children profit from spelling-sound correspondences. On each of four days, children participated in both a phoneme-analysis condition and a control condition. In the analysis condition, children learned to segment selected spoken syllables into an initial consonant and the remaining portion of the word (e.g., /hem/ was segmented into /h/ and /em/, /lig/ was segmented into /l/ and /ig/). In the control condition, children simply practiced repeating selected spoken syllables such as /diz/ and /vok/. The second phase (the "reading" phase) of each condition was essentially the same. Children were taught to associate the printed symbols with the spoken syllables. For example, in the analysis condition, children learned the letters and letter combinations that corresponded to the spoken sounds of /h/, /em/, the *related* syllable /hem/, and the *unrelated* syllable /lig/. In the control condition, children learned the letters and letter combinations that corresponded to the spoken sounds of /d/, /iz/, the *related* syllable /diz/, and the *unrelated* syllable /vok/. Results indicated that children in the phoneme analysis condition made fewer errors reading the related syllable (e.g., /hem/) than the unrelated syllable (e.g., /lig/). In the control condition a reverse pattern occurred (more errors on the related word than the unrelated word). The authors interpreted this finding to mean that children who had practiced phoneme analysis were able to make better use of spelling-sound correspondences than children in the control group.

In another kindergarten study (Fox & Routh, 1984), 31 children who could not segment syllables into phonemes were randomly assigned to one of three conditions: (1) segmenting, (2) segmenting and blending, and (3) no treatment. Ten additional children who could already segment served as a comparison group. Children were taught to segment words into the initial consonant and the remaining portion of the word (e.g., /man/ was segmented as /m/ and /an/) and to blend these two segments to form a word. Children were trained in groups of five or six for 15-minute sessions, four or five days per week for five weeks. Posttests included segmenting and blending tasks, learning to associate sounds with Gibson letterlike forms (e.g., $\hat{x}$ for *m*), and a word task to measure the ability to read words produced by combining these letterlike forms. Results indicated that those who learned both to segment (phoneme analysis) and to blend (phoneme synthesis) had significantly better scores on all posttests than the segmentation only and the control group. Fox and Routh concluded that segmentation training by itself did not enable children to decode words on the reading analog task using letterlike forms. Because Fox and Routh did not include a blending only condition in their study, it was not possible to determine whether the interaction of segmenting and blending, or the blending component itself, accounted for the superior performance of the group trained in both segmenting and blending. It is possible that training in phoneme analysis alone (e.g., segmenting) does not develop the range of skills in phonological awareness required for transfer to reading.

Classroom Studies

Several additional studies designed to develop phoneme awareness in kindergarten children have evaluated the influence of this training on the child's naturally developing reading and spelling ability (as opposed to laboratory simulations of these skills). In the first group of studies to be reviewed, phoneme awareness was trained without making explicit the connections to print (Olofsson & Lundberg, 1983, 1985; Lundberg, 1987; Tornéus, 1984). In the second group of studies, the incremental value of making print to sound connections was assessed as part of the phoneme awareness instruction (Ball & Blachman, in press; Bradley & Bryant, 1983, 1985; Bradley, 1987; Hohn & Ehri, 1983).

PHONEME AWARENESS WITHOUT LETTER-SOUND TRAINING. An extensive kindergarten training program was evaluated in Sweden (Olofsson & Lundberg, 1983). The program used games and other tasks emphasizing rhyme recognition, syllable segmentation, identification, addition or deletion of initial phonemes, segmentation of two- and three-phoneme words, and blending phonemes into words. For six to eight weeks, kindergarten children participated in one of three treatment groups that differed in the amount of structure provided in the phoneme awareness lessons. In the most structured group, lessons were introduced three to four times per week for 15 to 30 minutes per lesson. In the least structured group, teachers followed a more spontaneous approach and introduced the phoneme awareness activities within the normal play activities of the day. Teachers were to focus on phoneme awareness without teaching letter names and sounds. There were also two control groups, one in which children were instructed in general, nonverbal, auditory perception skills (to control for the extra attention given the experimental subjects) and a no treatment control group.

There was improvement from pretest to posttest for only the most structured of the three experimental groups. The children in that group who benefited the most were those with lowest pretest performance. The authors concluded that phoneme awareness can be developed in preliterate children. One year later the phoneme awareness (segmentation and blending) and reading and spelling skills of 83 of the original 95 children were measured (Olofsson & Lundberg, 1985). Although the experimental children were superior on a test of phoneme synthesis (blending), effects of the training on reading and spelling were harder to isolate.

In an effort to overcome some of the limitations of the earlier research (e.g., limited training period), Lundberg and his colleagues conducted a more recent study also designed to evaluate the effects on reading and spelling of training in phoneme awareness in kindergarten (Lundberg, 1987). The experimental group (n = 235) received training from September through May in daily 15- to 20-minute lessons. The control group (n = 155) received no special treatment. Results indicated that the children in the experimental group improved more than the children in the control group on the set of metalinguistic tasks. These included rhyme production, word segmentation, syllable segmentation and synthesis, deletion of initial phonemes, and segmentation and synthesis of phonemes. When reading and spelling were measured more than seven months after the beginning of the first grade year, results indicated that the experimental group outperformed the control group on a test of speed and accuracy of silent word decoding. This difference between the two groups, however, showed only trend level ($p < .10$) significance. On a dictated spelling test, the experimental group significantly outperformed the control group. To evaluate the specificity of the preschool training, a math test was also given in first grade. On this test the control children outperformed the experimental children, demonstrating that the influence of the kindergarten training was restricted to tasks measuring beginning literacy.

In another study completed in Sweden, Tornéus (1984) also found that training in phonological awareness had an impact on spelling. First graders received eight 20-minute training sessions over eight weeks in the spring of the first grade year. Activities included rhyming, alliteration, and training in blending and segmenting. The control group spent time in general language activities. The results indicated that among children with the lowest pretest scores on the metaphonological tests, treated children improved significantly more in spelling than control children. The difference in reading was not significant. The authors hypothesized that many of the children had adequate phonological awareness prior to the training, as evidenced by ceiling effects (especially on the segmentation test). For these children, additional training in phoneme analysis would not be expected to influence reading and spelling skills. However, for those children in the second half of first grade who were not yet proficient in phoneme analysis (segmentation) and synthesis (blending), training improved performance on these skills and on spelling as well.

It is of interest that the same reading measure was used by Lundberg (1987) and Tornéus (1984) and that neither study demonstrated a significant effect of phonological awareness training on reading. These researchers used a rather unusual measure of reading that assesses both speed and accuracy of silent word decoding. The test included a list of 400 isolated words, and each word was written next to four pictures. The children were given 15 minutes to put a line through the picture that represented each word. Because increased phoneme awareness might influence performance on one type of reading measure more than another, it is possible that the particular reading test used in these studies is less sensitive to the changes in reading achievement that are due to increased phoneme awareness. It is important to remember that the use of different reading achievement instruments may contribute to variation in training effects across studies.

It should also be noted that these intervention programs (Lundberg, 1987; Oloffson & Lundberg, 1983, 1985; and Tornéus, 1984) did not include training in letter names and sounds, although the first grade subjects in the Tornéus study were most likely getting some of this instruction in their first grade reading program. Olofsson and Lundberg (1985) reported, for example, that "during the training period the main problem for the teachers was to focus on phonemic tasks without using letters and letter names" (p. 32). The authors intentionally eliminated instruction in letter names and sounds in order to control for one of the possible confounding variables. However, it is possible that the effects of phoneme awareness training on reading would have been greater if the connections between the sound segments and printed symbols had been made explicit.

PHONEME AWARENESS WITH LETTER-SOUND TRAINING. The importance of making the connections between segmented sounds and the corresponding printed symbols has been addressed in several recent studies (Ball & Blachman, in press; Bradley & Bryant, 1983, 1985; Bradley, 1987; Hohn & Ehri, 1983). Hohn and Ehri (1983) found that for prereading kindergarten children who knew letter names, those who learned to segment using disks with letters on them performed better on segmenting *practiced* combinations than the group trained with unmarked disks. Both groups were superior to controls. On *unpracticed* combinations the two trained groups did not differ from one another, but both surpassed the performance of controls. It was concluded that segmentation training using disks, with or without letters, gave children an advantage over untrained controls, but those trained with letter marked disks had an additional advantage.

The value of creating a link between sound and symbol during instruction in phoneme awareness was also demonstrated in a combined longitudinal and experimental training study (Bradley & Bryant, 1983, 1985). In their longitudinal study, Bradley and Bryant found a significant relationship between performance on a sound categorization task administered to 368 four- and five-year-olds and the reading and spelling achievement of these same children three years later. During the second year of the study, 65 children who had low scores on the sound categorization pretest were divided into four groups matched on age, sex, IQ, and sound categorization ability. The first group was trained in sound categorization by learning to group pictures of objects according to shared-sound categories. For example, *hen* could be grouped with *men* and *pen* because they share the same end sounds (they rhyme). *Hen* could also be grouped with *hat* and *hop* because all three share the same beginning sound. The second experimental group in the study was also trained in sound categorization, but in addition they were taught to represent the common sounds with letters of the alphabet. A third group (a control group) was taught to categorize the same pictures by conceptual categories. For example, *hen* could be grouped with *dog* and *pig* because all are animals. The fourth group was a no treatment control group. Children in conditions one, two, and three each received 40 individual lessons spread over a two-year period. Results indicated that the children trained only in sound categorization had somewhat higher reading and spelling scores than children who did not receive this training. However, children who received sound categorization training plus training with alphabet letters had significantly higher reading and spelling scores than the children in the two control groups and had significantly higher spelling scores than children in the sound categorization only group. This study provided important evidence for a causal link between phonological awareness and reading and spelling.

In a recent follow-up study (Bradley, 1987), 63 of the original 65 children were located and tested four years after the original study ended. The gains made during the intervention were still evident during follow-up testing in reading and spelling. The children who were taught to make the connections between sound categories and letter strings maintained their superior position in reading and spelling.

One question not answered by these studies (Bradley & Bryant, 1983; Bradley, 1987) concerns the relative benefit of various aspects of the training. Because Bradley and Bryant did not include a group that received letter training only, it is not possible to determine whether it was the combination of sound categorization and letter instruction that influenced reading and spelling or the letter training itself. A recent study (Ball & Blachman, in press) addressed this question. Ninety kindergarten nonreaders were randomly assigned to either a treatment group or one of two control groups. Children in the treatment group received training in phoneme awareness and letter name and letter sound instruction. The children in the first control group received instruction in language activities (e.g., general vocabulary, listening to stories) and letter name and letter sound training that was identical to that received by the phoneme awareness group. A second control group received no treatment. Children in the phoneme awareness group and the language activities control group received instruction in groups of five for 20 minutes, four times a week, for seven weeks. Prior to the intervention, the three groups did not differ on age, sex, race, phoneme segmentation, letter name knowledge, letter sound knowledge, or reading ability as measured by scores on the Word Identification Subtest of the Woodcock Reading Mastery Tests (Woodcock, 1973).

After the intervention the phoneme awareness group significantly outperformed both control groups on phoneme segmentation. This finding provided additional evidence that kindergarten children can be trained to segment words into their constituent sounds. With regard to letter name knowledge, the three groups did not differ at the end of the study. Most children knew a high percentage of letter names by the end of their kindergarten year. Knowledge of letter sounds was also reassessed on a posttest. The results indicated that the phoneme awareness group and the language activities control group (that had letter sound training identical to the phoneme awareness group) did not differ from each other on letter sound knowledge. Both groups, however, had significantly higher scores on letter sound knowledge than the no treatment control. This finding suggests that letter sound knowledge in and of itself does not improve phoneme segmentation. Despite the fact that the language activities control group did not differ from the phoneme awareness group in letter sound knowledge, only the phoneme awareness group made significant gains in phoneme segmentation.

In order to assess the reading ability of these kindergarten children, reading was measured with the Word Identification Subtest (Woodcock, 1973) and a phonetically regular word list created for this study. This list included 21 words selected from the pool of real words generated by the nine graphemes taught during the letter name and letter sound instruction component of the training. Although the individual graphemes were used during the intervention, combinations of these graphemes that represented words were not introduced during training with either the phoneme awareness group or the language activities control group. After the intervention, children in the phoneme awareness group were able to read more words on both the Woodcock and the phonetically regular word list than children in either control group. It should be noted that although the language activities control group was comparable to the phoneme awareness group in letter sound knowledge, they were inferior to the phoneme awareness group in reading achievement. Thus, an increase in letter sound knowledge alone does not appear to have an impact on reading.

IMPLICATIONS OF TRAINING STUDIES

Several conclusions can be drawn from the training studies reviewed. First, it is possible to develop some aspects of phoneme awareness in kindergarten children. Children who have received this training demonstrate a greater awareness of the phonemic segments in words than children who have not received this training. The impact of this training on reading and spelling, however, depends to some extent on the specific components of the phoneme awareness instruction. Creating a link between the sound segments and the alphabet letters that represent those segments appears to be an important aspect of phoneme awareness training. Interventions that compare phoneme awareness with letter sound instruction to phoneme awareness without letter sound instruction have found groups receiving the combined instruction to be superior (Bradley & Bryant, 1983, 1985; Bradley, 1987). Researchers who have investigated phoneme awareness instruction without incorporating the letter sound connection (e.g., Olofsson & Lundberg, 1983, 1985; Lundberg, 1987; Tornéus, 1984) have not been able to demonstrate the impact on reading that is demonstrated when the printed letter symbols are connected to the sound segments in the word. It is also important to remember that other variables, such as the particular reading measure used and the duration of the training study, may contribute to the variation in treatment effects. Despite this, the evidence suggests that the value of phoneme awareness instruction is enhanced when explicit connections are made during training between the printed alphabet symbols and the sound segments in words.

CLINICAL SUGGESTIONS FOR TEACHING[1]

Although phoneme awareness appears to play an important role in early reading acquisition, activities to increase phoneme awareness have not routinely been incorporated into classrooms where beginning reading instruction takes place or into remedial programs with older students. Ideally, we want to develop phoneme awareness before children have failed in reading and spelling. This means that instructional procedures to enhance phoneme awareness should be incorporated into the earliest stages of preparing a child to read and should be reflected in the formal reading program that follows reading readiness activities.

READING READINESS ACTIVITIES

It has been suggested that word play in the form of nursery rhymes and rhyming games would help the prereading child discover sound similarities in spoken language (Liberman & Shankweiler, 1979). There is some recent evidence to support these suggestions (Maclean, Bryant, & Bradley, 1987). In a 15-month longitudinal study, beginning when the children were 3 years 3 months old, periodic assessments were made of knowledge of nursery rhymes, ability to detect and produce rhyme and alliteration, and ability to identify letters and read highly frequent words. The results indicated that knowledge of nursery rhymes at age three was related to the child's ability to detect rhyme (a measure of phoneme awareness) more than one year later. This was true even after differences in IQ and social background were controlled. Performance on rhyme and alliteration detection tasks was also related to beginning word reading. Maclean et al. (1987, p. 280) concluded that

> adults play a direct role in fostering the growth of phonological awareness in children with the help of informal linguistic routines. Nursery rhymes are one example of the informal way in which parents, for the most part unwittingly, draw their children's attention to the fact that words have separable component sounds.

---

[1]Some of the instructional procedures described in this section also appeared in Blachman (1984a, 1987) and Blachman and Ball (in press).

Once children have reached kindergarten there are many opportunities for the creative teacher or clinician to incorporate phoneme awareness activities into the daily routine. Ball and Blachman (in press) developed a 20-minute sequence of instruction that included a variety of phoneme awareness activities. The children began each lesson with a say-it-and-move-it segmentation activity (adapted from Elkonin, 1963, 1973). Each child in a group of five was given an 8 1/2-by-11-inch sheet of laminated paper. On the top half of this sheet was a picture (e.g., boat or clown) or geometric shape that served as a holding place for the disks that were used to represent the sounds in words. Children were told, for example, to put their disks in the square to indicate they were ready to begin. A thick black line divided the paper into two sections. Below the line was a black arrow going from left to right. The children were taught to move the appropriate number of disks down to this arrow to represent the individual sounds in a word pronounced by the teacher. During the training there was a slow progression beginning with the representation of one sound with one disk, followed by the representation of one sound repeated twice with two disks. Two-phoneme items were introduced next, and finally three-phoneme items were used. Children were shown that three-phoneme items could be built from previously segmented sounds. For example, disks were used to represent the sound /a/, then /at/, and finally /sat/. Phonemes could be deleted in a similar fashion (e.g., /sat/ became /at/ and then /a/). During the first few weeks of training, continuous sound letters were used in the initial position. After children were comfortable segmenting three-phoneme items beginning with continuous sound letters, stop consonants were used in the initial position.

A new item to be segmented was usually introduced and modeled by the teacher or a child. To demonstrate how to segment the word *sat*, the teacher first pronounced the word. She then said *ssssaaaat* in a drawn out fashion and moved one disk at a time from the square down to the arrow (carefully matching one sound to the movement of one disk). When all three disks were on the arrow, the teacher would sweep her finger across the three disks and repeat the word. The disks were then returned to the square and the children got ready to move their own disks. The teacher said the word *sat* again and then gave children the cue to begin by telling them to ''say-it-and-move-it.'' The children said the word in a drawn out fashion and moved one disk for each sound in the word.

To help children make the connection between the sound segments and the letters, graphemes can be added to individual disks once a particular sound-symbol correspondence is mastered. This provides an opportunity to individualize instruction, as each child does not need to work with the same letters or the same number of letters.

In addition to the say-it-and-move-it component of every lesson, a variety of other phoneme awareness activities were introduced (at least one per lesson). These included, for example, a game called "fix-it." A puppet was used to present segmented words to the children. The puppet might say *sssaaat* in a drawn out fashion, and the children would have to "fix-it." As part of this blending activity, the words were often embedded in sentences or short stories.

Another activity used in this part of the lesson was borrowed from the sound categorization activities used by Bradley and Bryant (1983, 1985). Children were taught to recognize the "odd one out" from a group of four pictures. Three of the pictures belonged together because they rhymed or because they shared a first, last, or middle sound. The children had to select the "odd one out" and explain why it did not belong. Rhyming sets (e.g., *men, ten, hen*) were introduced first, followed by sets that were grouped by initial sound similarities (e.g., *hat, hop, hen*). After both had been mastered, rhyming sets and initial sound sets were introduced in the same lesson, and children had to differentiate the rule for each set. This activity also provides an opportunity to make connections between sound segments and the letters that represent those segments. Letters can be used to represent the shared sound(s) in a given set of pictures. The teacher can demonstrate with the rhyming set, for example, that new words can be made by the deletion and addition of initial consonants.

During this component of the lesson, children also had an opportunity to practice their segmentation skills using an activity more like that originally developed by Elkonin (1963, 1973). Children were given 8 1/2-by-11-inch laminated sheets, each displaying a picture of a word to be segmented. Underneath the picture was a rectangle divided into the appropriate number of squares to represent the sounds in each word. Again children were given tiles (disks, blocks, or buttons) to represent the sound segments. The procedure was similar to that described in say-it-and-move-it, only now the children had the picture in front of them as a reminder of the word to be segmented.

Another component in each lesson involved instruction in letter sound correspondences. Children were taught to name the letter, to give the sound of the letter, and to give a word that begins with that sound. Each letter was accompanied by pictures of objects that begin with that sound (e.g., pictures of an apple and an ant were used to reinforce the sound of /a/). It is important to include the letter sound associations for the short vowels, as well as the consonants, even though the vowel sounds are not usually included in traditional kindergarten readiness activities. Knowledge of the short vowel sounds and a few consonants will enable children to read and spell a pool of phonetically regular words early in the instructional sequence, and this helps children to consolidate the connections they are making between print and speech.

Reading Instruction

A question not addressed in the literature concerns the type of reading program that should follow a reading readiness program that emphasizes phoneme awareness. As discussed previously, one of the earliest component skills of learning to read an alphabetic writing system is learning that speech can be segmented into the phonemic units represented in an alphabetic orthography (Liberman et al., 1980; Williams, 1986). The reader must then make the connections between these sounds and the symbols that represent them. This is sometimes referred to as "breaking the code" or learning to decode. It is this early stage of reading that is the most problematic for many children with reading disabilities (Chall, 1983; Gough & Tunmer, 1986). Consequently, an early emphasis on phoneme awareness in a reading readiness program should be followed by a reading program that emphasizes the alphabetic code.

There is already considerable empirical evidence to support the effectiveness of a code-emphasis approach to reading in the early grades (Chall, 1967, 1979, 1987; Williams, 1979b, 1985). This research was reflected in the strong recommendations in *Becoming a Nation of Readers: The Report of the Commission on Reading* (Anderson, Hiebert, Scott, and Wilkinson, 1985). One of the conclusions reached by this panel was that "the issue is no longer, as it was several decades ago, whether children should be taught phonics. The issues now are specific ones of just how it should be done" (p. 37). The commission suggested that children should be introduced to the alphabetic principle (that letters stand for sounds) as early and as simply as possible. An early emphasis on phoneme awareness will help children begin to make connections between sound and symbol, but for some children this may not be enough. That is, it may be critical that their first formal experience in reading build explicitly on this early awareness. Unfortunately, most beginning reading programs essentially ignore the alphabetic principle by emphasizing the memorization of whole words and by teaching word recognition strategies that rely on guessing.

One alternative to these traditional reading programs is to use a code-emphasis approach in the regular classroom before a child has experienced failure. One example of such an approach (Blachman, 1987) utilizes a simple five-step lesson plan that can be followed by classroom teachers and/or support personnel (e.g., reading teachers, resource teachers). Designed originally to be used by inner-city teachers who wanted an alternative program for low-achieving students, the five-step plan is easy to follow, takes 30 minutes of instructional time each day, and is appropriate for use with groups as well as individuals. Components of the program are borrowed from other code-emphasis approaches, and the five-step plan can be easily modified by the teachers and clinicians who use it. In an ongoing evaluation (Blachman and Ball, in preparation), this program is being used in first grade classrooms and will follow the kindergarten phoneme awareness model described earlier (Ball and Blachman, in press). The goal is to help children take advantage of the alphabetic principle by making explicit the systematic relationships between symbols and sounds.

The first component of this approach is a review of sound-symbol correspondences at the beginning of each lesson. This is followed in step two by instruction in phoneme analysis and blending. A simple procedure adapted from Engelmann (1969) is used to avoid the letter-by-letter blending approach that is often recommended. When children learn to pronounce *bat*, for example, as *buh-a-tuh*, it is often impossible for them to recover the original word regardless of how quickly they blend the sounds together (A. Liberman et al., 1967; Liberman, 1971; Liberman & Shankweiler, 1979). In the Engelmann procedure, the child is taught to produce a vowel followed by a consonant or a consonant (continuent) followed by a vowel as a single unit. The teacher represents the strategy on the board as

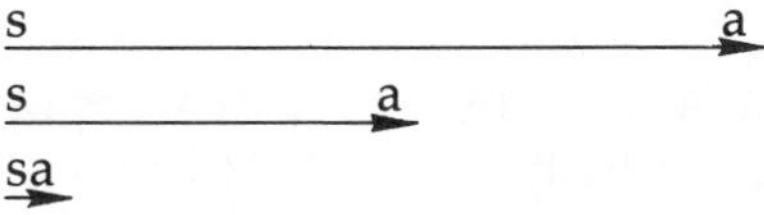

The teacher points to the first sound, and the child produces that sound until the teacher points to or writes the second letter. Its sound is then pronounced. The space between the two sounds is decreased until the child pronounces the combination as a single unit. By adding stop consonants in the final position, a pool of words is built (e.g., *sat*, *sap*).

A second technique is also used to help children avoid letter-by-letter blending. A small pocket-chart called a ''sound board'' (adapted from Slingerland, 1971) is used by each child to manipulate letters to form words. Consonants and vowels previously mastered by the children are placed in the top pocket. The teacher pronounces a word such as *mat* and asks the children to identify the vowel sound. The children then select the letter that represents that sound and places the color-coded vowel letter in the lower pocket. The teacher repeats the word and asks the children to select the letter card that represents the first sound in the word and to place that letter card in front of the vowel in the lower pocket. The teacher or another child then says "Now we have *ma*. The word we want to make is *mat*. What is the last sound we hear in *mmmaaat?*" The children select the *t*, place it at the end of the word in the lower pocket, and read the whole word. The teacher might then ask the children to change *mat* to *man* and *man* to *fan*. When other vowels are mastered, *fan* is changed to *fin*. Blends and digraphs are also incorporated into the lesson, and eventually *fin* becomes *shin*.

The third activity in this five-step plan gives the children an opportunity to develop more automatic recognition of words that they have practiced previously on the sound board. Once they can accurately read a pool of phonetically regular words (e.g., closed syllable words such as *ran* and *sat*), those words are written on flash cards and the children practice reading them fluently. High frequency sight words that have to be memorized (e.g., *said*) are also introduced. It helps to write in a different color those words that cannot be decoded.

Following this flash card drill, children are given an opportunity in step four to read connected text. This might involve the use of a linguistic reader, such as the *Basic Reading Series* (1976), published by Science Research Associations, and materials from *Primary Phonics* (Makar, 1977), published by Educators Publishing Service. A variety of other texts can be selected. What is important is having children read words in context (sentences, paragraphs, and stories) as soon as a small but adequate word pool is developed.

The fifth step in the lesson is a dictation activity. Children are asked to write several words from their story or words practiced earlier on the sound board. This activity is included to help children see that they can spell the words they can read and that reading and spelling are part of the same process. New skills continue to be introduced and incorporated in later parts of the lesson. After the introduction of closed syllables, other patterns are introduced (e.g., final "e" words, such as *cake* and *hike*; vowel team words, such as *boat* and *coin*).

Although the focus of these early activities is on developing accurate and automatic word recognition skills, vocabulary development and comprehension are not neglected. Children should know or be introduced to the meaning of all words they can read, and comprehension of stories both read and listened to should be monitored. However, the value of accurate and automatic word recognition skills should not be overlooked. There is considerable evidence that the development of fluent decoding skills is a source of difficulty for many poor readers and that comprehension is compromised without accuracy and fluency at the level of the individual word (Gough, 1984; Gough & Tunmer, 1986; Lesgold & Resnick, 1982; Perfetti & Hogaboam, 1975; Perfetti & Lesgold, 1977; Stanovich, 1982a, 1982b, 1986; Torgesen, 1986).

CLINICAL SUGGESTIONS FOR ASSESSMENT

Despite the role that phonological awareness appears to play in early reading ability, the traditional reading readiness tests or reading assessment batteries do not reflect an emphasis on this skill (Blachman, 1983, 1984a; Mann & Liberman, 1984). Measures of phonological awareness administered in kindergarten have been found to predict first grade reading ability as well as or better than measures of intelligence or reading readiness tests (Stanovich, Cunningham, & Cramer, 1984). Thus, assessment of a beginning reader or older nonreader should include a simple measure of phonological awareness (e.g., asking children to count or segment sounds; to categorize words by the beginning, middle, or end sound; or to perform the somewhat more difficult sound deletion task). Including other reading-related language measures in the assessment battery can further enhance predictive accuracy. For example, when measures of verbal short-term memory and rapid automatized naming (Denckla & Rudel, 1976) were used with a measure of phoneme awareness (phoneme segmentation), this set of tasks was found to account for more than 74 percent of the variance on a test of word recognition in first grade (Blachman, 1983). This is considerably better than the 50 percent accounted for by the better predictive instruments (Lindsay & Wedell, 1982; Pikulski, 1974).

In addition, much can be learned about the beginning reader by a thorough assessment of alphabet knowledge. This might begin with a simple matching task using alphabet letters, followed by letter recognition (i.e., child selects the letter named by the examiner from a multiple-choice array) and letter identification (i.e., child names each letter as it is presented). It is also useful to ask the child to identify the sound made by each letter and to provide a word that starts with each sound. Finally, the child should be asked to copy each letter and then to write each letter from memory.

To provide information about the word recognition skills of the beginning reader (particularly the student who is not yet able to read words on a standardized instrument), the examiner can attempt to assess recognition of words displayed in the child's environment. In the typical kindergarten or first grade classroom, for example, names of colors and numbers, months of the year, and names of the children in the class are often prominently displayed. Most children will recognize at least some of these words without having had any direct instruction. If the examiner has access to these words, they can provide a useful yardstick of the child's beginning reading ability (print awareness).

When a child who has been exposed to reading instruction demonstrates knowledge of consonant sounds but is still unable to read words, two trial teaching activities may be useful. The examiner can introduce the sound of /a/ (as in *cat*), and then introduce the word family *at*. To determine if the child can use knowledge of initial consonants, an initial consonant substitution drill can be presented. The examiner selects consonant sounds that the student has mastered and displays the following pattern on the board:

at
c*at*
s*at*
m*at*
f*at*
r*at*

If necessary, the examiner can pronouce /at/ and demonstrate how *at* becomes *cat*. The child is then asked to read the remaining words. A more difficult activity is to use the Engelmann (1969) blending technique described earlier under Clinical Suggestions for Teaching. Again, the examiner selects a consonant sound that the child has mastered and teaches the child the sound of /a/. Once the child can read a consonant and vowel as a unit (e.g., *ma*), final consonants are added to make a pool of words such as *ma*n, *ma*t, *ma*d. These two exercises may give the examiner some insight into the child's level of understanding of the function of letter sound correspondences in reading words. There are some young nonreaders and older remedial students who demonstrate knowledge of sound-symbol correspondences, but who have not been able to acquire a sight vocabulary even when the words have been constantly displayed in their daily environment (e.g., months of the year). It is often the students who have been unable to remember whole words by their visual configuration *and* who have not been given direct instruction in phoneme analysis and synthesis who remain nonreaders. The initial consonant substitution drill and trial teaching with Engelmann blending may be the first opportunity a student has had to see that his or her basic sound-symbol knowledge can be used in decoding simple words. This may give the student a glimpse, at least, of what it means to unlock the alphabetic code.

For a student who has some beginning reading skills, an assessment should include at least three basic components. First, a graded word list, which measures the student's ability to read high frequency words found in standard basal readers, can be used as an initial screening device. Particularly when little evidence is available to document a student's reading ability, a graded word list gives the examiner a rough estimate of the child's skill. Because graded word lists are readily available and easy to administer and score, they are sometimes the only instrument administered. It should be noted, however, that a graded word list samples a very narrow range of reading behavior and, used alone, does not provide an adequate assessment of a child's reading ability. Second, a separate measure of decoding skills should be administered. A decoding assessment will provide information about the child's ability to decode phonetically regular words (both real and nonsense words beginning with CVC trigrams).

Third, the child should be asked to read orally and silently in context. Comprehension of both oral and silent reading should be measured as well as listening comprehension. Although it would be possible to list numerous tests that might be used to assess each behavior, such lists are usually outdated before they can be published. What is more important than the names of specific tests is knowledge of the range of behaviors that should be assessed. A test battery to sample those behaviors can then be assembled.

A relatively new test, the Decoding Skills Test (Richardson & Di Benedetto, 1985), does deserve special mention. This measure samples a wider range of behavior than is typically measured by graded word lists and decoding tests. The authors use *decoding* in its broadest sense to refer to word recognition generally and not just the ability to read phonetically regular patterns. The test measures the development of a basal vocabulary, the ability to read phonetically regular patterns (both real and nonsense words), and the ability to use context as a cue in word recognition. The Decoding Skills Test was designed "to detect specific aspects of the reading problem that may be traced to poor decoding [word recognition]" (p. 1), and as such it is a welcome addition to the arsenal of reading tests currently available.

SUMMARY

The literature reviewed in this chapter suggests that phonological awareness plays a causal role in beginning reading achievement. In addition, early experience with phonological awareness activities appears to have a positive impact on reading and spelling, especially when connections are made between the sound segments of the word and the letters representing those segments. This training appears to be most beneficial for those who have poor phoneme awareness skills. We are still trying to determine whether one sequence of phonological awareness activities is better than another, how often and for how long training in these skills should take place, and the optimal design for the reading program that follows early phoneme awareness training. These are all questions that the creative clinician and teacher can help to answer.

REFERENCES

Anderson, R., Hiebert, E., Scott, J., and Wilkinson, I. (Eds.). (1985). *Becoming a nation of readers: The report of the Commission on Reading*. Washington, D.C.: National Institute of Education.

Ball, E., and Blachman, B. (in press). Phoneme segmentation training: Effect on reading readiness. *Annals of Dyslexia*.

Basic Reading Series, (1976). Chicago, IL: Science Research Associates, Inc.

Blachman, B. (1983). Are we assessing the linguistic factors critical in early reading? *Annals of Dyslexia, 33*, 91–109.

Blachman, B. (1984a). Language analysis skills and early reading acquisition. In G. Wallach and K. Butler (Eds.), *Language learning disabilities in school-age children*, 271–287. Baltimore, MD: Williams and Wilkins.

Blachman, B. (1984b). Relationship of rapid naming ability and language analysis skills to kindergarten and first grade reading achievement. *Journal of Educational Psychology, 76*, 610–622.

Blachman, B. (1987). An alternative classroom reading program for learning disabled and other low-achieving children. In R. Bowler (Ed.), *Intimacy with language: A forgotten basic in teacher education*, 49–55. Baltimore, MD: The Orton Dyslexia Society.

Blachman, B., and Ball, E. (in preparation). A kindergarten and first grade classroom reading program with an emphasis on phonological awareness.

Blachman, B., and James, S. (October, 1986). A longitudinal study of metalinguistic abilities and reading achievement in primary grade children. Paper presented at the meeting of the International Academy for Research in Learning Disabilities, Northwestern University, Evanston, IL.

Bradley, L. (November, 1987). Rhyme recognition and reading and spelling in young children. Paper presented at the Early Childhood Symposium on Preschool Prevention of Reading Failure at the meeting of the Orton Dyslexia Society, San Francisco, CA.

Bradley, L., and Bryant, P. (1983). Categorizing sounds and learning to read: A causal connection. *Nature, 301*, 419–421.

Bradley, L., and Bryant, P. (1985). *Rhyme and reason in reading and spelling*. International Academy for Research in Learning Disabilities Monograph Series, Number 1. Ann Arbor, MI: University of Michigan Press.

Brady, S. (1986). Short-term memory, phonological processing, and reading ability. *Annals of Dyslexia, 36*, 138–153.

Bruce, L. (1964). The analysis of word sounds by young children. *British Journal of Educational Psychology, 34,* 158–170.

Byrne, B., and Ledez, J. (1983). Phonological awareness in reading disabled adults. *Australian Journal of Psychology, 35,* 185–197.

Chall, J. (1967). *Learning to read: The great debate.* New York: McGraw-Hill.

Chall, J. (1979). The great debate: Ten years later, with a modest proposal for reading stages. In L. Resnick and P. Weaver (Eds.), *Theory and practice of early reading, 1,* 29–55. Hillsdale, NJ: Erlbaum.

Chall, J. (1983). *Stages of reading development.* New York: McGraw-Hill.

Chall, J. (1987). The importance of instruction in reading methods for all teachers. In R. Bowler (Ed.), *Intimacy with language: A forgotten basic in teacher education,* 15–23. Baltimore, MD: The Orton Dyslexia Society.

Content, A., Kolinsky, R., Morais, J., and Bertelson, P. (1986). Phonetic segmentation in prereaders: Effect of corrective information. *Journal of Experimental Child Psychology, 42,* 49–72.

Crain, S., and Shankweiler, D. (in press). Syntactic complexity and reading acquisition. In A. Davison, G. Green, and G. Hermon (Eds.), *Critical approaches to readability: Theoretical bases of linguistic complexity.* Hillsdale, NJ: Erlbaum.

Denckla, M., and Rudel, R. (1976). Rapid 'automatized' naming (R.A.N.): Dyslexia differentiated from other learning disabilities. *Neuropsychologia, 14,* 471–479.

Elkonin, D. (1963). The psychology of mastering the elements of reading. In B. Simon and J. Simon (Eds.), *Educational psychology in the U.S.S.R.,* 165–179. London: Routledge and Kegan Paul.

Elkonin, D. (1973). U.S.S.R. In J. Downing (Ed.), *Comparative reading,* 551–579. New York: MacMillan.

Engelmann, S. (1969). *Preventing failure in the primary grades.* Chicago: Science Research Associates.

Fox, B., and Routh, D. (1975). Analyzing spoken language into words, syllables, and phonemes: A developmental study. *Journal of Psycholinguistic Research, 4,* 331–342.

Fox, B., and Routh, D. (1980). Phonemic analysis and severe reading disability in children. *Journal of Psycholinguistic Research, 9,* 115–119.

Fox, B., and Routh, D. (1984). Phonemic analysis and synthesis as word attack skills: Revisited. *Journal of Educational Psychology, 76,* 1059–1064.

Gough, P. (1984). Word recognition. In P. Pearson (Ed.), *Handbook of reading research,* 225–253. New York: Longman.

Gough, P., and Tunmer, W. (1986). Decoding, reading, and reading disability. *Remedial and Special Education, 7,* 6–10.

Hohn, W., and Ehri, L. (1983). Do alphabet letters help prereaders acquire phonemic segmentation skill? *Journal of Educational Psychology, 75,* 752–762.

Juel, C., Griffith, P., Gough, P. (1986). Acquisition of literacy: A longitudinal study of children in first and second grade. *Journal of Educational Psychology, 78,* 243–255.

Lesgold, A., and Resnick, L. (1982). How reading difficulties develop: Perspectives from a longitudinal study. In J. Das, R. Mulcahy, and A. Wall (Eds.),

Theory and research in learning disabilities, 155–188. New York: Plenum Press.
Liberman, A., Cooper, F., Shankweiler, D., and Studdert-Kennedy, M. (1967). Perception of the speech code. *Psychological Review, 74*, 431–461.
Liberman, I. (1971). Basic research in speech and lateralization of language: Some implications for reading disability. *Bulletin of the Orton Society, 21*, 72–87.
Liberman, I. (1973). Segmentation of the spoken word and reading acquisition. *Bulletin of the Orton Society, 23*, 65–77.
Liberman, I. (1983). A language-oriented view of reading and its disabilities. In H. Myklebust (Ed.), *Progress in learning disabilties, 5*, 81–101. New York: Grune and Stratton.
Liberman, I., and Shankweiler, D. (1979). Speech, the alphabet, and teaching to read. In L. Resnick and P. Weaver (Eds.), *Theory and practice of early reading, 2*, 109–132. Hillsdale, NJ: Erlbaum.
Liberman, I., and Shankweiler, D. (1985). Phonology and the problems of learning to read and write. *Remedial and Special Education, 6*, 8–17.
Liberman, I., Shankweiler, D., Blachman, B., Camp, L., and Werfelman, M. (1980). Steps toward literacy. In P. Levinson and C. Sloan (Eds.), *Auditory processing and language: Clinical and research perspectives*, 189–215. New York: Grune and Stratton.
Liberman, I., Shankweiler, D., Fischer, F., and Carter, B. (1974). Explicit syllable and phoneme segmentation in the young child. *Journal of Experimental Child Psychology, 18*, 201–212.
Lindsay, G., and Wedell, K. (1982). The early identification of 'at risk' children: Revisited. *Journal of Learning Disabilities, 15*, 212–217.
Lundberg, I. (1987). Phonological awareness facilitates reading and spelling acquisition. In R. Bowler (Ed.), *Intimacy with language: A forgotten basic in teacher education*, 56–63. Baltimore, MD: The Orton Dyslexia Society.
Lundberg, I., Olofsson, A., and Wall, S. (1980). Reading and spelling skills in the first few years predicted from phonemic awareness skill in kindergarten. *Scandinavian Journal of Psychology, 21*, 159–173.
Maclean, M., Bryant, P., and Bradley, L. (1987). Rhymes, nursery rhymes, and reading in early childhood. *Merrill-Palmer Quarterly, 33*, 255–281.
Makar, B. (1977). *Primary phonics*. Cambridge, MA: Educators Publishing Service.
Mann, V. (1984). Longitudinal prediction and prevention of early reading difficulty. *Annals of Dyslexia, 34*, 117–136.
Mann, V., and Liberman, I. (1984). Phonological awareness and verbal short-term memory: Can they presage early reading problems? *Journal of Learning Disabilities, 17*, 592–599.
Mattingly, I. (1972). Reading, the linguistic process, and linguistic awareness. In J. Kavanagh and I. Mattingly (Eds.), *Language by ear and by eye*, 133–147. Cambridge, MA: MIT Press.
Morais, J., Bertelson, P., Cary, L., and Alegria, J. (1986). Literacy training and speech segmentation. *Cognition, 24*, 45–64.
Morais, J., Cary, L., Alegria, J., and Bertelson, P. (1979). Does awareness of speech as a sequence of phones arise spontaneously? *Cognition, 7*, 323–331.
Olofsson, A., and Lundberg, I. (1983). Can phonemic awareness be trained

in kindergarten? *Scandinavian Journal of Psychology, 24,* 35–44.

Olofsson, A., and Lundberg, I. (1985). Evaluation of long-term effects of phonemic-awareness training in kindergarten: Illustrations of some methodological problems in evaluation research. *Scandinavian Journal of Psychology, 26,* 21–34.

Perfetti, C. (1985). *Reading ability.* New York: Oxford University Press.

Perfetti, C., and Hogaboam, T. (1975). Relationship between single word decoding and reading comprehension skill. *Journal of Educational Psychology, 67,* 461–469.

Perfetti, C., and Lesgold, A. (1977). Discourse comprehension and sources of individual differences. In M. Just and P. Carpenter (Eds.), *Cognitive processes in comprehension,* 215–237. Hillsdale, NJ: Erlbaum.

Pikulski, J. (1974). Assessment of prereading skills: A review of frequently employed measures. *Reading World, 13,* 171–197.

Read, C., and Ruyter, L. (1985). Reading and spelling skills in adults of low literacy. *Remedial and Special Education, 6,* 43–52.

Richardson, E., and Di Benedetto, B. (1985). *Decoding skills test.* Parkton, MD: York Press.

Rosner, J. (1971). *Phonic analysis training and beginning reading skills.* Pittsburgh, University of Pittsburgh Learning Research and Development Center. (ERIC Document Reproduction Service No. ED 059-029).

Rosner, J. (1973). *The perceptual skills curriculum.* New York: Walker Educational Book Co.

Shankweiler, D., Liberman, I., Mark, L., Fowler, C., and Fischer, F. (1979). The speech code and learning to read. *Journal of Experimental Psychology: Human Learning and Memory, 5,* 531–545.

Share, D., Jorm, A., Maclean, R., Matthews, R. (1984). Sources of individual differences in reading acquisition. *Journal of Educational Psychology, 76,* 1309–1324.

Slingerland, B. (1971). *A multi-sensory approach to language arts for specific language disability children: A guide for primary teachers.* Cambridge, MA: Educators Publishing Service.

Stanovich, K. (1982a). Individual differences in the cognitive processes of reading: I. Word decoding. *Journal of Learning Disabilities, 15,* 485–493.

Stanovich, K. (1982b). Individual differences in the cognitive processes of reading: II. Text-level processes. *Journal of Learning Disabilities, 15,* 549–554.

Stanovich, K. (1986). Matthew effects in reading: Some consequences of individual differences in the acquisition of literacy. *Reading Research Quarterly, 21,* 360–407.

Stanovich, K., Cunningham, A., and Cramer, B. (1984). Assessing phonological awareness in kindergarten children: Issues of task comparability. *Journal of Experimental Child Psychology, 38,* 175–190.

Torgesen, J. (1986). Computer-assisted instruction with learning disabled children. In J. Torgesen and B. Wong (Eds.), *Psychological and educational perspectives on learning disabilities,* 417–435. Orlando, FL: Academic Press.

Tornéus, M. (1984). Phonological awareness and reading: A chicken-and-egg problem? *Journal of Educational Psychology, 76,* 1346–1358.

Treiman, R., and Baron, J. (1983). Phonemic-analysis training helps children benefit from spelling-sound rules. *Memory and Cognition, 11,* 382–389.

Wagner, R. (1986). Phonological processing abilities and reading: Implications for disabled readers. *Journal of Learning Disabilities, 19,* 623–630.

Wagner, R., and Torgesen, J. (1987). The nature of phonological processing and its causal role in the acquisition of reading skills. *Psychological Review, 101,* 192–212.

Wallach, M., and Wallach, L. (1976). *Teaching all children to read.* Chicago: University of Chicago Press.

Williams, J. (1979a). The ABD's of reading: A program for the learning disabled. In L. Resnick and P. Weaver (Eds.), *Theory and practice of early reading, 3,* 179–195. Hillsdale, NJ: Erlbaum.

Williams, J. (1979b). Reading instruction today. *American Psychologist, 34,* 917–922.

Williams, J. (1980). Teaching decoding with an emphasis on phoneme analysis and phoneme blending. *Journal of Educational Psychology, 72,* 1–15.

Williams, J. (1985). The case for explicit decoding instruction. In J. Osborn, P. Wilson, and R. Anderson (Eds.), *Reading education: Foundations for a literate America,* 205–213. Lexington, MA: Lexington Books.

Williams, J. (1986). The role of phonemic analysis in reading. In J. Torgesen and B. Wong (Eds.), *Psychological and educational perspectives on learning disabilities,* 399–416. Orlando, FL: Academic Press.

Woodcock, R. (1973). *Woodcock reading mastery tests.* Circle Pines, MN: American Guidance Service, Inc.

Vellutino, F. (1979). *Dyslexia: Theory and research.* Cambridge, MA: MIT Press.

6

Higher-Order Language Processes and Reading Disabilities

Froma P. Roth
& Nancy J. Spekman

In technologically advanced societies, both the comprehension of written language (reading) and its production (writing) are essential communication linkages between people. Reading requires the comprehension of printed text in its context of use. It is an active, constructive process, the goal of which is to determine and understand the meaning intended by the author. Successful readers bring to reading the sum total of their knowledge, and information processing and cognitive abilities. They also utilize linguistic knowledge that is both structural and conceptual in nature.

It is widely recognized that reading is a language-based skill (Gleitman & Rozin, 1977; Perfetti & Lesgold, 1977; Snyder, 1980; Vellutino, 1977, 1979, 1987). According to Catts and Kamhi (1986), different aspects of language are involved in both the decoding and comprehending of written text. The influence of lower-order language abilities (e.g., phonological processing) on decoding skills and early reading development was considered in Chapters 1 and 4.

The purpose of this chapter is to examine the relationship between higher-order oral language abilities and reading development in students with reading disabilities. We begin with a brief discussion of higher-order linguistic processes and their proposed relationship to reading. The main body of the chapter will address the higher-order language processing abilities of reading disabled students in three specific areas of oral language performance: (1) semantics, (2) syntax, and (3) discourse. Also included is a discussion of the potential impact of oral linguistic deficits on reading performance.

There is a large body of evidence that children with reading disabilities demonstrate significant problems with language tasks that involve higher-order operations. Deficits have been shown in the areas of semantics (Fry, Johnson, & Muehl, 1970; Rudel, Denckla, & Broman, 1981), morphology and syntax (Morice & Slaghuis, 1985; Vogel, 1974, 1977), and discourse (Feagans & Applebaum, 1986; Oakhill, 1984).

While some of the studies to be described later have specifically involved students diagnosed as reading disabled (RD), many have involved samples of students identified more broadly as learning disabled (LD). In such instances learning disability is defined as a discrepancy between intellectual ability and one or more areas of language development and/or academic achievement. It is reasonable to assume, however, that the majority of LD students were not identified on the basis of oral-language deficits (Donahue, 1986), and that the majority of them demonstrated underachievement at least in the area of reading. Given this assumption, and for the purposes of this chapter, the term RD will be used to refer to this population.

It is well documented that RD students represent a heterogeneous diagnostic group with respect to patterns of reading difficulties. Subtyping research has confirmed the existence of discrete subgroups of RD children and adolescents (Doehring & Hoshko, 1977; Fisk & Rourke, 1979; Lyon, 1978a, b; Lyon & Watson, 1981; McKinney, 1984; Petrauskas & Rourke, 1979; Rourke, 1978; Satz & Morris, 1981; Speece, McKinney, & Applebaum, 1985; Spreen & Haaf, 1986; also see Chapter 2 of this book). This work has shown that not all RD youngsters read poorly for the same reasons and therefore do not benefit from the same instructional methods (Johnson, 1978; Johnson & Myklebust, 1967; Lyon, 1983, 1985). Further, the psychological validity of subtyping has been demonstrated by intervention studies that have shown some differential effects of reading instructional methods among various subgroups of RD youngsters (Lyon, 1983, 1985; Lyon, Stewart, & Freedman, 1982).

Given the existence of distinct RD subgroups in the written language domain, it is probable that subtyping efforts with this population would reveal similar heterogeneity in the oral language domain. Moreover, it is likely that a relationship exists between performances in the oral and written language domains. Unfortunately, there are limited experimental data available that delineate the kinds of reading problems that result from specific patterns of oral language disabilities, especially concerning higher-order abilities. It is possible, however, to draw on existing theoretical, clinical, and empirical evidence to formulate viable hypotheses regarding differential reading patterns that might result logically from specific types of oral language problems.

Pronounced oral language difficulties are not exhibited by all students with reading disabilities; however, a high incidence of language deficits is apparent in this population (Vellutino, 1977). Moreover, there is the belief that many RD students have subtle language problems that do not reveal themselves on standard diagnostic batteries but that interfere significantly with the ability to read (Bryant & Bradley, 1981; Frith, 1981; Liberman, 1983; Treiman & Baron, 1981; Westby, Maggart, & Van Dongen, 1984).

Donahue (1986) has suggested the existence of at least three subgroups of language disorders within the RD population. The first group includes those students with relatively severe language problems who are identified early, typically during the preschool years. Evidence exists that many of these children will experience subsequent difficulty learning to read. The second group of students have language problems that are less obvious than those of students in the first group. These students may not be identified as having problems until they enter school. Some of these children may have phonological processing deficits that interfere with the development of word recognition skills. Others may only encounter difficulties as the linguistic and cognitive demands of the curriculum increase. For example, at about fourth grade the reading curriculum changes from a focus on "learning to read" to a focus on "reading to learn" (Chall, 1983). At this time, the content of the written material becomes less familiar, new vocabulary is introduced, units are longer and syntactically more complex, and higher levels of comprehension and integration are expected. At this point, many of these students begin to fall behind.

The third group proposed by Donahue (1986) might not be identified as language deficient until even later. This group is composed of students who enter school with age-appropriate oral language skills but who fall behind in reading for other reasons (e.g., problems in attention or motivation). The reading difficulties in turn lead to less exposure to the more sophisticated vocabulary and syntactic structure that is characteristic of written language. Thus, these youngsters do not make the same linguistic advances seen in normally achieving (NA) students in the later elementary years. Along a similar vein, reading difficulties also may contribute to failure to keep up with and add to world knowledge by depriving students of a frequently used channel for learning information. Obviously, this situation introduces a potentially vicious cycle in which linguistic limitations restrict the language level of written material that can be processed meaningfully, which in turn limits access to content knowledge. In this way, the level of oral language proficiency impacts on the development of reading, and reading ability in turn affects oral language processing. Eventually, it may be difficult to differentiate one group from another. Due to limited exposure to printed material, the end result for students in any of these groups may be the same. Their linguistic deficits affect reading, but also their reading deficits may adversely affect further language development.

HIGHER LEVELS OF LINGUISTIC PROCESSING AND READING

According to the model proposed by Catts and Kamhi (1986; also see Chapter 1), three levels of information processing are involved in the reception of both the spoken and the written word. The first level, *perceptual analysis,* involves the identification of the segmental and suprasegmental features of incoming stimuli. The second level, *word recognition,* involves the establishment of either a phonological or visual representation of the incoming stimuli and the subsequent activation of word meaning, or lexical access (Golinkoff, 1975–1976; Perfetti & Lesgold, 1977). The goal is to identify the incoming stimuli as familiar by matching it with an already stored representation in the lexicon, and access its meaning. Word meaning may be activated in different ways. A reader may proceed directly from a visual whole (word) matched to a stored visual representation and then to meaning. Alternatively, a reader may develop an intervening phonological representation. This may occur either by (1) ''saying'' a whole word or by (2) visually analyzing a stimulus into parts (morphemes, syllables, individual letters), developing a phonological representation for each part, and then blending (synthesizing) the sounds together.

The goal is to utilize the quickest, most efficient means. Developing skills and practice enable readers to recognize more words as visual wholes and to recognize them more automatically. Even sophisticated readers, though, may need to segment difficult, unfamiliar words (e.g., when reading technical material or reading material outside one's area of expertise). When word identification is especially difficult, readers may expend so much attention and energy on word identification that there are few resources available to be directed at encoding word meaning and text comprehension (LaBerge & Samuels, 1974; Perfetti & Lesgold, 1977). However, even with relative ease and accuracy of word identification, access to single word meaning is not guaranteed. Many readers are able to decode words for which they have limited or no stored meaning.

The third level of information processing, *higher-order processing,* involves the processing of units larger than a single word (i.e., sentences and extended texts). Just as accurate word identification does not guarantee accurate word meaning, accurate word meaning may be necessary but not sufficient for comprehension of longer text units. Beyond single word meaning, comprehension of text requires a wide variety of higher-level linguistic and problem solving skills such as the following:

- understanding relations between words and word parts that are signaled by word order and morphological endings
- understanding relations between sentences that are signaled by the use of such cohesive devices as anaphoric and cataphoric reference, ellipsis, and substitution
- identifying words based on familiarity with content and/or context
- determining vocabulary meaning (including the correct meaning of homophones, words with multiple meanings, and idiomatic usages) based on context
- understanding at different levels of abstraction including literal and inferential comprehension; determining main idea; summarizing; and making appropriate predictions regarding story events, character traits, and character emotions and motivations
- determining the author's communicative intent
- determining the information that is most relevant and retaining it for a sufficient period of time
- utilizing knowledge of narrative structure.

These and other higher-order linguistic processes that are involved in the areas of semantics, syntax, and discourse are most influential at the levels of word recognition and textual processing. The relationships between the different levels of information processing cannot be considered as either unidirectional or unilateral. Thus, in some instances, text-level processing occurs following both perceptual and word recognition stages. However, it is also true that higher-level language and cognitive processes in turn influence accurate word identification and meaning derivation. For example, word recognition may occur only when the word is embedded in a meaningful context that facilitates identification. One student, for example, consistently read *garden* as *grand* when the stimulus was presented in isolation, but read the word correctly when it was presented in a sentence such as "The flowers are growing in my *garden*."

Good readers appear to have many strategies available for processing written text and are able to utilize and shift these strategies flexibly depending on the content and difficulty of the material being read and their purpose for reading. According to Gibson and Levin (1975), readers direct their attention to material for processing in the most economical way available to them. This means, for example, that the largest units appropriate to the task are processed and that information relevant to a reader's purpose is selected for attention; information that is not needed or wanted is ignored. By using a variety of alternative strategies, good readers are able to take advantage of a continual reduction in the amount of information that needs to be processed (Gibson & Levin, 1975). For instance, context and grammatical structure provide a smaller message set, and thereby improve word recognition accuracy; meaning or word alternatives are reduced by using "old" information or world knowledge to comprehend "new" information. Thus, sophisticated readers can be described as moving flexibly among the different levels of information processing.

HIGHER-ORDER LANGUAGE ABILITIES

SEMANTICS

Semantic competence involves knowledge of (1) individual word meanings and (2) rules that govern the combination of word meanings for the formation of meaningful phrases and sentences. Semantics is the aspect of language that is most closely linked to the processes of memory and concept formation. Memory processes are involved in the structural organization of semantic information and are essential for the efficient storage and retrieval of knowledge. However, efficient information storage and retrieval are possible only when a meaningful organization structure is imposed on the information to be stored. Thus, the construction of well-organized conceptual structures or semantic networks depends on the individual's concept formation abilities (the ability to categorize). Individuals with deficient concept formation abilities necessarily will have less elaborate vocabulary and underlying semantic networks and be less able to store information in a manner so that it can be accessed easily.

It is logical to asume that language deficits in the area of semantics may be reflected in reading and interfere with reading in many ways. The stage at which such reading difficulties appear and the form and severity they may take is dependent on the nature and severity of the language deficits, the content and difficulty level of the reading material, and the nature of the early reading curriculum. For example, students with semantic deficits who are taught to read with a highly phonetic approach (in which sound-symbol relationships and word identification are stressed over comprehension) may develop proficiency in decoding. Their reading difficulties may not be identified until the time when comprehension assumes a more dominant position in the curriculum. Other students with semantic deficits, who begin with a more meaning based curriculum, may demonstrate word meaning and text comprehension problems from the very beginning. Others may progress through early levels, when reading material contains familiar vocabulary and is based on familiar experiences, but may demonstrate difficulty when expected to comprehend at more abstract levels and read material to learn new information and integrate at higher levels. As mentioned previously, reading disabilities themselves can impact negatively on the acquisition of semantic knowledge.

Lexical Processing

Studies that have investigated the semantic development of RD students have focused primarily on lexical knowledge. RD students have been found to demonstrate deficits on a variety of measures of lexical processing, including vocabulary and word associations and word retrieval.

VOCABULARY AND WORD ASSOCIATIONS. There appears to be a strong correlation between oral vocabulary and reading. The strength of this relationship is perhaps highlighted best by a report of a recent national literacy survey (National Assessment of Educational Progress, 1986), which concluded that the greater one's knowledge of word meanings, the better skilled the person is at reading comprehension.

The oral vocabulary skills of RD students have been examined using a variety of receptive and/or expressive tasks. Investigations of single word comprehension have produced mixed results. Some studies found that RD children and adolescents perform more poorly than NA peers on measures of nonrelational terms; that is, words that refer to tangible objects and events (Bryan, Donahue, & Pearl, 1981; Rudel, et al., 1981). In other cases, no significant group differences have emerged (Semel & Wiig, 1975; Wiig & Semel, 1973, 1974).

Experimental findings are more consistent regarding the comprehension of relational words and indicate that RD students display inferior comprehension of such terms (Kavale, 1982; Wiig, Becker-Redding, & Semel, 1983; Wiig & Semel, 1973). Relational words are terms for which there are no concrete referents in the real world. For example, many relational words encode concepts of space, time, location, and quantity. Relational words refer to relationships between objects and/or persons, and therefore represent a more abstract class of lexical items than nonrelational words. Unlike nonrelational terms, the comprehension of relational words requires the ability to hold in memory more than one referent and perform an internal comparison. Knowledge of relational words is deemed critical for early educational success. Failure to understand relational words can significantly impair a child's ability to follow teacher directions, learn classroom routines, and acquire reading and other academic skills.

The expressive vocabulary skills of RD students have been assessed primarily on structured tasks in which subjects are required to define a series of words. Experimental results indicate that the definitions produced by RD children and adolescents are less accurate and less sophisticated than those of their NA counterparts (Hoskins, 1983; Rudel, et al., 1981; Wiig & Semel, 1975). Hoskins (1983) noted that RD students usually provide descriptions and examples of vocabulary words rather than formal definitions.

Word associations are viewed as a measure of an individual's ability to organize word categories and concepts. Traditionally, development of word association skills has been examined by presenting a word to a child and requesting the child to say the first word that comes to mind. Children younger than six typically provide either (1) a syntagmatic response, which is a word or phrase that could precede or follow the stimulus word in a setence (e.g., *drink/milk*), or (2) a clang response, which is a word that has sound properties similar to the stimulus word such as rhyming words (e.g., *cat/mat*) (Ervin, 1961). In contrast, older children and adults provide a paradigmatic response, a word in the same grammatical class as the stimulus word (e.g., *cat/dog*). In normal developing children, the shift from a syntagmatic to a paradigmatic response pattern occurs between six and eight years of age, with proportional increases in paradigmatic associations continuing through adolescence.

Reliable information regarding the word association abilities of RD students is limited to the work of Israel (1980) and Shilo (1981). The results of these investigations reveal that RD students appear to follow the normal developmental sequence but at a delayed rate. Specifically, the RD students studied did not exhibit the age-expected paradigmatic shift and provided significantly greater proportions of nonparadigmatic associations than their NA peers even at 13 years of age (Shilo, 1981). In addition, Israel (1980) found that the RD group alone produced a relatively high proportion of clang responses, which are considered a primitive class of nonparadigmatic associations. The explanation for these findings is not clear-cut and probably involves one or more of a variety of factors, including, (1) a restricted vocabulary, (2) immature classification schemes for organizing lexical information, and (3) retrieval deficits.

The findings discussed above indicate that there are differences in the semantic development of some students identified as RD. Comparable experimental studies that have examined the single word comprehension skills of these students during reading are not available. While most reading is obviously textual in nature, word meaning tasks (e.g., match a stimulus word with a picture referent, provide a synonym or antonym for a stimulus word, or complete a word analogy) are common on most group and some individual achievement tests. Also unavailable is research that begins with students specifically identified as having oral semantic deficits and then examines their reading behaviors and error patterns. However, it is possible to draw on clinical experience to predict or describe the effect that a semantic deficit may have on both word identification and reading comprehension.

When reading, students with semantic-based deficits are more likely to rely on graphic, phonologic, orthographic, and syntactic information than on semantic and morphologic cues.[1] Thus, reading errors may have some degree of visual and/or phonologic similarity and fit in syntactically, but be semantically unrelated to the printed word and passage content. For example, when asked to read "The duck *dived* into the water," a 12-year-old student with semantic deficits read "The duck *drived* into the water." The same child read "The bird could not *believe* his eyes" as "The birds did not *belong* his eyes." Some reading errors may even result in nonsense words (e.g., *shapping* for *shaping*).

In many instances, these students will not attempt to self-correct their errors. They may be unaware that what they have read does not make sense, or they may be unable to derive a more reasonable substitution. In some instances, hearing oneself read may help to trigger an awareness of meaning distortions. It has been suggested that when self-corrections are made, the corrections may more likely reflect attempts to resolve reader-based inconsistencies (those that violate what the reader knows about the world) than text-based inconsistencies

---

[1] The kinds of cue utilized when confronted by an unknown word indicate the sources of information a reader is able to use (Pflaum & Bryan, 1982). When words are presented in isolation, the following sources of information are available to assist the reader in accurate word identification and subsequent lexical access: (1) graphic (visual features or visual patterns within words, such as word length, general configuration, and letter sequence), (2) orthographic (spelling regularities and constraints found within our alphabetic writing system; for example, *pro* is permissible, *nmr* is not; knowledge of silent *e* rule), (3) phonologic (sound characteristics and constraints; for example, *eigh* is pronounced /a/, *mp* is permissible at the ends of words but not at the beginning), and (4) morphologic (meaning contained within prefixes, suffixes, and root words). Two additional sources of information are available when words are contained within sentences and extended units of text. These are (1) semantic (the meaningful context surrounding the word, such as sentence and passage content) and (2) syntactic (the structural context, such as rules governing word order and subject-verb agreement).

(those that contradict or in some way violate preceding text information) (Reis & Spekman, 1983). Of course, the extent to which this happens is based on the reader's world knowledge and life experiences. When reading about topics that are not within personal experiences, both reader-based and text-based errors may not be corrected because the reader does not have the internalized knowledge with which to associate passage content. Even when prior knowledge does exist, a reader may need to be made consciously aware of it. Thus, prior to reading, a discussion of the topic and its relevance to the student may help the reader tap into whatever related information stores he or she might have.

Readers with semantic deficits may demonstrate difficulties in determining word meaning from text. A review of two reading curricula, for example, revealed that vocabulary development relied primarily on learning word meaning from sentences; however, the sentences used were typically inadequate for determining the meaning of the vocabulary word (Beck, McKeown, McCaslin, & Burkes, 1979). Thus, attention must be given to the contexts from which a student is expected to derive meaning. Readers also may experience difficulties on tasks requiring them to demonstrate word understanding via synonyms, antonyms, and analogies. More subtle problems with word comprehension may be evident when the student is reading words with multiple pronunciations. For example, *Joe will record* (ré cord) *his next* record (re córd) *soon*. Readers with semantic deficits also may have difficulty determining the correct or intended meaning for words with multiple meanings and connotations.

Comprehension may vary with length of reading passage. Extended units of text require that the reader first identify information that is likely to have relevance for subsequent events and then retain that informational focus long enough to utilize subsequent information (Roth & Perfetti, 1980). RD students may experience difficulty with one or both aspects.

Responses to comprehension questions and activities may vary with the type of question. In general, the difficulty experienced by readers with comprehension problems will increase as the abstraction level of the activity increases. Some may be able to correctly answer factual questions but have difficulty with tasks that require vocabulary definitions, inferential thinking, and interpretation of the information contained in the text. For example, this would involve predicting upcoming events, determining cause and effect, or understanding character motivations. It is reasonable also to assume that more abstract vocabulary and language usage (e.g., humor, idiom, slang, dialect, and simile and metaphor) will cause difficulties. Reading comprehension may be improved in instances when a reader recognizes the advantages of looking back in the text for information or clarification. (See Garner & Reis, 1981, for a discussion of text lookbacks.)

WORD RETRIEVAL. Word retrieval involves the ability to access an intended word from one's vocabulary or lexicon. The study of word retrieval skills has involved the use of tasks that require rapid and/or accurate naming of series of visual stimuli or of words within specified semantic categories.

RD students have been described historically as evidencing word retrieval deficits. Two decades ago, Johnson and Myklebust (1967) used the term *reauditorization* problems to codify clinical observations of verbal naming and word finding difficulties in RD students. Subsequent experimental findings have borne out their observations (Denckla & Rudel, 1976a, b; Denkla et al., 1981; German, 1979, 1982; Wiig et al., 1983; Wiig, LaPointe, & Semel, 1977; Wiig & Semel, 1975; Wiig, Semel & Nystrom, 1982; see Chapter 4, this volume). Students identified as dyslexic and RD have been shown to perform significantly more poorly than NA peers on word retrieval tasks. Their performance is characterized by a slower naming rate, a higher incidence of naming errors (particularly apparent on low frequency words), and longer response latencies on correct responses. Moreover, these difficulties can persist into adolescence (Wiig et al., 1977; Wiig & Semel, 1975; White, 1979; Wolf, 1979). Blachman (1984) found that the rapid automatic naming of colors and letters was a reliable predictor of reading achievement.

Interestingly, there is some evidence to suggest that RD students have more serious word retrieval problems than learning disabled (LD) students who do not possess a primary reading disorder. In addition to attaining inferior accuracy and latency scores, RD students have been found to display error patterns that are different from those exhibited both by nonreading impaired LD and NA students. The oral naming errors made by dyslexic subjects tend to be in the form of circumlocutions and phonetically related word substitutions. In contrast, the incorrect naming that typifies the error performance of nonreading impaired LD and NA subjects involves word substitutions that are not phonetically related, but may or may not be semantically related. This group is also less likely to circumlocute (Denckla & Rudel, 1976a, b; Denckla et al., 1981).

The underlying source of RD students' word retrieval difficulties is not agreed on by researchers. Some contend that it is a manifestation of a more generalized language disorder (Aaron, Baxter, & Lucenti, 1980; Denckla & Rudel, 1976a, b; Geschwind, 1967). Others (Harris, 1979; Leonard, Nippold, Kail, & Hale, 1983) support a view that RD students have incomplete meaning entries for vocabulary words in their lexicons. For example, they do not include peripheral items in a semantic category and have trouble recognizing ambiguous contexts of a word or the relationship between the meaning of one word and related lexical items (Fried-Oken, 1983; Wiig & Becker-Caplan, 1984). Still others hypothesize that the word finding difficulties of RD students are due solely to a problem of access. In this view, RD students have adequately developed lexical stores but cannot call up the information as accurately or automatically as NA students. This view is given some credence by the abundance of clinical examples describing (1) difficulties calling up high frequency familiar words and (2) the frequent use of circumlocutions. (See Chapter 4 for further discussion of the topic.)

The oral reading behaviors of students with word retrieval problems may be highly similar to their oral language patterns. First, when reading aloud, they may appear dysfluent with frequent hesitations and pauses, apparent stuttering, and/or frequent word or phrase substitutions. Second, similar to oral circumlocutions, clinical examples have been reported of students looking at printed words and defining them but without being able to call up the specific words. Third, word substitutions may be frequent. However, unlike the reading substitution errors of others with semantically based deficits, error analysis in cases of word retrieval problems frequently reveals a high proportion of substitutions that are semantically related to the intended word. For example, in relation to the intended word, substitutions seen clinically may be from within the same semantic category (mother/father, dogs/pets, air/sky, big/little), may be more closely synonymous (pond/lake, much/many, house/home), or may reflect other word associations (''Peter'' read as ''Pan''). In many instances, the substituted word actually may have little to no graphic or phonologic similarity with the printed text.

For those students with word retrieval problems who make semantically correct word substitutions, passage meaning may be less distorted than might otherwise be expected. Comprehension will be affected only to the degree that meaning has been changed or to the extent that working memory has been disrupted. However, the manner by which comprehension is measured may affect a student's ability to demonstrate comprehension. For students with retrieval problems, it may be necessary to measure comprehension with multiple-choice or other recognition type responses and/or allow the reader to look back in the text so as not to require a heavy emphasis on retrieval itself. Thus, while it is commonly assumed that facility with word retrieval is essential for deriving meaning from printed text, it is possible that students with retrieval difficulties are able to access word meaning but are not able to recall the name of the word. (This could present a problem, though, for working memory and in turn comprehension; see Chapter 4.)

FIGURATIVE LANGUAGE

In addition to lexical deficits, RD students demonstrate problems with figurative language forms. Figurative language forms are nonliteral language uses and include such forms as metaphors, similes, idioms, proverbs, and humor. Clearly, figurative language processing involves more than semantic knowledge; there are syntactic and discourse aspects involved as well. However, the area of figurative language is included here within the framework of semantics because it is so strongly meaning based. The comprehension and production of figurative forms require metalinguistic awareness because their accurate processing depends on the ability to objectify and manipulate language as an arbitrary linguistic code. Figurative language occurs frequently in conversations and in written materials for middle and upper elementary school students. Thus, facility with figurative language is considered necessary for optimal participation in communicative interactions and for academic achievement.

The extant literature indicates that RD students in elementary school grades have difficulty processing metaphoric language both at the level of comprehension (Lee & Kamhi, 1985; Nippold, Leonard, & Kail, 1984; Seidenberg & Bernstein, 1986) and production (Lee & Kamhi, 1985). Interestingly, Nippold and Fey (1983) found that preadolescents (9;5 to 11;7 years) with a reported resolved history of preschool language impairment also experienced significant difficulty understanding metaphors. These youngsters made significantly more errors when explaining a series of metaphors than a group of age-matched peers, and most of the interpretation errors were literal in nature.

RD students between 7 and 13 years of age also have been shown to exhibit reduced comprehension of similes (Seidenberg & Bernstein, 1986) and idioms (Strand, 1982). Finally, Fowles and Glanz (1977) reported that language activities involving humor posed difficulty for a group of 6- to 9-year old students who were identified as below average readers. In comparison to same-age above average readers, the slow reading group showed less appreciation of the humor in an experimental set of riddles and were less able to retell the riddles to another person or explain why the riddles were funny. The impact of oral figurative language problems on reading has not been investigated. It is logical to expect, however, that difficulties in the oral language domain would carry over to the domain of written language.

SYNTAX AND MORPHOLOGY

Syntactic competence involves knowledge of the structural aspects of the linguistic system and encompasses both morphological and syntactic rules. Morphological rules modulate meaning by signaling syntactic structure in individual words. Syntactic rules determine the order and combination of words in the construction of well-formed sentences. By the time children typically begin formal classroom instruction in reading, their oral language skills reflect mastery of most syntactic and morphological rules. Morever, knowledge of these rules appears to be integrally related to reading ability in that they serve as primary cues for deciphering written text and thus are instrumental in facilitating reading comprehension (Guthrie, 1973; Idol-Maestas, 1980; Vogel, 1974, 1977; Wanat, 1977; Weinstein & Rabinovitch, 1971).

The study of syntactic abilities of RD students has been motivated, in large part, by the belief that a general syntactic deficit underlies reading (Vellutino, 1979). The extant literature (Morice & Slaghuis, 1985; Vogel, 1974, 1977; Wiig et al., 1977; Wiig, Semel, & Crouse, 1973) indicates that many RD students perform significantly more poorly than NA peers on oral language tasks involving the comprehension and use of morphological units and syntactic structures.

In reviewing this body of work, it is important to note that the construct validity of many language tests is less than optimal. Several of the tasks on which syntactic deficits have been identified require linguistic behaviors that are not related to or that exceed the demands of everyday speaking and listening situations. A case in point is the Sentence Combining and Word Order subtests of the Test of Language Development—Intermediate (Newcomer & Hammill, 1982), a language test for children between 8;6 and 12;11 years. These subtests assess expressive syntax on the basis of a child's ability to (1) construct a complex grammatical sentence from a series of short sentences presented orally and (2) create a sentence from a series of four to seven words presented orally. Such tasks measure much more than syntactic knowledge; they are metalinguistic tasks with heavy emphasis on immediate auditory memory. Similarly, grammatical judgment tasks require a child to evaluate the relative well formedness of phrases or sentences. Here again, metalinguistic skills are necessary for successful performance. The child must make use of his or her linguistic knowledge to arrive at accurate judgments about the form of the language input. Thus, interpretation of a child's performance on these tasks is not clear-cut.

Deficits in morphological knowledge have been observed in numerous samples of RD children and adolescents on a variety of standardized and nonstandardized measures of language performance (Fletcher, Satz, & Scholes, 1981; Idol-Maestas, 1980; Kamhi & Catts, 1986; Klecan-Aker, 1984; Liles, Shulman, & Bartlett, 1977; Moran & Byrne, 1977; Morice & Slaghuis, 1985; Vogel, 1974, 1977; Wiig et al., 1977, Wiig et al., 1973). The most commonly cited rule violations exhibited by the disabled groups involved progressive and past tense verb forms, possessive markers, adjectival inflections, third person singular markers, and reflexive pronouns. It is generally agreed that the error patterns displayed by these youngsters reflect quantitative rather than qualitative differences. That is, RD students appear to proceed through the normal developmental stages of morphological rule acquisition but at a protracted or delayed rate.

RD and NA students also have been differentiated on measures of syntactic complexity. The conventional approach to the study of syntactic development has been the administration of standardized tests to groups of RD and NA students. The results of these studies indicate that RD students between seven years of age and adolescence demonstrate several characteristic problems, including (1) reduced sentence length, (2) a higher incidence of syntactic errors, and (3) a reduced ability to formulate and comprehend complex sentences, particularly, embedded sentences (e.g., Vogel, 1977; Wiig et al., 1983; Wiig et al., 1977; Wiig & Semel, 1975; Wiig et al., 1973).

Sentence comprehension problems have also been documented in RD students on experimental tasks. Specifically, RD children and adolescents have been shown to have difficulty understanding complex sentence types containing embedded clauses that deviate from canonical word order, such as relative clause constructions and infinitival and adverbial temporal complements (Byrne, 1981; Magee & Newcomer, 1978; Morice & Slaghuis, 1985; Stein, Carins, & Zurif, 1984; Wallach, 1984). Based on these studies, the inferior performance of the RD subjects has been attributed to their use of comprehension strategies that were developmentally less mature than those employed by the NA controls. Even at 14 years of age, RD subjects tended to rely mainly on semantic rather than syntactic information for sentence interpretation. Semantically based strategies are characteristic of young preschool children whose knowledge of syntax is just emerging (Bever, 1970). These strategies are relinquished by normally developing children in favor of syntactically based strategies prior to entry into the academic classroom. Morice and Slaghuis (1985) also found that the oral comprehension differences exhibited by their good and poor readers increased with age and contributed to a deterioration in the reading comprehension performance of the poor readers.

A recent approach to the study of oral expressive syntax has been the analysis of samples of narrative discourse. Narrative samples permit the examination of extended units of connected language and avoid some of the artificial constraints of traditional elicitation techniques. The results of this work have shown that narratives produced by elementary school-age RD students contain significantly higher rates of morphological and syntactic errors than those generated by NA counterparts (Doehring, Trites, Patel, & Fiedorowicz, 1981; Morice & Slaghuis, 1985; Purcell & Liles, 1985; Wren, 1981, 1982). The RD subjects tend to produce a greater proportion of simple sentences and far fewer embedded clauses. However, oral expressive syntax problems do not seem to be characteristic of all students with reading disabilities. For example, Roth and Spekman (1986a) and Klecan-Aker (1984) examined the syntactic complexity of narrative sequences produced by groups of RD and NA subjects between 8 and 14 years, and found equivalent RD-NA group performances on measures of clause length and clausal complexity. In addition, Roth and Spekman (1986a) reported that their RD and NA subjects demonstrated nearly identical rates of correct usage and highly similar *patterns* of usage of sentence constituents and sentence types.

As with semantic-based deficits, the relative impact of syntactic deficits on reading will depend on the nature (receptive and/or expressive) and severity of the problem and on the material being read. Students who have mastered most of the basic syntax forms orally may do well in early meaning-based reading programs. The syntax constructions in these programs are usually simple and reflect natural speaking patterns. Early reading materials in phonetically based reading programs, however, usually contain more stilted, less predictable semantic and syntactic patterns (e.g., *The fat cat sat on the mat with the rat*) that may make sentence processing more difficult. Later reading materials in both types of programs, however, utilize more complex and less familiar syntactic constructions (as do content texts that are introduced at this time). Thus, problems may become evident during the mid to late elementary years.

It is likely that receptive syntax deficits will be more debilitating than expressive problems. If the reader cannot determine the meanings and relationships that are signaled by morphological endings, word order, and syntactic patterns, reading comprehension probably will be affected regardless of the reader's prior knowledge and familiarity with the content. Morphological endings carry meaning with respect to aspects such as number (plural *-s*), tense (*-ed*, *-ing*, *-s*), and possession (*'s*). Word order can be used to determine meaning in certain active constructions (e.g., *The boy chased the girl* versus *The girl chased the boy*). However, the reader also must understand that a variety of syntactic patterns can be used to express the same idea and that attention to word order only may be misleading. The following examples are illustrative:

Active:	The teacher read to the child.
Passive:	The child was read to by the teacher.
Cleft:	It was the teacher who read to the child.
Pseudocleft:	The one who read to the child was the teacher.

Further, Roth and Perfetti (1980) note that the above four sentence types highlight different ways for indicating new versus old (given) information. In this case, the new information is "the teacher" and should be given primary focus by the reader. In sum, failure to accurately process the syntax of written text frequently results in failure to obtain the intended meaning.

It is reasonable to assume that expressive syntax deficits may have a more variable influence on reading comprehension. That is, despite errors noted during oral reading (e.g., failure to attend to word endings), the redundancy within our language may be sufficient for the reader to obtain meaning. For example, in the following sentence the past tense is signaled by the word *yesterday* and by the *-ed* ending: *Yesterday, I planted my tulip bulbs*. A reader's omission of *-ed* would not change sentence meaning.

In general, the oral reading of students with syntax disorders may reflect their oral language patterns. Their reading may be characterized by omissions, substitutions, or additions of word endings and whole words and by word order errors. Primary sources of information for word identification may be graphic, phonologic, orthographic, and semantic, with a reduced use of syntactic and morphologic information. Word substitutions may represent different grammatical categories than the stimulus words (e.g., adjectives substituted for verbs). A child who is unable to utilize internalized knowledge of syntax to predict or develop expectations may exhibit a word-by-word reading pattern. However, it is plausible that some students with only expressive deficits may derive benefit from hearing themselves read and self-correct syntactic errors; others may not self-correct because they are relying on their own expressive patterns. Finally, it is possible that some students with expressive syntax deficits will not make the errors described above. Such students may be aided by the concrete, visual representations of written language. They are able to use graphic, phonologic, and orthographic information to identify words with morphological endings and maintain correct word order. (See Johnson, 1985, for a discussion of the use of reading and writing to improve oral language skills.)

As indicated above, the reading comprehension of students with receptive syntax disorders likely will be affected to the degree that the written material contains unknown or unfamiliar syntactic patterns. The reading comprehension of students with expressive syntax disorders may or may not be affected. However, it is important to note that the means by which comprehension is measured may confound the clinician's interpretation of assessment data. For example, reading comprehension is frequently evaluated by asking the child to answer questions orally, to retell or summarize what has been read, to predict what will happen, or to describe such aspects as story setting and character attributes. The adequacy of a student's response may be influenced by his or her ability to provide concise and grammatically correct responses.

ORAL DISCOURSE

Discourse is the primary linguistic medium through which academic information is imparted and acquired. The two major forms of discourse that have received the most intensive study are conversation and narration. Conversation involves the maintenance of a dialogue over successive turns during which each partner alternately assumes speaker and listener roles. Narration involves extended units of text including stories and recounts of personal experiences. Conversation and narration share many similar characteristics. Both require a sense of purpose, the selection of relevant information, the clear and orderly presentation of this information, the ability to assume the perspective of the listener or audience, and the ability to make necessary repairs.

However, the requirements of narration differ from those of conversation in certain fundamental ways. First, narration involves the production (or comprehension) of extended units of text, whereas conversations are characterized by shorter units. Second, narratives are expected to contain an introduction and an organized sequence of events that lead to a logical resolution. Finally, narration requires that the speaker (writer) carry on a monologue. In monologues, speech is decontextualized; that is, the story typically is told out of the context of the event's occurrence. During monologues, the listener (reader) plays a relatively passive role and usually is not expected to provide informational support to the speaker. Thus, it is the responsibility of the speaker to present the information in a coherent and interesting manner so that it forms a unified whole (Roth and Spekman, 1986b). In contrast, the listener is expected to be more active during conversations by providing feedback to the speaker and by assuming the speaker role at appropriate junctures.

Deficits in discourse may impact significantly on all aspects of a child's academic performance, including the development of reading skills. Although the exact relationship between discourse and reading performance is yet to be determined, there is ample evidence that RD students manifest problems with both conversational and narrative discourse forms. For example, according to Westby and Martinez (1981), many RD students in mid elementary school have not attained the narrative skills characteristic of four- to five-year old children. The significance of this statement cannot be underestimated in light of the growing opinion that narrative language paves the way for the transition between oral language and literacy (Bruner, 1984; Westby, 1985; Westby et al., 1984). Moreover, there is some longitudinal data to indicate that narrative discourse proficiency is the most effective single linguistic predictor of reading comprehension achievement in elementary school–age RD students (Feagans and Applebaum, 1986) and of successful resolution of language impairment in preschool children with language disorders (Bishop and Edmundson, 1987).

The discourse difficulties identified in RD students occur in at least three related skill areas that underly both conversation and narration: (1) presupposition, (2) organizational rules and strategies, and (3) semantic integration.

PRESUPPOSITION

Presupposition involves information that is not necessarily explicit in a message but that must be shared by the discourse participants if a message is to be understood (Bates, 1976; Rees, 1978). Speakers and writers alike must determine their purpose for communicating (i.e., the information they wish to convey and/or the effect they wish to have on the receiver of their message) and the most appropriate form for their message. Assumptions are made with respect to word meaning, audience knowledge, audience characteristics (e.g., age, status, cognitive level) and the physical and social context in which the communication occurs (DeHart & Maratsos, 1984; Spekman & Roth, 1982). Listeners and readers also make assumptions or inferences as they attempt to determine the communicative intention and meaning of the speaker or author. This ability to presuppose or to take the perspective of another is also known as *role-taking*.

Units of text can be used to convey a wide variety of intentions. For example, messages may be used to comment, request, greet, protest, explain, or direct the behavior of others (Austin, 1962; Searle, 1969). During oral discourse activities, each intent can be expressed in a variety of forms, including the use of both direct and indirect linguistic, gestural, and paralinguistic means. It is not uncommon for a message to mean something other than its literal interpretation (e.g., a person at the bus stop who says "Do you have the time?" usually expects the listener to give the correct time rather than a yes/no response). It is also not uncommon for the various aspects of a message to be contradictory (e.g., "You look pretty" said with a sarcastic tone of voice). Thus, decisions regarding which form to use and the correct interpretation require varying degrees of presupposition.

The presuppositional abilities of RD students have been investigated primarily in oral conversational tasks, but some evidence is available also from oral narration tasks. Difficulties frequently occur in areas that require inferencing behavior such as (1) modification of communication style and (2) message informativeness.

Modification of communication style involves the ability to adjust one's speech style in appropriate and predictable ways according to the needs and attributes of a listener. Investigations of speech style modifications in RD students have examined several aspects of linguistic changes in accordance with a variety of listener-related variables. Overall, the results of these investigations indicate that despite adequate facility with the linguistic system per se, elementary school RD students demonstrate problems in modifying the syntactic and semantic complexity of their messages as a function of listener age (Bryan & Pflaum, 1978). In addition, they fail to adjust the degree of politeness or persuasiveness of their messages according to power and intimacy characteristics of different listeners (Donahue, 1981). Finally, they tend to be less tactful than NA peers in situations that normally engender sympathetic comments, such as delivering "bad news" to a classmate (Pearl, Donahue, & Bryan, 1983).

Aspects of communication style also involve the ability of a listener to determine the intended meaning. RD students have been found to respond like their NA peers to orally presented direct and indirect requests for information (Pearl, Donahue, & Bryan, 1979). However, no other empirical data have yet established the ability of RD students to comprehend the full range of direct and indirect communicative intentions.

Similar to oral language, written language is used to convey a wide variety of communicative intentions and thereby serves a variety of purposes. Creaghead (1986), for example, suggests that writing can be used "to request funds (instrumental), to request services (regulatory), to keep in touch (interactional), to create poetry (personal), to solicit advice (heuristic), to write novels (imaginative), and to give directions (informative)" (pp. 74–75). Written language can also be used to describe, to persuade or convince, and to deceive. (Also see Chapter 1, this volume.)

A reader's goal is to determine the communicative intentions of the author *and* of the characters within a story. Those with oral discourse deficits, especially those who have trouble identifying their own feelings and motivations, may have difficulty determining how a character feels in a given situation, what a character may do next in response to an event, what motivates a character to respond or react in a certain way, what a character *means* by his or her messages, and what certain behaviors or responses may indicate about the personality or character of this individual. When reading orally or acting out a story that has been read, readers with such deficits may not utilize different or appropriate voices for different characters and may not display appropriate emotions. Despite the importance of these skills, Creaghead (1986) suggests that the instructional emphasis in beginning reading programs (even some of the more meaning-based ones) is primarily on word identification and less so on the functional and communicative aspects of written language. Thus, RD students who do not receive early instruction with functional reading and writing may be in jeopardy for later years when they are expected to determine intended meaning and author intent independently and to respond appropriately (e.g., perform action, provide information, appreciate humor). It is also likely that, in reading, students will encounter a wide variety of indirect means for conveying intent, many of which are unfamiliar or infrequently experienced orally. Satire, sarcasm, humor, metaphors, idioms, and fables are all indirect means for conveying intended meaning. It is likely that RD students will require direct instruction in understanding such figurative uses of language.

Further, in reading, many of the cues typically used in speech situations for conveying and clarifying intention are either eliminated or marked differently. For example, in speech situations, linguistic cues are supplemented with information gained visually through observations of body language, gestures, and the situational context and auditorally via prosody and stress patterns. These sources of information are not available in written text. Instead, the reader must rely on the author's ability to convey the same information linguistically (via specific description of body language and gestures; e.g., "he bristles. . .") or with devices such as italics, underlining, and punctuation. Donahue (1984) reported that on oral language tasks, NA students between grades three and six (a stage at which normally developing children become fluent readers and writers) demonstrated a shift from the use of intonational features to the use of syntactic features for marking new information. In contrast, the RD students did not demonstrate this shift and continued to rely on intonational features. It appears that the RD students did not recognize that syntactic cues should be the primary means for marking new information. It is through printed text that syntactic cues are used primarily for marking new versus old information. Donahue hypothesized that the RD students' performance might reflect their more limited exposure to printed material and their failure to develop proficiency with written language.

Message informativeness refers to the degree to which essential information is conveyed. It is generally understood that, within any interaction, there is some information that is ''old'' or taken for granted and presupposed and some that is ''new'' or must be asserted. Shared information or knowledge can be established between partners in several ways: (1) by mutually monitoring some shared aspect of the physical settings (e.g., two people observing the same TV show), (2) by sharing some general knowledge of the speech situation itself or of one's communication partner (e.g., age, status, past experience), and (3) by mutually monitoring the preceding discourse (e.g., information already asserted might then be presupposed and assumed shared). Thus, when coding messages a speaker must make appropriate inferences about what information is shared and what information requires explicit statement. A speaker must also be able to revise unclear messages. To understand a message, a listener must agree about what information is already shared or established and what must be stated. A listener assumes responsibility for monitoring the information adequacy (amount of information and clarity of presentation) of a message. When the information provided by a speaker is insufficient or ambiguous, a listener must be able to request clarification, ideally in a manner that informs the speaker as to what aspect of the communication needs repair (e.g., volume, unidentifiable referent, confusing wording or vocabulary).

The performance of RD students in the area of message informativeness has been examined in both the speaker and listener roles. In the speaker role, evidence exists to suggest that RD subjects provide significantly less of the information required for successful task completion, and present information less precisely or efficiently than NA peers (Noel, 1980; Spekman, 1981). However, the hypothesis that these students are deficient in communicating essential information in messages is not entirely supported. Meline (1986) reported that eight- to nine-year-old RD subjects demonstrated the same degree of communicative effectiveness as their NA age-mates in describing novel figures to adult listeners.

As listeners, RD students appear to have difficulty monitoring the adequacy of information in the messages of others. The experimental findings available suggest that RD students in primary and middle grades do not take active responsibility as listeners by requesting clarification of messages that contain information insufficient for successful task completion or performance (Donahue, Pearl, & Bryan, 1980; Kotsonis and Patterson, 1980). Spekman (1981) reported that despite an equivalent number of questions asked by the RD and NA listeners, the RD listeners were less likely to clearly specify the nature of the information needed to provide clarification.

When confronted, in reading, with information that does not make sense, a competent reader might utilize one or more of the following "repair" strategies: (1) rereading the immediately preceding text, (2) looking back to earlier texts, (3) reading ahead, (4) calling up past relevant experiences, or (5) consulting a reference source (e.g., dictionary, encyclopedia, another person). However, students with discourse deficits who are not in the habit of seeking clarification for orally presented information also may not do so in reading. It is possible that they are unaware of their failure to comprehend, are unfamiliar with specific repair strategies, or are unable to determine when to utilize such strategies. This situation may be further compounded when students are taught to rely almost exclusively on phonic word attack strategies rather than to monitor for meaning and to apply specific strategies for gaining meaning.

In addition to message content itself, the informativeness of a message is also dependent on the appropriate use of specific linguistic devices such as deictic terms[2], indefinite/definite articles (*a/the*), and other forms of cohesion (e.g., substitution, ellipsis, and conjunction). In and of themselves, these terms are empty of meaning. Their interpretation depends on knowing something about the communication act in which they play a role (Fillmore, 1975); that is, their meaning is dependent on some aspect of the situation that may be external and/or internal to the discourse. For example, a competent speaker usually will first introduce a particular referent with an indefinite article (e.g., *a* dog) or a specific name (e.g., Fido). Once introduced, the referent can be presupposed or assumed to be shared and then may be referred to with a definite article (e.g., *the* dog) or a pronoun (e.g., *he, it*). Language impaired subjects have been shown to have difficulty with some of these linguistic devices (Liles, 1985), but little research is available involving RD subjects. Spekman (1978) reported that her RD subjects had more difficulty correctly using spatial deictic terms.

A reader's task also is to identify the specific information that has been presupposed. Such information should be readily available in the

[2] Examples of deictic terms are personal pronouns (*I, you*), demonstrative pronouns (*this, that*), terms of location (*here, there, left, right*), and of time (*then, now, before, after*).

text, easily inferred from the text, or already available within a reader's informational repertoire (world knowledge, shared experiences). If an author has appropriately identified the needs of an intended audience, the text should be written in a way that permits ready retrieval of the presupposed information. However, if a reader does not know how to locate the implied information, confusion and comprehension problems will result. Problems may be exacerbated further by common aspects of texts, such as a large number of characters, infrequent reference to minor characters or events, and complicated plot lines. Thus, in selecting reading material for students, teachers need to be sensitive to many factors beyond readability levels.

Another aspect of presupposition in text processing has to do with differentiating between given and new information within sentences. According to Roth and Perfetti (1980), each sentence within a unit of text performs two roles. First, every sentence has properties that identify the relevant portions of prior text (given information) and serve to stimulate a backward memory search to locate the information with which new information can be integrated. Second, each sentence has properties that dictate the information that will become active in a reader (new information). Thus, readers must make decisions regarding the information that should be retained, the material that needs to be kept in focus, the information that is likely to be most relevant for subsequent events, and ways to integrate new information with old. Considerable confusion will be experienced by readers who do not retain the necessary information, who elect to focus on information different from what the author intended, or who fail to integrate new information with old.

Organizational Rules and Strategies

In addition to presuppositional skills, discourse proficiency requires knowledge of organizational rules and strategies. To participate successfully in conversation and narration, a child must master the rule system underlying each of these forms and the rule strategies for regulating these different discourse activities. The literature indicates that during both unstructured and structured conversational activities, RD students engage in appropriate turn-taking behaviors, produce as many conversationl turns as their nondisabled peers, and talk as much as their partner. However, there do seem to be differences in the substance of their turns.

During spontaneous conversations with peers, the verbal contributions of RD students have been shown to contain more combative remarks and a greater proportion of negative and unsupportive comments in comparison to NA counterparts (Bryan, Wheeler, Felcan, & Henek, 1976; Smiley & Bryan, 1983a, b). As partners in structured conversational tasks, RD students between the first and eighth grades tend to assume a deferential interactional position. Their messages have been found to be less persuasive and less assertive. They are more likely to agree and less likely to disagree with classmates' opinions and rarely make bids to grab the conversational floor. Thus, their verbal contributions in group decision-making tasks seem to have little effect on the final outcome (Bryan et al., 1981; Donahue & Prescott, 1983). This deferential demeanor is also seen in dyadic conversational interactions with presumably nonthreatening listeners such as their mothers (Bryan, Donahue, Pearl, & Herzog, 1984). Finally, RD students have been shown to adopt an unassertive conversational posture even when they are assigned a speaker role that is considered socially dominant—that of a TV talkshow host (Bryan, Donahue, Pearl, & Sturm, 1981).

Oral narration also poses organizational problems for RD students. The main approach to the study of narrative processing has been the use of story grammars. Story grammars describe the internal structure of a story by specifying (1) the components of a story and (2) a set of rules underlying the order and relationships among the story components (Mandler & Johnson, 1977; Rumelhart, 1975; Stein & Glenn, 1979; Thorndyke, 1977). Story grammars presumably represent internalized knowledge of narrative structure, which is used to process narrative material such as narrative schema (Christie & Schumacher, 1975; Mandler & Johnson, 1977; Rumelhart, 1975; Stein & Glenn, 1979; Whaley, 1981).

Although several different story grammars have been proposed, all story grammars embody similar principles of content and organization. Stein and Glenn's (1979) story grammar, for instance, consists of a setting category and an episode system containing seven story grammar categories in the following order of occurrence: (1) *setting statements*, which introduce the protagonist(s) and describe the context of the story; (2) *initiating events*, which are occurrences that induce the protagonist to act; (3) *internal responses*, which describe the protagonist's internal reactions to the precipitating events; (4) *plans*, which indicate the protagonist's strategy for obtaining the goal; (5) *attempts*, which specify the overt actions of the protagonist to obtain the goal; (6) *direct consequences*, which indicate the protagonist's success or failure to attain the goal; and (7) *reactions*, which describe the protagonist's emotional response regarding the outcome. A story can consist of one or more episodes that are related to one another through sequential, temporal, causal, and embedded linkages.

Studies utilizing a story grammar framework have examined the narrative processing abilities of RD students in several areas including text memory, text comprehension, and spontaneous story production. The results of story recall studies reveal that RD students (elementary school grades through college) preserve the order of events in a story, demonstrate the same pattern of story organization, and engage in a similar proportion of plausible inferencing behavior as their normally achieving peers (Graybeal, 1981; Hansen, 1978; Spekman & Roth, 1987; Worden & Nakamura, 1982). Many studies, however, show that RD students frequently recall significantly less information from a story (Graybeal, 1981; Hansen, 1978; Johnston, 1982; Worden & Nakamura, 1982). In addition, they tend to include fewer linguistic markers that specify important temporal and causal relationships within a story (Spekman & Roth, 1987; Weaver & Dickinson, 1982). Thus, it appears that RD students possess implicit knowledge of narrative structure and apply this knowledge in the retrieval and reconstruction of texts in ways that are quite similar to nondisabled peers.

Despite their knowledge of narrative structure, RD students exhibit difficulties with the comprehension of text. For example, Hansen (1978) and Oakhill (1984) have shown that RD students in elementary school grades provide significantly fewer correct answers to factual questions that ask for literal information about a story passage than do NA controls.

Differences in narrative abilities between RD and NA students also exist at the level of story production. Some of the evidence in this area comes from investigations of the narrative structure and narrative style of self-generated stories. The construction of an original story is a far more complex and demanding task than retelling a story or answering questions about a story that has been heard. Story construction involves formulating ideas, planning and organizing the ideas, and encoding them linguistically (Merritt & Liles, 1987; Roth & Spekman, 1986b).

From a developmental perspective, the story production abilities of elementary and middle school–age RD students appear to be less mature than those of NA equivalents (Botvin & Sutton-Smith, 1977; Klecan-Aker, 1985; Westby et al., 1984). From a story grammar viewpoint, the existing evidence indicates that stories told by RD students between 7 1/2 and 13 years old tend to be significantly shorter, contain substantially fewer complete episodes, and contain far fewer minor setting statements than those of their NA counterparts (Liles, 1987; Roth & Spekman, 1986b; Westby et al., 1984). In addition, Roth and Spekman (1986b) found that RD subjects showed a reduced usage of response, plan, and attempt statements compared to NA controls and were significantly less likely to connect episodes with relations involving causality and simultaneity of events.

From the perspective of narrative content and style, stories produced by RD students in elementary school grades seem to be significantly less complex than those of average readers, with fewer elements of meaning included in each narrative clause. Moreover, their stories lack a literate-sounding quality, which is attributable, in part, to a reduced usage of modifiers and evaluative words and to a tendency to use a descriptive rather than narrative style (Westby et al., 1984). Thus, it appears that when faced with the task of generating their own stories, RD students have difficulty producing long and structurally complex narratives, and they exhibit problems in forming complete episodes within their stories. Further, these students do not seem to use an age-expected narrative style to relate story events.

The few studies (Feagans & Short, 1984; Merritt & Liles, 1987) that have compared story generation, recall, and comprehension abilities of RD subjects have yielded interesting results. It seems that some elementary school–age RD students demonstrate difficulties in both the comprehension and production of narrative sequences with respect to narrative content and linguistic form (Levi, Musatti, Piredda, & Sechi, 1984; Merritt & Liles, 1987), and in terms of story grammar knowledge and linguistic cohesion (Liles, 1985, 1987). Others appear to exhibit problems only at the level of production in the areas of story length and linguistic complexity (Feagans & Short, 1984). It has also been found that some RD students with story production deficits demonstrate similar problems at the level of story recall (Spekman & Roth, 1987).

Certain obvious differences exist between oral and printed conversations; some of these differences may cause difficulty in a reader's understanding of what is going on. For example, in print, conversational speech is indicated by quotation marks. The reader must attend to and understand the meaning of this punctuation form. Further, in written text the speaker is usually identified either by mention of the speaker's name or through use of a pronoun (e.g., *he* said); it is also possible that speaker identity is omitted over many conversational turns, and the reader must infer identity through the visual presentation; for example,

Mike said, "I'm bigger than you are!"
John replied, "No you're not!"
"Yes I am!"
"No you're not!"

Thus, establishing speaker identity and keeping track over many alternating turns (possibly with many participants) may be somewhat more difficult during reading activities.

It is logical to assume that knowledge of story structure is used in the comprehension and production of both oral and written stories. However, research in the area of narrative structure has typically utilized oral stories that are relatively short and uncomplicated. Roth and Spekman (1986b) utilized a story grammar framework to investigate the oral production of spontaneous stories, many of which were quite long and complex. The degree to which knowledge of story grammar structure was utilized to process lengthy and intricate plot structures was not clear.

It is clear, however, that readers benefit from well-organized passages in which context is clearly established and informative (Bransford & Johnson, 1972; Calfee & Curley, 1984). Ease of understanding may also be affected by the manner in which episodes or event sequences are connected and the number of embedded episodes. For example, episodes that are causally connected or connected via the simultaneity of events may be more difficult to understand (Roth & Spekman, 1986b). Instances in which episodes are embedded within one another may also create confusion for a reader. Roth and Perfetti (1980, p. 25) discussed the notion of "episodic closure." They suggested that episodes remain active in memory until resolved. In instances of incomplete resolution, competent readers are able to shift attention to new complications as they arise and then restore attention to the unresolved situation. It is highly likely that RD students with discourse deficits will experience considerable difficulty shifting and restoring the focus of their attention in a similar way. Stories containing many subplots may be especially difficult.

Semantic Integration

Semantic integration is a term used originally by Bransford and Franks (1971) to describe a constructive or inferential memory process employed by adults to organize and remember information from sets of sentences that are semantically related to one another. Using a research paradigm that has been replicated frequently, Bransford and Franks (1971) demonstrated that adults remember the meaning of sentences but not the actual sentences themselves. Their findings were interpreted as indicating that adults spontaneously integrate meaning across sentences and construct a unified semantic representation. It is this holistic semantic structure that is stored in memory and not the particular sentence forms in which the meaning is coded.

Developmental psycholinguistic research reveals that children between 6 and 12 years of age also engage in the constructive memory process of semantic integration (Paris & Carter, 1973; Paris & Lindauer, 1976). Moreover, it appears that elementary school children exhibit the same constructive memory strategies during reading in their efforts to remember and understand written information (Blachowicz, 1977).

Investigation of the semantic integration abilities of RD students is limited to one known study undertaken by Klein-Konisberg (1977). The RD subjects in this study performed in a strikingly different manner than their NA peers. Instead of retaining sentence meaning in the form of plausible inferences, the response patterns of the RD group were indicative of attempts at verbatim storage, an inefficient strategy for organizing and remembering information. The RD subjects appeared to have focused their efforts on retaining actual linguistic structures rather than forming and storing a unified meaning representation of the ideas expressed across the semantically related sentence sets. As Klein-Konisberg noted, the RD subjects may have been trying to remember "too much of the wrong thing" (p. 20).

It is likely that use of such an inefficient strategy interferes with the effective integration of incoming information and may be a factor that contributes to problems with inferential comprehension of oral and written text (Snyder & Downey, 1983). Oakhill (1984), for example, reported that a group of RD subjects made significantly more errors on a set of inferential comprehension questions calling for information that was not explicitly stated in the input story. Again, it appears as though the RD subjects did not use inferencing as a primary strategy for remembering and deriving meaning from story text. Westby (1985) suggested that the oral text comprehension difficulties experienced by RD students may be attributed, in part, to a reduced ability to identify the cause-effect relationships between events and feelings that are critical to understanding the motivations and actions of characters in a story.

SUMMARY

This chapter has explored the relationship between higher-order oral language processes and reading disabilities. For many years, researchers assumed that the relationship was unidirectional: from language deficits to reading deficits. In recent years, we have come to recognize the reciprocal nature of the relationship. Difficulties in reading also can cause higher-level language problems. Future studies need to specify the exact nature of the reciprocal relationships that exist between different aspects of higher-level language functioning and reading and how these relationships change throughout the developmental period.

One clear implication of this relationship concerns the changing roles that are being assumed by speech-language pathologists and special education professionals in the management of RD students. Traditionally, reading and oral language were considered as separate ability areas. As a result, reading disabilities were viewed as the purview of teachers and were managed in the classroom (or resource room) by special education professionals. On the other hand, oral language deficits were seen as the province of communication specialists and were handled outside the classroom by speech-language pathologists. The information presented in this chapter highlights the growing recognition that this traditional ''division of labor'' is no longer valid. Efficacious educational practices depend on informed and coordinated interdisciplinary efforts. Such efforts require that professionals in each discipline have a working knowledge of normal and disordered aspects of both reading and oral language development. This expertise then can be translated into effective educational management.

References

Aaron, P., Baxter, C., and Lucenti, J. (1980). Developmental dyslexia and acquired dyslexia: Two sides of the same coin? *Brain and Language, 11,* 1–11.

Austin, J. (1962). *How to do things with words.* Cambridge: Oxford University Press.

Bates, E. (1976). Pragmatics and sociolinguistics in child language. In D. Morehead and A. Morehead (Eds.), *Normal and deficient child language,* 411–563. Baltimore: University Park Press.

Beck, J., McKeown, C., McCaslin, E., and Burkes, A. (1979). *Instructional dimensions that may affect reading comprehension: Examples from two commercial reading programs.* (Tech. Report). University of Pittsburgh, Learning Research and Development Center.

Bever, T. (1970). The cognitive basis for linguistic structure. In J. Hayes (Ed.), *Cognition and the development of language,* 179–362. New York: Wiley.

Bishop, D., and Edmundson, A. (1987). Language impaired 4-year olds: Distinguishing transient from persistent impairment. *Journal of Speech and Hearing Disorders, 52,* 156–173.

Blachman, B. (1984). Relationship of rapid naming ability and language skills to kindergarten and first-grade reading achievement. *Journal of Educational Psychology, 76,* 610–622.

Blachowicz, C. (1977). Semantic constructivity in children's comprehension. *Reading Research Quarterly, 13,* 188–199.

Botvin, G., and Sutton-Smith, B. (1977). The development of structural complexity in children's fantasy narratives. *Developmental Psychology, 13,* 377–388.

Bransford, J., and Franks, J. (1971). The abstraction of linguistic ideas. *Cognitive Psychology, 2,* 331–350.

Bransford, J., and Johnson, M. (1972). Contextual prerequisites for understanding: Some investigation of comprehension and recall. *Journal of Verbal Learning and Verbal Behavior, 11,* 717–727.

Bruner, J. (1984). Language, mind, and reading. In H. Goelman, A. Oberg, and F. Smith (Eds.), *Awakening to literacy.* Exeter, NH: Heinemann.

Bryan, T., Donahue, M., and Pearl, R. (1981). Learning disabled children's peer interaction during a small group problem solving task. *Learning Disability Quarterly, 4,* 13–22.

Bryan, T., Donahue, M., Pearl, R., and Herzog, A. (1984). Conversational interactions between mothers and learning disabled or nondisabled children during a problem solving task. *Journal of Speech and Hearing Disorders, 49,* 67–71.

Bryan, T., Donahue, M., Pearl, R., and Sturm, C. (1981). Learning disabled children's conversational skills. *Learning Disability Quarterly, 4,* 250–259.

Bryan, T., and Pflaum, S. (1978). Linguistic, cognitive, and social analyses of learning disabled children's interactions. *Learning Disability Quarterly, 1,* 70–79.

Bryan, T., Wheeler, R., Felcan, J., and Henek, T. (1976). "Come on dummy": An observational study of children's communications. *Journal of Learning Disabilities, 9,* 661–669.

Bryant, P., and Bradley, L. (1981). Visual memory and phonological skills in reading and spelling backwardness. *Psychological Research, 43,* 193–199.

Byrne, B. (1981). Deficient syntactic control in poor readers: Is a weak phonetic memory code responsible? *Applied Psycholinguistics, 3,* 201–212.

Calfee, R., and Curley, R. (1984). Structures of prose in the content areas. In J. Flood (Ed.), *Understanding reading comprehension: Cognition, language, and the structure of prose.* Newmark, DE: International Reading Association.

Catts, H., and Kamhi, A. (1986). The linguistic basis of reading disorders: Implications for the speech-language pathologist. *Language, Speech, and Hearing Services in Schools, 17,* 329–341.

Chall, J. (1983). *Stages of reading development.* New York: McGraw-Hill.

Christie, D., and Schumacher, G. (1975). Developmental trends in the abstraction and recall of relevant vs. irrelevant thematic information from connected verbal material. *Child Development, 46,* 598–602.

Creaghead, N. (1986). Comprehension of meaning in written language. *Topics in Language Disorders, 6,* 73–82.

DeHart, G., and Maratsos, M. (1984). Children's acquisition of presuppositional usages. In R. Schiefelbusch and J. Pickar (Eds.), *The acquisition of communicative competence,* 237–293. Baltimore: University Park Press.

Denckla, M., and Rudel, R. (1976a). Naming of pictured objects by dyslexic and other learning disabled children. *Brain and Language, 3,* 1–15.

Denckla, M., and Rudel, R. (1976b). Rapid "automatized" naming (R.A.N.): Dyslexia differentiated from other learning disabilities. *Neuropsychologia, 14,* 471–479.

Denckla, M., Rudel, R., and Broman, M. (1981). Tests that discriminate between dyslexic and other learning disabled boys. *Brain and Language, 13,* 118–129.

Doehring, D., and Hoshko, I. (1977). Classification of reading problems by the Q-technique of factor analysis. *Cortex, 13,* 281–294.

Doehring, D., Trites, R., Patel, P., and Fiedorowicz, C. (1981). *Reading disabilities: The interaction of reading, language, and neuropsychological deficits.* New York: Academic Press.

Donahue, M. (1981). Requesting strategies of learning disabled children. *Applied Psycholinguistics, 2,* 213–234.

Donahue, M. (1984). Learning disabled children's comprehension and production of syntactic devices for marking given versus new information. *Applied Psycholinguistics, 5,* 101–116.

Donahue, M. (1986). Linguistic and communicative development in learning disabled children. In S. Ceci (Ed.), *Handbook of cognitive, social, and neuropsychological aspects of learning disabilities,* 263–289. Hillsdale, NJ: Erlbaum.

Donahue, M., Pearl, R., and Bryan, T. (1980). Conversational competence in learning disabled children: Responses to inadequate messages. *Applied Psycholinguistics, 1,* 387–403.

Donahue, M., and Prescott, B. (1983). *Young learning disabled children's conversational episodes in dispute episodes with peers.* Chicago Institute for the Study of Learning Disabilities.

Ervin, S. (1961). Changes with age in the verbal determinants of word associations. *American Journal of Physiology, 74,* 361–372.

Feagans, L., and Applebaum, M. (1986). Language subtypes and their validation in learning disabled children. *Journal of Educational Psychology, 78,* 358–364.

Feagans, L., and Short, E. (1984). Developmental differences in the comprehension and production of narratives by reading disabled and normally achieving children. *Child Development, 55,* 1727–1736.

Fillmore, C. (1975). Santa Cruz lectures on deixis 1971. Indiana University Linguistics Club, Bloomington, IN.

Fisk, I., and Rourke, B. (1979). Identification of subtypes of learning disabled children at three age levels: A neuropsychological multivariate approach. *Journal of Clinical Neuropsychology, 1,* 289–310.

Fletcher, J., Satz, P., and Scholes, R. (1981). Developmental changes in the linguistic performance correlates of reading achievement. *Brain and Language, 13,* 78–90.

Fowles, B., and Glanz, M. (1977). Competence and talent in verbal riddle comprehension. *Journal of Child Language, 4,* 433–452.

Fried-Oken, M. (1983). The development of naming skills in normal and language deficient children. Unpublished doctoral dissertation, Boston University, Boston.

Frith, U. (1981). Experimental approaches to developmental dyslexia: An introduction. *Psychological Research, 43,* 97–109.

Fry, M., Johnson, C., and Muehl, S. (1970). Oral language production in relation to reading achievement among select second graders. In D. Bakker and P. Satz (Eds.), *Advances in theory and method,* 123–159. Rotterdam: Rotterdam University Press.

Garner, R., and Reis, R. (1981). Monitoring and resolving comprehension obstacles: An investigation of spontaneous text lookbacks among upper-grade good and poor comprehenders. *Reading Research Quarterly, 16,* 569–582.

German, D. (1979). Word-finding skills in children with learning disabilities. *Journal of Learning Disabilities, 12,* 176–181.

German, D. (1982). Word-finding substitutions in children with learning disabilities. *Language, Speech, and Hearing Services in Schools, 13,* 223–230.

Geschwind, N. (1967). Neurological foundations of language. In H. Myklebust (Ed.), *Progress in learning disabilities.* New York: Grune and Stratton.

Gibson, E., and Levin, H. (1975). *The psychology of reading.* Cambridge, MA: MIT Press.

Gleitman, L., and Rozin, P. (1977). The structure and acquisition of reading, I: Relations between orthographies and the structure of language. In A. Reber and D. Scarborough (Eds.), *Toward a psychology of reading.* Hillsdale, NJ: Erlbaum.

Golinkoff, R. (1975–1976). A comparison of reading comprehension processes in good and poor readers. *Reading Research Quarterly, 11,* 623–659.

Graybeal, C. (1981). Memory for stories in language impaired children. *Applied Psycholinguistics, 2,* 269–283.

Guthrie, J. (1973). Reading comprehension and syntactic responses in good and poor readers. *Journal of Educational Psychology, 65,* 294–299.

Hansen, C. (1978). Story retelling used with average and learning disabled readers as a measure of reading comprehension. *Learning Disability Quarterly, 1,* 62–69.

Harris, G. (1979). Classification skills in normally achieving and learning disabled seven- and nine-year-old boys: A study in conceptualization. Unpublished doctoral dissertation, Northwestern University.

Hoskins, B. (1983). Semantics. In C. Wren (Ed.), *Language learning disabilities,* 85–111. Rockville, MD: Aspen.

Idol-Maestas, L. (1980). Oral language responses of children with reading difficulties. *Journal of Special Education, 14,* 335–404.

Israel, L. (1980). Free word associations of learning disabled and nondisabled children. Paper presented at the American Speech-Language-Hearing Association Convention, Detroit, MI.

Johnson, D. (1978). Remedial approaches to dyslexia. In A. Benton and D. Pearl (Eds.), *Dyslexia: An appraisal of current knowledge,* 397–421. New York: Oxford University Press.

Johnson, D. (1985). Using reading and writing to improve oral language skills. *Topics in Language Disorders, 5,* 55–69.

Johnson, D., and Myklebust, H. (1967). *Learning disabilities.* New York: Grune and Stratton.

Johnston, J. (1982). Narratives: A new look at communication problems in older language-disordered children. *Language, Speech, and Hearing Services in Schools, 13,* 144–155.

Kamhi, A., and Catts, H. (1986). Toward an understanding of developmental language and reading disorders. *Journal of Speech and Hearing Disorders, 51,* 337-347.

Kavale, K. (1982). A comparison of learning disabled and normal children on the Boehm Test of Linguistic Concepts. *Journal of Learning Disabilities, 15,* 160–164.

Klecan-Aker, J. (1984). The syntax of normal and learning disabled school-age children. Paper presented at the American Speech-Language-Hearing Association Convention, San Francisco, CA.

Klecan-Aker, J. (1985). Syntactic abilities in normal and language deficient middle school children. *Topics in Language Disorders, 5,* 46–54.

Klein-Konisberg, E. (1977). Semantic integration in normal and learning disabled children. Unpublished doctoral dissertation, the Graduate School and University Center of the City University of New York.

Kotsonis, M., and Patterson, C. (1980). Comprehension-monitoring skills in learning disabled children. *Developmental Psychology, 16,* 541–542.

LaBerge, D., and Samuels, S. (1974). Toward a theory of automatic information processing in reading. *Cognitive Psychology, 6,* 293–323.

Lee, R., and Kamhi, A. (1985). Verbal metaphor performance in learning disabled children. Paper presented at the American Speech-Language-Hearing Association Convention, Washington, D.C.

Leonard, L., Nippold, M., Kail, R., and Hale, C. (1983). Picture naming in language impaired children: Differentiating lexical storage from retrieval. *Journal of Speech and Hearing Research, 26,* 609–615.

Levi, G., Musatti, L., Piredda, M., and Sechi, E. (1984). Cognitive and linguistic strategies in children with reading disabilities in an oral storytelling test. *Journal of Learning Disabilities, 7,* 406–410.

Liberman, I. (1983). A language-oriented view of reading and its disorders. In H. Myklebust (Ed.), *Progress in learning disabilities,* 81–103. New York: Grune and Stratton.

Liles, B. (1985). Cohesion in the narratives of language disordered children. *Journal of Speech and Hearing Research, 28,* 123–133.

Liles, B. (1987). Episode organization and cohesive conjunctives in narratives of children with and without language disorder. *Journal of Speech and Hearing Research, 30,* 185–196.

Liles, B., Shulman, M., and Bartlett, S. (1977). Judgments of grammaticality in normal and language disordered children. *Journal of Speech and Hearing Disorders, 42,* 199–209.

Lyon, R. (1978a). Extension of learning disabled subgroup research: Contrasts with normal readers and varying racial proportions. Unpublished manuscript, University of Alabama, Birmingham.

Lyon, R. (1978b). The neuropsychological characteristics of subgroups of learning disabled readers. Unpublished doctoral dissertation, University of New Mexico.

Lyon, R. (1983). Subgroups of learning disabled readers: Clinical and empirical identification. In H. Myklebust (Ed.), *Progress in learning disabilities*, 103–133. New York: Grune and Stratton.

Lyon, R. (1985). Identification and remediation of learning disability subtypes: Preliminary findings. *Learning Disability Focus, 1*, 21–35.

Lyon, R., Stewart, N., and Freedman, D. (1982). Neuropsychological characteristics of empirically derived subgroups of learning disabled readers. *Journal of Clinical Neuropsychology, 4*, 343–365.

Lyon, R., and Watson, B. (1981). Empirically derived subgroups of learning disabled readers: Diagnostic characteristics. *Journal of Learning Disabilities, 14*, 256–261.

Magee, P., and Newcomer, P. (1978). The relationships between oral language skills and academic achievement of learning disabled children. *Learning Disability Quarterly, 1*, 63–67.

Mandler, J., and Johnson, N. (1977). Remembrance of things parsed: Story structure and recall. *Cognitive Psychology, 9*, 111–151.

McKinney, J. (1984). The search for subtypes of specific learning disability. *Journal of Learning Disabilities, 17*, 43–50.

Meline, T. (1986). Referential communication skills of learning disabled/language impaired children. *Applied Psycholinguistics, 7*, 129–140.

Merritt, D., and Liles, B. (1987). Story grammar ability in children with and without language disorder: Story generation, story retelling, and story comprehension. *Journal of Speech and Hearing Research, 30*, 539–552.

Moran, M., and Byrne, M. (1977). Mastery of verb tense markers by normal and learning disabled children. *Journal of Speech and Hearing Research, 20*, 529–542.

Morice, R., and Slaghuis, W. (1985). Language performance and reading ability at 8 years of age. *Applied Psycholinguistics, 6*, 141–160.

National Assessment of Educational Progress (1986). *Young adult literacy survey.* Princeton, NJ: ETS.

Newcomer, P., and Hammill, D. (1982). *Test of Language Development—Intermediate.* Austin, TX: Pro-Ed.

Nippold, M., and Fey, S. (1983). Metaphor understanding in preadolescents having a history of language acquisition difficulty. *Language, Speech, and Hearing Services in Schools, 14*, 171–180.

Nippold, M., Leonard, L., and Kail, R. (1984). Syntactic and conceptual factors in children's understanding of metaphors. *Journal of Speech and Hearing Research, 27*, 197–205.

Noel, M. (1980). Referential communication abilities of learning disabled children. *Learning Disability Quarterly, 3*, 70–75.

Oakhill, J. (1984). Inferential and memory skills in children's comprehension of stories. *British Journal of Educational Psychology, 54*, 31–39.

Paris, S., and Carter, A. (1973). Semantic and constructive aspects of sentence memory in children. *Developmental Psychology, 9*, 109–113.

Paris, S., and Lindauer, B. (1976). The role of inference in children's comprehension and memory for sentences. *Cognitive Psychology, 8*, 217–227.

Pearl, R., Donahue, M., and Bryan, T. (1979). Learning disabled and normal children's requests for clarification which vary in explicitness. Paper presented at the Fourth Annual Boston University Conference on Language Development, Boston.

Pearl, R., Donahue, M., and Bryan, T. (1983). The development of tact: Children's strategies for delivering bad news. University of Illinois at Chicago, Chicago Institute for the Study of Learning Disabilities.

Perfetti, C., and Lesgold, A. (1977). Discourse comprehension and sources of individual differences. In M. Just and P. Carpenter (Eds.), *Cognitive processes in comprehension*. Hillsdale, NJ: Erlbaum.

Petrauskas, R., and Rourke, B. (1979). Identification of subgroups of retarded readers: A neuropsychological multivariate approach. *Journal of Clinical Neuropsychology, 1,* 17–37.

Pflaum, S., and Bryan, T. (1982). Oral reading research and learning disabled children. *Topics in Language Disorders, 3,* 33–42.

Purcell, S., and Liles, B. (1985). Processing in discourse: Evidence from narrative analysis. Paper presented at the American Speech-Language-Hearing Association Convention, Washington, D.C.

Rees, N. (1978). Pragmatics of language: Applications to normal and disordered language development. In R. Schiefelbusch (Ed.), *Bases of language intervention,* 191–268. Baltimore: University Park Press.

Reis, R., and Spekman, N. (1983). The detection of reader-based versus text-based inconsistencies and the effects of direct training of comprehension monitoring among upper-grade poor comprehenders. *Journal of Reading Behavior, 15,* 49–60.

Roth, S., and Perfetti, C. (1980). A framework for reading, language comprehension, and language disability. *Topics in Language Disorders, 1,* 15–28.

Roth, F., and Spekman, N. (1986a). Syntactic abilities of learning disabled and normally achieving students: Some new findings. Paper presented at the Symposium on Research in Child Language Disorders, Madison, WI.

Roth, F., and Spekman, N. (1986b). Narrative discourse: Spontaneously generated stories of learning disabled and normally achieving students. *Journal of Speech and Hearing Disorders, 51,* 88–23.

Rourke, B. (1978). Reading, spelling, and arithmetic disabilities: A neuropsychological perspective. In H. Myklebust (Ed.), *Progress in learning disabilities,* 97–120. New York: Grune and Stratton.

Rudel, R., Denckla, M., and Broman, M. (1981). The effect of varying stimulus context on word finding ability: Dyslexia further differentiated from other learning disabilities. *Brain and Language, 13,* 130–144.

Rumelhart, D. (1975). Notes on a schema for stories. In D. Brown and A. Collins (Eds.), *Representation and understanding: Studies in cognitive science,* 211–236. New York: Academic Press.

Satz, P., and Morris, R. (1981). Learning disability subtypes: A review. In F. Pirozzolo and M. Wittrock (Eds.), *Neuropsychological and cognitive processes in reading,* 128–144. New York: Oxford University Press.

Searle, J. (1969). *Speech acts: An essay in the philosophy of language.* Cambridge, England: Cambridge University Press.

Seidenberg, P., and Bernstein, D. (1986). The comprehension of similes and metaphors by learning disabled and nonlearning disabled children. *Language, Speech, and Hearing Services in Schools, 17,* 219–229.

Semel, E., and Wiig, E. (1975). Comprehension of syntactic structures and critical verbal elements by children with learning disabilities. *Journal of Learning Disabilities, 8,* 53–58.

Shilo, V. (1981). Word associations in learning disabled children. Unpublished master's thesis, Emerson College, Boston, MA.

Smiley, A., and Bryan, T. (1983a). *Learning disabled boys' problem solving and social interactions during raft building.* University of Illinois at Chicago, Chicago Institute for the Study of Learning Disabilities.

Smiley, A., and Bryan, T. (1983b). *Learning disabled junior high school boys' motor performance and trust during obstacle course activities.* University of Illinois at Chicago, Chicago Institute for the Study of Learning Disabilities.

Smiley, S., Oakley, D., Worthen, D., Campione, J., and Brown, A. (1977). Recall of thematically relevant material by adolescent good and poor readers as a function of written versus oral presentation. *Journal of Educational Psychology, 69,* 381–387.

Snyder, L. (1980). Have we prepared the language disordered child for school? *Topics in Language Disorders, 1,* 29–45.

Snyder, L., and Downey, D. (1983). Pragmatics and information processing. *Topics in Language Disorders, 4,* 75–86.

Speece, D., McKinney, J., and Applebaum, M. (1985). Classification and validation of behavioral subtypes of learning disabled children. *Journal of Educational Psychology, 77,* 67–77.

Spekman, N. (1978). An investigation of the dyadic, verbal problem-solving communication abilities of learning disabled and normal children. Unpublished doctoral dissertation, Northwestern University.

Spekman, N. (1981). Dyadic verbal communication abilities of learning disabled and normally achieving fourth and fifth grade boys. *Learning Disability Quarterly, 4,* 139–151.

Spekman, N., and Roth, F. (1982). An intervention framework for learning disabled students with communication disorders. *Learning Disability Quarterly, 5,* 429–437.

Spekman, N., and Roth, F. (1987). Story recall abilities of learning disabled students. Paper presented at the American Speech-Language-Hearing Association Convention, New Orleans, LA.

Spreen, O., and Haaf, R. (1986). Empirically derived learning disability subtypes: A replication attempt and longitudinal paterns over 15 years. *Journal of Learning Disabilities, 19,* 170–180.

Stein, C., Cairns, H., and Zurif, E. (1984). Sentence comprehension limitations related to syntactic deficits in reading disabled children. *Applied Psycholinguistics, 5,* 305–322.

Stein, N., and Glenn, C. (1979). An analysis of story comprehension in elementary school children. In R. Freedle (Ed.), *New directions in discourse processing,* 53–120. Norwood, NJ: Ablex.

Strand, K. (1982). The development of idiom comprehension in language disordered children. Paper presented at the Symposium on Research in

Child Language Disorders, Madison, WI.

Thorndyke, P. (1977). Cognitive structures in comprehension and memory of narrative discourse. *Cognitive Psychology, 9,* 77–110.

Treiman, R., and Baron, J. (1981). Segmental analysis ability: Development and relation to reading ability. In G. MacKinnon and G. Waller (Eds.), *Reading research: Advances in theory and practice, 3.* New York: Academic Press.

Vellutino, F. (1977). Alternative conceptualizations of dyslexia: Evidence in support of a verbal deficit hypothesis. *Harvard Educational Review, 47,* 334–354.

Vellutino, F. (1979). *Dyslexia: Theory and research*. Cambridge, MA: MIT Press.

Vellutino, F. (1987). Dyslexia. *Scientific American, 256,* 34–41.

Vogel, S. (1974). Syntactic abilities in normal and dyslexic children. *Journal of Learning Disabilities, 10,* 35–43.

Vogel, S. (1977). Morphological ability in normal and dyslexic children. *Journal of Learning Disabilities, 10,* 292–299.

Wallach, G. (1984). Later language learning: Syntactic structures and strategies. In G. Wallach and K. Butler (Eds.), *Language learning disabilities in school-age children,* 82–102. Baltimore, MD: Williams and Wilkens.

Wanat, S. (1977). Developmental psycholinguistics: Implications for reading research. In S. Wanat (Ed.), *Language and reading comprehension*. Arlington, VA: ERIC Clearing House, Center for Applied Linguistics.

Weaver, P., and Dickinson, D. (1982). Scratching below the surface structure: Exploring the usefulness of story grammars. *Discourse Processes, 5,* 225–243.

Weinstein, R., and Rabinovitch, M. (1971). Sentence structure and retention in good and poor readers. *Journal of Educational Psychology, 62,* 25–30.

Westby, C. (1985). Learning to talk—talking to learn: Oral-literate language differences. In C. Simon (Ed.), *Communication skills and classroom success: Therapy methodologies for language learning disabled students*. San Diego, CA: College-Hill Press.

Westby, C., Maggart, Z., and Van Dongen, R. (July, 1984). Language prerequisites for literacy. Paper presented at the International Child Language Congress, Austin, TX.

Westby, C., and Martinez, B. (1981). Facilitating narrative abilities in mid-school students. Paper presented at the American Speech-Language-Hearing Association Convention, Los Angeles, CA.

Whaley, J. (1981). Readers' expectation for story structure. *Reading Research Quarterly, 17,* 90–114.

White, E. (1979). Dysnomia in the adolescent dyslexic and the developmentally delayed adolescent. Unpublished doctoral dissertation, Boston University, Boston, MA.

Wiig, E., and Becker-Caplan, L. (1984). Linguistic word retrieval strategies and word difficulties among children with language disabilities. *Topics in Language Disorders, 4,* 1–18.

Wiig, E., Becker-Redding, U., and Semel, E. (1983). A cross-cultural, cross-linguistic comparison of language abilities of 7- to 8- and 12- to 13-year-old children with learning disabilities. *Journal of Learning Disabilities, 16,* 576–585.

Wiig, E., LaPointe, C., and Semel, E. (1977). Relationships among language processing and production abilities of learning disabled adolescents. *Journal of Learning Disabilities, 10,* 292–299.

Wiig, E., and Semel, E. (1973). Comprehension of linguistic concepts requiring logical operations by learning disabled children. *Journal of Speech and Hearing Research, 16,* 627–636.

Wiig, E., and Semel, E. (1974). Logico-grammatical sentence comprehension by learning disabled adolescents. *Perceptual and Motor Skills, 38,* 1331–1334.

Wiig, E., and Semel, E. (1975). Productive language abilities in learning disabled adolescents. *Journal of Learning Disabilities, 8,* 578–586.

Wiig, E., Semel, E., and Crouse, M. (1973). The use of morphology by high risk and learning disabled children. *Journal of Learning Disabilities, 6,* 457–465.

Wiig, E., Semel, E., and Nystrom, L. (1982). Comparison of rapid naming abilities in language learning disabled and academically achieving eight-year-olds. *Language, Speech, and Hearing Services in Schools, 13,* 11–23.

Wolf, M. (1979). The relationship of disorders of word-finding and reading in children and aphasics. Unpublished doctoral dissertation, Harvard University, Cambridge, MA.

Worden, P., and Nakamura, G. (1982). Story comprehension and recall in learning disabled versus normal college students. *Journal of Educational Psychology, 74,* 633–641.

Wren, C. (1981). Identifying patterns of syntactic disorder in 6-year old children. *British Journal of Disorders of Communication, 16,* 101–109.

Wren, C. (1982). Identifying patterns of processing disorder in 6-year old children with syntax problems. *British Journal of Disorders of Communication, 17,* 83–92.

7

Assessing and Remediating Text Comprehension Problems

Carol E. Westby

> In a culture where written language is prominent and readily available, basic literacy is a natural extension of an individual's linguistic development. (Fillion & Brause, 1987, p. 216)

All language processes are dependent on the same superordinate cognitive abilities. The relations between oral language and written language are fundamental and reciprocal; reading and writing are initially dependent on oral language and eventually extend oral-language abilities (Flood & Lapp, 1987). Young children use their oral-language skills to learn to read, while older children use their reading ability to further their language learning—they read to learn. Once children are able to decode and read words and simple sentences, their focus should shift from the decoding of learning to read to the comprehension of reading to learn. In order to read to learn, students must learn how to learn from reading; they must learn how to use their language and cognitive abilities to comprehend text so they can acquire new knowledge (Brown, 1982).

Reading to learn, or comprehending texts, requires understanding a literate language style, which involves comprehension of novel words and increasingly complex sentences; yet more than comprehension of novel words and complex sentences is required for reading to learn. Readers must possess and acquire ever-increasing knowledge of their physical and social world, and they must know why they are reading; they must be aware of the communicative function or genre of the text (Brewer, 1980). A text may be a narrative with the purpose to entertain or teach, a description with the purpose to explain how to do something, an exposition with the purpose to present an organized body of information and develop a theory, or an argument with the purpose to persuade readers to change their opinion or ideas.

If students are to read to learn, they must also expect texts to make sense. Beaugrande (1984) proposed that reading to learn is dependent on one's having a model of, or purpose for, reading and on one's capacities for building models to organize the information encountered. To develop a model for the reading act and for gaining knowledge requires metacognitive processes; that is, the self-regulatory ability of students to design and monitor their own reading comprehension processes (Brown, 1982).

A major difference between good and poor readers is their view or model for the reading act and the way they build models for gaining knowledge during the act of reading. Good readers know that texts should make sense and that one reads to learn new information, while poor readers believe reading is sounding out words or saying the words fast, fluently, and with expression (Clay, 1973; Johns & Ellis, 1976; Myers & Paris, 1978; Reid, 1966). If students recognize the goal or purpose of reading as comprehending text, they are more likely to be actively involved in achieving this goal by monitoring their progress toward it. Effective readers must have some awareness and control of cognitive strategies they use while reading (Baker & Brown, 1984). Poor readers exhibit less awareness and use of these strategies (Bos & Filip, 1982; Meyer, 1987; Owings, Peterson, Bransford, Morris, & Stein, 1980; Willows & Ryan, 1981; Wong, 1982).

Chapter 1 discussed the various processes and knowledge involved in reading comprehension. In this chapter I will discuss how schema knowledge and metacognitive processing function in comprehending narrative and expository texts. The chapter will focus on assessment of schema knowledge and metacognitive processing and remediation of deficits in these areas. Methods for assessing and facilitating a literate language style, the development of the types of schema knowledge that underlie texts, the structure of texts, and the metacognitive or self-monitoring strategies of the comprehension process will be presented.

COMPREHENDING NARRATIVE AND EXPOSITORY TEXTS

INFORMATION USED IN TEXT COMPREHENSION

If readers are to make sense of texts beyond comprehending novel words and complex syntax, they must use three kinds of information: content facts, content schemata, and text grammars (Kieras, 1985). Content facts are the simple propositions that are conveyed by the texts (e.g., facts about ants or facts about a character in a story). At this level, information does not have any superordinate organizational content. If students recognize the vocabulary words used to present the facts, they can comprehend the individual pieces of information. To gain meaning from the overall text, however, a student must have a content schema, or be able to organize a content schema from the facts presented in the text. A content schema represents a superordinate organization of a mass of possible content facts. For example, one can have a content schema for the social structure of ant or bee colonies, the metamorphosis process of caterpillars and tadpoles, or the activities at a birthday party. The speed of reading and comprehension of a text becomes easier when the reader possesses intuitive knowledge of the text grammar structure of a text (Kieras, 1985). A text grammar or macrostructure is a schema that represents a frequent organizational pattern of textual elements that is independent of specific content.

The role of schemata in text comprehension has been extensively studied (Anderson & Pearson, 1984; Baker & Stein, 1981; Bartlett, 1932; Rumelhart, 1980; Stein & Glenn, 1979; Van Dijk & Kintsch, 1983). Schemata are hierarchically organized sets of facts or information describing generalized knowledge about a text, an event, a scene, an object, or classes of objects (Mandler, 1984). (*Note*: Some authors use the term *script* to refer to an event schema—the stereotypical knowledge structures that people have for common routines such as going to a restaurant, taking a subway, or going to a party [Beaugrande, 1980; Bower, Black, & Turner, 1979; Nelson, 1985; Schank & Abelson, 1977]. A script can be viewed as a specific type of schema.) Our schema knowledge enables us to behave appropriately in familiar situations, and when our schema information is applied to discourse (oral or written), it enables us to make the inferences necessary to comprehend the text—it enables us to read between the lines. If you have an elaborated schema or script for restaurants and you read the sentence *John was hungry. He looked in the yellow pages*, you know that John may be intending to call a restaurant for reservations or to order a pizza—you also know that he is not intending to eat the yellow pages.

Just as there are schemata for concepts that enable us to predict the specifics of content, there are also schemata for types of discourses or texts that enable us to predict the text genre and organization of information within the text. Each type of text has its own organization or macrostructure. When readers know the macrostructure of the text they are reading, they are better able to predict what will come next and comprehend the material (Horowitz, 1985a,b; Meyer, 1987; Scardamelia & Bereiter, 1984; Thorndyke, 1977).

NARRATIVE AND EXPOSITORY VARIATIONS IN TEXT GRAMMARS AND SCHEMA CONTENT

Research has shown that readers make use of story grammar or schema knowledge in the comprehension of narrative texts. Most stories conform to a stereotypical pattern. The reader uses knowledge of this pattern to make comprehension a very rapid and efficient process. It is not clear whether a story grammar is a content schema or a macrostructure text grammar (Mandler, 1982). Most stories follow certain content schemata having to do with events and goal-directed activities of characters. The text grammars specify how to take these events and activities and generate stories. Although the ordering of characters' activities may be modified to produce different stories, there is a strong relationship between the order of the story events and the order in which the events appear in the story text. The story content schemata and story text grammars or macrostructures facilitate students' abilities to recognize the gists or themes of passages. The gist or theme of a text represents the overall coherent topic of the text and its essential points. The macrostructure also facilitates readers' abilities to keep the gist or theme in mind and to use this information to construct text coherence by relating each sentence to preceding and following sentences and to the overall theme or gist. Recent literature on narrative abilities has shown that students with reading disabilities are not as knowledgeable or efficient in using story content schemata and text grammars to tell, retell, or comprehend stories. Students with reading disabilities tell shorter, less complete, less organized stories; comprehend and remember less of stories; and make fewer inferences about stories (Feagans & Short, 1984; Graybeal, 1981; Hensen, 1978; Liles, 1985, 1987; Merritt & Liles, 1987; Roth & Spekman, 1986; Weaver & Dickinson, 1979; Westby, Maggart, & Van Dongen, 1984).

As students advance in school, they are exposed to more and more expository texts (Otto & White, 1982). In early grades, the focus is on narrative texts. Even the material presented in history and science lessons is often presented in a narrative mode. By junior high and high school levels, however, narrative material usually appears only in literature/language arts courses. The information in all other classes is presented in a variety of expository formats. Students experience more difficulty understanding expository passages than they do narrative passages (Dixon, 1979; Hall, Ribovich, & Ramig, 1979; Lapp & Flood, 1978; Spiro & Taylor, 1987). Compared to expository prose, narratives are read faster, are more absorbing, and are easier to comprehend and recall (Freedle & Hale, 1978; Graesser & Goodman, 1985). Minimal research has been done exploring learning disabled students' abilities with expository text. Considering the difficulties they experience with narrative text, however, one would expect similar and likely greater difficulties with comprehension of expository texts.

Expository text usually contains content that is novel to the reader; consequently, the reader cannot readily apply content schema knowledge to aid comprehension (Kieras, 1985; Spiro & Taylor, 1987). Therefore, unlike comprehending narrative text, comprehending expository text is not primarily a matter of matching the content to a previously known pattern but rather involves dealing with the passage content at the level of individual facts. Once readers have processed the individual facts, they may organize them into schemata. Even if a content schema is available to the reader, this schema provides no strong expectations about the text grammar form of the material. For example, there are no textual rules that state in what order one must describe the facts about ant and bee colonies. This relative independence of content facts, content schemata, and text grammars marks a major difference between expository prose and stories. Because the content schema and text grammar are generally not available to the student prior to the first reading of an expository text, processing of expository texts is much more a bottom-up process than the top-down processing used in comprehending narrative texts, where the content schema and text grammar guide the reader's comprehension (Meyer & Rice, 1984). Bottom-up processing puts more of a load on the memory and integrative processes of readers because they must hold facts in memory, organize the facts into content schema, and attempt to search for a text structure that may facilitate their processing of the content schema (Beaugrande, 1984; Britton, Glynn, & Smith, 1985). Comprehending expository texts requires that readers use the individual facts of the text to construct a content schema, a text grammar or macrostructure, and the coherence relations among the sentences of the text.

Although the structure of expository texts is not as predictable as narrative text grammars, expository texts still follow some text grammar rules that govern the placement and order of information within text. A number of expository text grammar structures have been proposed.

Because the function and content of expository texts is so variable, unlike a story grammar, which can fit most content schemata, there must be different expository grammars for different types of texts. Common expository text grammars include structural organizations for comparison-contrast, problem-solution, cause-effect, temporal order, descriptive, and enumerative texts (Horowitz, 1985a, b; Meyer, 1987; Piccolo, 1987; Richgels, McGee, Lomax, & Sheard, 1987). The various expository text patterns are often signaled by headings, subheadings, and specific words (Finley & Seaton, 1987).

Narrative and expository texts differ not only in their text grammars, but also in the types of information in their content schemata. All texts can be analyzed in terms of content or idea units and relationships, which connect the content ideas (Black, 1985; Graesser, 1981; Graesser & Goodman, 1985). Content ideas are usually stated explicitly in the text and include the following:

1. Physical states: Statements that report ongoing states in the physical or social world (e.g., *The forest was cold, The king had three daughters*).
2. Physical events: Statements that report changes in the physical and social worlds (e.g., *The tornado destroyed the town, The monster killed the villagers*).
3. Internal states: Statements that describe the ongoing mental and emotional states of animate beings (e.g., *The big frog was jealous of the new baby frog*).
4. Internal events: Statements that refer to metacognitive or thought processes. (e.g., *The big frog knew he was in trouble, The lost duck forgot how to get home*).
5. Goals: Statements that refer to animate beings' attempts to attain future states and events (e.g., *The big frog wanted to get rid of the baby frog*).
6. Style: Statements that modify an action or a state (e.g., *The angry child screamed* furiously, *The lion crept* slowly *forward* inch by inch).

The following types of relationships can exist between the content ideas (the relationships between the content ideas often are not explicitly stated, but must be inferred):

1. Reason: This refers to the reasons that relate goals (e.g., *The villagers collected weapons to kill the monster.* There is a goal to collect weapons and a goal to kill the monster).
2. Initiate: Goals are created from somewhere. The initiate relationship links states, actions, and events, to goals (e.g., in the book, *One Frog Too Many* (Mayer & Mayer, 1975), the arrival of a baby frog

initiates a state of jealousy in the big frog and the state of jealousy initiates the big frog's attempts to get rid of the little frog).

3. Consequence: States, events, and actions can lead to other states and events by causally driven mechanisms (e.g., the ship's sinking is a consequence of its being hit by a torpedo).

4. Property: Objects and characters have attributes. Property relations are descriptive relations that link statements about how objects or characters look or relate to other objects and characters (e.g., *The jacket was brand new. It was made of real leather*).

5. Support: Support relations link general statement ideas that make assertions (e.g., in the statements, *Spiders are not insects; they have eight legs, whereas insects have only six*).

These content ideas and the relationships among the ideas represent the types of conceptual knowledge that students must possess to comprehend texts. Narrative and expository prose differ in the types of ideas and connections represented, and, consequently, these two types of texts require differing kinds of knowledge on the part of readers. Narrative texts unfold primarily in terms of goals and the reasons for these goals, whereas expository texts have more physical state ideas linked by consequences, property, and support relationships (Black, 1985; Graesser & Goodman, 1985). In order to understand texts, one must understand the content ideas and relationships among the content ideas that underlie the text. For narrative texts one must understand human motivations and goal-seeking behavior. For expository texts one must comprehend a variety of logical relationships (Black, 1985; Bruce & Newman, 1978; Voss & Bisanz, 1985).

METACOGNITIVE PROCESSING IN TEXT COMPREHENSION

Brown (1982) maintained that metacognitive abilities are essential for comprehending texts in order to read to learn. There are two aspects to metacognition. One aspect involves regulation of cognition, which involves planning and control of action. A second aspect involves knowledge about cognition and involves conscious access to one's own cognitive operations and reflection about those of others (Brown, 1987). Both types of metacognition are critical for reading comprehension.

Let us first consider how the use of cognition to plan and control actions is related to reading comprehension. Not all the information necessary to comprehend texts is available in scripts and schemata. Our ability to comprehend the theme of a story requires that we be able to figure out a character's plans and goals (Black & Bower, 1980; Bruce & Newman, 1978; Schank & Abelson, 1977; Voss & Bisanz, 1985). Bruce

(1980) maintained that perception of plans plays a major role in the way we structure our social reality. The research on plans and social actions in a number of fields has concluded that (1) understanding plans is a critical part of understanding actions, (2) the ability to understand plans is a very complex inferential task, and (3) children require many years to develop these skills (Miller, Galanter, & Primban, 1960; Piaget, 1932; Schmidt, 1976; Sedlack, 1974). In discussing the work of Sacerdoti (1975), Bruce noted that in order to interpret actions as being intentional, one needs the *ability to plan* (italics are Bruce's) and to recognize actions of others in terms of goals. He states that persons who have difficulty in recognizing plans and social actions in others will have difficulty comprehending texts that report such plans.

Many students with reading disabilities exhibit deficits in metacognitive abilities involving planning of their own behavior and in metacognitive awareness that planning is something that they or someone else might do (Baker, 1982; Hallahan, Kneedler & Lloyd, 1983; Wong & Wong, 1986). If students lack such metacognitive abilities, then they will likely not recognize planning on the parts of characters in texts, nor will they attempt to use metacognitive strategies to monitor their own comprehension of the text.

Reading to learn requires comprehension, and any attempt to comprehend must involve comprehension monitoring—a metacognitive behavior. Brown (1980) proposed the following metacognitive behaviors as essential for reading comprehension:

1. understanding the purpose of the reading assignment (e.g., for enjoyment, to be able to explain a principle, to compare one story to another, to complete a worksheet)
2. identifying the important aspects and main ideas of a message
3. focusing attention on major content rather than trivia
4. monitoring to determine if comprehension is occurring
5. engaging in self-questioning to determine if one's goals in reading are being achieved
6. taking corrective action when comprehension fails.

If students are using these strategies, then they will actively use information from content and text grammar schemata to facilitate comprehension by making predictions about what is to come in a text and by monitoring their comprehension to determine if their predictions are met (Meyer, 1987). For example, if you are reading a murder mystery, you are alert to clues that will lead you to discover the identity of the murderer. In expository text that begins with a topic sentence, you read to find information that supports the statement. You look for organizing words that signal sequence (*first, next, eventually*), cause-effect (*because, since, as a result of*), comparison-contrast (*similar to, however, although*), analysis (*characteristics, types, some features*), etc. (Finley & Seaton, 1987). If readers are unfamiliar with the structure of a text, they experience difficulty in determining what is and what is not important and the interrelationships among the information presented. Consequently, comprehension of the passage is limited.

The selection, maintenance, or changing of schemata during text comprehension requires monitoring (Pearson & Spiro, 1980). When we listen or read, we are matching the present information to our schema knowledge and attempting to determine if we have a schema for what is being presented. As new information arrives, one must determine if it fits the selected schema or if another schema is needed. For example, a group of students were reading a story in which the main character, Jim, suggested that rustlers were responsible for the rocks rolling down the mountains. If the students retrieved their schemata for rustlers, they should then expect some mention of cattle and perhaps a sheriff to appear as the story continued. If this is not forthcoming, then they must assume that they have selected the wrong schema and must look for other information to instantiate a different schema.

ASSESSING LANGUAGE AND COGNITIVE SKILLS FOR TEXT COMPREHENSION

The discussion in the first section of this chapter has summarized the language and cognitive skills that are essential for reading to learn—for comprehending text. They include a literate style of language, schema knowledge (including content schemata and text grammar schemata), and metacognitive processing. This section will address assessment of each of those aspects of language and cognition essential for text comprehension. Because little information is currently available on the development of comprehension of expository text, the focus will be on the assessment of the development of schema content and text grammar knowledge for narrative texts. The metacognitive strategies discussed are generally applicable to monitoring of both narrative and expository texts.

ASSESSING LITERATE LANGUAGE STYLE

Literate language style involves more explicit language and more complex syntactic sentence structures than oral conversational speech. Although there is no specific linguistic analysis system designed to identify a literate language style as opposed to an oral style, there are some systems that capture components of a literate style. In addition, there are some specific aspects of language associated with literate style that can be noted in a language sample.

Hunt's T-unit analysis has been a popular linguistic analysis system to code increasing syntactic development during the school years (Hunt, 1965). A *T-unit* is defined as a main clause plus any subordinate clauses or nonclausal structure that is attached to it. Subordinate clause structure is associated with a literate language style and has been shown to increase with a culture's exposure to literacy (Kalmar, 1985). T-unit length increases through adolescence largely as a result of increasing use of subordinate clauses.

Crystal's grammatical analysis system (LARSP) for language samples captures some of the aspects of literate language style (Crystal, 1979). This system is generally used with younger students, but it does code structures associated with a more literate style. The LARSP codes elaborations of noun phrases, coordinating conjunctions (*and, but, or, for*), subordinating conjunctions (*because, when, while, since, although*), relatives (*who, that, which*), adverbial conjuncts (which have a connective function such as *then, so, now, however, if-then, next, secondly, for a start, yet, lastly*), and adverbial disjuncts (which have a stylistic or attitudinal function such as *of course, really, probably, actually, practically, certainly*).

Pellegrini (1985) reported four aspects of children's language during play that were related to literate language style. These included temporal and causal conjunctions, elaboration of noun phrases, endophoric reference (i.e., linguistic ties between elements in the discourse, as opposed to exophoric ties, which link linguistic elements to items in the context), and verbs referring to mental processes and future events. A T-unit analysis accompanied by noting the following aspects of language occurring in each T-unit provides some sense of the degree to which a student is using a literate language style:

1. Conjunctions: *And then* and *and then* are not included in the tally because it cannot be determined if they are being used in their logical sense or only to keep the conversation going. Literate conjunctions coded include, but are not limited to *when, since, before, after, while, because, so, as a result, if, until, but, therefore, however,* and *although*.

2. Elaboration of noun phrases:

Modifiers: Note the words in the noun phrase immediately preceding the head noun (e.g., *The two, expensive, big, white* cockatoos).

Qualifiers: Note the words that follow the noun (e.g., The big white cockatoos *in the pet store window*).

3. Mental/linguistic verbs: These are verbs that denote cognitive and linguistic processes (e.g., *think, say, know, promise, forget, report*). Verb tenses other than present and present progressive.

4. Adverbs: Adverbs often code aspects of tone, attitude, and manner that in oral language would be coded through stress and intonation. Cook-Gumperz and Gumperz (1981) noted that adverbs provide information as to the necessary tone of voice to use when reading (*angrily, hotly, ominously*) and that children will recycle passages in which their previous reading intonation did not agree with the adverb.

ASSESSING KNOWLEDGE OF NARRATIVE CONTENT SCHEMATA AND TEXT GRAMMAR SCHEMATA

Two general questions need to be asked with respect to students' schema knowledge in relation to reading. First, do the students have the necessary schemata and can they retrieve the relevant schema information in response to visual and language cues so they can recognize or interpret the situation or comprehend the text or discourse? Second, can the students retrieve and organize schema information to initiate and carry out a task when little or no contextualized information is provided? In a sense these two questions represent aspects of receptive and expressive schema knowledge and use.

One can evaluate students' schema for a particular situation or concept and for a particular text genre. Evaluation of a students' narrative schema crosses both knowledge of world events and situations and knowledge of the structure of stories. As children develop, they acquire increasing understanding of their physical and social world. This knowledge is first coded in narrative texts and later in exposition and other genres. As their knowledge and understanding of the world increase and change, the structure of their narrative texts changes to reflect the changing construct of their thought. Children first read to learn through narrative, and research suggests that children learn more readily through narrative than through expository text (Freedle & Hale, 1979).

Traditionally, there have been two approaches to the assessment of children's narrative schema knowledge: (1) comprehension-based measures (e.g., asking questions about settings, characters, events) and (2) productive measures that require students to generate a story. Comprehension-based measures tend to tap students' schema understanding, while productive measures tend to tap students' ability to use schema knowledge to produce a text. In the literature, all productive measures have tended to be grouped together, whether the student is retelling a story, developing an original story with no stimulus provided, or describing the story in a wordless picture book. These do not, however, place the same demands on the storyteller. Telling a story from a wordless picture book requires only that a student recognize the story content schema. It does not require that the student generate story content schema and organize it into a text grammar structure. The pictures in the book lay out the story, and if students do little more than describe the pictures, their "story" contains the story grammar elements. For this reason, stories students tell when they are provided with highly structured stimuli (wordless picture books or films) are more similar to the comprehension-based measures because they focus on students' understanding or comprehension of content schema, but not on students' abilities to use story grammars. In this chapter, the narrative assessment section has been divided into (1) assessment of recognition/comprehension of narrative content schemata and (2) assessment of ability to organize content schema and text grammar in stories.

What conceptual knowledge is needed for a student's understanding and production of narratives? A narrative relates a time-ordered sequence of events that are interrelated in some way. The speaker/listener must, therefore, have an understanding of temporal relationships and two types of cause-effect relationships: physical and psychological. Physical cause-effect relationships obey the laws of the physical world (e.g., heavy rains cause floods or a dropped glass breaks). Psychological cause-effect relationships are the result of motivations or intentions of characters within the narrative. Behavior that is motivated or intentional is planned behavior. Understanding of planning or intentional behavior is essential for understanding story narratives because stories relate characters' plans to reach goals (Bruce, 1980; Wilensky, 1978). Recognition of the plans of characters in narratives requires (1) knowledge that people plan, (2) perspective taking (knowing what others are seeing), (3) person perception (knowing traits or attributes of others), and (4) role taking (knowing intentions, thoughts, and feelings of others).

Narratives also require that the story producer and receiver deal conjunctively with what happened in the action of the story and what the protagonists were thinking or saying. Preschool children begin to deal conjunctively with action and thought in play scripts when they alternate between describing the ongoing action and attitudes of characters in the play, taking on the roles of characters in the actual play activity, and acting as a stage manager (Wolf, 1986). The distinction between what is intended and what is actually done is a difficult one for young children, particularly when there is a disjunction between what is said and what is done (Bruner, 1985). Trickery tales—that is, tales of deceit—involve a disjunction between action and intention. Abrams and Sutton-Smith (1977) reported that children become fully able to comprehend trickster tales between 8 to 10 years of age. Appreciation of many television cartoons, such as the Roadrunner and the Pink Panther, is dependent on children's understanding of trickery. In addition to knowledge of temporal and cause-effect relationships, planning, and role taking, comprehension of trickster tales requires that the child (1) realize that deception can exist, (2) recognize that messages can be intentionally false and that the intention is more important than the content or consequence of the message, and (3) be able to detect deceit by noting visual and vocal cues that suggest that the speaker's words are not truthful and that the speaker is attempting to mask his or her true intentions (DePaulo & Jordan, 1982).

Table 7-1 presents aspects of the development of physical and social schema knowledge about the world in the left column and the development of the related narrative text grammars or structural schemata in the right column.

ASSESSING RECOGNITION/COMPREHENSION OF NARRATIVE CONTENT SCHEMATA

Assessing schema recognition involves evaluation of students' understanding of the information listed in the left-hand column of Table 7-1. A relatively quick way to evaluate students' ability to recognize and comprehend schema knowledge is to have the children tell stories from wordless picture books. Many of the wordless books by Mercer Mayer (such as *One Frog Too Many, Frog Goes to Dinner,* and *A Boy, A Dog, A Frog, and A Friend*) are especially useful for this purpose. Each story has several characters. The characters encounter a number of situations that trigger feelings that in turn trigger planned actions of the characters. The artist vividly depicts the characters' emotional experiences. To understand the stories, students must recognize what the characters are doing on each page. They must realize the relationships between activities on any two adjacent pages, as well as the relationships among all the actions in the book. They must understand temporal sequence and physical and psychological cause-effect relationships and plans and reactions of characters.

Evaluation of children's schema knowledge using wordless picture books can be done in two ways. In one method, the children are given the picture book and permitted to look through it and then told to tell the story that happened in the book as they go through the book page by page. The evaluator sits across from the child so that he or she cannot see the book and tells the child, "I can't see the book so make sure to tell the story so that I will understand it. Make it the kind of story we would read in a book." In a second method the clinician asks

TABLE 7–1.
Progression of Narrative Development

Shema Content	Text Grammar Structure
Preschool	
Ability to label.	Isolated description: labels or describes objects, characters, surrounding, and ongoing actions; no interrelationships among the elements mentioned.
Awareness of animate/inanimate distinction, that is, that animate beings act and inanimate objects are acted upon.	Action sequence: a list of actions that are not causally related, but which may be chronologically ordered based on perception; no interrelationships among the characters—characters act independently of each other; centering may be present—story may have a central character or a central theme (actions that each character does).
Awareness of physical cause-effect relationships; beginning of awareness of linear time for familiar sequences.	Reaction sequence: beginning of chaining—a set of actions or events that automatically cause other changes, but with no planning involved (e.g., a rock rolled down the mountain and the people ran).
Early Elementary School	
Awareness of psychological causality for primary emotions (happy, mad, sad, scared, surprised, disgusted); that is, awareness of situations that cause these emotions and what one might do because of these emotions, (e.g., brother takes toy → anger → hit brother); theory of mind (awareness that people think and feel, which allows for some perspective taking; ability to conceptualize near future; scriptal knowledge of common characters (e.g., wolves are bad and eat pigs; princes are good and save princesses from dragons).	Abbreviated episode: Both centering and chaining present; character(s) engage in cause-effect actions; story describes goals or intentions of characters, but planning must be inferred; story will have at least the components of initiating event, response, and consequence.

Further development of psychological causality (secondary or cognitive emotions; e.g., jealousy, guilt, shame, embarrassment); further perspective taking—awareness of interaction of character attributes with story elements of setting and events that enables child to comprehend/predict novel behaviors of characters; understanding of longer time frames (days, weeks); meta-awareness of the need to plan and how to plan; understanding of the need to justify plans.	Complete episode: Both centering and chaining present; describes the goals and intentions of the characters with some evidence of planning; story has at least an initiating event (problem), internal response (character's reaction to problem), plan, attempt (carrying out of plan), and consequence.
Late Elementary School Ability to perceive character change/growth (i.e., understand that character attributes change over course of story as result of events); ability to detect deception or trickery and to deceive or trick; awareness of time cycles (seasons, years); beginning awareness of multiple meaning for words and literal versus figurative meanings.	Elaborated stories: Stories may be elaborated in three ways: 1. Complex episode: A single episode story that may involve multiple plans, attempts, or consequences. 2. Interactive episodes: Story is told from the point of view of more than one character—results in parallel episodes. 3. Multiple episodes: The story has more than one "chapter," with each chapter having the story grammar elements of initiating event, response, plans, attempts, and consequences; in early stages, episodes are sequential, but in later development one episode may be embedded within another episode.
Adolescent/Adult Ability to engage in meta-narrative discussion; i.e. discussion of narrative structure and interpretation of characterization, themes, and plots; understanding of abstractions of time and space; ability to understand flashbacks; ability to understand allegories.	Metaphoric stories: The usual structure of stories may be intentionally modified in novel ways for humorous or metaphoric purposes.

questions that focus on a variety of schema relationships using guidelines for questions proposed by Tough (1981). This method is useful for younger children, for hesitant or shy children, and for children who have difficulty organizing extended verbal responses. The questions fall into four categories:

1. Reporting: What was the boy doing here? What happened here? Tell me about this picture.
2. Projecting: What is the boy saying to the big frog? What is the frog thinking? How does the boy feel?
3. Reasoning: Why is the frog thinking that? Why does the boy feel angry? Why did the big frog bite the little frog? Why did the tree fall down?
4. Predicting: What will happen next? What will the big frog do now?

The following stories exemplify students' differing schema recognition/comprehension abilities. The first story was told by a fourth-grade boy with high-average reading ability:

> Jerry Bert smiled when he found out that he had a new present. He looked at the tag and then he said, "Look, my name's on this. I'll open it up. Oh my gosh, another frog." [The other] the other frog, named Sandy, frowned. [um,] Then what was his name, what was the boy's name? [Examiner: Jerry]. Jerry lifted the baby frog out the box. His dog, his pet dog, Patty, looked at it. The other frog, Sandy, was very mad. He didn't want another frog in his life. Jerry Bert said, [um um,] "Sandy, meet my new frog. His name is Bert." Then all of a sudden, Sandy bit onto Bert's leg. Bert started crying and then, [um,] I keep forgetting, Jerry saved the little frog. He told Sandy not to ever do that again. And so they went for a little hike. They pretended they were all pirates and all part of a team. So they went down to a lake. Sandy frowned as she sat onto the turtle's back. [And] and Bert smiled. Sandy kicked Bert off. Bert started crying. Then Jerry said, "Sandy don't you dare do that again." Sandy was ashamed of herself. She didn't get to ride on the boat. They all got on the boat and went for a ride. Kerplunk. Sandy jumped onto the boat. Bert was a little scared when he saw this. Nobody else noticed. All of a sudden, Sandy kicked Bert off. Bert screamed as he flew off of the boat. The turtle looked at Sandy as he was very mad. Suddenly, [um] suddenly the turtle told Jerry. Jerry was mad. And then Jerry was surprised. He looked at Sandy and he was very very sad. So they went off looking for him. They couldn't find him anywhere, so they decided to go home. Everybody was mad at Sandy. Sandy was ashamed of herself. Jerry went home and he was very sad. He lied down on his bed and started crying. All of a sudden he heard something going "whee" in the sky. He saw something coming. It was flying toward him out of the window. It came right in and landed right on Sandy's head. Then they became friends.

Even without seeing the book, this story provides sufficient information for the listener to determine the theme and major activities of the characters. The student infers that a box with a ribbon and a tag is a present, identifies the expression on the character's faces, gives reasons for feelings, and infers the consequences of feelings. In so doing, the student is exhibiting the ability to project into the roles of the characters.

Students with a less developed schema knowledge will tell the story as a series of actions. They may realize that the book is presenting a story about several characters, but they appear unaware of the interrelationships of activities from one page to the next, and they do not recognize goal-directed behavior of the characters. Their stories consist of descriptions of the drawings, but with minimal interpretation. The following is part of the story told by a second-grade boy with an attention deficit disorder and language delay:

> The boy has a present and he's opening it. And he's looking at the tag. And the dog's sitting down and the frog's sitting down. And now after he opens it, [he] he has something. [And the and the] and the frog has a frown because he thinks it doesn't look good, and the turtle is sad because he can't see it. And the dog is happy. And the frog is happy, and the boy is happy. And now the boy had a bad face. A bad face on his face cause the big frog is biting the little frog's leg. And the turtle's sad and the dog is sad. And the turtle is taking both frogs walking. And now the turtle is taking both frogs and the big frog kicks the little frog off. And now the big frog is all alone in the forest. And someone got buried. I wonder who it was. The big frog maybe. And now they're in the water and the big one is jumping on that. The turtle is sleeping and the dog is sleeping. . . .

Although the child has labeled the expressions on the characters faces, he exhibits no awareness of the bases for the emotions.

Another approach to evaluating students' schema comprehension ability is to probe students' understanding as they read or listen to a story. At selected points in a story, questions can be asked that focus on concepts underlying the narrative, such as ''how does ______(character's name) feel?'' ''Why does he feel that way?'' ''What can ______(character's name) do? ''(to assess awareness of planning) ''What is the problem in the story?'' ''How was the problem solved?''

This approach was used to study the narrative comprehension of three groups of elementary school students, grades three through five (matched for grade, age, and sex) who differed in reading ability (Westby, Maggart, & Van Dongen, 1984). There were 12 children in each group—a group of average readers who were reading at grade level and were placed in the middle reading groups in their classrooms, and two groups of low readers, one in public school and one attending the university reading clinic. Both low reading groups were reading a year and a half below grade level, were placed in the lowest reading groups in their classrooms, were currently receiving no special-education services, and had not been identified as having any specific oral-language deficits on traditional assessment. The students attending the reading clinic were initially referred by their parents, who were not satisfied with their children's reading abilities and the lack of attention given to their reading delays in the public-school program.

The students in the three groups read stories on a variety of themes (a flood, a lost horse, a robbery, a diseased forest). The children were able to read the stories with at least 95 percent word accuracy. When they completed each story, they were asked how the main character felt about the problem or what went wrong in the story. Of the average readers' responses to the feelings questions, 87 percent were correct, whereas only 48 percent of the low and 39 percent of the clinic groups' responses were correct. Many of the children in the two low reading groups refused to answer because the story did not explicitly tell them how the characters felt, or they reported what their own feelings might be in a particular situation, regardless of the information about the character. This suggests that the low and clinic readers were less competent in perspective taking. If they were unable to recognize the character's feelings or emotional responses to the events in the stories, then it is likely that they also might not understand how and why the characters dealt wth the events.

Assessing Ability to Organize Narrative Schema Content and Text Grammars

If students are unable to tell a story from a wordless picture book or respond appropriately to questions asked about story content schemata, they will not be able to produce a coherent story themselves when no stimuli or stimuli with limited structure are provided (e.g., a single picture). Many students, however, are able to recognize the schematic information presented in wordless picture books and print and can comprehend questions asked about stories they have listened to or read, but are unable to retrieve and organize schematic knowledge when there is minimal environmental support. Ability to generate organized schematic knowledge can be assessed by having students tell stories when minimal contextual cues are available. Students can be asked to tell stories about poster pictures or can be given small figures and asked to make up a story about them. They can be asked to tell a story of a personal experience or to make up an imaginary story without any visual or toy supports. Producing stories of this type requires not only that the students have content schema knowledge of their physical and social world, but that they also have text grammar schema knowledge for the structure of narratives.

A number of story grammar analysis systems are available. Many of these systems are, like any linguistic analysis of a language sample, time-consuming in comparison to standardized tests. A more holistic approach is more practical for clinical purposes when large numbers of students must be assessed. Applebee (1978), Botvin and Sutton-Smith (1977), and Glenn and Stein (1980) have proposed hierarchies of story structures that are logically ordered from the least to the most complex. In the Glenn and Stein hierarchy, each structure includes all of the categories, functions, and relationships between categories found in the previous structures plus at least one additional one. Westby and her colleagues (1984, 1986) modified the Glenn and Stein system by including the information from Applebee and Botvin/Sutton-Smith. This modified structural hierarchy is presented in the right-hand column of Table 7-1. Analysis of narrative level can be done quickly by following the binary decision tree in Figure 7-1 (modified from Stein & Policastro, 1984). To use this binary decision tree, read through a child's story, then ask the following questions:

1. "Does the story have a temporally related sequence of events?" If it does not, then the story is an isolated description.

2. If the story does have a temporally related sequence of events, then ask, "Does the story have a causally related sequence of events?" If it has a temporally related sequence of events but does not have a causally related sequence of events, then the story is an action sequence.

3. If the story does have a causally related sequence of events, then ask, "Does the story imply goal-directed behavior?" If the story has a causally related sequence of events but does not imply goal-directed behavior, then the story is a reactive sequence.

4. If the story does imply goal-directed behavior then ask, "Is planning or intentional behavior made explicit?" If the story implies goal-directed behavior but does not make the planning of this behavior explicit, then the story is an abbreviated episode.

5. If the story does make the planning or intentional behavior explicit, then ask, "Is the story elaborated by having multiple attempts

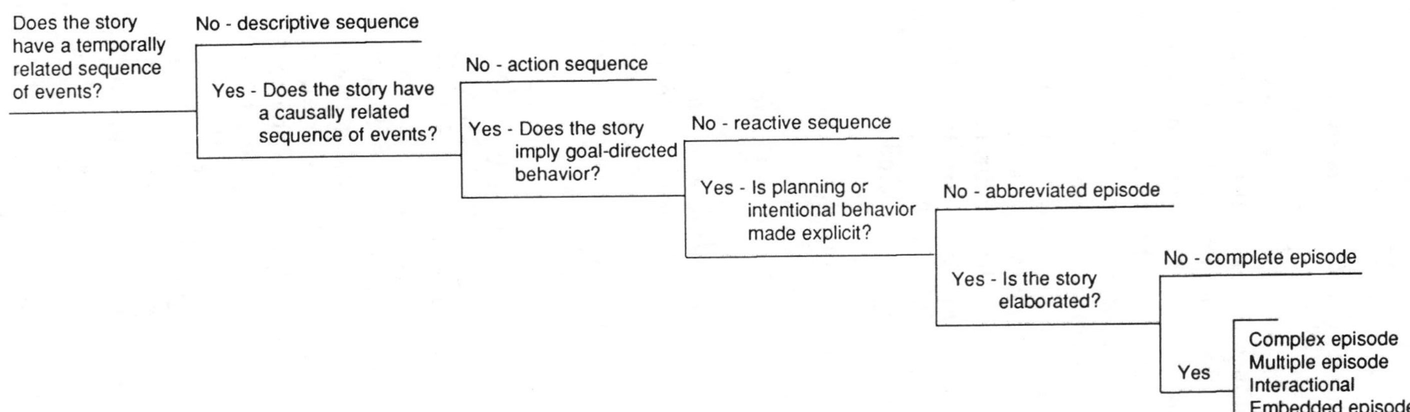

FIGURE 7-1. Story structure decision tree.

or consequences, multiple sequential episodes, or embedded episodes, or is the story told from the point of view of more than one of the characters?'' If the story does make intentional behavior explicit but is not elaborated, then the story is a complete episode.

6. If the story is elaborated, how is it elaborated? Is one aspect of the story elaborated? For example, is there an obstacle in the attempt path and multiple attempts? Does the story have multiple episodes—are they sequential or embedded? Is the story told from the perspective of more than one character?

This system has been used to analyze the narratives produced by the three groups of elementary school students differing in reading ability who were mentioned earlier in the comprehension section. The three reading groups were significantly different in the complexity of the stories they told in response to two poster pictures. Of the narratives told by the low readers in the reading clinic group, 62 percent were at the descriptive level and only 8 percent were elaborate structure narratives. Fifty-four percent of the average reading group's stories were elaborated structure narratives, and none of their narratives were of the descriptive type. The low reading school group exhibited a range of narrative structures, with the majority of their narratives (73 percent) falling in the middle range of narrative structures (action sequence, reactive sequence, abbreviated episode, complete episode); 16 percent of the low reading group's narratives were descriptions and 8 percent were elaborated structure narratives. Clearly, the low reading school group and the reading-clinic group students did not produce stories that were structurally as complex as the stories produced by the average readers. In their oral stories they made little or no reference to the intentions, plans, or goals of characters.

ASSESSING METACOGNITION

As mentioned earlier in this chapter, there are two aspects of metacognition. One aspect—regulation of cognition—involves planning and control of action. A second aspect—knowledge about cognition—involves conscious access to one's own cognitive operations and reflection about those of others (Brown, 1987). Both types of metacognition should be assessed. If students are to recognize intentional behavior of characters in stories, they must be able to plan their own behavior (Bruce, 1980). As students read, they must monitor their comprehension and know what actions to take to facilitate comprehension when comprehension fails (Brown, 1982).

In order to assess metacognitive abilities, one needs an understanding of their development. Metacognitive processes used to regulate behavior develop early. Luria (1961), one of the first to study the development of self-regulatory language, noted that children between 2½ to 4 years can use their own speech to initiate immediately following actions, but not to inhibit actions; by 4½ years, children can use their own speech both to initiate and inhibit their actions. Meacham (1979) also explored the development of preschool children's use of language to guide motor activity. In a first stage, the children may accompany their motor activity with overt verbal activity, but the two activities are independent. In the second stage, children engage in verbal activity to describe the outcome of their motor activities. Language does not, however, fulfill a guiding role, either to initiate or direct motor activity, or to facilitate the remembering of anticipated goals. Consequently, there is no evaluation of the outcome of motor activity. Language follows the activity and restates the events of the activity. In the third stage, language still follows the activity, but it is used to describe the anticipated goals of motor activities rather than the actual outcome. By describing anticipated goals the child is better able to remember them, and so it becomes possible to compare the remembered thought with the actual outcome and, hence, to evaluate the outcome. In the fourth stage, language precedes activity and plays a major role in planning and guiding the course of the child's motor activities. Until children use language to plan and control their behavior, they will not develop awareness of cognitive processes.

In order to develop conscious awareness of mental processes and metacognitive strategies, children must develop a theory of mind as separate and distinct from the body. The exact time of emergence of this awareness is controversial. Bretherton and Beegly (1982) suggested that it begins in infancy. Many others dispute this. Literature is available that indicates children are developing this awareness between ages three and seven. Wellman (1985) identified five different but overlapping sets of knowledge that form a person's metacognitive awareness.

1. Existence: The person must know that thoughts and internal mental states exist and that they are not the same as external acts or events.
2. Distinct processes: There are a variety of mental acts (e.g., remembering, forgetting, guessing, knowing, and daydreaming).
3. Integration: While there are distinctions among different mental acts, all mental processes are similar and related. For example, one can't remember or forget unless one first knew something. One can hope to remember, but think that one will not.

4. Variables: Any mental performance is influenced by a number of other factors or variables. For example, how much one comprehends depends on how familiar or novel the text is, the organization of the text, and the strategies used to comprehend the text.

5. Cognitive monitoring: The ability to read one's own mental states, or monitor their ongoing cognitive processes. Even young children often know when they understand and when they do not, or when they are fantasizing, dreaming, or imagining.

With this metacognitive awareness, children begin to be able to talk about their planning behavior. Pea (1982) interviewed children, ages 7 to 13 years to discover what they know about metacognition or planning of behavior. All the children knew that planning involves thinking about the future, and they knew when to plan, when not to plan, and why one must plan. The students reported that one must plan in order to do something and one must plan how to do something. They also stated that one must plan the specific conditions for doing something. They reported that one did not need to plan something you were just about to do, you don't plan if others plan it for you, and you don't plan if you already know what to do. One must plan because you have many actions to accomplish or because the activity won't work out if you don't plan. As indicated earlier, understanding of planning is essential in understanding the purpose or goal behind written text. If students do not plan for themselves, it is unlikely that they could interpret planning behavior of authors or characters in stories.

By early adolescence, students become conscious of the strategies they use to comprehend and remember information (Baker & Brown, 1984; Forrest-Pressley & Waller, 1984). They are aware of their own skills and of the ways the nature of the material to be learned (visual, linguistic, etc.), the task criteria (recognition, recall, problem solving), and the learning activities (attention, rehearsal, elaboration) will affect the strategies needed and their performance (Wong, 1985). This level of metacognitive processing is essential for comprehension of expository texts (Meyer, 1987). Comprehension of expository texts requires students to evaluate what knowledge they have about the topic and to use a variety of strategies (rereading, outlining, underlining) to comprehend and remember the material.

Assessing Regulation of Cognition

This can be evaluated in two general ways. First, one can determine if children give evidence of planning in their own behavior. One can observe a child's play and interview parents and teachers to determine if the child plans. A second approach is to present children with hypothetical problem situations requiring planning for the solutions.

Garvey (1982) maintained that symbolic role play is possible only when children conceive and plan an outcome and subsequently work toward that end (e.g., building a spaceship to travel to a distant planet where they will attack the snow monster). This outcome takes precedence over immediate sensory input, and it is the plan that guides children's response to the materials. Peers are able to join in pretend play only if they are able to recognize the others' pretend orientation and their particular plan. Sachs, Goldman, and Chaille (1984) noted that the amount of speech devoted to planning and organizing play is positively related to the content and complexity of children's narrative language. Pellegrini (1985) also reported that children with good symbolic play skills used a literate style of language and were consciously planning and organizing their fantasy play.

Observation of children's play enables us to observe planning in action. Westby (1980, 1988) developed a symbolic play scale that can be used to evaluate students' schema knowledge of their world and their manner of planning the use of this knowledge. Symbolic pretend play has a number of components. It involves (1) increasing decontextualization or decreasing reliance on concrete props and increasing reliance on verbal coding; (2) moving from representation of highly familiar themes to unfamiliar, novel themes; (3) increasing organization and preplanning of the play; and (4) increasing ability to engage in role taking. The organization category represents children's increasing ability to control and plan their behavior. The following sequence in development of organization and planning is noted:

- 17 to 19 months: The child moves quickly from one instance of pretending to another and engages in short, isolated play schemata. The child may pretend to sleep, then abruptly pretend to eat, with no links between events or elaboration of any of these schemata. Children do not announce what they are about to do nor comment on what they are doing or have done.
- 19 months to 2 years: Children begin to combine objects in play; they show awareness of things that go together and will look for them. For example, a child sees a plate and then looks for a spoon to use with the plate.
- 2 years to 3 years: Children elaborate familiar schemata. For example, the 2 1/2-year-old who is taking care of her baby will gather many of the items she needs. She will set the table with dishes, spoons, cups, and glasses and pull a highchair up to the table.

• 3 years to 4 years: Children produce an evolving sequence of events. At this point children will announce completed actions and actions that are to follow immediately. Now not only do they eat, but they first prepare the food, put it on the table, sit down and eat, clear the table, save the leftovers, wash the dishes, and then sit down to watch TV. The children do not plan these events ahead of time, but as they complete one aspect of the schema they automatically move into the next aspect.

• 4 years: Children plan their play in advance, and the planning phase may take as long or longer than the actual pretend play. They announce what they are going to play.

• 5 years: Children not only plan their own behavior, but they also plan and monitor the behavior of others. In play they assign roles to other children, list what the children are to do, and during the play periodically monitor what the other children are doing.

Although normally developing children from mainstream environments have well-developed symbolic play by age five to six years, older learning disabled students exhibit deficits in many aspects of symbolic representation that develop during the preschool years. My colleagues and I have used play evaluations with children from infancy through middle school (grades six to eight). Of the four aspects of symbolic play development, students with learning disabilities usually exhibited their greatest deficits in the area of organization. Many middle school students with learning disabilities do not exhibit the sequential organization of play that is present in normal three-year-olds' play. Currently we are analyzing narrative, play, and reading-comprehension data of fourth grade boys, 20 having high average reading ability and 20 having low average reading ability. The high average readers had stanine scores of 6–7 on the California Test of Basic Skills, and the low average readers had stanine scores of 3–4 on the same test. Preliminary results indicate that the poorer readers spend more time in simply manipulating the toys, while good readers work together and organize their play into thematic units. The poorer readers more frequently turned on the battery-operated toys and watched them shoot across the room and crash into the opposite wall. The better readers were more likely to announce that they were having races, imagine drivers in their cars, and evaluate why some of the vehicles traveled faster than others.

The age of the students should be considered when selecting the materials used in play evaluations with school-age students. For older students collections of various building sets (Legos, Construx), battery-operated vehicles (Stomper trucks, all-terrain vehicles), transformers, Mattel car sets (village, ore mine, service station), and Fisher-Price action sets are usually appropriate. Elementary school children may also enjoy these materials, but many students have not developed the ability to represent less familiar schemata or to decontextualize and use less realistic props. Consequently, play evaluation for elementary school children should include more realistic props and familiar materials such as household, store, and doctor materials.

One can also investigate students' planning abilities by presenting them with hypothetical problems. Goldman (1982) asked students to tell stories about how they might achieve goals such as getting out of doing chores, making friends, or wanting a dog and getting one. After the students responded to a task, such as telling a story about wanting a dog and getting one, they were asked to tell a story about wanting a dog but not being able to get one. They were asked what could stop them from getting a dog, or what could go wrong so they couldn't get one even though they wanted one. Following this response the students were asked "If that happened [child's obstacle], how could you still get a dog? How could you make that story into a story where you did get a dog?" (p. 283). Finally, they were asked if anything like this ever happened to them. Westby (1983) reported that many students with learning disabilities have marked difficulty with this task. Students who are successful with this task generally have dogs, and those who are unsuccessful do not have dogs. This result suggests that the task is ecologically valid; that is, that it is tapping a planning ability that students are using or not using in their lives.

Spivack, Platt, and Shure (1976) used somewhat similar procedures to explore the planning abilities of well-adjusted and poorly adjusted children who were identified as being impulsive, inhibited, or aggressive. They reported that well-adjusted four- and five-year-old children were able to give more alternative solutions to personal problems and could give more causes and consequences for the problems than poorly adjusted children. In elementary school, well-adjusted children were able to fill in the middle of problem-solving stories by giving multiple sequential steps to the solution and suggesting obstacles that might arise and ways around the obstacles. Well-adjusted adolescents were able to consider the thought processes of others in solving interpersonal problems. The Spivack, Platt, and Shure tasks can be useful in assessing interpersonal problem-solving skills and planning that underlie narratives.

For four and five-year-old students, they suggested presenting the child with the following type of problem: "Jimmy has been playing with the truck all morning and now George wants to play with it. What can George do or say to make sure he gets to play with the truck?"

Or "Michael just broke his mom's favorite vase. What can he do or say to keep his mom from getting mad?"

At the elementary school level the student is given the beginning and end of a story and asked to complete it. For example:

> Al (Joyce) moved into the neighborhood. He (she) didn't know anyone and felt very lonely. The story ends with Al (Joyce) having many good friends and feeling at home in the neighborhood. What happens in between Al's (Joyce's) moving in and feeling lonely, and when he (she) ends up with many friends? (p. 65).

The examiner evaluates the story in terms of the number of solutions generated, obstacles to various plans that are presented, and ways around these obstacles. Westby (1983) used this task with middle school learning disabled students and reported that many of them had no idea how the child could make friends.

At the adolescent level, the student is given the following type of task:

> Bill loves to go hunting, but he is not allowed to go hunting by himself. One weekend his parents go on a trip and he remains at home by himself. He has a new shotgun he received recently and a box of shells. He looks out of the window at the nearby woods and is tempted to go out hunting (p. 95).

The student is asked to tell everything that goes on in Bill's mind and then tell what happened. Westby reported that adolescents with learning disabilities seldom deal with the conflict between what Bill wanted to do and the restrictions given by the parents. Instead, they assumed that the boy would go hunting and then they discussed problems of not finding any birds to shoot or figuring out how to hide all the dead birds.

Story comprehension can also be used to assess a student's understanding of planning. An example of how understanding of planning behavior is related to story comprehension can be shown with the story *Harry and Shellbert* (Van Woerkman, 1977). The story begins with Harry, a hare, and Shellbert, a tortoise, having lunch. Shellbert relates the original story of the race between the tortoise and the hare. When Harry hears the outcome of the race, he becomes very angry and Shellbert challenges him to a race. Overconfident, Harry lies down to take a nap, placing a stick in the path with the long end pointing in the direction he is to run. He intends that Shellbert will trip over the stick and awaken him in time to win the race. Shellbert sees the stick, quietly passes the sleeping rabbit, and turns the stick in the other direction so that when Harry awakens, he runs the wrong way and loses the race.

The students read a portion of the story to the point at which the characters must take some action. The story is stopped at this point and the students are then asked what the character can do to accomplish his goal. For example, in the Harry and Shellbert story, after the two characters had decided to race, the students were asked, "What is something that Harry can do to make sure he will win the race?" When the students responded, they were told, "That's a good idea, what else could Harry do to make sure that he will win the race?" This was continued until the student could generate no more alternatives. The same procedure was followed with Shellbert. Student responses are scored for (1) number of plans, (2) number of steps in the plan, (3) if a justification of the plan is provided, and (4) feasibility of the plan.

This task was given to the high average and low average fourth-grade readers mentioned in the discussion of observing planning behavior in play. The two groups of readers did not differ in total number of plans given, but the high average readers gave significantly more plans that were judged as feasible and gave more justifications for their plans. Low average readers suggested activities that could not readily be associated with winning a race; for example, the turtle would wear sunglasses. The high average readers also gave more plans that focussed on activities that the character himself would do to win the race (such as running fast and not taking a nap), while the low average readers gave more plans in which one character got rid of the other character (by hitting him over the head, tripping him, or making him fall in a hole) (Westby, Van Dongen, & Maggart, 1986).

Assessing Knowledge of Cognition

Awareness of mental acts must precede the development of metacognitive strategies essential for children to comprehend and remember what they read. Children must be able to know when they know and when they don't know something if they are to interact appropriately with the teacher and are to be able to work independently. Wellman (1985) reported that by age seven, 80 percent of children exhibit the adult pattern of understanding mental terms such as *know, remember, forget*, and *guess*. Wellman developed several tasks that are useful in determining students' understanding or appreciation of these terms.

- Task 1: Knowing-remembering condition. Children see an item hidden in one of two containers. Then, after a brief delay, the children are asked to find the item. At that point they are asked "Did you know where the item was? Did you guess where the item was? Did you remember where it was?

• Task 2: Guessing condition. Children do not see where the item is hidden, and cannot know where it is, but must make a choice between the two containers.

• Task 3: Forgetting condition. Children watch a toy character who sees his coat put in one of two closets, and they are asked, "Does he know where his coat is? Why do you say he knows?" Later the character comes back looking for his coat and looks in the wrong closet. The children are asked "Did he know where his coat was? Did he remember? Did he forget? Why did you say he forgot?"

We present these tasks regularly in elementary classrooms for communicatively disordered students each year. Initially, the majority of the children respond randomly to these tasks. If children do not know when they know or don't know, they have no basis for deciding when they need to seek assistance with a task. As a consequence, many such children are content to complete entire activities incorrectly, while others develop a pattern of learned helplessness and approach the teacher for assistance and explanation of every task, even when they have done the task in the past and should know what is expected. Frequently, it is clear that they do know (but don't know that they know), because as soon as the teacher says, "We've done that before, you know how to do it," they return to their seats and complete the work without further explanation. Any work related to metacognitive monitoring of comprehension and performance on academic tasks is based on first understanding the concepts of knowing, remembering, forgetting, and guessing. If students are to monitor their comprehension, they must *know* when they are comprehending and when they are not comprehending. They must understand that they may be expected to *remember* the material they are reading, and they must know what they can do so they won't *forget*.

Jenkins (1979) proposed a model of learning that can be used to discuss types of metacognitive processing important for comprehension monitoring:

1. The characteristics of the learner; that is, what do the learners know about themselves—about their present knowledge, what is hard and what is easy for them, what they like and what they don't like.
2. The nature of the materials to be learned. This includes the learner's awareness of the organizational structure of the texts and the types of facts and content information that will appear in the texts.
3. The criterial task; that is, what is to be the end product of the learning. For example, is the student to retell the story, complete a multiple-choice test or essay test, or teach the material to someone else.
4. Learning strategies at one's disposal; that is, can one reread, does

one know how to outline or make semantic maps of the material, does one use visual imagery to remember the information, and so forth.

If students have awareness of these areas, they can use them to monitor their comprehension while reading. If students know something about themselves in relation to the topic or reading task, they can make decisions about how they will handle the task. For example, students might find history easy and know they can read and comprehend it in one reading while sitting in the cafeteria; on the other hand, they know that they find science difficult and must allow additional time to read the material and must read it in a quiet place.

If students are aware that texts can have organizational structure, they will use this knowledge to (1) identify the structural pattern of the text and (2) plan to use it strategically to identify the important aspects of the message, to focus attention on the main ideas rather than the trivia, and to predict the sequence of information in the text (Gordon & Braun, 1985).

If students are aware of the outcome requirements of the task, they can make adjustments in how they read and how well they need to comprehend. If they are reading for enjoyment or to provide a brief summary of the text to someone else, they do not need to devote a lot of attention to the task, and they do not need to comprehend everything in the text—just the main ideas. If they are to be able to write an essay about what they have read, they must understand the organization of the material and must understand the main ideas and how the other information supports the main ideas. This is clearly a task that will require more careful reading. Students who understand their own knowledge, abilities, interests, and the criterial nature of the reading task are able to choose the learning activities that will work best for them to comprehend the material at the level necessary for successful completion of the task.

One can gain insight into the comprehension monitoring strategies students use by having them read a story and stopping them periodically to ask what the story is about and to explain how they know this. With junior high students one can sample metacognitive awareness by asking what they do to remember and how they study for tests.

- If you have to remember something, what do you do?
- What do you do if you do not understand what you are reading?
- What do you do when you are going to have a test?
- What do you do when you say you study? Do you study differently for a math test than for a history test? For an essay test than for a multiple choice test?

Answering these questions is no assurance that the students actually use the strategies they say they do. Consequently, students should be observed during activities requiring strategy use (Cavenaugh & Borkowski, 1980). It is possible that the students who cannot respond to these questions may be using some unconscious comprehension and remembering strategies, but it is unlikely that they are using them effectively.

FACILITATING TEXT COMPREHENSION

Now that we know the types of linguistic and cognitive knowledge essential for text comprehension, what can be done to facilitate students' ability to comprehend what they read? Goodman (1973) proposed 12 easy ways to make reading difficult, and one difficult way to make reading easy. According to Goodman, to make reading easy for students, one must make reading easy. This can be done by providing students with interesting, comprehensible texts—texts that have a clear, higher-organizational structure, and texts that are matched to the level of the students' schema knowledge. The focus of this section of the chapter is to demonstrate how (1) high-quality children's literature can be matched to students' present cognitive and linguistic abilities so that students can comprehend the texts and at the same time gain additional knowledge from the texts, and (2) through student-teacher interactions, adults can facilitate the development of the metacognitive strategies students need to become independent learners.

DEVELOPING A LITERATURE LANGUAGE STYLE

FACILITATING EXPLICIT LANGUAGE USE

In Chapter 1, the differences between oral and written language were discussed. Compared to oral language, written literate-style language uses more specific vocabulary and more complex syntactic structures to specify the relationships among people, actions, and objects. A more literate style of language must be used anytime the speaker and listener or reader and writer are not in the same time and space and do not share familiarity with the topic. In order to develop a literate language style, children must hear literate language and have the opportunity to use it in meaningful communicative contexts. Children may be exposed to a literate style in the language spoken by adults around them and in stories that are read to them.

Barrier games have been a popular means to develop explicit

language. A child sits on each side of a barrier with shapes, figures, or Tinkertoys. The clinician or child makes a design or constructs a model and then must tell the student on the other side of the barrier what to do to make a design or construct the model.

Children need opportunities to hear and use literate language in conversation when minimal contextual cues are available. Show and Tell or Sharing Time serves this function in many kindergarten and first-grade classrooms. These activities are often difficult for students with reading disabilities because there are no concrete clues in the environment to help trigger what they can say and because they must maintain the discourse themselves. Sharing Time can be modified to ease the transition into literate monologue by beginning with a group discussion on a topic familiar to all students. The teacher writes a number of topics on cards and then has the students draw a card for discussion. We have chosen statements such as ''What would happen if you played ball in the street?'' ''What would happen if you invited someone home with you after school?'' or 'What would happen if you got two presents that were the same?'' The nature of these questions allows the teachers and children to begin by giving personal narrative examples and then to generalize to an expository form of what might generally happen in most conditions. Two adults lead the group. If no children initially respond, the adults engage in an informal discussion, for example, of a time when they invited someone home with them. If something one adult said is unclear to the other, the other adult requests clarification or further explanation. The children are permitted to interrupt at any time and add their own experience. As they do, they begin to talk about nonpresent objects and activities and must do so in a way that is understandable to others in the group. If the group discussion is about bringing a friend home after school and a child begins to talk about finding a car in the trash, an adult asks if this is related to the current topic and the child is reminded about the topic of the discussion. As the year continues, students begin to be able to ask each other questions to clarify information, and in so doing, all students become better able to talk about past experiences clearly.

Pretend play activities also provide opportunities for literate language use. The decontextualization or reduction in the need for concrete props that occurs in imaginative play requires increasing use of explicit language for the play to be shared with others. Pellegrini (1985) reported that children who exhibit higher levels of symbolic pretend play also exhibit more literate language styles. They make use of more adjectives, conjunctions, words referring to metacognitive functions (*I know, I think*), and more endophoric reference (reference to information in the text) as opposed to exophoric reference (reference to information in the context). In sociodramatic play children must communicate effectively with each other if the play is to proceed. As props become less realistic, the need for explicit language increases. If a child puts a box on the table and intends it to be a turkey that will be carved for dinner, the child needs to make his or her intention clear to other children in the play environment.

Facilitating Complex Structures

Children can be introduced to the literate style of texts through familiar stories that have repetitive or cumulative organization. Listen to the language style of *The Three Billy Goats Gruff* (Asbjornsen & Moe, 1957):

> Once on a time there were three billy goats who were to go up to the hillside to make themselves fat, and the name of all three was "Gruff." On the way up was a bridge over a river they had to cross, and under the bridge lived a great ugly troll with eyes as big as saucers and a nose as long as a poker. So first of all came the youngest Billy Goat Gruff to cross the bridge. "Trip, trap! trip, trap!" went the bridge.

or from *Millions of Cats* (Gag, 1928):

> Once upon a time there was a very old man and a very old woman. They lived in a nice clean house which had flowers all around it, except where the door was. But they couldn't be happy because they were so very lonely.

The beginnings of these stories have relative clauses (introduced by *who* and *which*), literate conjunctions (*because, but, except*), inverted sentence structure (*on the way up was a bridge over the river they had to cross*), and explicit vocabulary (*eyes as big as saucers, nose as long as a poker*).

Some stories make use of one or two aspects of literate language style. Such books can be used to highlight specific literate structures. Relative pronouns can be introduced through stories such as *There Was an Old Woman Who Swallowed a Fly* (Adams, 1973) or *The House That Jack Built* (Rogers, 1968). In *Millions of Cats*, each cat is described by a relative clause: "a kitten which was black and very beautiful, a cat which had brown and yellow stripes like a baby tiger, another cat which was so pretty he could not bear to leave it." The repetitive nature of the first two stories facilitates role playing by young children. The *Millions of Cats* story can be extended by having children look through cat calendars, choose the cat they like, and describe it using relative clauses (e.g., "I like this cat that has long orange fur and a short tail.").

Many stories use complex sentence structures. It has often been assumed that complex sentences are particularly difficult to comprehend. Actually, complex sentences with certain conjunctions are sometimes easier to understand than two simple sentences, because the conjunctions signal the important relationship existing between the sentence components (Armbruster, 1984; Pearson, 1974). If-then structures are presented in books such as *If I Were a Toad* (Paterson, 1977), in which a child says what she would do if she were different animals ("If I were a fish, I would be too smart to bite the hook"), and *If I Had* (Mayer, 1968), in which a boy tells what he would do with different animals ("If I had a snake, I'd put it in my toybox. Then my sister wouldn't mess up my toys."). The teacher can reinforce the concept through roleplay, asking the children to demonstrate what would they do if they were a kangaroo, a puppy, a horse, or if they had a porcupine or a lion.

A book such as *When I Was Young in the Mountains* (Rylant, 1982) can be used to introduce the temporal conjunction *when*. In this book the author reflects on the things she did when she was young and living in the mountains. This book experience can be extended by having children bring in pictures of themselves when they were younger and talking about them or making their own book of *When I was Young*. For young children, this can be followed with *When I Get Bigger* (Mayer, 1983), in which the main character talks about all the things he will do when he is bigger.

The conjunction *but*, which is difficult to explain, can be made clear in stories. For example, in *Just for You* (Mayer, 1975), the little monster is trying to be helpful, but always ends up creating problems ("I wanted to help you carry the groceries just for you, but the bag broke."). In *One Monday Morning* (Shulevitz, 1967), the king comes to visit a little boy, *but* he isn't home. Each day the king and more of his retinue come to visit, but the boy isn't home.

In *The Gillygoofang* (Mendoza, 1982) and *Bringing the Rain to Kapiti Plain* (Aardema, 1981), explicit descriptive language is combined with relative pronouns and conjunctions:

> The gillygoofang bewildered the giddyfish, a fish which could bounce up and down out of the water, not because it swam backward to keep water out of its eyes or changed colors to trick the bigger fish or whistled to warn the little fish or laid square eggs or slept in the weeds with one eye open, but because it couldn't bounce up and down out of the water.

> This is Ki-pat who watched his herd as he stood on one leg like a big stork bird; Ki-pat, whose cows were so hungry and dry, they mooed for the rain to fall from the sky; To green-up the grass, all brown and dead, that needed the rain from the cloud overhead—The big, black cloud, all heavy with rain, that shadowed the ground on Kapiti Plain.

Developing Narrative Schema Knowledge

Skilled language users draw simultaneously on several sources of schematic knowledge in comprehending text:

1. Domain: specific knowledge of topics, concepts, or processes for a particular subject matter.
2. General world knowledge: understanding of social relationships, causes and activities that are common to many specific situations and domains.
3. Knowledge of rhetorical or text grammar structures: conventions for organizing and signaling the organization of texts (McNeil, 1987).

The conceptual knowledge underlying narrative text involves awareness of temporal action sequences, cause-effect or reactive sequences (first physical causality and later psychological causality), planning, and understanding of the concept of trickery or deception.

Family Role in Narrative Development

In order to learn to comprehend and produce narratives, children must hear a variety of well-structured narratives. Children with limited narrative abilities frequently do not enjoy listening to or reading complex stories. To assure children's willingness to listen to or read stories, children must be provided with books that are comprehensible to them. By determining children's narrative abilities (using the guidelines presented earlier in this chapter) appropriate books can be made available. Books are arranged according to narrative level on separate shelves in the classroom bookcase. The shelves are labeled with the names of children for whom the books would be appropriate. Children are assigned to shelves that contain books at or preferably slightly above their present narrative level. We have found that children are much more willing to listen to and read stories when they have chosen them. Narrative structure arises from understanding of conceptual relationships. Consequently, one does not teach the structure, but instead, one facilitates students' comprehension by giving them experiences with the domain-specific and world knowledge that underlie any particular structure.

The relationship between listening to stories and reading competency is explained to the students' parents. Current research shows the critical role that early experience with books has on children's later school success (Clark, 1976; Durkin, 1966; Wells, 1986). For example,

Wells (1986) documented that the amount children were read to during the preschool years was the language variable most related to academic success at fifth grade. The teacher explains that the children will be bringing home books and that the parents are to read the books and help the child complete the book report form. Book report forms are matched to the child's level of narrative development. Table 7-2 presents the developmental sequence of questions asked on book report forms. Figure 7-2 shows a sample of a form used for a level 5 book report. The

TABLE 7–2.
Book Report Sequence

Book Report 1

1. Identify title either by naming or pointing to on cover.
2. Identify author either by naming or pointing to on cover.
3. Draw a picture of a favorite part of the story.
4. Describe the pictures in the book.

Book Report 2

1. Identify title either by naming or pointing to on cover.
2. Identify author either by naming or pointing to on cover.
3. Name the major characters.
4. Tell the first thing that happened in the story.
5. Tell how the story ends.

Book Report 3

1. Identify title either by naming or pointing to on cover.
2. Identify author either by naming or pointing to on cover.
3. Name the major characters.
4. Relate three things, in sequence, that happened in the story.
5. Retell the story using the pictures.

Book Report 4

1. Identify title by naming.
2. Identify author by naming or pointing to on cover.
3. Respond to a *why* question concerning physical actions. (e.g., Why did the boy get an umbrella?)
4. Relate three things, in sequence, that happened in the story.
5. Retell the story using the pictures.

Book Report 5

1. Identify title by naming.
2. Identify author either by naming or by pointing to on cover.
3. Identify a feeling exhibited by one of the main characters.
4. Explain how you know a character is experiencing a particular feeling.
5. Retell the story using the pictures.

(continued)

TABLE 7-2. *(continued)*

Book Report 6

1. Identify title by naming.
2. Identify author by naming or pointing to on cover.
3. Identify a feeling exhibited by one of the main characters.
4. Explain why the character feels as he or she does.
5. Retell the story without pictures.

Book Report 7

1. Identify title by naming.
2. Identify author by naming or pointing to on cover.
3. Tell problem in the story.
4. Tell how characters solved the problem.
5. Retell story without pictures.

Developed by Linda Costlow, Cynthia Garcia, and Carol Westby.

book report forms provide the parents with guidelines of what they can discuss about the book with their child.

Experiences with books must also be carefully scaffolded. Storybook reading with children is not a part of all cultures, and many children come to school with no exposure to this type of activity. Learning disabled students from mainstream families also often have had limited exposure to storybook activities. Families of these children report having tried to read stories to their children, but the children were uninterested and inattentive so the family did not pursue the activity. If books are carefully matched to the child's narrative comprehension level, however, nearly every child will enjoy listening to stories.

The sequence of questions presented in the book reports is based on information regarding adult-children interaction with books and on information about narrative development. Infants' first exposure to books generally involves a labeling activity. The adult asks, "What's this?" When the child does not respond, the adult provides the label and goes on to the next page (Ninio & Bruner, 1976). Eventually, children learn to take their turn and will even initiate the game by bringing the adult a book and asking, "What's this?" Snow and Goldfield (1981) documented the following hierarchy of questions/comments that a parent used with her child between ages two to four years:

- Item levels (What's that? Who's that?)
- Item elaboration (How many pigs? What color car?)
- Event (What happened? What's ______ doing?)
- Motive/cause (Why did he want an umbrella?)
- Evaluation/reaction (How did he feel when that happened? Wasn't that a bad thing to do?)

FIGURE 7-2. Sample book report form.

- Real-world relevance (The pig's taking a bath. You did that this morning.)

Through this type of interactive discourse, children learn how to discuss and interpret books. Parents can be trained to use this type of scaffolding in interacting with their learning disabled children when discussing personal experiences as well as when sharing books. Through such discussions parents can facilitate children's development of a literate-style oral language. At the beginning of the year, parents are provided with a scrapbook. Periodically throughout the year, a page with a photograph of the child participating in a school activity is sent home with the child. Under the photo the teacher writes the types of questions the parent can ask to elicit a personal narrative. For young or severely language handicapped children, the initial questions require only labeling, such as "Who made the piñata?" Later, questions requiring event description are added, such as "What did James do? What were you doing?" Still later, questions asking about motivation or cause are introduced, such as "Why did you make a piñata?" The photo album provides parents with information about what is happening at school and with systematic methods for facilitating their child's ability to talk about the school activities.

Developing Narrative Content Schema and Text Grammar Knowledge Through Literature

For school-age students with reading disabilities, the purpose of their first book reports is to familiarize them with the general nature of books and to play the question-answer game. In Book Report 1 in Table 7-2, children are asked to identify the title and author, describe the pictures in the book, and draw a picture of something in the book. Ability to do this results in "stories" with a descriptive structure. The books chosen for this level are those that have a central character or theme and a simple series of activities.

When children are able to describe the activities in the book, they are introduced to more concepts about the nature of a story and asked to tell how the story begins and how it ends. The children are introduced to the idea that books present a sequence of activities about a character and that one begins at the front of the book and finishes at the back of the book (Book Reports 2 and 3). Books in this category include *The Very Hungry Caterpillar* (Carle, 1969), a story about a caterpillar who eats its way through a variety of foods; *The Snowy Day* (Keats, 1962), about Peter's activities in the snow; and *Charlie Needs a Cloak* (dePaola, 1974), about the sequence of events involved in making a wool cloak for

Charlie. To facilitate relating of a series of sequential activities, children can participate in activities similar to those in the story. For example, after reading *The Very Hungry Caterpillar,* children can sample the foods that the caterpillar ate. To extend children's experiences with *The Snowy Day,* a speech-language pathologist in Albuquerque took her ice chests to the mountain one weekend to fill them with snow so that on Monday the children in her class could make snowmen and throw snowballs. In another instance, children were studying a unit on early New Mexico. After the teacher read *Charlie Needs a Cloak,* weavers came to the classroom. They brought wool and showed the children how to spin it, then threaded a small hand loom and allowed the children to weave strips of cloth for scarves. Children can be encouraged to retell not only the stories in the books, but also to relate their own experiences. Stories of this type will result in action sequence narratives.

As children become able to deal with the beginning-to-end temporal action sequences, it is time to introduce cause-effect sequences, which give rise to stories of the reactive sequence type. In temporal sequence stories, the exact order of activities is not always critical. For example, in *The Snowy Day,* it is not important whether Peter first makes a snowball or an angel in the snow. Cause-effect (reactive sequence) stories, however, must have a set sequence of events. For example, in *Round Robin* (Kent, 1982), a small robin eats and eats until he becomes obese. When the other robins fly south for the winter, he must hop because he is too fat to fly. Because he is hopping along the snowy ground, a fox almost catches him.

Pourquoi tales that explain the origins of aspects of nature or the characteristics of certain animals are helpful to develop understanding of cause-effect because they make explicit links between actions and reactions. For example, in *Why Mosquitoes Buzz in Peoples' Ears* (Aardema, 1975), a mosquito annoys an iguana by buzzing in his ear. The iguana puts sticks in his ears so he can't hear the mosquito. A python talks to the iguana, who cannot hear him because of the sticks in his ears. The python thinks the iguana is angry with him and runs into a rabbit hole. The rabbits run from their hole because they think the python is coming to eat them. The birds see the rabbits running and sound an alarm because they think there is danger. Hearing the alarm the monkeys swing swiftly through the trees. One of the monkeys falls on an owl's nest, causing the death of an owlet. In *Why the Sun and the Moon Live in the Sky* (Dayrell, 1968), the water refuses to visit the sun and the moon because their house is too small. The sun responds by building a bigger house. The water comes to visit; the water gets deeper and deeper, causing the sun and the moon to climb to the roof of their house and eventually causing them to flee to the sky. When reactive sequence stories are introduced, Book Report 4 is provided. Now, in addition to being asked to relate three things in sequence that happened in the story, the students are also asked questions that focus on the physical causality or the reason for the activity. *Why* questions are introduced, such as, "Why couldn't the robin fly?" "Why did the rabbits run from their holes?" or "Why did sun build a bigger house?"

Repetitive or cummulative stories, which often have more complexity than action or reactive sequences, can be used to assist children in developing understanding of temporal and cause-effect sequence. Although the children may not understand all of the nuances in some of these stories, the repetitive nature of the story and chantlike nature of the language facilitates children's remembering of the words and action-reaction sequences. *Brown Bear, Brown Bear, What Do You See?* (Martin, 1983), *The Little Red Hen* (Galdone, 1973), *The Three Pigs* (Galdone, 1970), and *Drummer Hoff* (Emberley, 1967) are excellent examples that lend themselves to children's joining in the reading.

Development of the abbreviated and complete episode structure requires understanding of psychological causality or an understanding of motivations for behavior. Students must become aware that characters have feelings that motivate behavior or that feelings can be elicited by events. By kindergarten, children can identify and give examples of situations eliciting the emotions happy, mad, sad, and scared (Harter, 1982). Stories that explicitly discuss feelings, such as *Feelings* (Aliki, 1984) or *The Feeling Fun House* (Morse, et al., 1985), or that elicit feelings, such as *The Quarreling Book* (Zolotow, 1963) are useful in this stage. A story such as *Franklin in the Dark* (Bourgeois, 1986) is useful for young children. Franklin is a young turtle who will not go into his shell because he is afraid of the dark. He visits a number of other animals who relate their fears, including a duck who wears water wings because he is afraid of deep water and a bird who wears a parachute because he is afraid of heights. Junior high children enjoy books such as *Scary Stories to Tell in the Dark* (Schwartz, 1981). Books such as these can provide children with the opportunity to discuss their own fearful experiences.

At this level, students also become alert to common scripts and character traits. To further scriptal development and awareness of character traits, a series of books having the same character or theme can be presented. Younger children will enjoy books about pigs and wolves. After children are familiar with *The Three Little Pigs* (Galdone, 1970), they can read such books as *Mr. and Mrs. Pig's Evening Out* (Rayner, 1976), in which the babysitter turns out to be a wolf, and *Garth Pig and the Ice Cream Lady* (Rayner, 1977), in which the ice cream lady is a wolf. The children can be encouraged to predict what they think will happen when they see the wolf appear at the door as the babysitter, or when Garth Pig enters the ice cream lady's truck. Older students enjoy stories about giants, trolls, and dragons. After several stories about dragons, the book *The Fourteenth Dragon* (Seidelman & Mintonye, 1968) can be read. In this book thirteen dragons are vividly described in words and pictures. On the last page is the fourteenth dragon, the dragon that the reader of the book is to draw. Book reports 5 and 6 are presented at this level.

The temporal sequence, physical causality, and psychological causality of the earlier stages are further elaborated in the complete episode stage. The role of planning in meeting the character's goals becomes important at this stage. Children now understand secondary emotions, such as shame, guilt, embarrassment, and pride. These emotions are dependent on higher cognitive functioning and awareness of social sanctions (Lewis & Michalson, 1983). Books that describe situations that elicit these feelings can be read and discussed. Understanding emotions should lead to a better understanding of characters' intentions and their attempts or plans to cope with their problems and emotions. The majority of stories require understanding of psychological causality and planning of characters. Some examples of such stories are described below.

In *Chester the Worldly Pig* (Peet, 1965), Chester is dissatisifed with his life on the farm and decides to better himself by learning a skill and joining the circus. Although he succeeds in this goal, he later encounters numerous other serious threats from which he must escape. In *Cross-Country Cat* (Calhoun, 1979), Henry the cat is left behind at his owner's winter cabin. In order to catch up with his owners he sets out on skis and must cope with several dangers he encounters along the way. In *Fin M'Coul: The Giant of Knockmany Hill* (dePaola, 1981), Fin is being chased by a giant who is bigger and stronger than he is, and he and his wife must devise a plan to save themselves. Book Report 7 requires the students to identify the problem in the stories and explain how the characters solved the problems.

Between ages 10 and 12, typical students produce stories that are elaborated in a variety of ways. Early elaborations involve multiple attempts in the characters' plans or multiple minichapters or episodes. Later elaborations involve stories told from the point of view of more than one character or stories embedded within stories. Underlying these narrative structures are perception of character growth and change, awareness of deception, awareness of cyclical time, and understanding of figurative versus literal word meanings.

Stories that rely heavily on characterization can be appreciated in the elaborated narrative stage. The book *Sarah, Plain and Tall* (MacLachlan, 1985) is an excellent introduction to this level. It contains several episodes but is short enough to be read in one long session or two short ones. This book is the story of a motherless pioneer family and the woman who answers papa's letter to come and be his wife. The changes in the emotional responses of each of the characters over the course of the story are critical to the events and outcome. Students can discuss the traits of each of the characters. For example, papa is lonely, thoughtful, industrious, sad; Sarah, the mail-order wife, is homesick, independent, optimistic, joyous, adventuresome; Caleb, the boy, is wistful, worrying, loving; and Anna, the girl, is hopeful, understanding, missing her mother. The story is told through the eyes of Anna. Students can be encouraged to retell the story through the eyes of the other characters.

By this stage, students appreciate books that require understanding of multiple meanings of words. These can be of two types: stories that involve a play on words or trickery tales. Many junior high students enjoy the books in the series *Not Quite Human* (McEvoy, 1985), which require appreciation of figurative and idiomatic expressions. In this series, a junior high teacher invents an android that can pass as a 12-year-old boy. The android's "father" sends him to school. The android has been programmed with an extensive vocabulary, but his comprehension is overly literal as is illustrated in the following excerpt:

> "My name is Chip," answered the android. "This is my first day at school."
>
> The man ran his hand through his thick black hair. "It's going to be your last day," he yelled, "or my name isn't Mr. Duckworth."
>
> "And if it isn't my last day," asked Chip, attempting to sort out the logic, "then what is your name?"
>
> "Your name is going to be mud if you don't tell me why you smashed my trophy case!"
>
> "My name will always be Chip," answered the mechanical boy. "It can't change. Although sometimes women change their names when they get married."

The concept of deception may be introduced with trickery tales. Students must be assisted in understanding that what a person says is not necessarily what he or she intends to do. The concept can be introduced to middle school students through trickery tales from different cultures, such as the coyote tales of the Southwest Indians, Anansi the Spider tales from Africa, raven tales from the Northwest, or the Uncle Remus tales from the South, as well as trickster tales from other cultures. Because these tales come from oral histories, they include frequent repetition and lend themselves to easy role playing. Students are given the roles of the characters in the stories, and initially the teacher takes the role of the inner thoughts of the trickster. For example, in the story, *The Crocodile's Tale* (Aruego & Aruego, 1972), a Philippino folktale, the crocodile is caught in a noose. He promises to give a boy a gold ring if he cuts him down. We know, of course, that the crocodile has no intention of giving the boy a ring, but rather intends to eat him. When a student playing the crocodile finishes saying he will give the boy a gold ring, the teacher snickers and in a loud whisper says, "I'm not really going to give him a ring. I'm just saying that. I'm really going to grab him and take him into the river and eat him." After several role-playing experiences with the teacher verbalizing the inner thoughts and actual intentions of the trickster, a student can be assigned this role.

The final stage of narrative development, metaphoric, does not result in additional complexity of narrative structure. The complexity is at the content level. The entire story may be allegorical and can be read for two levels of meaning. For example, *The Phantom Tollbooth* (Juster, 1961) may be read as the story of a boy's adventures in a strange land or as a story of a boy finding beauty and purpose in life. Similarly, the Narnia stories by C. S. Lewis, can be read as exciting adventures of a group of children or as a theological statement on the conflict between good and evil.

Normally developing adolescents can think of abstractions of time and space, and as a consequence will enjoy science fiction and fantasy tales that play with these concepts. Such stories frequently have multiple embedded plots that take place during different time frames. Susan Cooper's *The Dark Is Rising* (and its four sequels) and Madeleine L'Engle's *A Wrinkle in Time* (and its two sequels) are excellent examples of stories that manipulate time and space. Both move back and forth between the present situation and other times and places.

By this stage, students have a meta-awareness of narratives. They know what to expect from narratives and can compare and contrast narratives in terms of structure and theme. This ability to compare and contrast narratives can be furthered by having students read different versions of the same story or several books on a similar theme. One can begin with highly familiar stories and obvious variations. For example, *The Three Little Hawaiian Pigs and the Magic Shark* (Laird, 1981) and *Wili Wai Kula and the Three Mongooses* (Laird, 1983) are variations of *The Three Little Pigs* and *The Three Bears*. Students can study the geography and history of Hawaii and discuss the reasons for the variations in these stories. Many cultures have variants of the *Cinderella* tale; for example, the French version of *Cinderella* by Perrault (retold by Ehrlich, 1985), the German version by Grimm (1978), and the Chinese version *Yeh-Shen* by Louie (1982). Using their metanarrative skills, students can discuss the similarities and differences in these tales in terms of story grammar components such as settings, characters, problems (initiating events), type of magic, attempts to cope with the problem, and endings.

FACILITATING METACOGNITION

FACILITATING REGULATION OF COGNITION OR CONTROL OF BEHAVIOR

Not only must students have the necessary content and text grammar schemas to understand texts, they must also be actively involved in understanding, remembering, and learning from the texts. As indicated earlier, before students can monitor their text comprehension, they must be able to plan and monitor their motoric activities. To facilitate development of regulation of cognition, children must be involved in planning many of the activities that are carried out in the classroom. To plan their behavior children must (1) determine what the task is, (2) reflect on what they know or need to know, (3) devise a plan for dealing with the task, (4) monitor progress, and (5) evaluate the outcome. Initially, the teacher models this planning behavior by thinking aloud as an activity is conducted. Meichenbaum's (1977) self-instructional training paradigm provides guidelines for what the teacher would say. For example, when the class made cheese-lion sandwiches (open-face cheese sandwiches with celery for a face and grated cheese for manes), the teacher began by defining the task or the problem (''I'm going to make a cheese-lion sandwich''). She then focused her attention on the steps in the process (''I need a piece of bread and a slice of cheese; now I need to cut some celery for his face''). Next, she verbally reinforced herself (''I cut just the right size piece of celery''), verbally corrected errors (''I didn't slice enough cheese to cover the bread—I need to cut some more''), and commented on the outcome (''This lion looks good enough to eat''). Then she talked the children through the activity step by step. As the children cut the celery and grated the cheese, she verbalized their progress toward completion of the sandwich, and finally she talked with the children about the outcome of the project—how the sandwiches looked and tasted.

As children became familiar with the process of classroom projects, they became more responsible for the planning and execution of activities. When an activity was presented, the children had to determine what was needed and how they would proceed. Ralph the Bear pictures from the *Think Aloud* curriculum (Camp & Bash, 1981) were enlarged and displayed in the room. In this four-poster series, Ralph models the steps in self-guiding speech by asking (1) ''What is my problem'' or ''What am I supposed to do?'' (2) ''How can I do it?'' or

"What is my plan?" (3) "Am I using my plan?" and (4) "How did I do?" These posters helped the children remember the steps used in planning and carrying out an activity. By asking the children, "Are you following Ralph Bear's rules?" the teachers were able to reduce their overt monitoring of the children's behavior. Reduction of overt monitoring of the children's actions by the teacher is essential if children are to internalize the metacognitive monitoring process.

Symbolic play time (or creative dramatics) also provides an opportunity to plan. Elementary school children engage in play themes such as having a birthday party, going to a restaurant, visiting the doctor or hospital, or going on a camping trip to the International Balloon Fiesta. They must decide what roles are required for the theme, who will play each role, what events will happen, what problems might arise and how they will cope with them, what materials and props they need, and what time of day or year the event is taking place.

At the middle school level, simulation games are used as focus units. For example, in Albuquerque, in a classroom of 24 students with learning disabilities, team-taught by two special-education teachers and a speech-language pathologist, a nine-week period in language arts was devoted to the theme of pioneers. Pioneers were described as people who chose to travel to a new unsettled area. The unit was begun by having the students view the film *Seven Alone,* the true story of the Sager children who were orphaned on the Oregon Trail in 1844. The majority of the students in the class were not originally from Albuquerque. The teacher requested that the students interview their parents and grandparents to learn where they had moved from, why they had moved, and how they had moved. In small-group discussions, the students compared their families' reasons for and manner of moving with the Sager family's. Then the students began the simulation game Pioneers (Wesley, 1974). Pioneers is a simulation that allows students to vicariously participate in situations and events similar to those experienced by pioneers who headed west in early wagon trains. The teacher and student manuals for the game provide goals that must be accomplished and situations that the travelers will experience over the course of several weeks. The 24 students were divided into 3 wagon teams of 8 students. Each student represented a family head. Students were assigned identities and given families and stock. The individual students had to make decisions regarding what they would take in their wagons. They were given a large selection of items to choose from, but were limited in the weight of materials they could take. Consequently, they had to make decisions regarding specific items they would take. A wrong decision, such as omission of critical supplies, could create later difficulties.

As the simulation progressed, the wagon train groups had to make decisions, such as what to do about a lack of water, how to cross a flooded river, how to handle hostile Indians, and which trail to take. In coping with each problem that arose and arriving at a decision, the groups had to define *who* was involved, *where* the action took place, *when* the action took place, *what* the problem was, and *why* it was a problem. Then they had to discuss possible actions and the pros and cons of each action. Individual students and wagon trains gained points to move along the trail based on the wisdom of their decisions and by reading other books about pioneers and doing a variety of related projects, such as researching what to do in case of a snake bite, building model Conestoga wagons, and preparing a frontier meal for other class members (e.g., one class cooked buffalo meat stew). The students read from journals and diaries that were written by pioneers who had traveled on wagon trains. They also kept journals of the events they experienced during the simulation.

As the simulation progressed, students became more aware of the need to cooperate and make wise decisions. Students on one train argued heatedly and decided to split their train in two and go on separate trails. Within a few days it became clear that these two smaller trains could not survive. They did not have people with expertise in some areas; for example, one part of the train had the doctor, while the other part had the blacksmith. The smaller trains also did not have access to all of the tools or food necessary, and the students on the smaller trains could not read enough or do enough individual projects to collect sufficient points to move the train ahead quickly. The simulation activity provided students with consequential feedback on their planning and decision making.

Facilitating Metacognitive Thought or Monitoring Comprehension

As students progress in their ability to plan and control their behavior, they begin monitoring their progress toward a goal. Just as monitoring of behavior is important, so also is monitoring of conversation (Markman, 1981; Patterson & Roberts, 1982; Robinson, 1981). If students do not monitor their comprehension during conversation, they are unlikely to monitor their comprehension during reading. To encourage children to monitor what they were hearing, a teacher in an elementary classroom for students with language learning disabilities intentionally gave inappropriate instructions such as "Wash these paper napkins so we can use them tomorrow," or obviously wrong or impossible suggestions such as "Hurry and put your shoes on your heads so we can go out for recess." Initially, many children attempted to respond to these instructions, but they quickly learned that they had to listen carefully to the teacher and correct her because she made mistakes. It appeared that many of the students initially assumed that teachers were always right, and consequently they never challenged anything they were told. After catching the teacher in obvious errors, they became freer to question the teacher and let her know they did not understand what was expected. Gradually, the obviousness of the inappropriate instructions was reduced so that students had to listen more carefully.

Academically successful students read for meaning (to comprehend) and read to remember (to study) (Baker & Brown, 1984). As with other aspects of learning, metacognitive comprehension monitoring must be modeled meaningfully if students are to use it. Vygotsky (1978) pointed out that verbal social interaction plays a major role in the development of higher mental (metacognitive) functions. These functions first occur on an interpersonal (social) level and later on an intrapersonal (individual) level. Gavelek and Raphael (1985) proposed that the interactive discourse that occurs in questioning introduces children to metacognitive skills. By asking appropriate questions about texts, teachers carry out the metacognitive functions that students should eventually come to exercise themselves. Comprehension monitoring requires that students learn to ask themselves the questions that previously the teacher had asked. Postman and Weingartner (1969) stated that "Once you have learned how to ask questions, relevant and appropriate and substantial questions, you have learned how to learn and no one can keep you from learning whatever you want or need to know" (p.23).

Effective readers create meaning for a text in their own minds as they interact with passages (Tierney & Pearson, 1983). To construct a coherent meaning, readers must know what questions to formulate about a text and what questions they may expect to be answered (Fitzgerald, 1983). Comprehension monitoring can initially be practiced during a story reading time when the teacher is reading an interesting story to a group of children. By asking appropriate questions, teachers can facilitate students' retrieval of appropriate schemata and monitoring of their text comprehension to determine if they have selected the appropriate schema or if they must change their schema selection. Below, excerpts from the story *The Magic Finger* (Dahl, 1966) are used to show how this might be done. The teacher reads a passage (p. 18):

> "We must do it," said Mr. Gregg. "We've got to have somewhere to sleep. Follow me."
>
> They flew off to a tall tree and right at the top of it Mr. Gregg chose a place for the nest.

> "Now we want sticks," he said. "Lots and lots of little sticks. Off you go, all of you, and find them and bring them back here.

The teacher asks the students, "What do you think this story is about?" The students are required to justify any answer from information that has been provided in the text. For example, if they respond that the story is about birds, they should refer to the fact that Mr. Gregg flew to a tree and talked about a nest. These are things that birds could do. The teacher can challenge this response by noting that Mr. Gregg talked, and birds don't talk. Students may counter with the idea that in fantasy stories, birds do sometimes talk. The teacher continues reading, stopping and questioning the students regarding what the story is about and what is happening. Later in the story, the teacher reads (p. 21):

> "Oh, dear! Oh, dear!" said Mrs. Gregg. "They have taken over our whole house! We shall never get it back. And what are we going to eat?"
>
> "I will not eat worms," said Philip. "I would rather die."
>
> "Or slugs," said William.
>
> Mrs. Gregg took the two boys under her wings and hugged them. "Don't worry," she said. "I can mince it all up very fine and you won't even know the difference. Lovely slugburgers. Delicious wormburgers."
>
> "Oh no!" cried William.
>
> "Never!" said Philip.
>
> "Disgusting!" said Mr. Gregg. "Just because we have wings, we don't have to eat bird food. We shall eat apples instead. Our trees are full of them. Come on!"
>
> So they flew off to an apple tree.
>
> But to eat an apple without holding it in your hands is not easy. Every time you try to get your teeth into it, it just pushes away.

The information in this part of the text should cause listeners/readers to question their choice of a bird schema for the story. The teacher stops and asks what the students now think the story is about. If they still say it is about birds, she draws their attention to parts of the text. Did Mr. and Mrs. Gregg always live in a nest? She reminds them of Mrs. Gregg's comment about not being able to get back to her house. She also notes that these birds don't like the usual bird food. Perhaps they do not like worms because they are fairy-tale birds, but she also notes that they also did not seem to know how to eat apples because they did not have hands. Even if they were fairy-tale birds, they should have been able to eat apples with their mouths.

A variant of this procedure is the Directed Reading Thinking Activity

(DRTA) (Richek, 1987; Stauffer, 1969). In using the DRTA, students listen to or read a portion of a text. Then they stop and are asked to orally predict what will happen next and to give reasons for these predictions. After this justification, they listen to or read another section of the text, noting whether or not their predictions have been confirmed. Then they report which predictions were confirmed by referring to the text for support. Students can be encouraged to make predictions about a story by using cues in the title and the picture on the book cover.

Helping students in comprehension monitoring is a worthwhile activity for all older elementary and middle school and high school students. Different types of stories and text genres provide different types of cues, and the teacher needs to demonstrate the use of these cues as she asks questions that focus students' attention on the cues. Modeling of comprehension monitoring and guiding students in comprehension monitoring appears to be even more essential for expository than narrative texts. Hardy (1978) has stated that narrative is a primary act of mind, and Bruner (1985) has added that narrative is a primary mode of thought. Perhaps because of this primacy of the narrative mode, less comprehension monitoring is necessary to comprehend narratives. It appears likely, however, that the unfamiliar concepts and structures of expository text require much more active metacognitive processing to be comprehended. In the section on narrative assessment, I indicated that the structure of narratives arises from the content schemata of the narratives. If one understands human goal-directed behavior, one will also understand and recognize the structure of a good story. Expository texts, however, have no preordained structure. Readers must discover the text grammar structure of each expository text if they are to use it to facilitate their comprehension.

To facilitate metacognitive monitoring of expository texts, teachers can explain the functions of different types of expository texts, identify the different types of texts, the organization of the types, and the key words that students can look for (Finley & Seaton, 1987; McGee & Richgels, 1985; Piccolo, 1987). Some examples follow.

	Function	**Key Words**
Descriptive	Does the text tell me what something is?	No key words
Sequence	Does the text tell me how to do something or make something?	first . . . next . . . then second . . . third following this step finally

Cause/effect	Does the text give reasons for why something happens?	because, since, reasons, then, therefore, for this reason, results, effects, consequently, so, in order to, thus, then
Problem/solution	Does the text state a problem and offer solutions to the problem?	a problem is, a solution is
Comparison/contrast	Is the text showing how two things are the same or different?	different, same, alike, similar, although, however, on the other hand, but, yet, still, rather than, instead of
Enumerative	Does the text give a list of things that are related to the topic?	an example is, for instance, another, next, finally

The teacher can read a text aloud, modeling her or his own thought processes while doing so. The teacher can present the students with a passage, have them scan the passage for key words and make predictions about the structure of the paragraph.

Reciprocal peer or cooperative teaching is another helpful method to develop comprehension monitoring strategies in students (Dansereau, 1987; Palincsar & Brown, 1984). Cooperative teaching can be approached in two ways. In one method two students read the same passage. When both are finished, one student summarizes what he or she has read and the other student corrects any errors he or she has noted in the summary. In a second method, two students read different passages. Then one student summarizes the passage and the other student asks clarifying questions. Then the students switch roles. These particular cooperative teaching methods have been useful with older students in junior high and beyond who have some metacognitive monitoring skills in place.

For younger students, those with more advanced narrative abilities can be used to facilitate other students' development of narrative skills. Students who are working on level 7 book reports can usually work effectively with children who are using Book Reports 1 through 4. The younger child may have a parent read the story, or in some instances the older peer tutor reads the story to the younger child. Then the older student asks the questions on the book report form to the younger child and judges the younger child's response.

SUMMARY

Comprehending text is essential if students are to become independent learners. There are many tests available to measure text comprehension, but only recently are attempts truly being made to teach comprehension. We cannot teach comprehension unless we understand what cognitive and linguistic abilities underlie the comprehension process. For many years it was assumed that if students were able to decode rapidly, comprehension would automatically follow. Although this does indeed appear to be the case for many normally developing students, it is not the case with reading disabled students.

In this chapter, procedures to assess and facilitate text comprehension were described. Adequate assessment would include evaluation of students' (1) literate language style, (2) physical and social world knowledge, (3) ability to organize this conceptual knowledge into coherent texts such as stories, and (4) ability to monitor their own motoric activities and their text comprehension.

In order to assist students with learning disabilities in developing their reading-comprehension abilities, we must first facilitate their understanding of the linguistic and cognitive concepts that occur in texts. To do this, texts must be presented that are interesting and comprehensible to the students. We must then assist the students in developing the metacognitive monitoring strategies that will enable them to learn from text without the support of a teacher.

ACKNOWLEDGMENTS

Information on narrative development and suggestions for narrative assessment have emerged from a research project currently being jointly conducted by this author and Dr. Zelda Maggart and Dr. Richard Van Dongen at the University of New Mexico. Many of the practical activities in this chapter have been suggested and implemented in the classroom by Linda Costlow, Cynthia Garcia, and Barbara Stirbis.

REFERENCES

Abrams, D., and Sutton-Smith, B. (1987). The development of the trickster in children's narrative. *Journal of American Folklore, 90,* 29–47.

Anderson, R., and Pearson, P. (1984). A schematic-theoretic view of basic processes in reading comprehension. In P. Pearson (Ed.), *Handbook of reading research*. New York: Longman

Applebee, A. (1978). *The child's concept of story.* Chicago: Chicago University Press.

Armbruster, B. (1984). The problem of "inconsiderate text." In G. Duffy, L. Roehler, and J. Mason (Eds.), *Comprehension instruction.* New York: Longman.

Baker, L. (1982). An evaluation of the role of metacognitive deficits in learning disabilities. *Topics in Learning and Learning Disabilities, 2,* 27–35.

Baker, L., and Anderson, R. (1982). Effects of inconsistent information on text processing: Evidence for comprehension monitoring. *Reading Research Quarterly, 17,* 281–294.

Baker, L., and Brown, A. (1984). Metacognitive skills and reading. In P. Pearson (Ed.), *Handbook of reading research.* New York: Longman.

Baker, L., and Stein, N. (1981). The development of prose comprehension skills. In C. Santa and B. Hayes (Eds.), *Children's prose comprehension.* Newark, DE: International Reading Association.

Bartlett, F. (1932). *Remembering: A study in experimental social psychology.* Cambridge: Cambridge University Press.

Beaugrande, R. (1980). *Text, discourse, and process.* Norwood, NJ: Ablex

Beaugrande, R. (1984). Learning to read versus reading to learn: A discourse-processing approach. In H. Mandl, N. Stein, and T. Trabasso (Eds.), *Learning and comprehension of text.* Hillsdale, NJ: Erlbaum.

Black, J. (1985). An exposition on understanding expository text. In B. Britton and J. Black (Eds.), *Understanding expository text.* Hillsdale, NJ: Erlbaum.

Black, J., and Bower, G. (1980). Story understanding and problem solving. *Poetics, 9,* 223–250.

Bos, C., and Filip, D. (1982). Comprehension monitoring skills in learning disabled and average readers. *Topics in Learning and Learning Disabilities, 2,* 79–85.

Botvin, G., and Sutton-Smith, B. (1977). The development of structural complexity in children's fantasy narratives. *Developmental Psychology, 13,* 377–388.

Bower, G., Black, J., and Turner, J. (1979). Scripts in memory for texts. *Cognitive Psychology, 11,* 177–220.

Bretherton, I., and Beegly, M. (1982). Talking about internal states: The acquisition of a theory of mind. *Developmental Psychology, 18,* 906–921.

Brewer, W. (1980). Literary theory, rhetoric, and stylistics: Implications for psychology. In R. Spiro, B. Bruce, and W. Brewer (Eds.), *Theoretical issues in reading comprehension.* Hillsdale, NJ: Erlbaum.

Britton, B., Glynn, S., and Smith, J. (1985). Cognitive demands of processing expository text: A cognitive workbench model. In B. Bruce and J. Black (Eds.), *Understanding expository text.* Hillsdale, NJ: Erlbaum.

Brown, A. (1982). Learning how to learn from reading. In J. Langer and M. Smith-Burke (Eds.), *Reader meets author: Bridging the gap.* Newark, DE: International Reading Association.

Brown, A. (1987). Metacognition, executive control, self-regulation, and other more mysterious mechanisms. In F. Weinert and R. Kluwe (Eds.), *Metacognition, motivation, and understanding.* Hillsdale, NJ: Erlbaum.

Bruce, B. (1980). Plans and social action. In R. Spiro, B. Bruce, and W. Brewer

(Eds.), *Theoretical Issues in Reading Comprehension*. Hillsdale, NJ: Erlbaum.
Bruce, B., and Newman, D. (1978). Interacting plans. *Cognitive Science, 2,* 195–233.
Bruner, J. (1985). Narrative and paradigmatic modes of thought. In E. Eisner (Ed.), *Learning and teaching the ways of knowing*. Chicago: University of Chicago Press.
Camp, B., and Bash, M. (1981). *Think aloud: Increasing social and cognitive skills—A problem-solving approach*. Champaign, IL: Research Press.
Cavenaugh, J., and Borkowski, J. (1980). Searching for metamemory-memory connection: A developmental study. *Developmental Psychology, 16,* 441–453.
Chafe, W. (1982). Integration and involvement in speaking, writing, and oral literature. In D. Tannen (Ed.), *Spoken and written language*. Norwood, NJ: Ablex.
Clark, M. (1976). *Young fluent readers*. London: Heinemann.
Clay, M. (1973). *Reading: The patterning of complex behavior*. Portsmouth, NH: Heinemann.
Cook-Gumerz, J., and Gumperz, J. (1981). From oral to written culture: The transition to literacy. In M. Farr (Ed.), *Variation in writing: functional and linguistic differences*. Hillsdale, NJ: Erlbaum.
Crystal, D. (1979). *Working with LARSP*. New York: Elsevier.
Dansereau, D. (1987). Transfer from cooperative to individual studying. *Journal of Reading, 30,* 614–619.
DePaulo, B., and Jordan, A. (1982). Age changes in deceiving and detecting deceit. In R. Feldman (Ed.), *Development of nonverbal behavior in children*. New York: Springer-Verlag.
van Dijk, T., and Kintsch, W. (1983). *Strategies of discourse comprehension*. New York: Academic Press.
Dixon, C. (1979). Text type and children's recall. In M. Kamil and A. Moe (Eds.), *Reading research: Studies and applications*. Clemson, SC: National Reading Conference.
Durkin, D. (1966). *Children who read early*. New York: Teachers College Press.
Feagans, L., and Short, E. (1984). Developmental differences in the comprehension and production of narratives by reading disabled and normally achieving children. *Child Development, 55,* 1727–1736.
Fillion, B., and Brause, R. (1987). Research into classroom practices: What have we learned and where are we going? In J. Squire (Ed.), *The dynamics of language learning*. Urbana, IL: ERIC.
Finley, C., and Seaton, M. (1987). Using text patterns and question prediction to study for tests. *Journal of Reading, 32,* 124–142.
Fitzgerald, J. (1983). Helping readers gain self-control over reading comprehension. *The Reading Teacher, 37,* 249–253.
Flood, J., and Lapp, D. (1987). Reading and writing relations: Assumptions and directions. In J. Squire (Ed.), *The dynamics of language learning*. Urbana, IL: ERIC.
Forrest-Pressley, D., and Waller, T. (1984). *Cognition, metacognition, and reading*. New York: Springer-Verlag.
Freedle, R., and Hale, G. (1979). Acquisition of new comprehension schemata for expository prose by transfer of a narrative schema. In R. Freedle (Ed.),

New directions in discourse processing. Norwood, NJ: Ablex.

Garvey, C. (1982). Commmunication and the development of social role play. *New Directions in Child Development, 18,* 81–101.

Gavelek, J., and Raphael, T. (1985). Metacognition, instruction, and the role of questioning activities. In D. Forrest-Pressley, G. MacKinnon, and T. Waller (Eds.), *Metacognition, cognition,and human performance.* Orlando: Academic Press.

Glenn, C., and Stein, N. (1980). Syntactic structures and real-world themes in stories generated by children. (Tech. Report). Urbana: University of Illinois.

Goldman, S. (1982). Knowledge systems for realistic goals. *Discourse Processes, 5,* 279–303.

Goodman, K. (1973). On the psycholinguistic method of teaching reading. In F. Smith (Ed.), *Psycholinguistics and reading*. New York: Holt, Rinehart, and Winston.

Gordon, C., and Braun, C. (1985). Metacognitive processes: Reading and writing narrative discourse. In D. Forrest-Pressley, G. MacKinnon, and T. Waller (Eds.), *Metacognition, cognition, and human performance.* Orlando: Academic Press.

Graesser, A. (1981). *Prose comprehension beyond the word*. New York: Springer-Verlag.

Graesser, A., and Goodman, S. (1985). Implicit knowledge, question answering and the representation of expository text. In B. Britton and J. Black (Eds.), *Understanding expository text*. Hillsdale, NJ: Erlbaum.

Graybeal, C. (1981). Memory for stories in language impaired children. *Applied Psycholinguistics, 2,* 269–283.

Hall, M., Ribovich, J., and Ramig, C. (1979). *Reading and the elementary school child*. New York: Van Nostrand.

Hallahan, D., Kneedler, R., and Lloyd, J. (1983). Cognitive behavior modification techniques for learning disabled children: Self-instruction and self-monitoring. In J. McKinney and L. Feagans (Eds.), *Current topics in learning disabilities*. Norwood, NJ: Ablex.

Hansen, C. (1978). Story retelling used with average and learning disabled readers as a measure of reading comprehension. *Learning Disability Quarterly, 1,* 62–69.

Hardy, B. (1978). Narrative as a primary act of mind. In M. Meek, A. Warlow, and G. Barton (Eds.), *The cool web.* New York: Atheneum.

Harter, S. (1982). Children's understanding of multiple emotions: A cognitive developmental approach. In W. Overton (Ed.), *The relationship between social and cognitive development*. Hillsdale, NJ: Erlbaum.

Horowitz, R. (1985a). Text patterns: Part I. *Journal of Reading, 28,* 448–454.

Horowitz, R. (1985b). Text patterns: Part II. *Journal of Reading, 28,* pp. 534–541.

Hunt, K. (1975). *Grammatical structures written at three grade levels*. Champaign, IL: NCTE Research Report 3.

Jenkins, J. 91979). Four points to remember: A tetrahedral model and memory experiments. In L. Cermak and F. Craik (Eds.), *Levels and processing in human memory.* Hillsdale, NJ: Erlbaum.

Johns, J., and Ellis, D. (1976). Reading: Children tell it like it is. *Reading World, 16*:2, 115–128.

Kalmar, I. (1985). Are there really no primitive languages? In D. Olson, N. Torrance, and A. Hildyard (Eds.), *Literacy, language, and learning.* Cambridge University Press: New York.

Kieras, D. (1985). Thematic processes in the comprehension of expository prose. In B. Britton and J. Black (Eds.), *Understanding expository text*. Hillsdale, NJ: Erlbaum.

Lapp, D., and Flood, J. (1978). *Teaching reading to every child*. New York: Macmillan.

Lewis, M., and Michalson, L. (1983). *Children's emotions and moods*. New York: Plenum.

Liles, B. (1985). Cohesion in the narratives of normal and language disordered children. *Journal of Speech and Hearing Research, 28,* 123–133.

Liles, B. (1987). Episode organization and cohesive conjunctives in narratives of children with and without language disorder. *Journal of Speech and Hearing Research, 30,* 185–196.

Luria, A. (1961). *The role of speech in the regulation of normal and abnormal behavior.* New York: Liveright.

Mandler, J. (1982). Some uses and abuses of a story grammar. *Discourse Processes, 5,* 305–318.

Mandler, J. (1984). *Stories, scripts, and scenes: Aspects of schema theory.* Hillsdale, NJ: Erlbaum.

Markman, E. (1981). Comprehension monitoring. In W. Dickson (Ed.), *Children's oral communication skills*. New York: Academic Press.

McGee, L., and Richgels, D. (1985). Teaching expository text structure to elementary students. *The Reading Teacher, 38,* 739–748.

McNeil, J. (1987). *Reading comprehension: New directions for classroom practice.* Glenview, IL: Scott, Foresman.

Meacham, J. (1979). The role of verbal activity in remembering the goals of actions. In G. Zivin (Ed.), *The development of self-regulation through private speech*. New York: Wiley.

Meichenbaum, D. (1977). *Cognitive-behavior modification: An integrative approach*. New York: Plenum.

Merritt, D., and Liles, B. (1987). Story grammar ability in children with and without language disorder: Story generation, story retelling, and story comprehension. *Journal of Speech and Hearing Research, 30,* 539–552.

Meyer, B. (1987). Following the author's top-level organization: An important skill for reading comprehension. In R. Tierney, P. Anders, and J. Mitchell (Eds.), *Understanding readers' understanding*. Hillsdale, NJ: Erlbaum.

Meyer, B., and Rice, G. (1984). The structure of text. In P. Pearson (Ed.), *Handbook of reading research*. New York: Longman.

Miller, G., Galanter, E., and Primbran, K. (1960). *Plans and the structure of behavior.* New York: Holt, Rinehart, and Winston.

Myers, M. (1987). The shared structure of oral and written language and the implications for teaching writing, reading, and literature. In J. Squire (Ed.), *The dynamics of language learning*. Urbana, IL: ERIC.

Myers, M., and Paris, S. (1978). Children's metacognitive knowledge about reading. *Journal of Educational Psychology, 70,* 680–690.

Nelson, K. (1985). *Making sense: The acquisition of shared meaning.* Orlando: Academic Press.

Ninio, A., and Bruner, J. (1976). The achievement and antecedants of labeling. *Journal of Child Language, 5,* 1–15.

Otto, W., and White, S. (Eds.) (1982). *Reading expository material.* New York: Academic Press.

Owings, R., Peterson, G., Bransford, J., Morris, C., and Stein, B. (1980). Spontaneous monitoring and regulation of learning: A comparison of successful and less successful fifth graders. *Journal of Educational Psychology, 72,* 250–256.

Palincsar, A., and Brown, A. (1984). Reciprocal teaching of comprehension-fostering and comprehension-monitoring activities. *Cognition and Instruction, 1,* 117–175.

Patterson, C., and Roberts, R. (1982). Planning and the development of communication skills. *New Directions in Child Development, 18,* 29–46.

Pea, R. (1982). What is planning development the development of? In D. Forbes and M. Greenberg (Eds.), *Children's planning strategies.* San Francisco: Jossey-Bass.

Pearson, P. (1974). The effects of grammatical complexity on children's comprehension, recall, and conception of certain semantic relations. *Reading Research Quarterly, 10,* 155–192.

Pearson, P., and Spiro, R. (1980). Toward a theory of reading comprehension instruction. *Topics in Language Disorders, 1,* 71–88.

Pellegrini, A. (1985). Relations between preschool children's symbolic play and literate behavior. In L. Galdo and A. Pellegrini (Eds.), *Play, language, and stories.* Norwood, NJ: Ablex.

Piaget, J. (1932). *The moral judgment of the child.* London: Kegan Paul.

Piccolo, J. (1987). Expository text structure: Teaching and learning strategies. *The Reading Teacher, 40,* 838–847.

Postman, N., and Weingartner, C. (1969). *Teaching as a subversive activity.* New York: Delacorte Press.

Reid, J. (1966). Learning to think about reading. *Educational Research, 9,* 56–62.

Richek, M. (1987). DRTA: 5 variations that facilitate independence in reading narratives. *Journal of Reading, 30,* 632–636.

Richgels, D., McGee, L., Lomax, R., and Sheard, C. (1987). Awareness of four text structures: Effects on recall of expository text. *Reading Research Quarterly, 22,* 177–197.

Robinson, E. (1981). The child's understanding of inadequate messages and communication failure: A problem of ignorance or egocentrism. In W. Dickson (Ed.), *Children's oral communication skills.* New York: Academic Press.

Roth, F., and Spekman, N. (1986). Narrative discourse: Spontaneously generated stories of learning disabled and normally achieving students. *Journal of Speech and Hearing Disorders, 51,* 8–23.

Rumelhart, D. (1980). Schemata: The building blocks of cognition. In R. Spiro,

B. Bruce, and W. Brewer (Eds.), *Theoretical issues in reading comprehension*. Hillsdale, NJ: Erlbaum.

Sacerdoti, E. (1975). Nonlinear nature of plans. Proceedings of the Fourth International Joint Conference on Artificial Intelligence. Tbilisi, Georgia, U.S.S.R.

Sachs, J., Goldman, J., and Chaille, C. (1984). Planning in pretend play: Using language to coordinate narrative development. In A. Pellegrini and T. Yawkey (Eds.), *The development of oral and written language in social contexts*. Norwood, NJ: Ablex.

Scardamelia, M., and Bereiter, C. (1984). Development of strategies in text processing. In H. Mandl, N. Stein, and T. Trabasso (Eds.), *Learning and comprehension of text*. Hillsdale, NJ: Erlbaum.

Schank, R. (1982). *Reading and understanding*. Hillsdale, NJ: Erlbaum.

Schank, R., and Abelson, R. (1977). *Scripts plans goals and understanding*. Hillsdale, NJ: Erlbaum.

Schmidt, C. (1976). Understanding human action: Recognizing the plans and motives of other persons. In J. Carroll and J. Payne (Eds.), *Cognition and social behavior.* Hillsdale, NJ: Erlbaum.

Sedlak, A. (1974). An investigation of the development of the child's understanding and evaluation of the actions of others. Tech. Report No. NIH-CBM-TR-28). New Brunswick, NJ: Department of Computer Science, Rutgers University.

Snow, C., and Goldfield, B. (1981). Building stories: The emergence of information structures from conversation. In D. Tannen (Ed.), *Analyzing discourse: Text and talk*. Washington, D.C.: Georgetown University Press.

Spiro, R., and Taylor, B. (1987). On investigating children's transition from narrative to expository discourse: The multidimensional nature of psychological text classification. In R. Tierney, P. Anders, and J. Michell (Eds.), *Understanding readers' understanding*. Hillsdale, NJ: Erlbaum.

Spivack, G., Platt, J., and Shure, M. (1976). *The problem-solving approach to adjustment*. San Francisco: Jossey-Bass.

Stauffer, R. (1969). *Teaching reading as a thinking process*. New York: Harper and Row.

Stein, N., and Glenn, C. (1979). An analysis of story comprehension in elementary school children. In R. Freedle (Ed.), *New directions in discourse processing, II*. Norwood, NJ: Ablex.

Stein, N., and Policastro, M. (1984). The concept of story: A comparison between children's and teacher's viewpoints. In H. Mandl, N. Stein, and T. Trabasso (Eds.), *Learning and comprehension of text*. Hillsdale, NJ: Erlbaum.

Thorndyke, P. (1977). Cognitive structures in comprehension and memory of narrative discourse. *Cognitive Psychology, 9*, 77–110.

Tierney, R., and Pearson, P. (1983). Toward a composing model of reading. *Language Arts, 60*, 568–580.

Tough, J. (1981). *Talk for teaching and learning*. Portsmouth, NH: Heinemann.

Voss, J., and Bisanz, G. (1985). Knowledge and the processing of narrative and expository text: Some methodological issues. In B. Britton and J. Black (Eds.), *Understanding expository text*. Hillsdale, NJ: Erlbaum.

Vygotsky, L.S. (1978). *Mind in Society.* Cambridge, MA: Harvard University Press.

Weaver, P., and Dickinson, D. (1979). Story comprehension and recall in dyslexic students. *Bulletin of Orton Society, 28,* 157–171.

Wellman, H. (1985). The origins of metacognition. In D. Forrest-Pressley, G. MacKinnon, and T. Waller (Eds.), *Metacognition, cognition, and human performance.* Orlando: Academic Press.

Wells, G. (1986). *The meaning makers.* Portsmouth, NH: Heinemann.

Wesley, J. (1974). *Pioneers.* Lakeside, CA: Interact.

Westby, C. (1980). Assessment of cognitive and language abilities through play. *Language, Speech and Hearing Services in Schools, 11,* 154–168.

Westby, C. (1983). Language in planning and problem solving. Paper presented at the American Speech-Language-Hearing Association Convention, Cincinnati, OH.

Westby, C. (1988). Children's play: Reflections of social competence. *Seminars in Speech and Language, 9*:1, 1–14.

Westby, C., Maggart, Z., and Van Dongen, R. (1984). Oral narratives of students varying in reading ability. Paper presented at the Third International Congress for the Study of Child Language, Austin, TX.

Westby, C., Van Dongen, R., and Maggart, Z. (1986). The concept of trickery: Its development and role in culture and reading. Paper presented at the International Reading Association Convention, Philadelphia, PA.

Wilensky, R. (1978). Why John married Mary: Understanding stories involving recurring goals. *Cognitive Science, 2,* 235–266.

Willows, D., and Ryan, E. (1981). Differential utilization of syntactic and semantic information by skilled and less skilled readers in the intermediate grades. *Journal of Educational Psychology, 73,* 607–615.

Wolf, D. (1986). "I'm the pirate," he said. Symbolic play as a context for learning about types of discourse. Paper presented at the International Reading Association Convention, Philadelphia, PA.

Wong, B. (1982). Strategic behaviors in selecting retrieval cues in gifted, normal achieving, and learning disabled children. *Journal of Learning Disabilities, 15,* 33–37.

Wong, B. (1985). Metacognition and learning disabilities. In D. Forrest-Pressley, G. MacKinnon, and T. Waller (Eds.), *Metacognition, cognition, and human performance.* Orlando: Academic Press.

Wong, B., and Wong, R. (1986). Study behavior as a function of metacognitive knowledge about critical task variables: An investigation of above average, average, and learning disabled readers. *Learning Disabilities Research, 1,* 101–111.

CHILDREN'S BOOKS

Aardema, V. (1975). *Why Mosquitoes Buzz in People's Ears.* New York: Dial.

Aardema, V. (1981). *Bringing the Rain to Kapiti Plain.* New York: Dial.

Adams, P. (1973). *There Was an Old Woman Who Swallowed a Fly.* Wilts, England: Child's Play.

Aliki (1984). *Feelings.* New York: Greenwillow.

Aruego, J., and Aruego, A. (1972). *The Crocodile's Tale*. New York: Scholastic.
Asbjornsen, P., and Moe, J. (1957). *The Three Billy Goats Gruff*. New York: Harcourt Brace Jovanovich.
Bourgeois, P. (1986). *Franklin in the Dark*. New York: Scholastic.
Calhoun, M. (1979). *Cross-Country Cat*. New York: Mulberry Books.
Carle, E. (1969). *The Very Hungry Caterpillar*. New York: Philomel.
Cooper, S. (1973). *The Dark is Rising*. New York: Atheneum.
Dahl, R. (1966). *The Magic Finger*. New York: Harper and Row.
Dayrell, E. (1968). *Why the Sun and the Moon Live in the Sky*. New York: Houghton Mifflin.
dePaola, T. (1974). *Charlie Needs A Cloak*. Englewood Cliffs, NJ: Prentice-Hall.
dePaola, T. (1981). *Fin M'Coul: The Giant of Knockmany Hill*. New York: Holiday House.
Ehrlich, A. (1985). *Cinderella*. New York: Dial.
Emberley, B. (1967). *Drummer Hoff*. Englewood Cliffs, NJ: Prentice-Hall.
Frazer, N. (1984). *Stout-Hearted Seven*. Seattle: Pacific Northwest National Parks and Forest Association.
Gag, W. (1928). *Millions of Cats*. New York: Coward, McCann, and Georhegan.
Galdone, P. (1973). *The Little Red Hen*. New York: Scholastic.
Galdone, P. (1970). *The Three Little Pigs*. New York: Clarion Books.
Grimm (1978). *Cinderella*. New York: Larousse.
Juster, N. (1961). *The Phantom Tollbooth*. New York: Random House.
Keats, E. (1962). *The Snowy Day*. New York: Viking.
Kent, J. (1982). *Round Robin*. Englewood Cliffs, NJ: Prentice-Hall.
Laird, D. (1981). *The Three Little Hawaiian Pigs and the Magic Shark*. Honolulu: Barnaby Books.
Laird, D. (1983). *Wili Wai Kula and the Three Mongooses*. Honolulu: Barnaby Books.
L'Engle, M. (1962). *Wrinkle in Time*. New York: Dell.
Louie, A. (1982). *Yeh-Shen*. New York: Philomel.
MacLachlan, P. (1985). *Sarah, Plain and Tall*. New York: Harper and Row.
Martin, B. (1983). *Brown Bear, Brown Bear, What Do You See?* New York: Holt, Rinehart, and Winston.
Mayer, M. (1968). *If I Had*. New York: Dial.
Mayer, M. (1974). *Frog Goes to Dinner*. New York: Dial.
Mayer, M. (1983). *When I Get Bigger*. Racine, WI: Western Publishing Co.
Mayer, M. (1975). *Just for You*. Racine, WI: Western Publishing Co.
Mayer, M., and Mayer, M. (1971). *A Boy, A Dog, A Frog, and A Friend*. New York: Dial.
Mayer, M., and Mayer, M. (1975). *One Frog Too Many*. New York: Dial.
McEvoy, S. (1985). *Not Quite Human: Batteries Not Included*. New York: Archway.
Mendoza, G. (1982). *The Gillygoofang*. New York: Dial.
Morse, J., Gouge, B., Tate, D., and Eickmeyer, J. (1985). *The Feeling Fun House*. Dallas: Family Skills, Inc.
Paterson, D. (1977). *If I Were a Toad*. New York: Dial.
Peet, B. (1965). *Chester the Worldly Pig*. Boston: Houghton Mifflin.
Rayner, M. (1976). *Mr. and Mrs. Pig's Evening Out*. New York: Atheneum.
Rayner, M. (1977). *Garth Pig and the Ice Cream Lady*. New York: Atheneum.

Rogers, J. (1968). *The House That Jack Built*. New York: Lothrop, Lee, and Shepard.
Rylant, C. (1982). *When I Was Young in the Mountains*. New York: E. P. Dutton.
Schwartz, A. (1981). *Scary Stories to Tell in the Dark*. New York: Harper and Row.
Seidelman, J., and Mintonye, G. (1968). *The Fourteenth Dragon*. New York: Harlin Quist.
Shulevitz, U. (1967). *One Monday Morning*. New York: Scribners.
Van Woerkman, D. 91977). *Harry and Shellbert*. New York: Macmillan.
Zolotow, C. (1963). *The Quarreling Book*. New York: Harper and Row.

8

Learning to Write: Context, Form, and Process

Cheryl M. Scott

Along with reading, writing is an area of great difficulty for a majority of children with learning disabilities. Writing remains as a major concern for adults who seek help for learning disabilities. In a study of 93 adults with learning disabilities, Blalock and Johnson (1987) asked subjects to discuss educational problems and concerns. Most of the group reported difficulty writing papers, including problems with spelling, grammar, punctuation, summarizing main points, organization, and planning. They worried about being dependent on others to edit their writing. Frequently, they cited problems taking notes in class because of their inability to comprehend and write simultaneously. The adults' perceptions of their writing problems were verified in formal tests and observations (Johnson, 1987). To these individuals, writing problems loomed as major obstacles to personal, academic, and vocational development. In light of the mounting evidence of writing problems as a major component of persistent learning disablities, language clinicians and special educators need to be increasingly concerned with written as well as spoken language.

Heightened awareness of writing problems coincides with recent interest in children's writing as an integral part of linguistic and cognitive development. Writing is integral in the sense that the child develops insights about writing prior to and alongside formal teaching. Thus, there are ''naturally unfolding'' as well as explicitly taught components to the development of writing (Emig, 1981; Himley, 1986, Scinto, 1986). Recent research emphasizing the unique forms and functions of writing has resulted in an appreciation of the naturalistic side of learning to write. Children apparently learn many of these unique properties of writing without explicit instruction (Perera, 1986a).

When the linguistic and cognitive nature of writing are emphasized, questions about relationships between writing and other linguistic activities assume a more central role. Thus, in a book about children with reading problems, it is appropriate to ask questions about writing, the other side of the literacy coin. Although reading and writing have typically been investigated as isolated entities, more recent accounts of literacy development stress connections between the two (Dobson, 1988).

This chapter and the following one offer an introduction to the topic of developmental writing problems and related clinical and teaching concerns. Because writing problems of children and adolescents with language and learning problems have received considerably less attention than reading disability, the present chapter attempts to lay a foundation for the discussion of writing problems. The first section presents a framework for considering the major components of writing; topics include context and purpose, linguistic form (text, sentence, and word structures), and process. The subsequent section on writing development is organized according to this scheme. Chapter 9 examines the nature of writing problems using the same scheme and then takes up the topic of assessment and intervention of writing problems. The aim of the two chapters together is to present an overview of writing problems across a wide age range, with sensitivity to recent literature on writing and writing development. Another goal is to address relationships between writing and reading.

THE COMPONENTS OF WRITING

CONTEXT AND PURPOSE

Writing takes place in many different situational and social contexts, for many different purposes. Context and purpose are related in many cases. Thus, writing that is a demonstration of one's knowledge—for example, an essay examination—would be unlikely at home, and a chatty letter to a friend would be unlikely at school. The dependencies are far from rigid, however. As Wignell (1987) observed, secondary school projects and papers are usually written at home, as a solitary activity, because there are inadequate blocks of time at school and teachers want to see the student's ''own'' work. Likewise, more than one letter to a friend has undoubtedly been written on school time. Although there are potentially as many places for writing as there are places for people, three prominent settings are the home, the school, and for adults, the work place. Writing could take place in a variety of social contexts (e.g., joint student-teacher or student-student constructued texts) or as an entirely solitary activity from initial planning to final editing.

All writing is done for an audience (self or others) and has purpose. The purposes of writing derive from the fact that writing and reading are ultimately interactive social and communicative processes. Thus, writing accomplishes many of the same communicative purposes as speaking (e.g., informing, as in a newspaper article; persuading, as in an opinion essay; consoling, as in a diary or letter). Writing, however, is also used for several unique purposes that derive directly from the permanency of the medium. These include the functions of information storage, labeling, literary form expansion (e.g., a novel as opposed to an oral story), and academic analysis (Olson, 1977; Perera, 1984).

Something is written to be read. The reading audience may be indeterminate (Rubin, 1987) in a specific way for some tasks (e.g., writing copy for a pamphlet about state tourism opportunities), but even young school children know they are writing for a teacher who has certain expectations (e.g., ''she expects me to fill three lines'' [Himley, 1986]). For many types of mature writing, particularly expository writing, the writer must anticipate the thoughts, feelings, and beliefs of eventual readers, a feat requiring social cognition of some magntitude (Rubin, Piche, Michlin, and Johnson, 1984). Undoubtedly, the ability of the writer to construct the reader's response affects every level of the writing process (Fredericksen & Dominic, 1981).

Contexts and purposes of writing change with development. Examples of early contexts for writing are drawing and play (Gundlach, 1982). Emergent writing activities are more social to the extent that a listener is often present to hear children talk while they write and ''read'' what they write (Cioffi, 1984; Sulsby, 1986). Children may have surprisingly few opportunities to compose actual texts during the first few years of elementary school when spelling and punctuation drills account for a large portion of the writing curriculum. Of the total language arts curriculum in the early grades, considerably more time is devoted to reading than to writing. In the later elementary years, children have begun to write reports as well as stories, and almost all school assignments are done during school hours. Some children write at home; thank-you notes, letters, stories, and lists are typical home-produced texts.

Secondary school writing has a narrow focus of audience and function (Applebee, 1984). Text-level writing is usually in the form of generalized summary or analysis (88 percent of all writing exercises) and done for the teacher-as-examiner (90 percent). The information for such writing most often comes from the teacher or from textbooks. Students entering the postsecondary system encounter similar contexts for writing, although the texts they produce are frequently longer.

After high school and college, writing contexts change dramatically for most people in terms of context, purpose, and amount. Although the literary essay is a major genre of secondary and postsecondary writing, according to Corbett (1981) only 1 percent of the population will ever write another literary essay following graduation. A minority of literate people write ''regularly and seriously in connection with their jobs'' (Corbett, 1981, p. 47). For that minority, however, there is evidence that the amount of writing is increasing. Such writing takes the form of in-house memoranda and, for an even smaller minority, production of the vast amount of printed matter consumed by other adults and children (e.g., newspapers, magazines, books, brochures, ads, solicitations).

LINGUISTIC FORM

TEXT STRUCTURE: GENRE

For purposes of this chapter, *text* is defined broadly as a piece of writing done for a particular purpose. For a young child, a text might be a few words printed on a drawing. An older child's story of a few sentences or a few pages is a text, as is a story written in response to the teacher's instruction to ''write a story using your ten spelling words.'' This chapter is a text. *Genre* is a distinctive type of text, for example narrative text, expository text, persuasive text, and so forth. Genre categories can be broad or narrow. Thus, a personal experience story is a particular type of narrative, but a personal experience story with a moral is an even finer subdivision.

A genre is distinctive from the standpoint of both linguistic form, and social action (Himley, 1986). In terms of linguistic form for example, two narratives have similar text structure properties, including a setting and initiating event, and similar grammatical forms both within and across sentences. Narratives typically are written or told with simple past tense verb forms and a restricted set of intersentence connectivity markers such as *and then* or *so* (cf. Scott, 1984, 1987). Expository texts are organized along logical rather than temporal lines; text structure possibilities include problem/solution, main point/supporting examples, compare/contrast, and classification. Grammatical forms unlikely in narratives (e.g., passive verb forms and adverbials like *in conclusion* and *therefore*) are more common in expository texts.

In addition to linguistic form similarity, genre implies a distinctive type of social action. Thus, texts within a genre occur in a recurrent social situation, to accomplish a particular purpose. Letters of recommendation, user manuals, and the half-page essay examination answer are examples of texts with particular purposes. Because linguistic form *and* social action properties are included in the definition, genre spans *both* function and form components of writing. As indicated previously in the discussion of context and purpose, the genres of interest change dramatically across a wide developmental span.

SENTENCE STRUCTURE

Traditionally, sentence level grammar has concerned writers and students of writing. In any text, one of the most common observations that can be made is whether the sentences are grammatical. For any school child, a large part of learning to write means learning to write grammatically correct sentences.

Sentence level grammar in any text is a product of both genre and channel. *Channel* refers to whether the text is spoken or written. As discussed in Chapter 1, certain features of the written medium—for example, the lack of prosody—dictate certain syntactic features, such as word order variations for theme and focus (Perera, 1986a). Further, the genre affects sentence level grammar, as discussed above. Thus, although it may be convenient to refer to "prototypical" written versus spoken language structure (Rubin, 1987), real written texts show the combined structural effects of both channel and genre. Biber's (1986) recent descriptive work in text analysis is an example of an attempt to account for a wide range of channel and genre effects.

The student of writing development is interested in how and when children learn to use structures known to be particulary prominent in written language (Perera, 1984, 1986a, 1986b). Sentence structure in texts produced by children and adolescents needs to be examined with genre and channel effects in mind.

WORD STRUCTURE: ORTHOGRAPHY

Spelling is a major component of learning to write. Although teachers frequently characterize English orthography as nonphonetic and/or erratic (i.e., full of "exceptions"), recent discussions emphasize orthographic regularities designed to reveal meaning relations.

Morphographemic rules describe the ways that meaning similarities are marked through spelling. A common example is the marking of past tense with *ed* even though the pronunciation varies depending on the phonetic properties of the verb stem. Another example is the *g* in *sign*, which is not pronounced but nevertheless reveals a semantic connection with *signature* where it is pronounced. Just as proficiency in sentence structure requires considerable abstraction of linguistic rules, proficient spelling appears to place similar demands on the writer's ability to abstract patterns. Developmental stages from logographic (visual), to alphabetic (phonetic), to mature orthographic spelling have been identified for both spelling and reading (Snowling, 1985). Possible distinctions between the reading and spelling of individual words in terms of required levels of phonemic awareness are also of interest in the study of emerging literacy.

THE WRITING PROCESS

Recent accounts of the writing process stress its difficulty (Scardamalia, 1981), its opaque nature (Donaldson, 1984), and its fluidity (Nystrand, 1986). Nystrand (1986, p. 18) captured these qualities with his comment that

> writing is not a straightforward skill like eating or swimming or typing. . . no one learns to write fluently once and for all in the way people drive cars and work lawnmowers. . .written discourse is not the well-oiled engine of written speech production nor the well-regulated cybernetic system of cognitive scripts and well-formed permissible text types.

Models of the cognitive processes involved in writing have nevertheless proliferated in the last 10 years (Bereiter & Scardamalia, 1987; Hayes & Flower, 1980, 1987). Such models apply to relatively mature writing (secondary level and above) of expository forms of text and deal with text-level rather than word-level (e.g., spelling) processes. Complete models would therefore need to be expanded to consider less mature forms of writing, a variety of genres, and lower level processes. Steinberg (1980) notes that it would be odd if one model fit all kinds of writing.

One of the major research paradigms used in the development of such models is protocol analysis (Hayes & Flower, 1980, 1987). Subjects are given writing assignments designed to last approximately one hour. During this hour they are asked to think, read, and write aloud as they write. Verbatim transcripts, along with written notes produced during the task, are then examined. Hayes and Flower (1980) compared protocol analysis to tracking a porpoise. Both the porpoise and writing processes are "deep and silent," but occasionally the porpoise breaks the surface. Similarly, the protocols provide surface-breaking moments in writing. Other methods of investigating the writing process include retrospective reporting and pause analysis (Black, 1981).

The protocols, in the main, validate a model of writing portrayed schematically in Figure 8-1. Writers have goals, which they arrange hierarchically. They then plan, generate text (write), and revise. In the planning phase, writers select and organize their knowledge about a topic for an effective presentation. Subprocesses of planning include (a) generating relevant information by retrieving it from long-term memory, (b) organizing the retrieved information, and (c) setting goals for the text (Black, 1981). During planning, writers actively draw on their knowledge of writing strategies. For example, they apply knowledge of genre conventions or generate new conventions (problem solve) when faced with unique writing needs. Topic knowledge alone does not necessarily ensure clear writing. The active application of knowledge about writing strategies is also required.

The text generation phase of writing (also called the translation phase) is when "pen is put to paper" and text is produced. In this phase, writers must choose the actual language forms that encode meaning at the same time that ideas are being expanded. Hayes and Flower (1987) reported that ideas noted in an outline are expanded by mature writers on the average by a factor of 8 in the final essay. Writers work by producing a part of a sentence, pausing, generating the next part, pausing, in a left to right manner. They rarely go back and rework parts generated two or three units back (Hayes & Flower, 1987). Daiute (1984) studied the loci and types of errors made by writers as they generate text. She proposed that writers, like speakers, produce sentences in clause-by-clause sequences, with simultaneous production of one clause and monitoring of the preceding clause. The previous clause is already in a "recoded" state when monitoring occurs. When working memory is taxed—for example, when generating longer and more complex sentences—the recoded previous clause is lost, leading to error in the clause under construction. Daiute noted that even though writers, unlike speakers, have the previous clause available for review, it is not routinely reread. The occurrence of overlapping errors, in which a portion of a clause is traced to two different clauses, supports this view of memory constraint in the generation phase. In the following example (Daiute, 1984, p. 209), the overlapping portion is italicized:

> Four years ago was the best time of my career which *I wasn't in a position to know* that then.

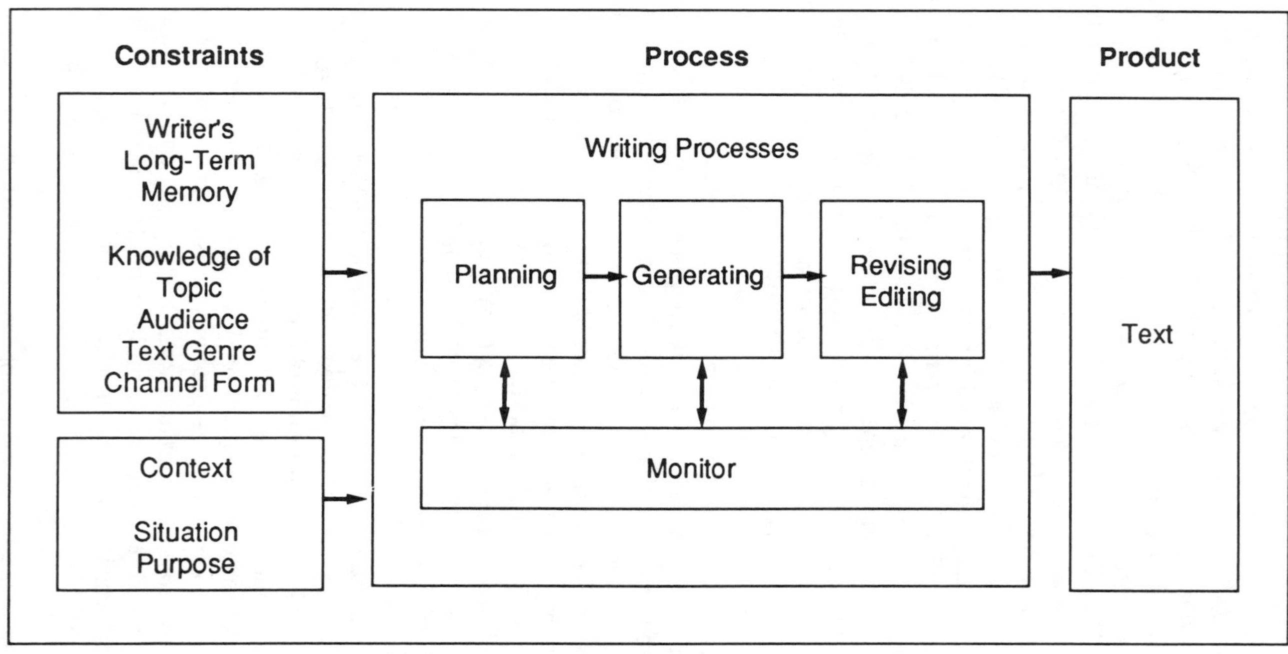

FIGURE 8-1. A simplified schematic of the writing process, based on the Hayes and Flower (1980, 1987) model.

Revising is the last stage of the three-stage linear model of the composing process. Recent research challenges the view of revision as an end-stage process, stressing instead the recursive nature of revising (Witte, 1983). Older and more expert writers devote proportionally more time to revising and make changes involving larger stretches of discourse and text meaning. Revisions of younger writers (nonadult) are directed to the sentence level and generally do not change meaning. Writers are relatively less adept at finding errors and faults in their own texts, compared with texts written by others. Several treatments of this phase recommend the separation of editing and revising processes. ''Editing'' is the term reserved for detecting and correcting errors in grammar, syntax, punctuation and spelling, while ''revising'' involves changing a text to alter its meaning or structure (Hull, 1987).

Just as one model is insufficient to account for all genres or ages, a single model is unlikely to account for different levels of expertise, interest, and commitment to writing. Bereiter and Scardamalia (1987) distinguish two models of the writing process, the *knowledge-telling model* and the *knowledge-transforming model*. The knowledge-telling model is similar to the one sketched above. Writers approach a writing task, either self-chosen or assigned, in a fairly straightforward manner. They first identify topics and form notions about appropriate genre. For example, given the assignment to write about a 12-month school calendar, topic identifiers might include *comparison of U.S. and Japanese students* and *forgetting information during summer vacations*. The genre would be an opinion essay. The knowledge-telling writer can get started on the task and turn out a text fairly quickly. The model allows for differences among outcomes depending on the writer's topic and genre knowledge. The knowledge-transforming writer, on the other hand, uses writing to rework thoughts. In so doing, this writer essentially ''discovers'' new thoughts, or comes to view something in a different manner. Presumably, the discoveries would not have come about without the act of writing. Revision is more extensive and recursive in such texts. Differences between the two approaches to writing are observed in longer start-up times, and more extensive note-taking and think-aloud protocols for knowledge-transforming writing (Bereiter & Scardamalia, 1987). Distinctions between the two approaches are not necessarily tied to age, although older writers probably employ a knowledge-transforming model more frequently. Apparently, some writers never use this approach.

Most models of writing, including the Hayes and Flower (1987) model, are concerned with the specifics of producing a coherent text rather than the ideas that motivate and surround a text. Accordingly, Collins and Gentner (1980) stress the importance of distinguishing between *text production* and *idea production* in a theory of writing. Both are subprocesses of writing, but there are important differences. Ideas are much more opaque than text and the number of allowable relations between ideas is greater than those in text. The basic form of ideas may be quite different from linguistic predications (i.e., text elements of approximately clause size). Ideas are first captured, then manipulated in various ways (e.g., simulations, taxonomies, critical-case generation). The importance of the distinction for purposes of this chapter and the following is that elements of some writing problems may lie with idea production, not text production. When students write about topics they know little about, have not previously thought about, and have little interest in, their text production processes operate on impoverished "raw material." For a particular problem writer, contributions from idea, text, or combined levels of processing are unquestionably difficult to untangle, but the distinction remains an important one in principle.

Although it is possible to imagine a general sequential schematic of planning, generating, and revising, the sequence is far from rigid and there are many points of interaction and recursive cycling (as represented by the monitor in Figure 8-1). In addition, as Nold (1981) argued, there is a constant tension between global plans (the writer's ability to keep overall meaning, purpose, and audience in focus) and local plans (the writer's knowledge of syntax, vocabulary, othography). Writing is difficult because of the number of different processing components and their *simultaneous* application. Trying to satisfy structure, content, and purpose constraints at one time is demanding for the best of writers (Collins & Gentner, 1980). It is not surprising that writing can sometimes cause problems for most people and usually causes major problems for individuals with learning disabilities.

LEARNING TO WRITE

Compared to spoken language and reading, the history of research in developmental writing is short. Perera (1986a) explained that because writing was viewed as an overlaid linguistic skill explicitly taught to children, it was less interesting to developmentalists. Recent accounts, however, stress writing (like reading) as an individually learned developmental activity as well as a socially taught linguistic system (Gundlach, 1982; Olson, 1984; Smith, 1984; Sulsby, 1986). The fact the some children begin writing words and sentences before any formal instruction underscores the individual, tacit side of early writing. Evidence that children extract many principles of writing on their own is also found in later developmental periods. Writing development is ultimately an interaction between individual cognitive processes invoked in the learning of writing and enabling contexts, both educational and cultural (Collins, 1984).

Emergent Writing, 4 to 6 Years

Context and Purpose

Spontaneous occurrences of writing prior to school instruction, or concurrent with early instruction, have been observed by several investigators (Bissex, 1980; Cioffi, 1984; Donaldson, 1984; Gundlach, 1982; Himley, 1986). Unlike the older writer who composes silently with few "extraneous" behaviors, the emergent writer frequently draws, says words out loud as they are written, and talks to others nearby.

Many observers of child writing have noted that children frequently draw and write on the same page. At first, drawing covers most of the page and writing is limited to one or several words that are often labels for drawn objects. Eventually, proportions shift so that a longer text is accompanied by smaller pictures that are added after the text is written. According to Gundlach (1982), the child "builds a bridge" between the familiar activity of drawing to the less familiar writing. In the author's observations, many children continue to draw small pictures with a broad spectrum of their written work—school writing excercise sheets, letters, and stories—into the third grade and beyond. Although the co-occurrence of writing and drawing are directly observable, the processes served by such combinations are not well understood (Gundlach, 1982). Perhaps the drawing helps the child sustain the writing effort. Or perhaps the drawing contributes to the text-making potential of the piece by "filling-in" information.

Some early texts have discernible communicative or personal purposes. As early as five years, and often by age six or seven, many children write messages for others, labels, lists to help themselves store and organize information, and longer texts of narrative form. Texts may have clearcut and sometimes even urgent purposes. Consider the now classic RUDF (are you deaf?) message presented by five-year-old Paul Bissex to his mother, when more conventional ways of getting her attention had failed (Bissex, 1980). Gundlach (1982) provided an example of a child's organizational writing, which appears to be more personal than social. After receiving a notepad for his seventh birthday, the child wrote at the top of a sheet *thig's with weel's,* and beneath he wrote, on separate lines, *Train's/ Truck's/ car's/ wagon's/ modersicle's/.*

It is not clear that all child writers have the same grasp of audience and purpose as Paul Bissex. Read (1981) observed that children are sometimes uninterested in the effects of their writing. They might write messages that they do not expect to be read (e.g., messages of the *keep out* variety for younger siblings who are nonreaders). Young children are also less likely to keep their own writing (as is well known to any parent interested in children's writing).

Text Structure: First Genres

Two text types, the *Book* genre (a form of narrative) and the *Draw and Write* genre have been observed in emergent writers. Both types of texts combine drawing with writing. Even though the written portion of the text may be limited to single words or word groups, the children nevertheless demonstrate that their knowledge of text structure extends across larger units of text.

The kindergarten classroom has provided many examples of early narrative writing. Dyson (1986) studied children's spontaneous story writing at a "writing center" in the kindergarten classroom. She cited the case of Ashley, who alternated between telling his story and planning his drawing and writing activities; for example; "Here go Spiderman. I'm writing both of 'em in real life [Spiderman and his unnamed friend]" (p. 210). Sulsby (1982, 1986) examined the differences between story telling and story dictation in 24 kindergarten children with a mean age of 5;10. Twelve children clearly distinguished dictated from told stories, as indicated by the use of reading-like intonation and written language wording for the dictated story.

Himley (1986) provided additional evidence that children grasp the boundaries of various text types before they write fully formed texts. She followed the development of the Book genre and the Draw and Write genre in a kindergarten child, Samantha. The child's early "books" had a title page with a title in capital letters (e.g., The Smile Book), numbered pages, and left-to-right/top-to-bottom orientation for the contents of the book (different types of faces and a repeated set of two identical graphic forms). Draw and Write was a teacher-initiated activity in which the children received a piece of paper with lines on the bottom half. The children were instructed to first draw on the top half, then write "anything" on the bottom half. Samantha's early writing on this assignment consisted of working to fill an arbitrary length requirement of three lines (she had observed that children who didn't write enough had their papers returned). There was little syntactic relation between words on one line or from one line to the next. With time, however, as the child persevered in both genres, she moved from texts that merely "looked like" (or in the case of Sulsby's dictated stories, "sounded like") a particular genre to texts that actually "read like" the intended genre (Himley, 1986, p. 157). Himley concluded that genre has a generative effect on young children's writing.

Word Structure and Underlying Process

The fundamental discovery that the child must make is that "one can draw not only things, but also speech" (Vygotsky, 1978, p. 115). Before this discovery, however, three- and four-year-old children often include letterlike forms (shapes bearing more or less resemblance to conventional letters) with their drawings, either spontaneously or when asked to "put letters with it."

Ferreiro (1984) investigated this earliest period of emergent writing in a group of Mexican children aged three to five years. Employing a Piagetian interview paradigm, she studied the children's responses to queries about their drawing and writing. To a child this age, Ferreiro found, letters are viewed as objects that have names. The question "What does it say?" is meaningless to such a child, who gives answers such as "letters" or "fives," because letters are not viewed as being symbolic. At this stage (letters as objects), there is no discernable relationship between the placement of letters and drawings on the page; letters may even appear inside the drawn object.

Eventually the child realizes that letters are substitute objects that "name" something else (letters as substitute objects). One sign of the change is the contrastive use of definite articles to refer to the picture of an object and the omission of the article when referring to the letters. Thus, the child answers *a chair* when shown a picture of a chair and *chair* when the adult points to the printed word "chair." Although letters now represent other objects, they do not yet represent the *sound pattern* of that object, as indicated by the lack of a consistent set of letters for a particular object. At this stage, writing is still a first-order symbol system (Dyson, 1986). Referring to Ferreiro's research, Donaldson (1984) drew attention to the fact that children are adept at symbolizing static objects with their letter-like forms, but that dynamic events are not represented. In this way, early writing differs from early speech in which children routinely encode movement and change (e.g., *allgone, up*). In fact, the association of writing and drawing with only static objects may make it hard for children to "break free" and discover the power of the written word for representing events as well as objects.

For writing to become a second-order symbol system, one equally suited to objects and events, the child must realize that written symbols designate speech sounds symbols—that writing, in essence, "draws" speech. An appreciation of the alphabetic nature of writing takes time to develop. Along the way, some children adopt a quantity strategy in which the names of different objects are distinguished by the number of ''letters.'' Later, a syllabic hypothesis—the notion that a letter represents a syllable—is evident, but consistent letter-syllable correspondence may still be lacking. Eventually, the aphabetic principle is discovered. Ferreiro (1984, p. 171) emphasized the similarities in the constructive aspects of learning to write and the construction of other logical schemes:

> Trying to understand the writing system, children face problems of a logical nature. There are problems of one-to-one correspondence, of the relationship between a totality and its constituent parts, of serial order, of identity and conservation of meaningful attribution, of classification, and of permutation and commutation. These problems arise in literacy development, just as they arise in many other domains, when children try to understand the world but the world resists the assimilation schemes of the growing subject.

In a project similar to Ferreiro's research, Sinclair (1984) asked children between the ages of 3;1 and 4;5 to write ''whatever they liked'' and then talked with the children about what they wrote. In terms of actual form, the children's graphic productions were of three types. Some children produced a continuous line of scribble, usually for peoples' names. Others produced strings of identical isolated forms (e.g., vertical lines, circle-like forms, or half-circle forms). The third writing style in this age range was strings of varied letter-like forms. Three of Sinclair's 21 subjects were reported to understand that writing represents sound, and made one mark per syllable. The other children's writing represented the range of symbolic levels of objects and people described by Ferreiro (1984). As reported by Sulsby (1986), the same child may use different types of graphic systems (e.g., scribbling, letter-like forms, and invented spelling) for different tasks and in different settings. Gradually, writing takes on more and more characteristics of invented and conventional spelling (Read, 1981, 1985, 1986).

Writing and Reading

The relationship between early writing and reading is interesting for practical as well as theoretical reasons and can be addressed from several perspectives. One question is whether writing and reading are similar but inverse processes. Another perspective examines aspects of early literacy activities for common roots and mutually beneficial effects. Answers to such questions should have an impact on writing and reading pedagogy. As it now stands, writing and reading instruction are separate portions of many language arts programs. Given a better understanding of possible relations, activities that are mutually beneficial for writing and reading might be designed. Examples of such activities are discussed in Chapter 9.

Writing and reading are frequently described as message encoding and decoding, implying an inverse relationship. A weak version of the inverse-relation view requires only that they have opposite general effects, for example, messages are constructed (written) and then reconstructed (read) at some later point. A stronger notion of the inverse relation would require that writing and reading "proceed through the same steps in opposite directions; that is, that every step of one process must be the inverse of a corresponding step of the other" (Read, 1981, p. 106).

According to Read (1981), young children's reading and writing are not inverses in either the weak or the strong sense. He observed that children frequently cannot read their own writing, and, as indicated previously, they may be less aware of the purposes and value of writing. Children at times seem to be more concerned with the *process* of writing than the *product* (Read, 1981). Evidence that the spelling and reading of words are not inverse processes can be found in the study of invented spellings. Read (1981, 1986) studied the spelling of familiar words in children between the ages of four and six. The children spelled words in a segment-by-segment manner (or syllable-by-syllable), drawing from both the letter's common sound values and the names of the letters. Read (1981) noted that the children *created*, rather than retrieved, the spelling of a word. Moreover, the same word was sometimes created afresh on each new spelling, because there was considerable variation from one spelling to the next. Bryant and Bradley (1980) reported evidence of the opposite type—that children can also spell words they are unable to read. Apparently, then, the types of phonological insights that underly phoneme-grapheme decoding are not identical to the types of insights required for spelling, an encoding process.

Galda (1984) analyzed those aspects of early literacy activities that presumably underly both writing and reading and are mutually facilitative. First, both emergent reading and writing activities in the home environment are emulative rather than instructional. The child selects items to learn (whether a bedtime story or a session with crayons and paper) and caretakers react with pleasure. Second, concepts about print relevant to the task of both reading and writing are formed (e.g., directional arrangement of letters and words on a page, spaces between words, conventional ways of writing words). Another similarity is seen in the hypothesis-testing nature of early reading and writing. Both the invented spellings characteristic of writing and the types of reading errors revealed in miscue analysis can be interpreted as indications of hypothesis testing. Finally, children are learning that both reading and writing are done for a purpose and carry meaning. Indeed, it is difficult to see how one activity could *not* inform the other.

According to Olson (1984), both reading and writing are well served in homes where parents use a "metalanguage" (the use of language about language). Such homes are literate homes in which parents treat language as an object and believe that it can be taught to children. Olson (1984) traced the types of book-sharing activities that encourage the child to view language as an object composed of words, both nouns and verbs. Of some interest is Olson's view that parents believe they are teaching the child to *talk* during such routinized book activities. What they are actually planting is a common root system for reading and writing, which, more than speaking, depend on metalanguage facility.

A recent study by Dobson (1988) supplied some of the most direct evidence of important developmental connections between writing and reading. Dobson reported results of a two-year project involving bimonthly sampling of planned observations and interactions with children in a naturalistic writing/reading context. The children were followed from the beginning of kindergarten through the end of the first grade. In each session the children were asked to draw a picture, "write" about the picture, and "read" their work; they also chose and read storybooks from preselected materials. The goal of the project was to identify naturally developing strategies used by the children as they approximated writing and reading. Dobson (1988, p. 4) identified five levels of advancing print awareness:

- Level 1: The contents of books are meaningful and can be read as such.
- Level 2: Spoken text matches with the written text (time-space match).
- Level 3: The alphabetic principle is used to match speech and print and thus produce a stable wording.
- Level 4: Words appear on a page as units of print, separated by space.
- Level 5: Morphemes (word, base, or affix) have a constant spelling but can be combined to form new units of meaning.

Dobson then sought to show how certain developments in reading and writing were related to each level of print awareness. To illustrate, she observed that Level 2 awareness was *first* evident in the context of the children's *own* writing; when asked to "read" their "writing," the children began to match written and spoken units. For example, they might make a unit-to-unit match between the words in the message and printed letters accompanying their picture, or they might track a line of print several times until the spoken message ended. The point of interest is that the children first used the strategy in reading their own writing; it was some time before they used a similar strategy when "reading" the storybooks. Dobson (1988, p. 12) concluded that "reading and writing are mutually supportive and connected at each step to learners' functional knowledge of the written language system and how it works."

ELEMENTARY SCHOOL WRITING, 7 TO 12 YEARS

An adequate account of writing development in the school years would have to deal with the same topics addressed for emergent writing (i.e. context, purpose, genre, spelling) plus additional ones. The older child begins to use conventions unique to written language; for example, punctuation. As texts become considerably longer and the variety of text types increase, genre analysis for older children is considerably more extensive. Moreover, as the child produces longer texts, the processes of planning, generating, and editing begin to be of interest. Longer texts also permit an analysis of the child's knowledge of syntactic structures more characteristic of written language. At this point in time, significant progress in each of these topics is underway, but there is as yet no well developed theory of developmental writing (Bereiter, 1980; Shuy, 1981).

CONTEXT AND PURPOSE

What are the occasions of writing for elementary school children? In the early elementary years, classroom contexts include copying single words from the board, writing single words from dictation, copying phrases and sentences from the board, generating sentences that incorporate certain words, generating stories that incorporate a set of words, generating stories in response to topics suggested by the teacher, and Draw and Write texts of the type described in the previous section. Children are gradually given assignments to write stories about personal experiences (the Recount genre, after Christie, 1986) and to make up stories about selected topics. In later elementary years, children may be expected to write biographical or historical narratives as well as procedural and expository texts. At home, children write letters, stories, and diaries.

Many elementary school writing assignments are done for an audience of one—the teacher. Although most school texts are written for the purpose of demonstrating knowledge, assigments vary according to the type of knowledge under scrutiny. Some assignments, especially in the early elementary years, are read for content only (note the "read but not corrected" stamp on school papers). With others, the content seems less important than the form. Whatever conclusions the child draws about the purpose of school-produced texts, the effects of such restrictions are not well understood. Largely in reaction to the contrived contexts and purposes of school writing, Graves (1983) advocates the writing of texts for larger audiences beyond the teacher. Children in such classrooms actually "publish" their work and read the texts of their peers. Text 1, *The Deadly Snake,* from the author's files, is an example of such a publication. Written as a class project by a nine-year-old third grader, the dedication, story, and "about the author" sections were bound in a hardback cover made from cardboard and contact paper. The story is a fictional piece with obvious *Star Wars* connections. Notable features include the polished punctuation and spelling, presumably the result of editing activities preceding the final draft.

TEXT STRUCTURE: GENRE

The ages between early and late elementary grades span a considerable period of growth in the length and types of different text genres produced. Draw and Write texts, discussed previously, continue as an early genre for school children. Examples include the sentence *I'm rasing wiv Dean in the smiig pool,* written beneath a picture of children in a swimming pool, and the sentence *Popcorn is delicious yummy and crunchy,* written after a classroom popcorn-making experience (Christie, 1986, p. 124). Texts 2 and 3 are recount and fictional narrative texts written by children in the early elementary years (from Christie, 1986, pp. 128–129). In the recount text (Text 2), the child reconstructs a series of events from personal experience. The store structure includes a setting ("On Wednesday"), a series of events, and a closing ("The End"). Connectivity markers appropriate for temporally related events include *and, and then,* and *so.* Text 3 is similar but adds a true problem (the disappearance of the baby bear), which would be more characteristic of fictional narratives.

The ability to produce different types of texts suitable for particular contexts is an important mark of writing development. The development of genre-specific writing in older elementary children has been studied in single-function and cross-function projects. In a single function study of narrative writing, Yde and Spoelders (1985) found significant growth in cohesion (after Halliday and Hasan, 1976) and compactness (after Scinto, 1983) in a two-year period between 9 and 11 years.

TEXT 1

the Deadly Snakes
by: Chris Marks

I dedicate this story
to my dog, Wicket

Once there were three guys. One was named Herman, one was named Bill, and one was named Leo. They decided to take a hike. They went on a hike. They were walking, and they came to a cave.

"Lets go in the cave" said Bill.

"But it looks so dark in there" said Herman.

"So what" said Leo.

"Oh well" said Herman. They killed 10 snakes before they got out. The snakes followed them. One almost bit Bill but the snakes head hit a rock and he died. Then Herman sliced another snake into 9 pieces. "Remember you guys use the force" said their grandfather. Ching ching. They killed all the snakes but one. They all swung at it and they all yelled at the same time "It's metal"

But then they saw a electric wire that was sticking out of it "chop it" said Herman. zzzzzz They killed that last snake. They were heros' then but now there's Superman.

About the Author

Chris Marks grew up loving monsters, and danguros things. Now he is 9 years old and still loving monsters and dangerus things:

TEXT 2

Anakie Gorge (spelling corrected)

On Wednesday we went to Anakie Gorge and when we went we went past Fairy Park and when we got there we walked down the path and we saw a koala and we saw a lizard and there was dead foxes hanging on the fence and we walked on to the picnic place and then we climbed up the mountain and I nearly slipped so I went down and when everyone was down we had lunch and then we had a play and then we went for a walk to the creek and found stones and boys were throwing stones in the water and when we were combing back Jeffrey fell in the creek and before we went we made daisy chains. The End.

TEXT 3

Climb Away Susy Koala

One day there was a mother with her baby and they were looking for some food and the little baby went away from her mother and she saw that her baby was gone and she went looking for her and she met one of her friends hullo have you seen my baby no and the koala said do you want to help me look for her yes so off they went and on the way they met another friend hullo have you seen my baby no so the mother said do you want to help yes and they got very scared because there was parrots and they found her behind the tree looking for food and they lived happily ever after. The End.

Several cross-function projects have investigated developing sensitivity to genre in children's writing. Hidi and Hildyard (1983) compared narrative and opinion essay writing in third and fifth grade children. In terms of general facility with one or the other genre, fifth graders wrote well-formed narratives, but only a few produced well-formed opinion essays. In grade three there were fewer well-formed narratives, but the students able to write good narratives were also able to write good opinion essays. For both groups, narratives were better formed, more cohesive, and longer than opinion essays. Compared to narratives, neither third or fifth grade students had the text-specific organizational strategies required to produce good opinion essays (e.g., discourse elements such as positive and negative rational factors). Such text-specific difficulties, however, were not limited to writing; similar problems occurred in speaking, indicating that channel is not the primary source of difficulty. The reasons why children's nonnarrative texts lag behind are not clear. With reference to expository texts, Christie

(1986) argued against the common assertion that nonnarrative texts are inherently more difficult for children to write. Children's lack of experience with such texts, she believes, is the more likely explanation (see also Martin, Christie, and Rothery, 1987).

A different comparison, between persuasive and narrative writing, was carried out by Pellegrini, Galda, and Rubin (1984). Third and fifth grade children in their study demonstrated sensitivity to genre as indicated by the types of conjunctions used. Children used more causal conjunctions in the persuasive writing and more additive conjunctions in the narrative writing. Growth in the ability to organize persuasive texts along causal lines occurred between the third and fifth grades.

Sentence Structure

Children's written sentences have been examined in some detail. In the 1960s, several large scale projects analyzed children's school writing according to sentence length, degree of subordination, and frequencies of syntactic structures, particularly types of dependent clauses (Hunt, 1965, 1970; Loban, 1976; O'Donnell, Griffin, & Norris, 1967, as discussed in Scott, 1988b). More recently, Perera (1984, 1986a) published extensive reviews of the structural features of children's written language, as distinct from spoken language; comparisons of written and spoken language of children between the ages of 8 and 12 were the focus of her own research (Perera, 1986b).

From a structural perspective, children's written sentences resemble their spoken utterances until the later elementary years. Quantitative measures of syntactic complexity reveal that both spoken and written sentences increase in length between the third and sixth grades, from approximately 7.5 words per T-unit (a structurally defined unit consisting of a main clause and any attached subordinate clauses) to 9.5 words. O'Donnell et al. (1967) found that written sentences were slightly shorter in the third grade; by fifth grade, however, a crossover had occurred and written sentences were longer (9.34 words compared with 8.90 words). Measures of subordination density (e.g., main + subordinate clauses/T-units) also reveal changes in the upper elementary grades, from approximately 1.1 to 1.3 clauses per sentence. (See Scott, 1988b for commentary on the use of sentence length and subordination measures.)

Kroll (1981) proposed four periods in the evolution of spoken/written form relationships. During a *preparation phase*, children concentrate on spelling and the mechanics of writing. Spontaneously written texts in this period are not up to the standard of spoken language; for example, sentences are shorter and grammatical errors (usually omissions) occur that would not be heard in speech. In a *consolidation phase,* writing more closely resembles speech. In the following first grade text from Read (1981, p. 111), words seem to role off the pen just as they might role off the tongue:

TODAY IS FALL NO TOMAERO IS FALL
YES TODAY IS FALL WEL JAST FRGT IT
THE LEEVS AER FALLING
THE LEEVS AER FALLING
AND TAY TRNE DIFRINT COLRS

At the age of 9 or 10, many children enter a *differentiation phase* in which structures more characteristic of written language are found. Differentiation occurs in the following areas: (1) the absence of distinctly oral structures, (2) fewer coordinated main clauses and more subordinate clauses and parenthetical constructions, and (3) the appearance of structures specific to written language (e.g., passive voice and nonfinite verb forms) (Perera, 1986a; Scott, 1988b). Further, patterns of written text organization begin to appear (e.g., word order changes for theme and focus). This is a somewhat awkward period; elements of the previous phase may continue so that a given text might ''swerve erratically from over-formality to colloquialism and back again'' (Perera, 1984, p. 208).

Text 4, from the author's files, is such a text. Written by a second grade child at the age of 7; 8, the narrative is a fantasy piece written in the first person. Punctuation is erratic—a colon (line 8) coexists with many omissions of periods. There are several structures characteristic of mature writing including a series construction (lines 8–11) and adverbial fronting (line 13, *there stood a little tiger cub*), but several spoken forms (e.g., *well* in line 19) are also present. There are traces of phonetic spelling (*privace, thermas, follod*).

Finally, in the *integration phase,* writers move easily between oral and written form, adapting structure to fit the needs of a variety of text types. Rubin (1987) refers to the most advanced writing of this phase as ''reconverged'' (i.e., writing and speaking). Writers can now draw on an oral style in their writing when they wish to convey a particular effect to the reader. According to Perera (1984) and Rubin (1987), many writers never reach the integration phase. Instead, they continue to write in a manner characteristic of earlier phases. Some may write in a ''hypercorrect'' manner (Rubin, 1987), to the detriment of their continuing development as writers (see p. 312, line 21, in Chapter 9 for an example).

TEXT 4

TIGER CUB

One hot Summer I was walking in the field Just me, privace at last. Feeling proud of myself I sat down with a little sac lunch I had made. I opend my thermas and set out my blanket. as I ate my lunch I planned what I was going to do. I was going to: pick some wild flowers, swim in the field lake, and biuld things in the fields Sandpile I heard this little new new. I looked behind me there stood a little tiger cub. he sat down beside me. new new he said. I stroked his Soft tiger fur After I hat done my three tasks I noticed the tiger cub had follod me. Well I did the thing most children would do I decied to ask my folks if I could have him. When I got home I asked my dad why he was mewing? My dad Studeyd his mewing for a minuit

(Story continues as follows)

He needs a home he said. So the tiger cub stayed at my house from then on. I named him Stripey.

SENTENCE PUNCTUATION

Whereas the examination of children's invented spellings provides evidence of intutitive knowledge about phonology, the study of children's punctuation errors reveals developmental changes in syntactic knowledge. Cazden, Cordeiro, and Giacobbe (1985) analyzed the use of the possessive apostrophe, quotation marks, and periods in the spontaneous writing of a first grade class that served as one of the sites for Donald Graves' research on the conference approach to writing instruction (1983). First graders supplied periods in approximately half the opportunities. What interested the authors more than omissions, however, were errors of *commission*—the children's incorrect use of periods. These errors were far from random and appeared to reflect several hypotheses about the constituent structure of English. With development through the elementary years, the ''sentence fragments'' created by erroneous period placement remain relatively stable in number and change qualitatively. To illustrate, sixth graders studied by Weaver (1982, p. 442) produced fragments consisting of noun clauses, for example,

> I wanted to know one thing. If you would please come with me to the High Wheeler soon.

which never appeared in the writing of younger children. Weaver (1982) concluded there is much to learn from the study of children's use of period ''errors.''

JOHN, AN 11-YEAR-OLD WRITER

Texts 5 and 6 illustrate several points made thus far in relation to writing of elementary school–age children. The texts are part of an ongoing investigation on the development of written and spoken genre in fifth and eighth grade normally developing and learning disabled youngsters (Scott, 1987). Text 5 is a narrative, and Text 6 is an expository piece (a report); both were written in response to a request to summarize videotaped programs. The writer, John, is a normally developing 11-year-old boy. Quantitative data for the texts are shown in Table 8-1. In this project the children also summarized the films orally; corresponding spoken data are also available, therefore, and are shown in parentheses in Table 8-1.

Several interesting differences attributable to genre and channel are found. Although John spent more time writing the report text than the narrative text (28 minutes as opposed to 25 minutes), the report text is considerably shorter, both in total words and in number of T-units.

TEXT 5

This third story is about this kid named yanis they lived on a island yanises fiamly was all farmers yanis was a dedicated farmer one day yanis was taking the sheep to the meadow and a lamb went wild it ran up the mountian when he got to the top he saw the sea for the first time the sea that surrounded his island From then on yanis dreamed of being a fisherman his father noticed that yanis was not himself yanis told his father his dream his father took him to the elder of the town the elder said to try new jobs first he tried baking the water they baked with made him think of the sea. Then he shoe making the leather made him think of a sail on a ship. Last he tried woodworking the wood made him think of building a ship. Finaly his dad let yanis go his dad thought yanis would find out how hard it is to be a fisherman then come home to be a farmer. Yanis traveled for two days then came to the town on the coast, He told kids what he was going to do they laughed at him; But a woman took pitty on yanis and took yanis to her home the woman told yanis he would have to work to stay there anymore. Yanis looked for a job but he could not find one they made fun of him. He made a fishing pole. One day he met a man named Crostos and he thought him the way to fish. One day a fisher-man got real sick Crostos talked the fisherman into taking yanis the fisherman found out yanis was a good fisherman and they hired him.

Nevertheless, the report (Text 6) is syntactically more complex than the narrative, which is reflected in substantially longer T-unit length and a higher degree of subordination. Text 6 contains several structures characteristic of planned written text, including adverbial fronting (lines 1, 19, 27), a series construction (lines 13–16), and appositive contructions (*bushes mainly cactuses, animals like the badger*). The chronological organization of the narrative text (e.g., *one day, from then on, first, last, finally*) is not found in the report text. Comparing written and spoken versions of the narrative, the spoken T-units are longer and the subordination index is slightly higher than the written measures. This relationship is reversed in the report, however. Longer and more highly subordinated written T-units are present for this child, but are specific to expository texts. The point that genre and channel *together* determine form is supported in these comparisons. Conventional punctuation is largely absent from both texts. (The variation in punctuation among Texts 1, 4, and 5 and 6 is notable. Inasmuch as Text 1 was a "published" classroom project, the author in all likelihood had help from the teacher, particularly with the quotation marks).

In spite of the complexity of the report text (Text 6) at the sentence level, John does not convey the text structure in an explicit manner. The main point (that the desert is surprisingly lively) remains unstated.

TEXT 6

In the mountians the air goes down the side of the mountian and gets hot and forms a desert. The desert has one main tree called the soursos tree opens up when it rains and traps the water so it can live off the water later. The desert has bushes mainly cactuses there are many kinds of cactuses. There are alot of animals who live in the desert like turtles, rabbits, wild boars, scorpians, spiders, desert foxes, many kinds of insects, and lots of lizard's. The animals look for food in the day and look for caves or dig holes at night. In the cool soil a foot down in the soil it can be 25° cooler in the hole than outside. But animals like the badger and the hog nosed skunk know just where to find them. They dig them out of the ground then eat them. When it rains in the desert there is uasaly a good chance of flash flooding becaus the soil is so dry and hot that it can't take in very much wate There are rivers in the deser uasaly there are oasis next to the river an oasis a place where bushes and trees grow.

Table 8-1.
Quantitative data for Texts 5 through 11 including the total number of words in the text, the number of T-units, the average T-unit length in words, and the degree of subordination (clauses, main + subordinate/T-unit).

	Total words	Total T-units	Words/T-unit	Clauses/T-unit
Text 5 Narrative 11 years	292 (295)	37 (30)	7.89 (9.83)	1.68 (1.77)
Text 6 Report 11 years	187 (225)	15 (22)	12.46 (10.23)	1.93 (1.68)
Text 7 Narrative 14 years	337 (653)	33 (61)	10.20 (10.70)	1.88 (2.02)
Text 8 Report 14 years	174 (422)	15 (33)	11.60 (12.79)	1.80 (1.85)
Text 9 Narrative 14 years, LLD	104 (281)	13 (23)	8.00 (12.22)	1.77 (2.26)
Text 10 Report 14 years, LLD	56 (144)	6 (12)	9.50 (12.00)	1.33 (1.83)
Text 11 Report 15 years, LLD	320	22	14.54	2.00

The point that plants and animals have learned to adapt is also unstated. John's report is comprehensive—he reports facts about how the desert was formed, its plants, its animals, and its climate, but there is no overall text structure (e.g., several main points supported by examples). Apparently, John had no main point in mind at the beginning of this task and none developed as he wrote. His narrative, on the other hand, is well formed according to text structure expectations, containing setting statements, a clearly stated beginning event, and fully developed episodes.

THE PROCESS: PLANNING, GENERATING, AND REVISING TEXT

The research of Bereiter and Scardamalia, much of it summarized in their 1987 book, approaches children's writing from a process rather than a structural (product) perspective. They are particularly interested in how children cope with the cognitive demands of expository writing. The end of writing development, in their view, is the attainment of complex coordinations of ideas (Scardamalia, 1981). It takes a great deal of planning, as discussed previously, to accomplish the coordination of ideas. Moreover, during planning, the writer of an expository text needs to take into account the "inward debate" that the text will stimulate in the reader (Britton, 1982). In this regard, expository writing contrasts with narrative writing in which the story proceeds without the same degree of reader anticipation.

Bereiter and Scardamalia have worked with fourth, sixth, and eighth grade children between 10 and 14 years of age. In one set of experiments (Scardamalia, 1981), children were asked to convey in writing the information found in four cells of a matrix. The information in each cell could be presented independently or it could be related to information in one or more other cells (see Figure 8-2). For a second task the children wrote an opinion essay on the topic of children choosing their own subjects to study in school. Written products on both tasks were characterized according to four levels representing increments in simultaneous idea coordination. Examples of Level 1 and Level 4 productions for both tasks, found in Scardamalia (1981), appear in Figure 8-2. Level 4 performance, which calls for the simultaneous coordination of four ideas, was achieved by only one of 80 eighth grade students, the highest grade tested. All four levels of performance are analyzed in detail in Scardamalia (1981).

Bereiter and Scardamalia (1987) examined planning more directly with another group of 10- to 14-year-old children who were asked to write the same opinion essay. They reasoned that the observed tendency of children to do little planning in advance of writing was perhaps a school habit rather than a more basic developmental constraint. Therefore, to induce the children to do more planning, the children were given specific planning instructions prior to writing in an effort to experimentally separate the act of planning from actual writing. One analysis centered on a comparison of notes generated prior to writing and the final text. Whereas the 14-year-olds' notes listed "gists" of ideas that were expanded into complete ideas in the text, the notes of the 10-year-olds were already complete sentences, which then recurred practically unchanged in the text. The product of planning for the younger children was the text itself, not an intermediate plan. In an

TASK 1

	Michigan	California
Climate	cool	warm
Fruit Crop	apples	oranges

Level 1: In the state of Michigan the climate is cool. In the state of Michigan the fruit crop is apples. In the state of California the climate is warm. In the state of California the fruit crop is oranges.

Level 4: In Michigan's cool climate they harvest apples but with California's warm climate oranges may be grown.

TASK 2

Should students be able to choose what things they study in school?

Level 1: (preserving child's spelling and punctuation) In School We Should Be Able To Do Any Kind Of We Want To Do We Are Free We Could Do Anything We want God Us Free We Could Do Anything We Want To Do I'd Like Spelling And Math In School We Should Do It Any Time We Want.

Level 4: Chose is an important thing but a very tricky thing to fool with. I feel that chose of school subjects should be something that is done carefully. A young child given a chose would pick the easy subjects with no foresight into his future. But choose in his later years could be very important. To develop his leadership qualities. To follow and develop his interests and charictor to his fullest. So with these facts I come to the conclution that chose of subjects should not be given until about the age of fifteen. You can not condem or praise what you know little about. Until the age of choise a full and general cericulum should be given. It is not up to the school board to decide your life and until you are old enough to decide it is not your dission ether.

FIGURE 8-2. Examples of Level 1 and Level 4 coordination of ideas on the matrix task (Task 1) and the thesis defense task (Task 2), from Scardamalia (1981).

analysis of the think-aloud protocols from the planning period, the number of idea units generated was found to double between the ages of 10 and 14. Another sign of change was in the recognition of planning. Ten-year-olds could not recognize elements of planning when modeled by an adult, but performance had substantially improved by age 12. With age, then, there is increasing differentiation of planning from text production. Bereiter and Scardamalia (1987) stressed that the more mature planning "consists of thinking *about* the composition rather than planning that consists of mentally rehearsing or creating the composition" (p. 210).

WRITING AND READING

Once children are writing and reading at levels beyond the emergent period, it becomes possible to examine the relation between these two major components of literacy from a number of additional perspectives. Several studies, reviewed by Stotsky (1983), have looked for correlations between measures of writing ability and reading achievement or experience. From the middle elementary grades through postsecondary levels, the correlation studies show that better writers are usually better readers and read more than poor writers. Further, better readers produce more syntactically mature writing than poor readers (Stotsky, 1983, p. 636). Good readers/poor writers (and vice versa) are not infrequent however; such cases of literacy "mismatch" accounted for approximately 20 to 25 percent of the students in Loban's study (1963). The exceptions notwithstanding, it would be odd indeed if the correlation studies yielded different results. Although these studies establish a relationship, they do not go far toward explaining the nature of the relationship.

Other investigations have attempted to (1) improve writing (or reading) and have measured the effects on the other literacy component, or (2) improve writing (or reading) *through* the use of the other literacy component. Stotsky (1983) provided a review of these experimental studies as well. Researchers have studied children in the later elementary grades through postsecondary levels. Positive results are generally found for two types of studies. First, studies that have used writing activities to improve comprehension and retention of new information show reading recall and achievement above levels attained in repeated reading or question/answer paradigms. Examples of writing activities include outlining, taking notes, paraphrasing, and summarizing. Positive results have also been found in studies attempting to improve writing by providing reading experiences in lieu of grammar lessons or additional writing practice.

The direct influence of reading as a structural model for writing is apparently evident as early as second grade. Eckhoff (1983) analyzed writing samples in two second grade classrooms that used distinctly different types of basal reading texts. One basal series used shorter T-units, less subordination, and generally simpler sentences than the other series. These same differences were reflected in the writing samples from the two classrooms. The effects were diminished but not entirely eliminated for above-grade level readers exposed to the simpler basal series.

Attempts to actually explain the nature of the relationship between writing and reading are advanced by investigations that examine similarities in the two processes. In the period of emergent writing, spelling and decoding processes have been compared. For older children, who are writing and reading extended texts, the relation question can be posed for text-level processing. Bereiter and Scardamalia

(1987) looked for evidence that processing strategies used in writing and reading problematic (logically incongruent) texts were similar. For a reading task, sixth and tenth grade children read and thought out-loud as they read. The think-aloud protocols were then analyzed. On a production task, the same children arranged sets of sentences into a coherent text and again thought out-loud as they worked. There were age-specific similarities in the strategies applied across tasks. On both tasks, the younger children used a ''single-pass'' strategy, which allowed them to read through the text or arrange the sentences on an item-by-item basis. The older students' strategies on both tasks were more ''cyclical,'' revealing evidence of recursive processing, revision, and gist construction. Thus, although spelling and decoding processes for beginning writers are dissimilar in at least some respects, as discussed previously, higher-level text processing strategies used by older writers and readers are thought to be more alike.

SECONDARY SCHOOL WRITING

The secondary student faces new challenges as a maturing writer. By this time a certain amount of writing fluency is neccessary in order to meet new requirements such as essay examination answers and term paper analyses. Topics for writing are rarely self-chosen, creating additional burdens because of an information base that may be less familiar or unmotivating or both. Genre development in expository and persuasive texts will be extensive.

The young secondary writer has learned to spell words, generate successive clauses, and punctuate more or less automatically. To these skills, maturing secondary writers develop further as *communicative* and *unified* writers (Bereiter, 1980). The communicative writer sets out to have a particular effect on a reader and is able to translate more general social cognitive skills to the written product. The ability to anticipate the ''inner debate'' of the reader, as previously discussed, becomes critical in persuasive and expository writing. Whereas the communicative writer considers *other* readers' views, the unified writer considers his or her *own* perspective as a reader. In effect, an internal feedback loop is established (writer-self with reader-self). As a result, personal standards of writing are developed along with personal style, viewpoints, and rewards for writing (Bereiter, 1980).

CONTEXT AND PURPOSE

Several projects have investigated secondary school contexts for writing. Britton and his colleagues studied writing done in British schools between the ages of 11 and 18 (Britton, Burgess, Martin, McLeod, & Rosen, 1975). More recently in the United States, Applebee (1984) reported results from a study of ninth and eleventh grade school writing. Both investigations found that most secondary school writing (85–90 percent of all writing exercises) is done for the teacher in the role of examiner (i.e., for an audience of one, for the purpose of demonstrating knowledge). Students observed by Applebee (1984) spent an average of 3 percent of their school day and homework time writing material of paragraph length or longer. Most of their writing was informational, either analytic or summary in nature; only 12 percent was personal or imaginative. Interestingly, students identified as poor writers did proportionally more personal and imaginative writing and less informational writing than those students whose writing was considered to be stronger. The information for the students' writing came from teachers and textbooks in most instances, and from personal experience much less frequently (27 percent).

Text and Sentence Structure

Genre effects on form have been demonstrated in a number of studies (Crowhurst & Piche, 1979; Rubin, 1982; Scott, 1987). Presumably, the high school graduate would be capable of integrative writing, as discussed previously, in which structure varies appropriately according to genre and context.

Quantitative studies of syntactic complexity in writing during the secondary years indicate slow, steady increases, as reflected in average length of T-units and degree of subordination (Hunt, 1965, 1970; Loban, 1976). Hunt (1970) studied the writing of fourth, sixth, eighth, tenth, and twelfth graders and of adults in a sentence-combining task, which, in certain respects, resembled the matrix task of Scardamalia (1981), as discussed previously and illustrated in Figure 8-2. In the Hunt task, students were asked to rewrite "in a better way" series of simple sentences (e.g., *Aluminum is a metal. It is abundant. It has many uses.*) Hunt (1970) was interested in syntactic changes rather than the coordination of ideas (Scardamalia's focus), but, as shown by studying the essay in Figure 8-2, the two types of development are associated. Hunt's results documented continuing growth through the twelfth grade, as indicated in longer sentences, longer clauses, and more subordination.

Matthew, a 14-Year-Old Writer

Several of these structural developments are illustrated in Texts 7 and 8, written by a 14-year-old boy in response to the same films

TEXT 7

The movie Yanis and his dream was about a young Greek boy and his dream in life.

It starts out with Yanis at his home in a small village on an island. He works on a farm with his family. He doesn't really enjoy what he does but he knows that his place in the world is to be a farmer just like his fathier.

One day he chases a runaway goat up a mountain and sees, for the first time, the sea. He dreams about it that night. He tells his father about it and his father tells him to forget about it. He is a farmer and that's all.

Yanis doesn't give up on his dream. His father takes him to an important man in the community to try to get him to stop wanting to go to the sea. The man suggests he try other jobs to help his community. Yanis tries several jobs and does good work but each one reminds him of how much he wants to go to the sea.

Finally he returns home and tells his parents he still wants to go. After a discusion they agreed.

Yanis travels very far just to be turned down by everyone he asks for a job. A woman takes him to her house and lets him stay. She warns him not to be a fisherman because her husband died at sea.

After continually being turned down Yanis tries to mcke his own fishing pole. He isn't succesful with his new pole until he meets an old fisherman named Costos. Costos shows Yanis how to fish better.

Yanis and Costos were fishing and they meet a fishing boat and one of the fisherman was sick. They needed another fisher badly. They took Yanis reluctantly but he proved himself to the older men.

Yanis told his parents of his achievements and they expected him to return home but Yanis was finally happy.

discussed in connection with the texts by the 11-year-old. Quantitative data are found in Table 8-1. Matthew's report (Text 8), like John's, is shorter than the narrative (Text 7). Average T-unit length is longer for the report text, however. Developmental effects for syntactic complexity (as revealed in T-unit length and subordination measures (are seen in the narrative texts (a comparison of Texts 5 and 7) but not for the report texts (a comparison of Texts 6 and 8). Nevertheless, Matthew's report is better developed from the standpoint of overall text structure. Unlike John, Matthew states the main point explicitly at the outset (the point that the desert is not just rocks) and reiterates the same point at the end of the text. He mentions the food chain, a point that connects the several animals shown in the film. He uses explicit connectives including the enumerative *also* (line 25) and the concluding *in all* (line 31). Matthew ties the text together with the repeated statement *the film (it) showed . . .* (termed *metastatements* by Kintsch & van Dijk, 1978). A final comparison involves punctuation, which is much improved in the 14-year-old's texts. As these texts illustrate, writing has progressed considerably in a three-year span.

THE PROCESS: PLANNING, GENERATING, AND REVISING TEXT

As the secondary student becomes a unified writer, planning and revision phases are undergoing considerable change. Think-aloud

TEXT 8

The film "The Desert" was interesting because it showed that the desert isn't just rocks. It showed that there are many plants but they are just more spread out. They are spread out because there is less water and so the plants must have larger roots to absorb enough water to survive under the hot circumstances

It also showed that animals live in the desert. Animals such as lizards, snakes, birds, and some mamals live there.

It showed the food chain. It Starts out with the rodent eating a plant. Then the snake or lizard eats the rodent. Next the big birds, such as hawks, eat the snake or lizard. Finally the Scavengers like the Vulture eat the remains ~~of~~ dead animals.

The film also showed how when it rains the ground is so hard from the heat of sun that the water can't sink in and a flash flood occurs.

In all the film showed that there was an environment in the desert with living animal and plants. The film also showed that the desert isn't just a bunch of big rocks.

protocols of students aged 10, 12, 16, and 18 were studied by Hayes and Flower (1980). The 18-year-olds produced more diverse types of comments, including statements about spelling, grammar, and text organization. When Burtis, Bereiter, Scardamalia, and Tetroe (1983) compared college undergraduates with 10-, 12-, and 14-year-olds in their study of advanced planning, they found that the undergraduates did considerably more planning. Their planning notes were very condensed, with arrows drawn between units, and they made explicit comments about text structure; for example, "I'll start with the idea that . . ." (p. 170). Emig (1971) studied the composing process in 16- and 17-year-olds as they composed aloud. Students did very little planning or revising overall, but they did more of each when writing reflexive material than during extensive composing. Reflexive composing included writing for the self as audience (poetry and autobiographical material); extensive composing was usually a teacher-directed writing task.

Hayes and Flower (1987) recently reviewed the developmental literature on the revision phase of writing. They noted that adult and more expert writers devote proportionally more time to revising. Adults also look on revising from a more global perspective, as a way of "molding the argument." By way of contrast, secondary students devote little time to revision, and when they do revise, changes are largely limited to the sentence level (correcting/changing grammar and punctuation). Sometimes their changes are harmful rather than helpful.

Planning, generating, and revising are components of writing models that generally assume that writing is created "afresh," either entirely from within the writer's mind or from many text sources. In reality, many writing assignments at the secondary level are summaries of other texts. Kintsch and van Dijk (1978, p. 376) refer to such texts as *second-order discourses*, which they define as "discourses with respect to another discourse, such as free-recall protocols or summaries." What developmental trends are found in the ways that writers condense text?

In their model of text production, Kintsch and van Dijk (1978) describe three rules (deletion, generalization, and integration) that operate on the propositions of the input text to produce the summarized version. Drawing on the Kintsch and van Dijk model, Brown and Day (1983, p. 3) studied students' summarization of expository texts that were specifically designed to elicit the following five summarization rules:

1. *deletion* of unimportant or trivial information
2. *deletion* of redundant information

3. *superordination* of lists, that is, substitution of a category name for instances of a category
4. *selection* of a topic sentence, that is, near verbatim use of a topic sentence from the text
5. *invention*, that is, creation and use of a topic sentence that did not appear in the text but easily could have

After reading the text three times, fifth, seventh, tenth grade and college students wrote summaries of two 500-word expository passages. They could refer to the original text and any notes as they wrote. Brown and Day found that deletion rules (numbers 1 and 2) were used by all subjects, even fifth graders. There were significant age differences in the use of the other three rules, however. The invention rule, which could be termed ''say it in your own words,'' was the strongest differentiator of age and the least used by all subjects. Fifth and seventh grade students made very little use of this rule, and college students used it in only half of all opportunities. Developmental trends are interpreted as compatible with the extent to which the rules depart from the favored *copy-delete* strategy used by previously studied fifth an seventh graders (cf. Brown, Day, & Jones, 1983). In a follow-up experiment, junior college students performed on a level with seventh graders, which appeared to confirm the notion that such students have difficulty with text related academic tasks. In another follow-up experiment, two graduate students (teachers of freshman composition classes) used the higher-level rules in almost all opportunities. Interestingly though, these graduate students could not verbalize the nature of these five rules when interviewed about what they considered to be basic rules of good summarization. However, the five rules were mentioned more frequently when the two students were asked to think aloud about what they were doing during the summarization task itself. Brown and Day (1983) concluded that on-line reporting is more successful than posthoc interviewing for eliciting metacognitive accounts of the summarization process.

SUMMARY

Writing development has been summarized beginning with emergent writing and continuing through high school. Perhaps the reader has the impression that the majority of children traverse these stages with ease. This writer is not aware of studies that address the number of children who do. Whereas almost all children have been talking for some time when they enter kindergarten, an equally large proportion cannot be assumed to produce spontaneous writing of the types described in the section on emergent writing (Donaldson, 1984; Gundlach, 1982). Even after a period of school instruction, many children fail to become fluent writers, and even more fail to become the types of writers implied by the adjectives *knowledge-transforming, integrative,* and *unified*—terms used in previous sections to denote the highest levels of writing skill.

In light of information reviewed thus far, a number of themes seem critical for the discussion of writing problems that follows in the next chapter. One is the inherently difficult nature of writing for all of us. Writing is difficult because there are so many simultaneous demands involved in the coordination of complex ideas on paper. Writing is increasingly recognized as a lifelong endeavor that for many people "remains a difficult process, avoided at some length, and enjoyed most (if at all) only in the completion" (Applebee, 1984, p. 1). A second theme is the difficulty children must experience in finding reasons to write—or at least, to write longer texts. Many of the unique functions of writing—for example, information storage and academic analysis—are outside the grasp of children. Neither situation is apparently resolved during secondary school years in which a large portion of writing involves repeating or summarizing information previously organized by textbooks and teachers, for the purpose of demonstrating knowledge. Students are rarely asked to extend and integrate new information through their writing (Applebee, 1984). A final theme is that any piece of writing done by a child or adolescent is a text within a context. The purpose of the text, the circumstances of its actual production, and the particular genre it represents, will all affect written form.

REFERENCES

Applebee, A. (1984). *Contexts for learning to write.* Norwood, NJ: Ablex.

Bereiter, C. (1980). Development in writing. In L. Gregg and E. Steinberg (Eds.), *Cognitive processes in writing,* 73–93. Hillsdale, NJ: Erlbaum.

Bereiter, C., and Scardamalia, M. (1987). *The psychology of written composition.* Hillsdale, NJ: Erlbaum.

Biber, D. (1986). Spoken and written textual dimensions in English: Resolving the contradictory findings. *Language, 62,* 384–414.

Bissex, G. (1980). *GYNS AT WRK: A child learns to write and read.* Cambridge, MA: Harvard University Press.

Black, J. (1981). Psycholinguistic processes in writing. In C. Frederiksen, M. Whiteman, and J. Dominic (Eds.), *Writing: The nature, development, and teaching of written communication,* 199–216. Hillsdale, NJ: Erlbaum.

Blalock, J., and Johnson, D. (1987). Primary concerns and group characteristics.

In D. Johnson and J. Blalock (Eds.), *Adults with learning disabilities: Clinical studies*, 31–46. New York: Grune and Stratton.

Britton, J. (1982). Spectator role and the beginnings of writing. In M. Nystrand (Ed.), *What writers know*, 149–169. London: Academic Press.

Britton, J., Burgess, T., Martin, N., McLeod, A., Rosen, H. (1975). *The development of writing abilities (11–18)*. Schools Council Research Studies. London: MacMillan.

Brown, A. and Day, J. (1983). Macrorules for summarizing texts: The development of expertise. *Journal of Verbal Learning and Verbal Behavior, 22*, 1–14.

Brown, A., Day, J., and Jones, R. (1983). The development of plans for summarizing texts. *Child Development, 54*, 968–979.

Bryant, P., and Bradley, L. (1980). Why children sometimes write words which they do not read. In U. Frith (Ed.), *Cognitive processes in spelling*, 355–372. London: Academic Press.

Burtis, J., Bereiter, C., Scardamalia, M., and Tetroe, J. (1983). The development of planning in writing. In B. Kroll and G. Wells (Eds.), *Explorations in the development of writing*, 153–176. New York: John Wiley.

Cazden, C., Cordeiro, P., and Giacobbe, M. (1985). Spontaneous and scientific concepts: young children's learning of punctuation. In G. Wells and J. Nicholls (Eds.), *Language and learning: An interactional perspective*, 107–124. London: The Falmer Press.

Christie, F. (1986). Writing in the infants grades. In C. Painter and J. Martin (Eds.), *Writing to mean: Teaching genres across the curriculum*, 118–135. Applied Linguistics Association of Australia, Occasional Papers, No. 9.

Cioffi, G. (1984). Observing composing behaviors of primary-age children: The interaction of oral and written language. In R. Beach and L. Bridwell (Eds.), *New directions in composition research*, 171–190. New York: Guilford Press.

Collins, J. (1984). The development of writing abilities during the school years. In A. Pellegrini and T. Yawkey (Eds.), *The development of oral and written language in social contexts*, 201–211. Norwood, NJ: Ablex.

Collins, A., and Gentner, D. (1980). A framework for a cognitive theory of writing. In L. Gregg and E. Steinberg (Eds.), *Cognitive processes in writing*, 51–72. Hillsdale, NJ: Erlbaum.

Corbett, E. (1981). The status of writing in our society. In M. Whiteman (Ed.), *Writing: The nature, development, and teaching of written communication: Vol. 1. Variation in writing: Functional and linguistic-cultural differences*, 47–52. Hillsdale, NJ: Erlbaum.

Crowhurst, M., and Piche, G. (1979). Audience and mode of discourse effects on syntactic complexity in writing at two grade levels. *Research in the Teaching of English, 13*, 101–109.

Daiute, C. (1984). Performance limits on writers. In R. Beach and L. Bridwell (Eds.), *New directions in composition research*, 205–224. New York: Guilford Press.

Dobson, L. (1988). *Connections in learning to write and read: A study of children's development through kindergarten and grade one*. Champaign, IL: Center for the Study of Reading, Technical Report No. 418.

Donaldson, M. (1984). Speech and writing and modes of learning. In H. Goelman, A. Oberg, and F. Smith (Eds.), *Awakening to literacy,* 174–184. London: Heinemann.

Dyson, A. (1986). Children's early interpretations of writing: Expanding research perspectives. In D. Yaden and S. Templeton (Eds.), *Metalinguistic awareness and beginning literacy,* 201–218. Portsmouth, NH: Heinemann.

Eckhoff, B. (1983). How reading affects children's writing. *Language Arts, 60,* 607–616.

Emig, J. (1971). *The composing process of 12th graders.* Champaign, IL: National Council of Teachers of English, Research Report No. 13.

Emig, J. (1981). Non-magical thinking: Presenting writing developmentally in schools. In C. Frederiksen and J. Dominic (Eds.), *Writing: The nature, development, and teaching of written communication: Vol 2. Writing: Process, development, communication,* 21–31. Hillsdale, NJ: Earlbaum.

Ferreiro, E. (1984). The underlying logic of literacy development. In H. Goelman, A. Oberg, and F. Smith (Eds.), *Awakening to literacy,* 154–173. London: Heinemann.

Fredericksen, C., and Dominic, J. (1981). *Writing: The nature, development, and teaching of written communication: Vol. 2. Writing: Process, development, communication.* Hillsdale, NJ: Earlbaum.

Galda, L. (1984). The relations between reading and writing in young children. In R. Beach and L. Bridwell (Eds.), *New directions in composition research,* 191–204. New York: Guilford Press.

Graves, D. (1983). *Writing: Teachers and children at work.* London: Heinemann.

Gundlach, R. (1982). Children as writers: The beginnings of learning to write. In M. Nystrand (Ed.), *What writers know,* 129–148. New York: Academic Press.

Halliday, M., and Hasan, R. (1976) *Cohesion in English.* London: Longman.

Hayes, J., and Flower, L. (1980). Identifying the organization of writing processes. In L. Gregg and E. Steinberg (Eds.), *Cognitive processes in writing: An interdisciplinary approach,* 3–30. Hillsdale, NJ: Erlbaum.

Hayes, J., and Flower, L. (1987). On the structure of the writing process. *Topics in Language Disorders, 7,* 19–30.

Hidi, S., and Hildyard, A. (1983). The comparison of oral and written productions in two discourse types. *Discourse Processes, 6,* 91–105.

Himley, M. (1986). Genre as generative: One perspective on one child's early writing growth. In M. Nystrand (Ed.), *The structure of written communication,* 137–157. New York: Academic Press.

Hull, G. (1987). Current views of error and editing. *Topics in Language Disorders, 7,* 55–65.

Hunt, K. (1965). *Grammatical structures written at three grade levels.* Champaign, IL: National Council of Teachers of English, Research Report No. 3.

Hunt, K. (1970). Syntactic maturity in school children and adults. *Society for Research in Child Development Monographs,* No. 134, *35,* No. 1.

Johnson, D. (1987). Disorders of written language. In D. Johnson and J. Blalock (Eds.), *Adults with learning disabilities: Clinical studies,* 173–204. New York:

Grune and Stratton.

Kintsch, W. and van Dijk, T. (1978). Toward a model of text comprehension and production. *Psychological Review, 85,* 363–394.

Kroll, B. (1981). Developmental relationships between speaking and writing. In B. Kroll and R. Vann (Eds.), *Exploring speaking-writing relationships: Connections and contrasts,* 32–54. Champaign, IL: National Council of Teachers of English.

Loban, W. (1963). *The language of elementary school children.* Urbana, IL: National Council of Teachers of English, Research Report No. 1.

Loban, W. (1976). *Language development: Kindergarten through grade twelve.* Champaign, IL: National Council of Teachers of English, Research Report No. 18.

Martin, J., Christie, F., and Rothery, J. (1987). Social processes in education: A reply to Sawyer and Watson (and others). In S. Eggins, J. Martin, and P. Wignell (Eds.), Writing Project, Working Papers in Linguistics, No. 5, Linguistics Department, University of Sydney, Sydney, Australia.

Nold, E. (1981). Revising. In C. Frederickesen and J. Dominic (Eds.), *Writing: The nature, development, and teaching of written communication: Vol. 2. Writing: Process, development, communication,* 67–79. Hillsdale, NJ: Erlbaum.

Nystrand, M. (1986). *The structure of written communication: Studies in reciprocity between writers and readers.* New York: Academic Press.

O'Donnell, R., Griffin, W., and Norris, R. (1967). *Syntax of kindergarten and elementary school children: A transformational analysis.* Champaign, IL: National Council of Teachers of English, Research Report No. 8.

Olson, D. (1977). From utterance to text: The bias of language in speech and writing. *The Harvard Educational Review, 47,* 257–281.

Olson, D. (1984). "See! Jumping!" Some oral language antecedents of literacy. In H. Goelman, A. Oberg, and F. Smith (Eds.), *Awakening to literacy,* 185–192. London: Heinemann.

Pellegrini, A., Galda, L., and Rubin, D. (1984). Context in text: The development of oral and written language in two genres. *Child Development, 55,* 1549–1555.

Perera, K. (1984). *Children's writing and reading.* London: Basil Blackwell.

Perera, K. (1986a). Language acquisition and writing. In P. Fletcher and M. Garman (Eds.), *Language acquisition,* 2nd ed., 494–533. Cambridge: Cambridge University Press.

Perera, K. (1986b). Grammatical differentiation between speech and writing in children aged 8 to 12. In A Wilkinson (Ed.), *The writing of writing,* 90–108. London: The Falmer Press.

Read, C. (1981). Writing is not the inverse of reading for young children. In C. Frederiksen and J. Dominic (Eds.), *Writing: The nature, development, and teaching of written communication: Vol. 2. Writing: Process, development, communication,* 105–115. Hillsdale, NJ: Erlbaum.

Read, C. (1985). Effects of phonology on beginning spelling: some cross-linguistic evidence. In D. Olson, N. Torrance, and A. Hildyard (Eds.), *Literacy, language, and learning,* 389–403. Cambridge: Cambridge University Press.

Read, C. (1986) *Children's creative spelling.* London: Routledge and Kegan Paul.

Rubin, D. (1982). Adapting syntax in writing to varying audiences as a function of age and social cognitive ability. *Journal of Child Language, 9,* 497–510.

Rubin, D. (1987). Divergence and convergence between oral and written language communication. *Topics in Language Disorders, 7,* 1–18.

Rubin, D., Piche, G., Michlin, M., and Johnson, F. (1984). Social cognitive ability as a predictor of the quality of fourth-graders' written narratives. In R. Beach and L. Bridwell (Eds.), *New directions in composition research,* 297–307. New York: Guilford Press.

Scardamalia, M. (1981). How children cope with the cognitive demands of writing. In C. Frederiksen and J. Dominic (Eds.), *Writing: The nature, development, and teaching of written communication. Vol 2. Writing: Process, development, communication,* 81–103. Hillsdale, NJ: Earlbaum.

Scinto, L. (1983). The development of text production. In J. Fine and R. Freedle (Eds.), *Developmental issues in discourse,* 225–268. Norwood, NJ: Ablex.

Scott, C. (1984). Adverbial connectivity in conversations of children 6–12. *Journal of Child Language, 11,* 423–452.

Scott, C. (1987, April). Summarizing text: Context effects in language disordered children. Paper presented at the First International Symposium on Specific Language Disorders, Reading, England.

Scott, C. (1988a). The development of complex sentences. *Topics in Language Disorders, 8,* 44–62.

Scott, C. (1988b). Spoken and written syntax. In M. Nippold (Ed.), *Later language development: Ages 9 through 19,* 49–95. San Diego, CA: College-Hill Press.

Shuy, R. (1981). Toward a development theory of writing. In C. Frederiksen and J. Dominic (Eds.), *Writing: The nature, development, and teaching of written communication: Vol. 2. Writing: Process, development, communication,* 119–132. Hillsdale, NJ: Earlbaum.

Sinclair, A. (1984, July). Three-year-olds' writing behavior. Paper presented at the Third International Congress for the Study of Child Language, Austin, TX.

Smith, F. (1984). The creative achievement of literacy. In H. Goelman, A. Oberg, and F. Smith (Eds.), *Awakening to literacy,* 143–153. London: Heinemann.

Snowling, M. (1985). The assessment of reading and spelling skills. In M. Snowling (Ed.), *Children's written language difficulties,* 80–95. Windsor, England: Nfer-Nelson.

Steinberg, E. (1980). A garden of opportunities and a thicket of dangers. In L. Gregg and E. Steinberg (Eds.), *Cognitive processes in writing,* 155–167. Hillsdale, NJ: Erlbaum.

Stotsky, S. (1983). Research on reading/writing relationships: A synthesis and suggested directions. *Language Arts, 60,* 627–642.

Sulsby, E. (1986). Young children's concepts of oral and written text. In K. Durking (Ed.), *Language development in the school years,* 95–116. London: Croom-Helm.

Vygotsky, L. (1978). Mind in society: The development of higher psychological processes. M. Cole, V. John-Steiner, S. Scribner, and E. Souberman, Eds.

and Trans., Cambridge, MA: Harvard University Press.

Weaver, C. (1982). Welcoming errors as signs of growth. *Language Arts, 59,* 438–444.

Wignell, P. (1987). In your own words. In S. Eggins, J. Martin, and P. Wignell (Eds.), Writing Project, Working Papers in Linguistics, No. 5, Linguistics Department, University of Sydney, Sydney, Australia.

Witte, S. (1983). Topical structure and revision: An exploratory study. *College Composition and Communication, 34,* 313–341.

Yde, P., and Spoelders, M. (1985). Text cohesion: An exploratory study with beginning writers. *Applied Psycholinguistics, 6,* 407–415.

9

Problem Writers: Nature, Assessment, and Intervention

Cheryl M. Scott

Teachers and clinicians working with language learning problems, whether spoken or written, depend on basic work in language learning for direction. Within the past 10 years, a considerable body of information on the nature of writing and its development has become available; much of this information has been summarized in Chapter 8. The reader will recognize topics and themes from that chapter throughout Chapter 9. Here, an overview of the nature of writing problems is followed by discussion of assessment and intervention principles and techniques. Following the organization of information in Chapter 8, writing problems are discussed in terms of context, structure, and process. Unlike reading disabilities, which have an extensive literature and long tradition in standarized assessment, writing problems are less clearly defined. For this reason, terms such as *writing disorders* or *writing disabilities* have been avoided.

Problem Writers

Writing is a difficult task, a fact detailed in Chapter 8. The difficulty of writing is compounded for problem writers. For those with persistent problems, writing must seem

> but a line that moves haltingly across the page, exposing as it goes all that the writer doesn't know, then passing into the hands of a stranger who reads it with a lawyer's eyes, searching for flaws. (Shaughnessy, 1977, p. 7, as cited by Gundlach, 1982, p. 134)

Fortunately for those with writing problems, awareness of such difficulties has increased considerably in the last 15 years. There is a widespread perception that the writing of school children and college students in the United States has deteriorated. This perception is reflected in articles in popular magazines such as the 1975 *Newsweek* article entitled "Why Johnny Can't Write" (Sheils, 1975). Although writing pedagogy has always been a topic of lively debate in regular education circles, articles in the popular media intensify the debate and add a sense of urgency to efforts to find more effective ways to test and teach writing. Awareness of writing problems has also increased in special education circles and among language clinicians who deal with spoken language disorders and reading disabilities. This is due in part to longitudinal research indicating that (1) children identified as language disordered in preschool frequently have major academic difficulties in elementary secondary school (Aram, Ekleman, & Nation, 1984), and (2) writing problems persist into adulthood as a major component of adult learning disabilities. Indeed, writing problems continue to occur well after spoken language and reading have shown significant improvement (Johnson, 1987).

Unfortunately the study of writing problems is not straightforward. One set of issues is definitional. When does a problem in writing, which we all have in degrees, become a problem requiring special remedial efforts (a question of presence-absence)? For problem writers, can degrees of writing proficiency be discerned (a question of degree)? What are the differences between learning disabled writers, basic writers, and low ability writers (a question of type)? It must be stated at the outset that standard criteria for defining "a writing problem," or degrees and subtypes of writing problems, do not exist presently. An example of the circularity of definition is the description of basic writers as "any student of average mental ability who is not learning disabled and who is underachieving in written language" (Gregg, 1983, p. 334). (The term *basic writer* was introduced by Shaughnessy in 1977 to describe many students who entered the City University of New York under the open-admissions policy of the late 1960s). In this section, characteristics of problem writers who have been identified as learning disabled are discussed along with results for individuals labeled as basic writers or simply poor writers. The common characteristic shared by such writers is a discrepancy between basic ability and performance in writing.

Information is also available on the writing of acquired aphasic students (Cromer, 1978) and deaf adolescents (Charrow, 1981), but this information will not be reviewed here.

Another set of issues centers on the developmental changes in the course of writing problems. Writing problems are not routinely identified until children are attempting to write longer texts—in other words, well into the later elementary years. Consequently, the seeds of writing problems have been given little attention. What kinds of emergent writing behaviors, or lack of, were observed several years ago in today's problem writers? Although there have been a few longitudinal projects on writing (Loban, 1976), to this author's knowledge, no one has studied problem writers longitudinally over a long period of time in a comprehensive manner. At present, the nature of writing difficulties in secondary and postsecondary students and adults has received more attention than problems of elementary students.

A final issue concerns the limited focus in studies of problem writers. Available research has concentrated predominantly on structural aspects of writing. Narrative texts, produced under experimental conditions, have received the most attention, almost to the exclusion of other genres. Observations of processes used by problem writers in the planning, generation, and revision of text are underrepresented in the literature.

The following overview of writing problems is organized according to the components of writing discussed in the previous chapter (i.e., text structure, sentence structure, word structure, process). Within each section, when possible, findings are discussed separately for younger and older writers. A summary of structural findings is shown in Table 9-1 where the studies surveyed are also listed along with a brief statement of design. There is little uniformity across the projects in subject selection criteria. The Loban (1976) and Hunt (1970) investigations took place in the 1960s before school children were routinely identified as learning disabled. Hunt (1970) identified low-achieving subjects on the basis of achievement tests only; Loban's low-ability subjects were identified on the basis of teacher ratings on several spoken and written language parameters. In a typical research paradigm, subjects were asked to write narratives in response to a picture, a film, or a story opener (Anderson, 1982; Barlett, 1984; Johnson, 1987:, Morris & Crump, 1982; Myklebust, 1973). Loban (1976) analyzed school compositions; the Hunt (1970) and Gregg (1983) investigations used a sentence-combining task. Information in Table 9-1 should be interpreted as a survey of possible findings rather than as a description of any one text or a description of any individual with a writing problem. Indeed, one of the hallmarks of this type of problem is the heterogeneity among individuals (Johnson, 1987).

TABLE 9–1.
Linguistic characteristics of children and adults with writing problems.

A summary of linguistic characteristics of problem writers

PRODUCTIVITY

Limited (fewer words and sentences) when compared with normals on controlled writing tasks (1, 3, 8, 10)

TEXT STRUCTURE: GENRE

Lack of coherence and text organization (6)

Narrative

Conclusions less likely (3)
Fewer temporal conjunctions and cohesive ties (3)
Opening sentences too vague or too specific (3)
Less anaphoric adjustment in easy/difficult contexts (2)
Inappropriate pronoun person (beginning story in third person, switching to first person (1)

Exposition

Fewer cohesive ties (8)
Fewer adverbial connectives (10)
Overuse of sentence-initial *and* (10)

SENTENCE STRUCTURE

Less complex as indicated by shorter T-units (words/unit) (5, 6, 10)
Less complex as indicated by lower subordination index (5, 6, 10)
Less complex as indicated by shorter clause length (words/clause) (5)
Omitted words, word endings, and punctuation (1, 3, 4, 8)
Noun-verb agreement errors (8)
Fragments and run-ons (3)
Limited range of conjunctions (3, 10)
Inappropriate use of *if, because, since* (3)
Fewer adverbial clauses of concession (e.g., *unless, although*) (6)
Fewer nonfinite verbs (6)
Inappropriate noun-phrase premodification (e.g., *the parents* for *his parents*) (1)
Overuse of *and* as sentence connector (1,5)

SPELLING

Both phonetic and nonphonetic errors, but nonphonetic errors predominate in poorest spellers (3)
Morphographemic spelling errors (3)
Word boundary difficulties in text writing (3)
Letter transpositions (more in spontaneous writing) (3)

LEXICON

Limited variety, as measured by type/token ratio (7)

A Summary of linguistic characteristics of problem writers

HANDWRITING
Appear to *draw* letters (no automatic motor plan) (3)
Poor letter closure (e.g., *day* looks like *clay*) (3)
Inappropriate letter heights (*e* looks like *l*) (3)
Faulty connections between letters (3)
Faulty spacing (no clear beginnings/endings to words) (3)
Uneven pressure (3)
Mixed manuscript and cursive writing (3)
Mixed upper/lowercase letters (3)
Idiosyncratic rule systems (3)
Inconsistency (3)

1 Anderson (1982): five learning disabled fourth graders, narrative in response to picture
2 Barlett (1984): 19 fifth grade and 17 seventh grade below-average writers, narrative response to cartoon sequence pictures
3 Johnson (1987): 93 learning disabled adults, mean = 26.5 years, narrative in response to PSLT picture and letter samples, WRAT for spelling analysis
4 Gregg (1983): learning disabled college students, expository essay and sentence-combining task
5 Hunt (1970): 17 low-achieving students in grades 4, 6, 8, 10, and 12, sentence-combining task
6 Loban (1976): 35 low-ability students, followed from grade four through grade twelve, school writing
7 Morris and Crump (1982): 72 learning disabled children, age 9–15 years, narrative response to silent film
8 Morris and Stick (1985): 60 learning disabled high school students, expository reports
9 Myklebust (1973): reading disabled and learning disabled school children, narrative in response to PSLT picture
10 Scott (1987): 1 language learning disordered fifth grader, 2 language learning disabled eighth graders, narrative, persuasive, and expository summary

PRODUCTIVITY

One of the most consistent findings for problem writers across a wide age range is the production of shorter texts compared to control subjects. What is more, in studies that correlate countable features of students' writing with teacher evaluation of writing, text length (in words) is a better predictor of superior ratings than sentence (or T-unit) length (Freedman, 1982). Text length is also a good predictor of teacher ratings of other parameters of scholastic aptitude including number work, general knowledge, oral ability, and use of books (Richardson, Calnan, Essen, & Lambert, 1976). Because short texts do not present the same opportunities for text structure development as longer texts, the findings for productivity and genre inadequacies should be seen as related.

Text Structure: Genre

The picture of *narrative text* produced by problem writers is far from complete, but evidence suggests that young writers have particular problems with anaphoric reference. In a study of five fourth grade writers with learning disabilities (LD), Anderson (1982) found that LD writers, more often than matched controls, began their story using third person reference but then switched to first person. Bartlett (1984) asked fifth and seventh grade good and poor writers to write stories in reponse to two sets of picture sequences. One set required the writer to distinguish between three same-age, same-gender characters—a difficult pronoun referencing problem; the other set was not problematic. The poor writers made fewer appropriate anaphoric adjustments in the difficult context condition. Additional narrative text problems cited for young writers include an overreliance on *and* connectives (Anderson, 1982).

Johnson (1987) examined narrative texts written by a large group of young adult LD individuals. The texts were written in response to the picture stimulus for the Picture Story Language Test (Myklebust, 1965). The stories were described as lacking in explicit temporal connectives and other cohesive ties. Opening sentences were frequently too vague or too specific, and a fourth of the narratives lacked identifiable endings. The LD adult texts were shorter in terms of total words and number of sentences than texts of high school students.

Decreased productivity has also been observed as characteristic of *expository texts*. In a study comparing 60 normal and LD high school students on an expository writing task, Morris and Stick (1985) found that the LD writers' texts were shorter and contained fewer lexical and grammatical cohesive ties. Scott (1987) reported that the productivity difference for expository text was marked in a comparison of three LD youngsters (fifth and eighth grade) with matched controls. In two (of three) comparisons, the LD students wrote less than half the total words written by normal students. Scott also observed that expository and persuasive texts of LD students contained fewer logical adverbial clauses per sentence. Neither the productivity nor the adverbial clause differences were evident in narrative text writing. A third area of difference for Scott's LD writers was the use of more sentence-initial *and* connectives in expository and persuasive writing (23 and 13 percent of all sentences, compared with 0 and 7 percent for the control students). There were no differences, however, on narrative texts. Both normal and LD students began approximately 25 percent of all narrative sentences with *and*.

Regardless of their difficulties with any particular text genre, evidence from a limited number of cross-function studies indicates that LD writers are not insensitive to genre influence. In a study of LD sixth, eighth, and tenth grade students, Blair and Crump (1984) found that *argumentative texts* were structurally more complex than *descriptive texts*. Comparing narrative, persuasive, and expository summary writing in three LD students (fifth and eighth grade), Scott (1987) reported that persuasive texts were more complex than narrative texts (as measured by T-unit length and subordination ratio). Expository texts, however, were less complex than narratives. Control subjects wrote more complex sentences in *both* persuasive and expository pieces. Thus, results suggest that while LD writers make some appropriate adjustments in text complexity depending on genre requirements, different text types are controlled with more or less skill. Specifically, relative to matched controls, LD students appear to have inordinate difficulty with expository writing. Because normal younger children usually write more complex narrative than expository texts (Kress, 1982), this finding for older LD children is not unexpected.

Sentence Structure

As shown in Table 9-1, sentences produced by problem writers are less complex as indicated by average length in words, the extent of subordination, and the use of more literate structures such as nonfinite verb forms. Loban's (1976) findings for poor writers are particularly noteworthy. In a longitudinal study, Loban collected school compositions of children from the fourth through twelfth grades. The compositions of children consistently rated by teachers as low in language ability were then compared to those with high ratings. The metric of comparison was a structural complexity index that was the sum of weighted scores for a variety of structures. The point to emphasize is that the index included several structures in addition to subordinate clauses (e.g., appositives, parenthetical constructions, verb phrase auxiliaries, and modals). The index consistently differentiated between the high and low ability students across all grades. However, use of subordination as a *single* measure of complexity failed to distinguish the groups in the higher grades. Apparently the low ability writers controlled a more limited repertoire of complex structures. Although subordination is an important index of grammatical complexity at the sentence level, Loban's results underscore the importance of examining a wider variety of structural systems for problem writers.

Errors listed in Table 9-1 include omitted word endings and words (including major clause elements such as subjects) and punctuation. Noun-verb agreement problems are sometimes cited. Unfortunately, it is difficult to construct a developmental composite for error types, given gaps and methodological variations in the data base.

SPELLING

Spelling is a problem for almost all problem writers. In a recent review of the literature on spelling abilities in LD students, Gerber and Hall (1987) established spelling as a "robust" weakness among LD students, one that emerges early and persists as a serious problem throughout secondary school. Poplin, Gray, Larsen, Banikowski, and Mehring (1980) found that of the several subtests of the Test of Written Language (TOWL) (Hammill & Larsen, 1978), spelling scores were the most consistent differentiators of normal and LD students in grades three through eight. There are now several studies on the spelling abilities of various groups of disordered children including those with phonological disorders (Stackhouse, 1985), reading disability (Carpenter, 1983; Snowling, 1980), acquired severe aphasia (Cromer, 1980), and deafness (Dodd, 1980).

A substantial number of projects have explored patterns of spelling errors among the learning disabled. An example is the work of Carpenter (1983) who studied third and sixth grade LD children with word recognition scores at least two years below grade level. Compared to grade level readers, the LD children's spelling errors consisted of proportionally more omissions, unrecognizable words, medial position errors, and fewer phonetic substitutions on predictable (phonetically regular) words. A slightly different pattern characterized the LD children's errors on unpredictable words, but fewer phonetic substitutions remained as a distinguishing characteristic.

The distinction between phonetic (e.g., *institoot/institute*) and nonphonetic (e.g., *instut/institute*) errors is a recurring theme in the literature on LD writers. Although most problem writers make both types of spelling errors, nonphonetic errors account for proportionally more errors in the poorest older spellers (Johnson, 1987). The phonetic/nonphonetic (sometimes called "bizarre") error distinction is not without its critics, however. As Gerber and Hall (1987) point out, simplified error schemes based on the experimenter's judgments of phonetic equivalence may mask some of the more inventive and even logical "errors" applied by LD students.

Recent treatments of developmental spelling stress the cognitive and linguistic side of learning to spell, as discussed in the previous chapter. This orientation is reflected in several investigations of poor spellers that have interpreted errors in terms of developmental stages in the abstraction of word structure patterns. For example, Schwartz (1983) studied the ability of 8-, 9-, and 10-year-old LD children to abstract spelling patterns in real and nonsense words. Analysis of error patterns indicated a wide range of error types that traversed errors typical of preschool/beginning spellers to those more typical of children in a transitional stage between alphabetic and orthographic spelling. To Schwartz, this suggested a slower but similar sequence of spelling development for LD youngsters compared to the normal sequence. Gerber and Hall (1987) provided a review of information processing approaches to the study of deficient spelling; these approaches attempt to model the spelling *process*, taking cognitive as well as linguistic parameters into account.

SPOKEN AND WRITTEN FORM IN WRITING

As discussed in the previous chapter, it takes time for children to learn that written language is not simply spoken language written down; slowly, children develop a distinctly written style. Do problem writers plateau in Kroll's (1981) consolidation phase where writing resembles speech (see p. 282, line 1, in Chapter 8)? Phelps-Terasaki, Phelps-Gunn, and Stetson (1983, p. 349) apparently took this view when they stated that "weak writers rely on speech to direct their writing." Three projects studying spoken and written form in LD students provide some evidence on the issue of spoken-written form differentiation. Only a small number of students have been studied thus far; ages range from fifth grade to college level.

The fifth grade LD student studied by Scott (1987) produced more complex spoken versions in three of four spoken-written comparisons (two narrative, one persuasive, and one expository summary), as measured by the amount of subordination. By comparison, the control subject produced written texts with more subordination in three of four comparisons. Another sign that the LD student's writing resembled speaking was the use of first and second person commentary. For example, the last two sentences in the expository summary were

> the waters cause flash floods
> *you* wouldn't think that.

and the first two sentences of the persuasive summary were

> They try to make things look bigger in shape and size to trick *you*, But *I* think they should keep them like they are and compare it to things. (Punctuation used by the writer has been preserved in citations.)

Two studies that compared the spoken and written language of college problem writers indicate that, with time, some poor writers do learn unique conventions of written language. Cayer and Sacks (1979) asked four basic writers to both discuss and write their views of a current social problem. (Basic writers, as defined previously, are those with average mental ability who are underachieving writers but who are not identified as learning disabled). The students' written sentences were longer, more highly subordinated, and contained more adverbial and adjectival modifiers. Furthermore, distinctly oral structures such as *right, well,* and *I think* were less common in writing.

Farr and Janda (1985) reported results from a case study of an 18-year-old basic writer who was a speaker of Black English Vernacular. A lengthy oral interview was compared to the written corpus generated in a 10-week composition class. Both texts were analyzed for typically literate forms (e.g., passive voice, nominalization, series constructions) and typically oral forms (e.g., coordinating conjunctions). The student used the respective structures of spoken and written language in a manner similar to speakers and writers observed by Chafe (1982) and others. Moreover, Black English forms that occurred orally were absent from writing. What, then, was wrong with the student's writing? In addition to grammatical errors (e.g., *situations that deals with violence, I dare not to display them, you certainly have gave me challenge*), a truncated, formal quality permeated the written samples. For example, on a class assignment, the student wrote,

> People should not smoke for three reasons, and in this passage I will focus on all three. First of all people should not smoke because it is fatal. The reason for this statement is because smoking is the main cause of lung cancer. Many people die from lung cancer every year. One good example that supports my factual statement is . . . (Farr and Janda, 1985, p. 66)

Farr and Janda (1985, p. 66) reasoned that the student ''seemed to be attempting to generate language which fills an appropriate form rather than language which is an authentic vehicle for his own intended meaning.''

Rubin (1987) described the writing of problem college writers as ''hypercorrect''—an adjective that would presumably apply to Farr and Janda's subject. Some writers, Rubin believes, have an unrealistic stereotype of written language as a formal, ''correct'' grammatical system. In terms of Kroll's (1981) stages in the evolution of spoken-written relations, such writers would be functioning in the differentiation stage in which writing is structurally distinct from speaking. The problem, according to Rubin (1987), is that the problem writer plateaus at this level. The problem writer never becomes an integrative writer (Kroll's highest level), one who balances spoken and written features in accordance with the demands of the writing task at hand.

KEVIN, A 14-YEAR-OLD LEARNING DISABLED WRITER

Texts 9 and 10 illustrate some of the difficulties of problem writers. (For continuity, texts in this chapter are numbered consecutively following texts in the previous chapter.) Texts 9 and 10 were written by Kevin, a 14-year-old LD eighth grade writer. Kevin participated in the same study (Scott, 1987) as John and Matthew (Texts 5 through 8, as described in Chapter 8). Quantitative measures of overall length, T-unit length, and degree of subordination are found in Table 8-1 of the previous chapter. When compared to the respective narrative and expository texts produced by 14-year-old Matthew (Texts 7 and 8), the difference in productivity is striking. Kevin's texts are approximately one-third the length of Matthew's. Sentences in both texts are shorter and less subordinated than those of Matthew (comparisons of Texts 7 and 9, and 8 and 10), but they are grammatically correct with one exception (Text 9, lines 2–3). Kevin's handwriting is good, but note the change from cursive writing in line 1 to printing in line 2 of Text 10. Spelling is generally correct; in fact, there are only three misspelled words in the combined texts (*cacktuses, there/their, is/his*). Punctuation is poor, however. Kevin omits periods and frequently fails to capitalize; there are no errors of commission, resulting in sentence fragments, as previously discussed. In light of the fact that sentence fragments are still found in texts written

TEXT 9

After he finished school Yanis helped is dad farm and one day while he was out whith the goats and saw the sea. From then on he wanted to be a fisherman. he told His dad and he tried to convince him to be a farmer but it wouldnt work so he ventured off to go to the sea. When he got there nobody wanted him to go with them. So he traveled to many towns with nobody that wanted him. Finally he met a guy and he taught him the ways and one day a fisherman got sick and Yanis got to go

TEXT 10

all the cacktuses hold water and grow
1 inch per year. There can be a temendous
amount of Temperature drop under the soil
deserts are found in areas where mountains
have eroded. Birds will make there nests
in cactuses for protection. most animals
stay in doors during the day.
there are always rivers in the desert
for water.

by 17-year-olds, and these fragments can be interpreted positively as evidence of new structural systems entering the writing system (see Weaver, 1982), Kevin's lack of such "errors" is difficult to interpret.

There are many differences between Kevin and his age-matched control Matthew at the text level. Kevin's narrative is cast in the past tense, whereas Matthew narrates in the more mature present tense. The narrative (Text 9) progresses appropriately with temporal connectives (*and one day, from then on, finally*). On the other hand, both opening and closing statements are weak compared to Matthew's narrative:

Kevins's opener:	After he finished school Yanis helped is dad farm
Matthew's opener:	The movie Yanis and his dream was about a young Greek boy and his dream for life.
Kevin's closing:	and one day a fisherman got sick and Yanis got to go
Matthew's closing:	Yanis told his parents of his achievements and they expected him to return home but Yanis was finally happy.

Differences in the boy's knowledge of text structure become even more apparent in the expository report on deserts. Kevin's desert report (Text 10) is a set of six sentences related only by general content. Because there is no text structure, the sentences could be rearranged and presented in another order just as easily. Rearrangement of Matthew's sentences (Text 8), however, would destroy his well-crafted text structure. In summary, Kevin's strengths as a writer are in spelling and sentence level grammar. Sentence grammar "strength" for Kevin means the lack of grammatical errors, but this must be interpreted conservatively in light of his relatively simple sentences. Kevins's weaknesses are in higher level text structure. The distinction raised earlier between text generation and idea generation (p. 270, line 1, of Chapter 8) may well apply to Kevin's writing. His report-writing abilities on other topics and in different tasks (e.g., self generated as opposed to summary tasks) would need to be assessed before concluding that his problems stem from a lack of expository text structure knowledge.

PAUL, A 15-YEAR-OLD LEARNING DISABLED WRITER

A comparison of Paul's desert text (Text 11) with Kevin's (Text 10) underscores the heterogeneity in writing problems. Paul is a 15-year-old LD student enrolled in the ninth grade. Paul's desert text is three times as long as Kevin's. Paul writes in longer sentences (greater T-unit length), which contain more subordinate clauses, than either Kevin or Matthew. Only 3 of 22 T-units contained grammatical errors (lines 10–11, 23, 25–26). Structures that are inappropriate in formal report writing (e.g., *mostly*) occur, but there are also structures that are distinctly more literate (e.g., *are said to be*). Unlike Kevin, Paul is a poor speller and his handwriting is only moderately legible. There were 25 misspelled words, 18 of which involved vowel errors. Several words (*cactus,*

TEXT 11 *

Descrts were formed By erosion and
Dry weather. most Rivers are underground
or seasonal Rivers and Rain comes
in large quantities and causes flash
[illegible] flouding and causes animals,
spiders, or insects to flee. To Higher
ground to keep from drownding or being
swept away, when Rain does come the
Plant life compeats to collect as
much as possible and save of it
to [illegible] Contribit to oases and
River and such. the plant life consists
of cactuses and leafy plants mostly
thorney Plants the thorns are to
Protect the water supply of the plants
the cactuses Root System is Horizonl
to suport its weight and to collect
water over a long distance, most of
the leafy plants are located at
[illegible] or By the oases and Rivers.
Two plants growing side by side are
Said to be norsering one another
(cactuses and trees) one get shade
and water a vise versa from
one another. climate or weather
are dry, hot and windy at some times)
clowds are formed over mountins
and are Blown and worked down the
side of the mountains and then are
Dumped down on the desarts.
animals are mostly small and are
lizerds, snakes, and insects But there are
some animels or mamils such as
Hedge Hogs, mice, Rats, cyotes, wolves,
tigers, and Rynosed organtos, these animals
eat one another for food and the Hedge
Hog eats cactuses for food and water
But most of the animels go to oases
and rivers to drink, mamels seek
natrual caves, ledges and Hollows to stay
out of the Heat during the hot part
of the day and go out at the
evening or night to search for food or
drink. Birds are a part of the
enviroment and they live in the cactus
or tree than one might peck a Hole
in side of one and the other might Build
[illegible] nest in the middle of the top
of one for protection from other
animals.

*This text appears in typed form on page 344.

mammal, animals) had variable spellings in the text. In terms of text structure, Paul's desert summary lies somewhere between that of Matthew and Kevin. There is no mention of the main point, and no closing, but the text is structured topically; Paul first discusses desert formation, then plants, followed by climate, and finally animals. Sentences could not be rearranged as freely as Kevin's. Punctuation is very poor; there are only seven periods and seven capitals in the entire text. Paul's interest in biology probably contributed to the length of the text.

RESEARCH DIRECTIONS

In comparison to information about the structural characteristics of texts, less is known about the planning, text generation, and revision processes employed by problem writers. Several avenues of inquiry may be fruitful. One approach would be to study *error patterns* of problem writers. Like Kevin and Paul, many problem writers have relative strengths and weaknesses. Weaknesses would undoubtly vary from one writer to the next, however, with the result that valuable information could be gained by studying the co-occurrence of error types. Perera (1985) provided an example of 12-year-old writer that illustrates this point. This child omitted function words such as *a, on, in the,* and *you* in writing but not in speech. The most likely explanation for the discrepancy is that the physical act of writing is inordinately difficult. As the child's thoughts "outpace the hand," words that carry less meaning are omitted. The next step would be to observe the child in the act of writing. Poor handwriting and/or slow rate of writing would be likely to co-occur with omission of function words. Thus, when a writing problem is scrutinized for weakness patterns, which may stem from a common base, underlying processes may surface more readily.

Research paradigms found useful in the study of writing processes—for example, think-aloud protocol analysis— have not yet been routinely applied in the study of children and adolescents with writing problems, although there are some studies with college-level basic writers. Compared to successful writers, problem college writers spend less time in planning activities and their revisions address surface text characteristics that preserve meaning, for example, punctuation and rewording with synonyms (see Humes, 1983, for a review of processing studies in college writers). There would be no reason to expect distinctly different findings from younger LD students, but this remains to be verified. One prediction might be that poor writers, when forced to preplan, behave like Bereiter and Scardamalia's (1987) youngest writers who planned in a data-driven (i.e., single-pass) rather than a cyclic manner (see p. 291, line 8, in Chapter 8). The extent to which the processes used by poor writers are similar to those of younger writers is unknown at present.

Attempts to categorize errors and understand their sources (as well as their syntax) should also contribute to an understanding of processes used by problem writers (e.g., Daiute, 1984; Hull, 1987, Shaughnessy, 1977). Daiute's (1984) study of sixth to twelfth grade students' errors in relation to locus and broader context provides a model of error analysis with potential application to the study of errors in problem writers (see p. 267, line 27, in Chapter 8). Text generation, according to Daiute, places considerable demand on memory, and many types of errors (e.g., overlapping sentences) have their onset after a clause sequence that taxes working memory. The theme that some errors are *positive* indications of new systems entering a student's writing has emerged in several recent treatments of developmental and problem writing.

Much remains to be learned about the nature of writing problems. Linguistic analyses to date permit the construction of "lists" of broad structural characteristics but little else. Studies of problem writers across several genres and longitudinally across several years should contribute important information in the future. The interpretation of errors within a developmental framework (cf. Hull, 1987) and the analysis of error patterns will be instructive. There is a need to study problem writers as processors—during the planning, generating, and revising stages of writing. Finally, inasmuch as any writer will persevere only when there is a reason to write, the contexts for writing, both in and out of school, should be explored in greater detail.

ASSESSMENT OF WRITING PROBLEMS

REGULAR EDUCATION PERSPECTIVES

Although a substantial body of literature exists on the assessment of spoken language disorders and reading disability, the literature on assessing developmental writing problems is extremely sparse by comparison—reflecting no doubt the lack of basic work on the nature of writing problems. In regular education, on the other hand, writing assessment has been debated for many years. The controversy derives in part from the lack of agreement on the definition of writing competence and ultimately from the lack of a theory of writing development that would guide assessment assumptions. Areas of concern include the specific subskills that should be evaluated, whether such subskills are in fact separable and whether they can be reliably judged.

In the last decade, however, a consensus view that writing is more than surface structure seems to be emerging. As a result, there has been a trend away from assessment procedures that concentrate exclusively on sentence level structural conventions (e.g., grammar and punctuation) toward those that take into account textual properties including overall text structure, cohesion, and meaning (Greenberg, 1987).

Three general approaches to writing assessment can be distinguished. In an *indirect* approach, students' ability to recognize correct and incorrect form is assessed, usually in a multiple-choice format. This format is typically found in standardized achievement tests. The procedure is indirect because students are not asked to write but only to recognize correct form. Although indirect procedures measure some aspects of editorial skill, they are not valid tests of writing performance (Cooper & Odell, 1977). *Direct* approaches to writing assessment require that the student generate some type of textual writing sample, which is then evaluated. The evaluation approach can be *holistic* or *analytic*. Holistic techniques require the evaluator to make more or less subjective judgments of several dimensions of a writing sample (e.g., content, style, organization), usually in the form of a rating. Reliability can be increased by careful training of raters. Analytic approaches look at countable features of a writing sample; for example, the number of words, the number and type of connectives, and the extent and type of subordination. Holistic and analytic approaches could, of course, be combined.

Even if evaluators could agree on the general approach, several formidable problems remain. One problem is the lack of procedures applicable to younger writers, or problem writers, who are not yet producing multisentence texts. Another is the issue of impromptu versus planned writing. Most procedures require an impromptu writing sample; the student is shown a stimulus picture, or given a topic, and begins to write immediately. How well such impromptu samples predict a student's ability to write in situations when a text evolves over a period of time is unknown. To address this concern, some experts recommend the evaluation of samples that are written over several days and allow ample time for revision, whereas others recommend a portfolio approach in which several different written genres are assessed (Greenberg, 1987).

NORM-REFERENCED TESTS OF WRITING IN SPECIAL EDUCATION

For many years the Picture Story Language Test by Myklebust (1965) was the most widely used writing test with learning disabled students. The test uses a picture prompt to elicit a narrative, which is then scored for total words, total sentences, words per sentence, syntax, and an abstract-concrete dimension. The syntax measure is a score reflecting the number of errors in grammar, morphology, word usage, and punctuation. Thus, sentence level surface grammar conventions are assessed with this measure. An adolescent who wrote a story entirely in correct but simple (one-clause) sentences would receive a higher syntax score than a cohort whose story was written with longer, more complex sentences containing several errors. As discussed in Chapter 8, recent interpretations of certain types of developmental "errors" may be positive rather than negative.

At the present time, the Test of Written Language (TOWL) (Hammill & Larsen, 1978) is frequently used to test writing in students with language and learning disabilities. The standardization sample ranged in age from 9;0 to 14;5 years. There are four major parts to the test: (1) a spontaneously produced writing sample, (2) a dictated spelling test, (3) a cloze text of inflectional morphemes and pronoun case, and (4) a test that requires application of capitalization and punctuation conventions. For the writing sample, youngster are asked to write a story about a series of three pictures. Planning is encouraged by telling the children to take five minutes to think about the story first and to plan "the whole story" before beginning to write. The goal is for the child to write a story of approximately 50 words, filling the space provided (9 lines). The stories are scored for vocabulary, thematic maturity, thought-units, and handwriting. Thematic maturity is scored by a 1 or 0 (present/absent) decision for 20 items. Although some of the items are indicative of text structure (e.g., the story has a definite ending), other items appear more arbitary and are not supported by developmental research (e.g., the items "writes in paragraphs" and "gives personal names to spacelings"). The thought-unit score is a measure of the child's ability to write in complete sentences. Although the manual states that thought-units are not exactly the same as T-units (after Hunt, 1965), the differences are not explained.

Although the TOWL draws the evaluators' attention to several important components of writing (grammatical form, spelling, and punctuation), the thematic maturity scoring procedure is not an insightful way to view text structure. Aspects of text and sentence structure not evaluated include connectivity, syntactic structures characteristic of written form, types of subordination, and complete narrative structure. Because the writing task elicits a fictional narrative in a contrived context, the ability to generalize the results to other genres and contexts is uncertain. For purposes of forming remedial teaching goals, text analyses derived from the developmental writing literature are recommended.

Several norm-referenced tests of spelling are available. As indicated, the TOWL contains a spelling-to-dictation subtest. The students hear each word used in a sentence before they attempt to spell it. The Test of Written Spelling (Larsen & Hammill, 1986), a test limited to spelling, divides test words into those that are predictable and those that are unpredictable. Predictable words follow spelling rules that apply across many words (e.g., dog, spring, salute); unpredictable words (e.g., pardon, awful) do not conform to general rules. The test was standardized on children between the ages of 6 and 18. Like the procedure on the TOWL, children hear the word both in isolation and in a sentence. The relative strengths shown by a child on either the predictable or unpredictable words, if any, contribute to intervention planning, according to the test authors.

Because spelling of single words and spelling in text writing may be different (Grubgeld, 1986), both text-level and dictated word spelling should be analyzed. Dictated words, for older children, should include polysyllabic as well as monosyllabic words and words that require morphological knowledge, both inflectional (e.g., *-s*, *-ing*) and derivational (e.g., *-tion*). Writers should be given an opportunity to identify and correct their spelling errors (Johnson, 1987).

THE EVALUATION OF WRITING SAMPLES

SAMPLE TYPES

Considering the theme in the previous chapter of context and genre effects on writing, it follows that writing assessment should strive to sample a variety of contexts and genres; which genres would depend on the developmental level of the child or adolescent. At developmental levels of mid-elementary age and above, genres should include at a minimum a text type that is chronologically based (e.g., a narrative) and one that is organized logically (e.g., an opinion essay or expository report). A clinician might evaluate various pieces of school writing as well as samples gathered in a clinic setting or pieces written at home. Because students write best about things they know, they can be given a choice of two or three topics in a particular genre. In a project evaluating the writing of children between the ages of 7 and 13, Wilkinson, Barnsley, Hanna, and Swan (1979) used the following four types of samples:

1. *Autobiographical narrative*: "The happiest/saddest day of my life," or "The best/worse experience I ever had."
2. *An account of a process written from authority*: how to play a particular game or sport.

3. *A fictional story*: writer selects one of three pictures.
4. *Discussion/persuasion*: "Would it work if children came to school when they liked, and could do what they liked there?"

The evaluation of writing on entirely self-chosen topics is also recommended. At the mid- to upper-elementary level, self-chosen topics will usually be personal narratives or informal reports (Calkins, 1983). Unless a child is accustomed to this type of writing, however, the request to write something entirely of one's own choosing can be initially dumbfounding for many children (Calkins, 1983).

Freedman (1982), following a review of several types of variables that affect writing, concluded that the accuracy of determining writing capability increases with the number of samples collected. Similarly, Scott (1988) recommended a portfolio approach in the evaluation of children's complex language, both written and spoken.

SAMPLE CONDITIONS

The issue of the sample environment for problem writers is critical. Good writers may learn over the years to perform well in writing "test" situations even when there is little commitment to truly communicate a message. Even at a young age, children become quite skilled in learning what is valued by the educational system. Calkins (1983, p. 50) told the story of observing as a researcher in a first grade classroom in which the teacher, in the Graves (1983) writing process tradition, emphasized content and revisions over form and neatness. One six-year-old in the class approached Calkins with the question "Mrs. Giacobbe likes good stories and yucky writing. What do you like?" Poor writers may be "less savvy" (Freedman, 1982). Therefore, special sampling conditions and inducements may be necessary to elicit a good effort.

Because problem writers frequently produce short texts, special encouragement to extend the text is in order. For example, students might be asked to "try to write at least two pages," or short breaks could be suggested. In clinic settings, once a general developmental level of writing has been determined, a writing portfolio can be extended by asking children to write certain types of texts at home under more relaxed conditions. Younger writers might be encouraged to write more if they are told to draw along with their writing. Time constraints should not be imposed.

Observations about the process of writing are as important as observations about the finished product. For older students, notations of planning and revising behaviors, whether spontaneous or suggested, should be made. Freedman (1982) illustrated the potentially interesting and important information gained from such observations in an anecdotal account of a fifth grade child. When first observed on a class writing task, the child appeared to be a problem writer. One day before the assignment was due, the girl produced a very inferior product after much fretting, crying, and complaining. Freedman's offers of help in the form of idea-generating suggestions were rejected. The next day the child decided, on her own, to approach the topic differently. The resulting product was a marked improvement, even in surface areas such as legibility and the absence of grammatical errors. During this second attempt, the child asked Freedman to serve as an instant dictionary for the spelling of difficult words, with the result that the text generation phase proceeded in a relatively uninterrupted manner. Reflecting on the experience with this child, Freedman (1982, p. 38) observed the following:

> On the first day, the writer had not decided how to approach the writing task, and she allowed the close deadline to unnerve her; on the second day, she decided on an approach and used the even closer deadline to her advantage. This anecdote shows the potentially deceptive nature of the written product in the assessment of writing skills.

A permanent videotape of the writing effort can supply information at the process level, including the amount of time the student writes and pauses (better writers pause more frequently and pause for longer periods of time as they write).

Writing assessment for some young children with language disorders begins even before there are texts of several sentences to analyze. Interviews with parents and teachers will reveal whether the child engages in any of the emergent writing behaviors that precede text-level writing. Parents can be asked to keep papers that contain drawings and letterlike forms. The types of literacy events in the home can be analyzed. Parents and children can be observed in book reading routines to determine whether parents adopt the ''active interpreter'' role (Wells, 1985) and the metalanguage (Olson, 1984, as discussed in Chapter 8) known to facilitate both writing and reading.

Sample Analysis

Several different sytems for analyzing samples have been proposed. A system proposed by Isaacson (1985), for example, includes the analytic evaluation of fluency, syntactic maturity, and vocabulary (i.e., counts of various items). Fluency is a measure of productivity (in number of words), a frequent shortcoming of texts produced by problem writers.

Syntactic maturity involves the calculation of T-unit length and the number of sentences that are fragments, simple, compound, and complex. Content is rated holistically in Isaacson's system.

Wilkinson, Barnsley, Hanna, and Swan (1979) criticized analysis procedures that count surface forms on the grounds that not all important developments in writing result in countable items that increase over time. They described four scales of writing development, which are applied to several different sample types. The scales are used as a series of guided judgments (holistic) covering stylistic, affective, cognitive, and moral aspects of writing. For example, the cognitive scale includes describing, interpreting, generalizing, and speculating. Development within each of these cognitive domains is then detailed. The authors illustrate the application of the scale with complete texts written by 7-, 10-, and 13-year-old British children.

The potential list of analyses that could be applied to any one text, whether analytic or holistic in nature, is indeed long. The evaluator's knowledge of writing components and their development, the topics reviewed in the previous chapter, will be the best guide for selecting a set of analyses. First, the clinician explores the contexts and purposes of writing for a problem writer. Second, samples of typical genres can be analyzed according to text, sentence, and word structure (spelling), with attention to indications of spoken/written form differentiation. Any of these structural analyses could be more or less detailed, depending on the nature of the problem. Third, a description of developmental levels of planning, generating, and revising text is indicated for students capable of producing longer texts. Holistic, descriptive, or quantitative methods can be selectively applied. For example, conveying a writer's sense of audience is likely to be a descriptive item in an analysis, but the degree of complexity as indicated by the amount of subordination can be quantified more easily. In the wake of recent interest in developmental writing, many specialized analysis procedures can also be culled from the literature, including, for example, error analysis following Dauite (1984) or Hull (1987), and level of complex idea coordination (Scardamalia, 1981). Finally, information about attitudes toward writing is important. Suggestions for attitude surveys (e.g., "what I like least/most about writing") are found in Giordano (1984a, 1984b), but evaluator-constructed interviews that fit particular circumstances may yield more information.

As language clinicians and teachers begin to prepare for more active involvement in the assessment of problem writing, two guidelines are offered for consideration. The first is to continue to study examples of texts written by child and adolescent writers in order to develop a sense of developmental levels and change. There are several excellent sources that include publication of child texts "in the child's own hand." Calkins (1983), for example, included many examples of third and fourth grade writing from a classroom using the writing workshop approach. Because the writing difficulties that qualify a child as a problem writer will usually be ones of degree, a firm grasp of the wide spectrum of writing possibilities is essential. The second guideline is to approach assessment with the goal of discovering the reason and logic of the writer's problems. Shaughnessy's (1977) work with basic college writers remains as one of the best models of the discovery process.

INTERVENTION WITH WRITING PROBLEMS

Much like the situation in assessment, intervention with writing problems is an undeveloped topic compared with that of spoken language disorders and reading disabilities. Even in regular education, books and papers devoted to writing instruction are meager compared to those concerned with reading. A study completed in 1976 by Graves revealed that for each dollar spent on writing instruction, one hundred dollars went into reading instruction (as reported by Calkins, 1983, p. 152). Ten years plus later, the gap has perhaps narrowed. The regular education literature on writing instruction is of course applicable for problem writers. In recognition of the regular education base for work with problem writers, this section begins with a brief review of general trends in writing pedagogy. Guidelines and procedures appropriate for young emergent writers are then presented, followed by procedures appropriate for students who are writing longer texts. The chapter closes with a discussion of several intervention topics applicable across a wide range of writing development.

TRENDS IN THE TEACHING OF WRITING

The recent interest in writing development has stimulated both debate and substantive changes in the teaching of writing at elementary, secondary, and postsecondary levels of education. Hairston (1982) asserted that the changes qualify as a *paradigm shift*, a term coined by Kuhn (1963) to refer to major changes in scientific fields that occur when old methods no longer solve new problems. In fact, the yearly repetition found in language arts writing programs is testimony to the ineffectiveness of many procedures (Calkins, 1983; Phelps-Terasaki et al., 1983). Several points of contrast between old and new approaches to writing include the following (Emig, 1981; Hairston, 1982):

OLD	NEW
Emphasis on product	Emphasis on composing process
Writers know what they will say at the outset	Writers sometimes discover what they will say in the process
Composing is a linear process	Composing is a recursive process
Children must be taught from parts to wholes (sentences before discourse)	There is an interplay between local and global concerns
Emphasis on lower-level processes (spelling, grammar, punctuation)	More emphasis on higher-level processes (text macrostructure)

Of course, some (e.g., Emig, 1981) would argue that the "old" still reigns in many classrooms. Others would argue that the "new" isn't new enough. For example, Martin, Christie, and Rothery (1987) propose that the writing-as-craft approach, fueled by frequent conferencing between writer and teacher (Graves, 1983), may produce children who *enjoy* writing more but who nevertheless fail to *develop* as writers. The reason, these authors state, is that text types (genre) must be made more obvious to children. They recommend a genre-based approach to the teaching of writing.

TEACHING WRITING TO EMERGENT WRITER/READERS

For children with language disorders, writing is a concern as early as the developmental age of four or five years. This is the age when children are exposed to the metalanguage of writing *and* reading (Olson, 1984). Also at this age, children form concepts about print, progressing from letters-as-objects to letters-as-symbols to letters-as-speech (Ferreiro, 1984). Language clinicians can program activities that encourage insights about print and writing, in one-on-one interactions with children or in groups. Parents can be taught to do the same.

Since children begin to write at the same time or even before they read, the potential efficacy of programs designed to integrate writing and reading seems obvious. Rather than separating reading and writing as distinct parts of the early literacy curriculum, they can be taught together in a variety of activities such as typing and other keyboard work, journalism, and creative dramatics (Moxley, 1982). Additional activities include dictating and the language experience approach to reading (but see Pinnell, 1988, for caveats regarding the language experience approach). Spelling words can be taken from the children's own dictated material. Contrary to the practice of always controlling spelling and decoding words according to word families, the inclusion of a wider variety of words (e.g., *dinosaur* as well as *egg*) might be predicted to stimulate the child's own hypothesis-generating strategies. Experience with print (writing and reading) *outside* the basal readers is recommended. Short but interesting texts such as greeting cards, party invitations, menus, and steps-in-a-process texts such as recipes, games, and crafts can be written as well as read. Earlier experiences with expository texts (Christie, 1986) and a wide variety of nonfiction materials (Paice, 1985) are recommended. Several sources have many suggestions for early curricula that combine reading and writing (Goulandris, 1985; Moxley, 1982; Stackhouse, 1985). For example, Boutwell (1983) described an experimental program with an eight-year-old child that centered on (a) reading what the child wrote and, later, (b) writing at difficult places in the text.

Two programs, one devised for kindergarten level children and the other for first grade, illustrate recent teaching approaches specifically designed to integrate early writing and reading. Kawakami-Arakaki, Oshiro, and Farran (1988) describe a kindergarten program in which writing and reading are combined in two daily activities. In a *morning message activity,* the teacher writes the date on the board, spelling out letters and numbers while encouraging the children to join in. Next, she writes a message of at least a sentence about something of interest that day. Even though some children are reading only a few words, they are all encouraged to go to the board to point out anything of interest about the message. This step was designed to actively draw the children's attention to the conventions of writing. The authors provide an illustration of a morning message routine from the later part of the year (Kawakami-Arakaki et al., 1988, p. 4). The message on the board was,

> April 17, 1985
> Good Morning, It's Wednesday, an art day. There's no music at 1:30 today because we are invited to a Spring Fling. Older boys and girls will be dancing and jumping rope. Please be on your best behavior.

Children then called attention to the following items in the message:

1. The contraction *it's* means it is.
2. The letter *s* in *boys* and *girls* makes these words plural.
3. The root word *day* is in Wednesday and today.
4. The word *be* is found twice in the message.
5. *Spring* and *Fling* rhyme.
6. The word endings *-ed, -ing,* and *-er* are used in *invited, dancing, jumping,* and *older.*

The second activity is an adaptation of the Graves and Hansen (1983) approach for first graders. This *writing process session* follows the morning message for 35 minutes. Hallmarks include child-generated writing topics and the development of a set of guidelines in the coaching of early writing (e.g., initial and/or final consonants used in conjunction with a blank line appear to encourage first picture labels and other types of word construction). Each session begins with the request for the children to write a message for the teacher on paper. Three phases of the session are prewriting and discussion, writing and conferring, and sharing. Drawings are acceptable messages for children unable to write any letters or words.

Pinnell (1988) adapted Marie Clay's (1979) Reading Recovery program for use with educationally at-risk first grade children. The program appears to be the emergent literacy analogue of early spoken language incidental teaching approaches. Children read and write "whole" texts with the teacher acting as a facilitator for child-initiated literacy behaviors. The components of a typical lesson as described by Pinnell (1988, p. 6) are as follows:

> Reading Recovery lessons are individual half-hour sessions which include several components. First, the child rereads several books which he has read before. This process allows him to work on reading in a context that is easy and full of meaning. The stories are natural language texts. Each day, the teacher keeps a running record of the new book that was introduced to the child the day before. This record is a kind of shorthand reproduction of the exact reading behavior on that text. While an accuracy record is calculated, that is not the most important information from the running record. This useful tool provides a way of analyzing behavior to determine whether the child is developing effective reading strategies. The lesson also includes writing a message. The child, helped by the teacher, constructs words he needs. The teacher encourages the child to hear sounds in words and to represent them with letters. The message is then read many times and is copied on a sentence strip which is cut apart and reconstructed by the child. These "cut apart" words are not used out of context but are always read as part of the whole message. Finally, the teacher introduces a new book by first talking about it and then asking the child to read it. This new book will be read independently the next day while the teacher takes a running record.

Analysis of session videotapes convinced Pinnell that children used information gained in one area (e.g., reading) to help solve problems in the other area (writing). Specifically, she identified a number of behaviors indicative of the formation of reading-writing connections. For example, children used previously read texts for writing material (specific words and phrases and character names). Through reading, they checked their construction of cut-up sentences and sometimes corrected their work on their own. Also, the children used the visual information gained in writing to help problem solve in reading (e.g., a child encountered *how* in reading, wrote *cow* on a piece of paper, then returned to reading able to read *how*). Pinnell's anecdote illustrates the point that the full cues required for spelling can be expected to have beneficial effects on reading, which requires only partial cues (Snowling, 1985).

The efficacy of the Pinnell (1988) program was evaluated by comparing the year-end performance of experimental children with others who received more typical types of reading skills instruction. On seven of nine language measures, the experimental children scored significantly higher. Of particular interest for this chapter is the fact that one of the improved scores was narrative writing. Blind evaluators, using a holistic scoring method, rated stories written by the Reading Recovery children significantly higher.

Both the kindergarten and first grade programs, by stressing the meaning potential of writing, are designed to cultivate children's sense of purpose in writing. Opinion is unanimous that children should be encouraged to discover significant uses for writing. As previously discussed, even though children are surrounded with print and people using print, the uses of such print may not be obvious. Taylor and Vawter (1978) offered suggestions for increasing the awareness of print function within the normal activities of an elementary classroom. For example, children wishing to feed the guinea pig must look to see when the last feeding occurred, and they must record the present feeding (the record-keeping function of print). The child who carries the lunch count information to the cafeteria sees the message potential of writing. Letter writing encourages the insight that writing is basically a social act. The social nature of writing becomes more obvious when writers receive feedback on their writing—feedback that responds to ideas as well as form.

Two themes, then, have emerged from applications of basic research in early developmental writing (as summarized in Chapter 8). The first is that children develop insights about writing and reading in an integrated manner, using knowledge gained in one domain to enlighten the other. The second is that even young children have the potential to write meaningful texts, even though the "text" may be short by adult standards and require adult participation for interpretation. Both themes are well represented in a book written specifically for parents and teachers of young children entitled *Write from the Start: Tapping Your Child's Natural Writing Ability,* by Graves and Stuart (1985). Pinnell's (1988) research, summarized above, provides evidence that the same principles are successful in accelerating writing and several other language domains in educationally at-risk children.

TEACHING WRITING TO OLDER CHILDREN AND ADOLESCENTS

When teachers and clinicians work with older problem writers, activities might be classified as structural (product) or process-oriented. Structural activities are those that teach explicit recognition and production of text, sentence, or word structure. Frequently, structural activities are done apart from the actual generation of text; for example, sentence-combining exercises might be expected to have a favorable impact on text writing at a later time. Process activities are those that teach explicit aspects of planning, generating, and revising text.

THE TEACHING OF STRUCTURE

The value of grammar lessons in producing better writing has been questioned in recent years. The criticism is usually directed at sentence-level grammar lessons; for example, underlining prepositional phrases in a set of unrelated sentences. Such lessons probably do not hurt writing, but their value in *helping* writing has not been demonstrated. Recent findings in text-level structure, and in genre and channel variation, suggest the use of different approaches to grammar teaching, including the explicit teaching of (1) genre and channel structural patterns, (2) text-level grammatical systems, and (3) complex sentence patterns.

According to Perera (1985), problem writers need explicit instruction in channel differences—the ways speech and writing differ and *the reasons why* they differ. Presumably, if students understood the reasons for structural patterns in writing (e.g., word order takes the place of prosody), they might be more likely to incorporate such patterns in their own writing. One suggestion for highlighting spoken and written differences is to record the writer in casual speech and then jointly construct a verbatim transcript from the tape.

Results from several projects lend support to the practice of explicit instruction in genre, or text structure, as a facilitator of expository writing. Armbruster, Anderson, and Ostertag (1986) studied the effect of teaching problem-solution structure on the ability of fifth grade students to write high quality summaries. Compared to fifth graders who received a more traditional approach consisting of discussion and answering questions about text material, the students in the experimental group recalled more information on an essay test and wrote summaries that included more main ideas. Their summaries also received higher ratings for organization, focus, integration, and support/elaboration. A finding of importance for language clinicians was that the training was, in the main, as beneficial for low ability students as for high ability students (ability was defined by reading comprehension scores).

Taylor and Beach (1984) documented beneficial training effects of a hierarchical summarization task on reading recall and text writing. Seventh grade students were given seven one-hour lessons in producing summaries of social studies passages. Opinion essays written by the students were rated before and after the training. When compared to a control group, the students' post-training essays received significantly higher ratings. The fact that the training had an impact on a slightly different genre (opinion essays) should be emphasized. Summary training may be a skill which, once learned, generalizes across several types of texts.

Stotsky (1983) provided a synthesis of earlier research on the explicit teaching of expository text structure. In general, research has demonstrated improved performance in *both* reading and writing following a variety of instructional techniques designed to make expository text structure more obvious.

An Australian team of linguists and educators at the University of Sydney (Eggins, Martin, & Wignell, 1987; Martin & Rothery, 1986; Painter & Martin, 1986) are presently studying genres in a variety of curriculum materials read and produced by students through the secondary level. They believe that better ways to teach writing will depend on more detailed descriptive work on genre. Their approach is summarized in the following statement:

> To be in control of their writing, students need to know the generic structure potentials of the genres in which they are expected to write. This implies, of course, that teachers first need to know what genres they expect and the characteristics of those genres. Such knowledge about genre(s) cannot be plucked out of the air, but will evolve from careful analysis of successful text creation. (Rothery & Gerot, 1986, p. 163)

Explicit teaching of narrative text structure has received considerable attention in spoken language (Page & Stewart, 1985; Westby, 1985). By comparison, written narrative text improvement has received less attention. Stewig's book (in press, 3rd ed.), however, is an extensive source of information on the teaching of narrative form throughout the elementary grades. The writing exercises/goals described in the book are reproduced in Table 9-2 (see pp. 335-337). Stewart (1985) has also offered suggestions for teaching narrative and expository structure.

Another type of structural activity is the explicit teaching of text-level grammatical systems of cohesion. These structural categories are found across genres, although there may be variations depending on the genre. Examples include verb tense/aspect maintenance, pronominal reference, and adverbial connectivity. Once students understand the general nature of these systems, practice generating appropriate forms can begin. Scott and Rush (1985) presented several formats for teaching adverbial connectives; they utilized cloze and paraphrase formats among others. Practice materials that *tax* the writer's grammatical knowledge are useful. For example, pronominal reference is taxed when there are two or more same sex characters of equal importance in a story.

A third and final category of structural goals involves teaching complex sentences. Mature writing requires complex sentences, defined here as sentences containing one or more subordinate clauses or other nonclausal complex structures (Scott, 1988). Sentence-combining exercises have been used for many years as a way to increase syntactic fluency and variety (Humes, 1983). A student is required to combine two or more short simple sentences into one longer complex sentence. Various degrees of cueing are possible (Gregg, 1983). A considerable body of literature reveals that students trained in sentence-combining transfer their knowledge of complex sentences to spontaneous writing (Hunt, 1977; Phelps-Terasaki et al., 1983). Daiute (1984) suggested that sentence combining and other types of complex sentence exercises are most beneficial to writers at the ages of 12 through 14 years, a time of rapid increase in the complexity of written language output. By increasing the familiarity and fluency of complex sentence patterns, writers are able to generate complex sentences with less burden on working memory; hence, there are fewer mistakes (Daiute, 1984). Task formats in addition to sentence combining—for example, sentence completion—may accomplish similar goals (see Wiig & Semel, 1984, for additional examples of task formats). Clinicians should carefully program a wide variety of complex sentence types specific to written language (cf. Perera, 1984; Scott, 1988)

The Teaching of Process

In contrast to structural activities, process procedures are those that occur in any of the three phases of writing; namely, planning, generating, or revising. The basic goal is to encourage the development of higher-level behaviors characteristic of older or expert writers. Planning and revising have received the most attention.

PLANNING. Much of the work in the facilitation of planning centers on teaching students to self prompt. Bereiter and Scardamalia (1987, p. 305) described a procedure used with students between the ages of 10 and 14 years. Students were taught to both select and respond to planning cues that were grouped into function categories. Examples of cues for opinion essay writing included:

New Idea:
  An even better idea is . . .
  No one will have thought of . . .
Elaborate:
  The reason I think so . . .
  Another way to put it would be . . .

The self prompts were incorporated into think aloud planning sessions. The students first observed the procedure as modeled by teachers. Bereiter and Scardamalia (1987) found significant differences between experimental and control groups in pre- and post-test expository and opinion essay writing. Harris and Graham (1985) discussed the successful use of self-control strategy training with two 12-year-old learning disabled writers.

Humes (1983) outlined several techniques designed to help students generate and arrange ideas in the planning stage of writing; these include word association, simile frames (e.g., the ______ is like ______), idea generating questions (e.g., why is this topic important?), matrix constructing (a chart for generating and recording ideas), and arrangement plans (e.g., descriptions of things can be arranged from top to bottom, or outside to inside). Rubin (1987) discussed procedures that draw on the writer's better developed oral rhetorical skills. The writer literally ''talks through'' ideas and then commits them to paper. This approach could be individually oriented or it could be done in groups, at which point it is similar to Grave's (1978) dyadic or group conferencing approach (1978).

REVISING AND EDITING. One of the most active areas of applied writing research deals with revision. The emphasis on revision is timely in light of Applebee's (1984) finding that ninth and eleventh grade students rarely treated their writing as texts that could be improved by revision. Neither, apparently, did the students' teachers. The infrequent teacher comments on student's texts tended to be general and unhelpful (e.g., ''You have some good ideas, but you need to be more careful about your word choice and your sentence structure. Make your sentences grammatically correct and as precise in vocabulary as possible'' Applebee, 1984, p. 106). Three important principles have emerged that shape revision activities: (1) the view that writing does not stop with the generation of a text—in other words, revision is a critical part of the text; (2) the view that errors are part of the learning process (Hull, 1987); and (3) the view that revising can be managed better by focusing on one type of error at a time (Hull, 1987; Perera, 1985).

As discussed in Chapter 8, changes that span large amounts of text and alter or redirect meaning seem to be the most difficult types of revisions for young writers and problem writers. Meaning and organization altering revision is the cornerstone of the writing-as-process approach of Graves (1978, 1983) and Calkins (1983). The writing workshops described by Calkins (1983) were designed in collaboration with third and fourth grade classroom teachers. The children spent 1 hour and 20 minutes three times per week (during their alert morning time) writing. (Meaningful text-level writing cannot be sandwiched into 20-minute slots of time.) For the first 10 minutes, the teacher presented some type of writing mini-lesson (e.g., the do's and don't's of selecting a good topic, mapping a possible text structure, how to "show but not tell" with words). Then came 50 minutes of actual writing and teacher-child conferencing (the teacher circulating to various children), followed by a final sharing time when the children discussed their writing together. Revision was central to the philosophy and the procedure, with the children writing successive drafts of most pieces. Calkins (1983) documented the changes in revision strategies that occurred over a two-year period from the beginning of the third grade through the fourth grade. The important finding of Calkin's research was that mid to late-elementary school children are capable of substantive revisions of their self-chosen topic texts in this type of supportive environment. Some children, however, found it difficult at first to overcome an aversion for "messing up" their texts by revising.

Scardamalia and Bereiter (1985) advocated a self prompting program for encouraging content and organization revisions. Sixth and twelfth grade students, supplied with a set of 13 diagnostic cues (e.g., "weak reason" and "hard to tell what the main point is"), made more revisions concerned with higher-level text reorganization than control groups not given the cues.

The literature contains several accounts of methods for encouraging editing—the last phase of the writing process. Changes made in this phase are less global and are directed at surface structure grammar, punctuation conventions, and spelling. In Calkin's (1983) third and fourth grade classrooms, editing was the last step of the final draft; it took place at a special "editing" table, aided by editing checklists (a form of self prompting). Discussing teacher-child editing interactions, Graves (in Graves & Stuart, 1985, p. 177) drew a sharp distinction between approaches that help children develop insight into written conventions versus the mere correction of errors:

> Telling writers they've made a mistake is not teaching. If the child can already do what I've corrected, then correcting is only reminding. And reminding is not teaching. If the child doesn't understand the error, then correcting it isn't enough. Many errors have to be ignored simply because children can only take in so much at one time. When I choose one type of error to work on, then I use what the child already knows to help him or her learn the new skill.

Graves goes on to illustrate the point by relating the case of the child who writes dialogue without quotation marks. Graves would first find out if the child knows what a conversation is. If so, can the child find the places where the speaker starts and stops talking? If the answer is yes again, the child is ready to learn about quotation marks (a symbol for something already known). Graves would also explain how quotation marks help the reader understand text meaning.

Editing of grammatical errors begins with the detection of errors and error patterns (Daiute, 1984; Hull, 1987). Presumably, the verbatim oral reading of text errors would prompt error recognition. Poor writers, however, are frequently poor error detectors. As they read their texts out loud, they skim over parts, drawing from long-term memory, and inadvertently "correct" errors as they read out loud. As an antidote, Perera (1985) suggested directing the writer to read the text at a slower rate.

Once errors are detected, writers can work with teachers and clinicians to uncover patterns in errors. The fact that errors are not random suggests that an underlying cause might be found that would direct further error detection efforts. The discovery of error patterns would counteract the tendency of poor writers to correct errors based on idiosyncratic "rules." Hull (1987) provided the example of a writer who crossed out a sentence final *however,* insisting that *however* cannot occur at the end of a sentence.

Possible motivators in the revision/editing process were suggested by Perera (1985). These included the use of different colored pens for different types of errors and teaching writers some of the symbols used by professional editors. Humes (1983) suggested using different colors of paper for successive drafts as another potential motivator. Further, several drafts can be required for "publication," or even for a grade on a particular piece. The main obstacle to improving revising behaviors may be attitudinal—the student's idea that the first draft is the only draft (Humes, 1983).

THE EFFECTS OF READING ON WRITING

Reading and writing connections in the development of writing and in programs designed for younger children have been emphasized in these chapters. A common theme in discussions of the "why Johnny can't write" variety is the perception that children who are poor writers do not read and are not "read to" by adults. A considerable body of research substantiates the claim that good writers read more than poor writers (see Stotsky, 1983, for a review). Many elementary teachers set aside time to read stories out loud to children. As it stands, this is a good habit, but it is rarely done often enough, over a long enough period of time (i.e., into the higher grades), and in genres other than narrative. As previously indicated, some writing researchers attribute expository text shortcomings in children's writing to *a lack of exposure* rather than inherent inability (Christie, 1986).

Experience with a variety of genres is especially important for children with reading disabilities. Good readers are not totally dependent on outside sources for text models; they can read good text themselves. Because poor writers are likely to be poor readers, however, they are more dependent on outside sources (teachers and parents) for exposure to good text models, particularly if they have been "raised" on a diet of the stilted prose in many remedial reading books (Eckhoff, 1983; Perera, 1985).

Several authors stress that the need for good text models continues well into the secondary years (Shuy, 1981). For some reason, older students are sometimes expected to induce the requirements of good text entirely on their own, and furthermore, they are expected to produce good text under pressure conditions (e.g., essay exams). Stotsky (1983) summarized several investigations that succeeded in improving writing by substituting reading experiences (largely unstructured) in place of grammar study or additional writing practice. Although high school and college students were the focus in most projects, one study by DeVries (1970), cited by Stotsky (1983), demonstrated similar effects for fifth graders.

A program specifically predicated on the assumption that children transfer knowledge from reading to writing is entitled Read to Write: Using Children's Literature as a Springboard for Teaching Writing (Stewig, in press, 3rd ed.). The program foundation is an active experience with literature that continues throughout elementary school. By *active,* the author refers to experiences that go beyond passive absorption, including talking, reflecting, arguing, and questioning. The techniques outlined in the book apply to narrative writing. As noted above, the outline of the program is shown in Table 9-2.

TABLE 9–2.
An outline of the learning activities recommended by Stewig (in press, 3rd ed.) for the teaching of narrative and other forms of creative writing.

Oral language

Teacher tells an oral story

Class discusses voice qualities of tellers on tapes/records

Discussing similarities/differences in folktale variants.

Dictates group stories based on
- (a) field exploration
- (b) classroom visitors
- (c) classroom experiences
- (d) pictures

Dictates questions prior to field experience

Child dictates a story:
- (a) any (a through d) above,
- (b) retells favorite story
- (c) makes up original tale

Characterization

Listening to author's description of character:
- (a) physical
- (b) physical and psychological
- (c) as established through language

Observing and composing:
- (a) writing physical description of self
- (b) writing physical description of "secret friend"

Writing physical/psychological description of character in a book

Shifting from third to first person (assuming a persona)

Adding a character to a story

Creating new character based on pattern in literature (distinctive traits)

Writing about a made-up character who stays the same

Writing about a made-up character who changes

Setting

Listening to author's description of setting:
- (a) visual
- (b) aural
- (c) spatial/tactile
- (d) olfactory
- (e) combination

Sensory exploration and writing about:
- (a) the classroom
- (b) the school environment
- (c) the home

Writing based on literature: descriptive writing about weather, time of day, seasons

Plot

Parallel plot: discussion and writing

Adapted plot:
- (a) rename characters
- (b) change number or type of characters
- (c) change nature of characters
- (d) change events

Plot completion

Plot creation; extending plot given in story:
- (a) backward in time
- (b) forward in time
- (c) relocate plot in another time/place

Fable: writing a plot to fit the moral

Character as it affects plot:
- (a) more fully develop a character already in the story
- (b) add a new character

Sequence in plot: writing flashbacks

Types of conflict as a base for writing:
- (a) type one: person versus person
- (b) type two: person versus fate
- (c) type three: person versus self

Figurative language

Literature input: reading poems/stories that include similes and/or metaphors

Writing similes:
- (a) writing simile stems
- (b) writing complete similes
- (c) incorporating similes into composition based on literature
- (d) incorporating similes into original compositions

Writing metaphor

Poetry

Reading poetry:
- (a) incidental (topical) sharing
- (b) "Poet-of-the-Month" approach

Writing unrhymed forms:
- (a) haiku
- (b) cinquain
  1. syllabic
  2. line
- (c) other:
  1. sept
  2. septet
  3. lanterne
  4. vignette

Writing rhymed forms: limericks

Concrete (visual) poetry

Poetry ideas (K. Koch)

Editing

Concurrent editing (choices made the child is writing)

Completion editing (choices made after the writing is completed)

Listening to stories/discussing the exploring words
- (a) choosing alternatives words
- (b) choosing alternative verbs

Changing compositions
- (a) adding words
- (b) changing word choices
- (c) combining sentences
- (d) sequence in composition
- (e) coherence in composition (filling in the gaps)
- (f) deletions

Conversation
- (a) listening to dialect
- (b) editing conversation

[1]From J.W. Stewig, (in press). Read to write: Using children's literature as a springboard for teaching writing, (3rd ed.). New York: Holt, Rinehart, and Winston. Reprinted by permission.

THE VALUE OF WRITING

Perhaps a good place to conclude these two chapters about writing is to think again of the LD adults with persistent writing problems mentioned at the beginning of Chapter 8. After years of writing struggle, frequently confined to tasks such as punctuation, sentence level grammar, and spelling, it is possible that many of these individuals have lost sight of the potential value of writing, whether social or individual. The benefits of writing for the individual are the most likely to be overlooked.

The major benefit to the individual is captured in again considering the knowledge-telling versus the knowledge-transforming model of writing (Bereiter & Scardamalia, 1987). The knowledge-transforming view of writing highlights the potential of writing as a ''tool of thought'' and a ''process of discovering.'' The model is an intentional model of writing, one that stresses the place of writing within a more generalized intentional cognitive mode of operating. In contrast to the knowledge-telling writer who depends on evoked memories and external assistance, the intentional writer sets cognitive goals to be achieved through writing, then actively pursues those goals (Bereiter & Scardamalia, 1987, p. 361). Even the writing-as-process approaches, which attempt to make writing meaningful for students, may not foster such writing. Bereiter and Scardamalia (1987, p. 360) have reminded us that ''mature writers are able to make writing tasks meaningful for themselves and *that this is part of their competence.*'' The central problem in education today, according to these authors, is finding ways to foster a more active, intentional cognition in general. Writing instruction can be part of the solution, so long as students are aware of the full extent of the composing process and achieve independence in managing the process. Writing can be the agent of cognitive, personal, and aesthetic development. A narrow functional view of writing is ill-advised (Perera, 1986).

Some students, particularly problem writers, lose sight of the potential value of their written ideas in a school context dominated by the use of writing to demonstrate mastery of textbook information. (If the information presented is wrong, it will not be judged as valuable.) Valuable and even profound ideas do not always require complex, perfect written form. As Scardamalia (1981) reminded, complex ideas and certainly valuable ideas can be stated in simple sentences with simple vocabulary. One of Johnson's (1987, p. 180) LD adults illustrated this point quite well when he wrote, in handwriting that was barely legible,

> As you can tell my handwriting
> is atrocious it has held me back
> throughout my entire life.

The last point about the value of writing brings us back to reading. Calkins (1983) stated that through writing, students become ''makers of reading.'' The tendency of children to impune blind authority to school texts might be neutralized as they gain a better understanding of the writer behind the texts they read. In the process, reading may become less intimidating. Calkins (1983, p. 157) drew an analogy for adult professionals who read material like the present chapters. Try writing such material, she recommends. Only then will you know first-hand the gaps and shortcomings.

REFERENCES

Anderson, P. (1982). A preliminary study of syntax in the written expression of learning disabled children. *Journal of Learning Disabilities, 15,* 359–362.

Applebee, A. (1984). *Contexts for learning to write.* Norwood, NJ: Ablex.

Aram, D.M., Ekelman, B.L., and Nation, J. (1984). Preschoolers with language disorders: Ten years later. *Journal of Speech and Hearing Research, 27,* 232–244.

Armbruster, B., Anderson, T., and Ostertag, J. (1986). *Does test structure/summarization instruction facilitate learning from expository text?.* Champaign, IL: Center for the Study of Reading, Technical Report No. 394.

Bartlett, E. (1984). Anaphoric reference in written narratives of good and poor elementary school writers. *Journal of Verbal Learning and Verbal Behavior, 23,* 540–552.

Bereiter, C., and Scardamalia, M. (1987). *The psychology of written composition.* Hillsdale, NJ: Erlbaum.

Blair, T., and Crump, W. (1984). Effects of discourse mode on the syntactic complexity of learning disabled student's written expression. *Learning Disability Quarterly, 7,* 19–29.

Boutwell, M. (1983). Reading and writing process: A reciprocal agreement. *Language Arts, 60,* 723–730.

Calkins, L. (1983). *Lessons from a child: On the teaching and learning of writing.* London: Heinemann.

Carpenter, D. (1983). Spelling error profiles of able and disabled readers. *Journal of Learning Disabilities, 16,* 102–104.

Cayer, R., and Sacks, R. (1979). Oral and written discourse of basic writers: Similarities and differences. *Research in the Teaching of English, 13,* 121–128.

Chafe, W. (1982). Integration and involvement in speaking, writing, and oral literature. In D. Tannen (Ed.), *Spoken and written language: Exploring orality and literacy,* 35–53. Norwood, NJ: Ablex.

Charrow, V. (1981). The written English of deaf adolescents. In M. Whiteman (Ed.), *Writing: The nature, development, and teaching of written communication: Vol. 1. Variation in writing: Functional and linguistic-cultural differences,* 179–187. Hillsdale, NJ: Erlbaum.

Christie, F. (1986). Writing in the infants grades. In C. Painter and J. Martin (Eds.), *Writing to mean: Teaching genres across the curriculum,* 118–135. Applied Linguistics Association of Australia, Occasional Papers No. 9.

Clay, M. (1979). *The early detection of reading difficulties.* Auckland, New Zealand: Heinemann.

Cooper, C., and Odell, L. (1977). *Evaluating writing: Describing, measuring, judging.* Urbana, IL: National Council of Teachers of English.

Cromer, R. (1978). The basis of childhood dysphasia: A linguistic approach. In M. Wyke (Ed.), *Developmental dysphasia,* 85–134. London: Academic Press.

Cromer, R. (1980). Spontaneous spelling by language disordered children. In U. Frith (Ed.), *Cognitive processes in spelling*, 405–422. London: Academic Press.

Daiute, C. (1984). Performance limits on writers. In R. Beach and L. Bridwell (Eds.), *New directions in composition research*, 205–224. New York: Guilford Press.

Dodd, B. (1980). The spelling abilities of profoundly pre-lingually deaf children. In U. Frith (Ed.), *Cognitive processes in spelling*, 423–440. London: Academic Press.

Eckhoff, B. (1983). How reading affects children's writing. *Language Arts, 60,* 607–616.

Eggins, S., Martin, J., and Wignell, P. (1987). Writing Project, Working Papers in Linguistics, No. 5, Linguistics Department, University of Sydney, Sydney, Australia.

Emig, J. (1981). Non-magical thinking: Presenting writing developmentally in schools. In C. Frederiksen and J. Dominic (Eds.), *Writing: The nature, development, and teaching of written communication: Vol 2. Writing: Process, development, communication*, 21–31. Hillsdale, NJ: Earlbaum.

Farr, M., and Janda, M. (1985). Basic writing students: Investigating oral and written language. *Research in the Teaching of English, 19,* 62–83.

Ferreiro, E. (1984). The underlying logic of literacy development. In H. Goelman, A. Oberg, and F. Smith (Eds.), *Awakening to literacy*, 154–173. London: Heinemann.

Freedman, S. (1982). Language assessment and writing disorders. *Topics in Language Disorders, 2,* 34–44.

Gerber, M., and Hall, R. (1987). Information processing approaches to studying spelling deficiencies. *Journal of Learning Disabilities, 20,* 34–42.

Giordano, G. (1984a). Analyzing and remediating writing disorders. *Journal of Learning Disabilities, 17,* 78–83.

Giordano, G. (1984b). *Teaching writing to learning disabled students*. Rockville, MD: Aspen

Goulandris, N. (1985). Extending the written language skill of children with specific learning difficulties—supplementary teaching techniques. In M. Snowling (Ed.), *Children's written language difficulties*, 134–146. Windsor: Nfer-Nelson.

Graves, D. (1978). *Balance the basics*. New York: The Ford Foundation.

Graves, D. (1983). *Writing: Teachers and children at work*. London: Heinemann.

Graves, D. and Hansen, J. (1983). The author's chair. *Language Arts, 60,* 176–183.

Graves, D., and Stuart, V. (1985). *Write from the start: Tapping your child's natural writing ability*. New York: E. P. Dutton.

Greenberg, K. (1987). Defining, teaching, and testing basic writing competence. *Topics in Language Disorders, 7,* 31–41.

Gregg, N. (1983). College learning disabled writer: Error patterns and instructional alternatives. *Journal of Learning Disability, 16,* 334–338.

Grubgeld, E. (1986). Helping the problem speller without suppressing the writer. *English Journal, 75,* 58–61.

Hairston, M. (1982). The winds of change: Thomas Kuhn and the revolution of the teaching of writing. *College Composition and Communication, 33,* 76–88.

Hammill, D., and Larsen, S. (1978). *The test of written language,* Austin, TX: Pro-Ed.

Harris, K., and Graham, S. (1985). Improving learning disabled student's composition skills: Self-control strategy training. *Learning Disability Quarterly, 8,* 27–36.

Hull, G. (1987). Current views of error and editing. *Topics in Language Disorders, 7,* 55–65.

Humes, A. (1983). Putting writing research into practice. *The Elementary School Journal, 84,* 3–17.

Hunt, K. (1985). *Grammatical structures written at three grade levels.* Champaign, IL: National Council of Teachers of English, Research Report No. 3.

Hunt, K. (1980). Syntactic maturity in school children and adults. *Society for Research in Child Development Monographs,* No. 134, *35,* No. 1.

Hunt, K. (1977). Early blooming and late blooming syntactic structures. In C. Cooper and L. Odell (Eds.), *Evaluating writing,* 91–105. Urbana, IL: National Council of Teachers of English.

Isaacson, S. (1985). Assessing written language skills. In C. Simon (Ed.), *Communication skills and classroom success,* 403–424, San Diego, CA: College-Hill Press.

Johnson, D. (1987). Disorders of written language. In D. Johnson and J. Blalock (Eds.), *Adults with learning disabilities: Clinical studies,* 173–204. New York: Grune and Stratton.

Kawakami-Arakaki, A., Oshiro, M., and Farran, D. (1988). *Research to practice: Integrating reading and writing in a kindergarten curriculum.* Champaign, IL: Center for the Study of Reading, Technical Report No. 415.

Kress, G. (1982). *Learning to write.* London: Routledge and Kegan Paul.

Kroll, B. (1981). Developmental relationships between speaking and writing. In B. Kroll and R. Vann (Eds.), *Exploring speaking-writing relationships: Connections and contrasts,* pp. 32–54. Champaign, IL: National Council of Teachers of English.

Kuhn, T. (1963). *The structure of scientific revolutions.* Chicago: IL: University of Chicago Press.

Larsen, S., and Hammill, D. (1986). *The test of written spelling.* Austin, TX: Pro-Ed.

Loban, W. (1976). *Language development: Kindergarten through grade twelve.* Champaign, IL: National Council of Teachers of English, Research Report No. 18.

Martin, J., Christie, F., and Rothery, J. (1987). Social processes in education: A reply to Sawyer and Watson (and others). In S. Eggins, J. Martin, and P. Wignell (Eds.), Writing Project, Working Papers in Linguistics, No. 5, Linguistics Department, University of Sydney, Sydney, Australia.

Martin, J., and Rothery, J. (1986). Writing Project, Working Papers in Linguistics, No. 4, Linguistics Department, University of Sydney, Sydney, Australia.

Morris, N., and Crump, W. (1982). Syntactic and vocabulary development in the written language of learning disabled and non-disabled students at four age levels. *Learning Disability Quarterly, 5,* 163–172.

Morris, N., and Stick, S. (1985, November). Oral/written language analysis of learning disabled and normal high schoolers. Paper presented at the annual meeting of the American Speech-Language-Hearing Association, Washington, D.C.

Moxley, R. (1982). *Writing and reading in early childhood*. Englewood Cliffs, NJ: Educational Technology Publications.

Myklebust, H. (1965). *Development and disorders of written language, Vol. 1, Picture story language test*. New York: Grune and Stratton.

Myklebust, H. (1973). *Development and disorders of written language: Vol. 2: Studies of normal and exceptional children*. New York: Grune and Stratton.

Olson, D. (1984). "See! Jumping!" Some oral language antecedents of literacy. In H. Goelman, A. Oberg, and F. Smith (Eds.), *Awakening to literacy*, 185–192. London: Heinemann.

Page, J., and Stewart, S. (1985). Story grammar skills in school-age children. *Topics in Language Disorders, 5*, 16–29.

Paice, S. (1985). *Reading and learning*. In C. Moon (Eds.), *Practical ways to teach reading*, 46–54. London: Ward Lock Educational.

Painter, C., and Martin, J. (1986). *Writing to mean: Teaching genres across the curriculum*. Sydney: Applied Linguistics Association of Australia, Occasional Papers No. 9.

Perera, K. (1984). *Children's writing and reading*. London: Basil Blackwell.

Perera, K. (1985). "Do your corrections"—How can children improve their writing? *Child Language Teaching and Therapy, 1*, 5–16.

Perera, K. (1986). Grammatical differentiation between speech and writing in children aged 8 to 12. In A. Wilkinson (Ed.), *The writing of writing*, 90–108. London: Falmer Press.

Phelps-Terasaki, D., Phelps-Gunn, T., and Stetson, E. (1983). *Remediation and instruction in language*. Rockville, MD: Aspen.

Pinnell, G. (1988). *Success of children at risk in a program that combines writing and reading*. Champaign, IL: Center for the Study of Reading, Technical Report 417.

Poplin, M., Gray, R., Larsen, S., Banikowski, A., and Mehring, T. (1980). A comparison of components of written-expression abilities in learning disabled and nonlearning disabled students at three grade levels. *Learning Disability Quarterly, 3*, 46–53.

Richardson, K., Calnan, M., Essen, J., and Lambert, L. (1976). The linguistic maturity of 11-year-olds: Some analysis of the written compositions of children in the National Child Development Study. *Journal of Child Language, 3*, 99–115.

Rothery, J., and Gerot, L. (1986). Writing in the junior secondary school. In C. Painter and J. Martin (Eds.), *Writing to mean: Teaching genres across the curriculum*, 150–173. Sydney: Applied Linguistics Association of Australia, Occasional Papers No. 9.

Rubin, D. (1987). Divergence and convergence between oral and written language communication. *Topics in Language Disorders, 7*, pp. 1–18.

Scardamalia, M. (1981). How children cope with the cognitive demands of writing. In C. Frederiksen and J. Dominic (Eds.), *Writing: The nature, develop-*

ment, and teaching of written communication: Vol. 2. Writing: Process, development, communication, 81–103. Hillsdale, NJ: Earlbaum.

Scardamalia, M., and Bereiter, C. (1985). Development of dialectical processes in composition. In D. Olson, N. Torrance, and A. Hildyard (Eds.), *Literacy, language, and learning: The nature and consequences of reading and writing*, 307–329. Cambridge: Cambridge University Press.

Schwartz, S. (1983). Spelling disability: A developmental linguistic analysis of pattern abstraction. *Applied Psycholinguistics, 4*, 303–316.

Scott, D. (1987, April). Summarizing text: Context effects in learning disordered children. Paper presented at the First International Symposium on Specific Language Disorders, Reading, England.

Scott, C. (1988). The development of complex sentences. *Topics in Language Disorders, 8*, 44–62.

Scott, C., and Rush, D. (1985). Teaching adverbial connectivity: Implications from current research. *Child Language Teaching and Therapy, 1*, 264–280.

Shaughnessy, M. (1977). *Errors and expectations: A guide for the teacher of basic writing*. New York: Oxford University Press.

Sheils, M. (1975). Why Johnny can't write. *Newsweek*, December 8, 58–65.

Shuy, R. (1981). Toward a developmental theory of writing. In C. Frederiksen and T. Dominic (Eds.), *Writing: The nature, development, and teaching of written communication: Vol. 2: Writing: Process, development, communication*, 119–132. Hillsdale, NJ: Earlbaum.

Snowling, M. (1980). The development of grapheme-phoneme correspondence in normal and dyslexic readers. *Journals of Experimental Child Psychology, 29*, 294–305.

Snowling, M. (1985). The assessment of reading and spelling skills. In M. Snowling (Ed.), *Children's written language difficulties*, 80–95. Windsor, England: Nfer-Nelson.

Stackhouse, J. (1985). Segmentation, speech, and spelling difficulties. In M. Snowling (Ed.), *Children's written language difficulties*, 96–116. Windsor, England: Nfer-Nelson.

Stewart, S. (1985). Development of written-language proficiency. In C. Simon (Ed.), *Communication skills and classroom success: Therapy methodologies for language-learning disabled students*, 341–364. San Diego, CA: College-Hill Press.

Stewig, J. (in press). *Read to write: Using children's literature as a springboard for teaching writing*, 3rd Ed. New York: Holt, Rinehart, and Winston.

Stotsky, S. (1983). Research on reading/writing relationships: A synthesis and suggested directions. *Language Arts, 60*, 627–642.

Taylor, B. and and Beach, R. (1984). The effects of text structure instruction on middle-grade student's comprehension and production of expository text. *Reading Research Quarterly, 19*, 134–146.

Taylor, N., and Vawter, J. (1978). Helping children discover the functions of written language. *Language Arts, 55*, 941–945.

Weaver, C. (1982). Welcoming errors as signs of growth. *Language Arts, 59*, 438–444.

Wells, G. (1985). Preschool literacy-related activities and success in school. In

D. Olson, N. Torrance, and A. Hildyard (Eds.), *Literacy, language, and learning: The nature and consequences of reading and writing,* 229–255. Cambridge: Cambridge University Press.

Westby, C. (1985). Learning to talk, talking to learn: Oral-literature language differences. In C. Simon (Ed.), *Communication skills and classroom success: Therapy methodologies for language-learning disabled students,* 181–213. San Diego, CA: College-Hill Press.

Wiig, E., and Semel, E. (1984). *Language assessment and interaction for the learning disabled.* Columbus, OH: Charles E. Merrill.

Wilkinson, A., Barnsley, G., Hanna, P., and Swan, M. (1979). Assessing language development: The Crediton project. *Language for Learning, 1,* 59–79.

APPENDIX: A TYPED VERSION OF TEXT 11 (P. 315)

1. Deserts were formed by erosion and
2. dry weather. most rivers are underground
3. or seasonal rivers and rain comes
4. in large quantities and causes flash
5. flouding and cases animals,
6. spiders, or insects to flee to Higher
7. ground to keep from dronding or being
8. swept away, when rain does come the
9. plant life compeats to collect as
10. much as possible and some of it
11. to to comtrubit to oases and
12. river and such. The plant life consists
13. of cactises and leafy plants mostly
14. & horney Plants the thorns are to
15. protect the water supply of the plants
16. the cactises root system is Horizonl
17. to support its weight and to collect
18. water over a long distance, most of
19. the leafy plants are loacated at
20. or By the oases and rivers.
21. Two plants growing side by side are
22. said to be nurseing one another
23. (cactises and trees) One get shade
24. and water or vise versa from
25. one another., climate or weather
26. are dry, hot and windy (some times)
27. cloweds are formed over mountains
28. and are blowen and warmed down the
29. side of the mountains and then are
30. dumped down on the deserts.
31. animals are mostly (unintelligible) and are
32. lizerds, snakes, and insects But there are
33. some animels or memils such as
34. Hedge Hogs, mice, rats, cyotes, wolves,
35. tigers, and pignosed skunkes, these animels
36. eat one another for food and the Hedge
37. Hog eats cactuses for food and water
38. But most of the animels go to oases
39. and rivers to drink, memels seek
40. neutrul caves, ledges and Hollows to stay
41. out of the heat during the Hot part
42. of the day and go out at the
43. evening or night to scout for food or
44. drink. Birds are part of the
45. eniroment and they live in the cacticus
46. or on them one might peck a Hole
47. in side of one and the other might build
48. a next in the middle of the top
49. of one for protection from other

10

Issues in Determining Eligibility for Service: Who Does What to Whom?

Frank M. Cirrin

In recent years, educators and specialists from several professions have displayed increased interest in reading problems of children. Ideally, optimal services would be provided to children with reading problems by making the best use of the professionals who have interest and expertise in aspects of reading disabilities. Realistically, there are many barriers that limit or prevent the realization of this goal. These factors include economic and political constraints, education agency eligibility regulations, issues of professional territoriality, and a reluctance to move away from traditional service delivery models. Provision of optimal services to children with reading disabilities is also complicated by the heterogeneity of children with reading problems as well as the educational and theoretical biases of individual professionals.

The problem of "who does what to whom" cannot be answered simplistically. The uppermost concern should be that the reading disabled child receive the services he or she needs, regardless of which professionals can provide those services. Although a surge of optimism has recently swept through many professional fields regarding the use of multidisciplinary approaches to reading disabilities (Alley & Deshler, 1979; Catts & Kamhi, 1986; Lerner, 1985), all too frequently discipline boundaries fragment coordinated interaction between professionals.

Cooperative planning among professionals and administrative support for multidisciplinary intervention programs are essential in providing optimal services to children with reading problems. Professionals must recognize that each one alone cannot meet all of the needs of all reading disabled students, but that through cooperative planning their collective efforts have a much greater chance of meeting the student's needs (Alley & Deshler, 1979).

The purpose of this chapter is to identify the factors that determine the involvement of professionals who provide remedial services to children with reading problems. The following issues are discussed in the first section of this chapter: (1) constraints placed on practice by government regulations, (2) professional territoriality, and (3) service delivery models. In the second section, suggestions will be presented for speech-language pathologists, classroom teachers, learning disabilities specialists, and reading specialists to provide optimal services to children with reading problems.

In this chapter the term *reading disabilities* will be used as a broad term to describe children whose reading level is not consistent with grade level or chronological age. It is recognized that children with reading problems are a heterogeneous group and that a child's specific reading difficulties and the presumed underlying basis for those difficulties will influence which professionals serve the child. The professionals most likely to serve children with reading problems include the classroom teacher, the reading specialist, the learning disabilities specialist, and the speech-language pathologist.

EDUCATION AGENCY REGULATIONS

The principal regulatory function of federal, state, and local education agencies is to specify which children qualify for special services. Economic and political factors play an important role in devising these regulations, whereas administrative and bureaucratic factors play an important role in determining how these regulations are actually implemented and carried out. These factors may place constraints on professional practice to the extent that optimal service plans, based on the individual needs of the child, may be compromised. More specifically, regulatory and administrative factors may limit the number of reading disabled children that qualify for special services. Education agency regulations may prevent specialists from using their professional expertise to plan and carry out an optimal individualized intervention program for a child with reading problems. A variety of regulatory factors influence which children are identified as reading disabled, including economic constraints, eligibility criteria, regulations on assessment methods, categorical funding labels, and the structure of child study teams.

Economic Constraints

Most education agencies are faced with restricted financial resources. Consequently, many agencies have sought ways to limit special education costs. One common approach has been to limit the number of children eligible for special education, including resource room and other services for children with reading problems. Some state legislatures have accomplished this by setting funding caps on services to these children (Boyan, 1985). Typically, monies for programs to serve additional children must be paid by each district without additional state aid. Consistent with the agenda of limiting special education costs, some education agencies have adopted regulations that limit the number of children eligible for special services.

Eligibility Criteria

Education agencies may adopt preestablished eligibility criteria to define a learning or reading disability. One way this is done is to base eligibility for special services on mandatory discrepancy formulas. Chalfant (1984) reviewed approaches that attempt to quantify the existence of a severe discrepancy between actual achievement and expected achievement for children with learning disabilities. Many education agencies determine eligibility for reading problems by using scores from reading achievement tests in conjunction with various discrepancy formulas. There are four major approaches used to determine discrepancy: (1) grade-level expectancy formulas, (2) achievement-level expectancy formulas, (3) standard score discrepancy formulas, and (4) regression models (Chalfant, 1984).

Grade-level expectancy formulas compare the student's grade-level placement and achievement scores to determine whether or not a discrepancy exists. The determination of deviation from grade level may be based on a constant level of deviation, such as achievement of one or two years below grade placement, or on a graduated deviation that increases as the grade placement increases, such as one year for intermediate grades, one and a half years for junior high school, and two years for senior high school. Grade-level expectancy formulas tend to overidentify students who are slow learners and underidentify students with high IQ scores.

Achievement-level expectancy formulas use mental age or IQ to determine whether a severe discrepancy exists between achievement and ability. The student's discrepancy score is then compared to an arbitrary severity-level cutoff. Achievement-level expectancy formulas identify severe cases of discrepancies but are dependent on questionable scores from intelligence tests. These formulas have many statistical problems and rely on an arbitrary severity level.

Standard score discrepancy models are used by many states to circumvent many of the criticisms leveled at grade or age expectancy formulas. In this method, all test scores are converted into standard scores with the same mean and standard deviation. A standard score states the position of a score with respect to the mean of the distribution and uses the standard deviation as the unit of measurement. The conversion of raw scores to standard scores allows for the comparison of scores across tests, subtests, age, and grade levels.

While simple standard score discrepancy models allow for comparisons among different tests, they do not take into account the effects of regression of IQ on achievement. Unless regression is taken into account, students scoring above the mean will tend to obtain achievement scores lower than expected, while children scoring below the mean will obtain scores higher than expected. This will lead to overidentification of children with IQs above 100 and an underidentification of children with IQs below 100. Several complex regression models have been proposed that take into account the phenomenon of regression toward the mean and thus seem more statistically appropriate for quantifying severe discrepancy between aptitude and achievement. However, there are several major concerns about the use of regression models. These include (1) the use of sophisticated statistical techniques on tests that are gross measures of behavior (Lerner, 1985); (2) the use of intelligence tests with low reliability; (3) errors in the understanding, use, and interpretation of regression procedures by administrators, special-education personnel, and parents; (3) selection of an arbitrary severity level; and (4) difficulty in determining when special services should be discontinued. Several excellent discussions of these approaches to determining discrepancy are available (see, for instance, Lerner, 1985; Salvia & Ysseldyke, 1988).

Regardless of the approach one uses to determine discrepancy, the exclusive use of discrepancy formulas to identify disabled readers is problematic (Council for Learning Disabilities, 1986; Lerner, 1985). There are several problems with discrepancy formulas. First, discrepancy formulas may contribute to inaccurate conclusions when based on assessment instruments that lack adequate reliability or validity. Second, many learning disabled and reading disabled individuals' intelligence test scores are depressed so that the resulting difference between intelligence and reading achievement scores may not be large enough to meet the discrepancy criterion; such individuals may therefore be denied acccess to, or may be removed from, needed reading services. Third, many underachieving individuals obtain significant discrepancies between intelligence and reading achievement test scores for motivational and other reasons. Fourth, the use of discrepancy formulas often creates a false sense of objectivity and precision among diagnosticians who feel that their decisions are statistically based. Fifth, in practice, discrepancy formulas are often used as the primary criterion for determining legal eligibility for reading services. Finally, although promoted as a procedure for increasing accuracy in decision making, discrepancy formulas often represent a relatively simplistic atempt to reduce incidence rates of reading disabled and other learning disabled children (Council for Learning Disabilities, 1986).

In addition to these problems, state and local education agencies have experienced great difficulty in trying to formulate criteria for determining at what point a reading disability represents a handicapping condition (Chalfant, 1984). Depending on such factors as the amount of funding available for special services and incidence caps for reading disabilities, education agencies may set discrepancy criteria as stringently as they deem necessary. Of course, all predetermined criteria are arbitrary and are related to the education agency's underlying agenda. Regulations may specify a stringent criteria for discrepancy that must be met before a child is considered eligible for reading services. For example, some agencies use a deficit criterion of 1.5 standard deviation units on certain standardized reading tests for eligibility for special education services in basic reading skills or reading comprehension (Boyan, 1985). A student may be reading disabled and still may not qualify for special education services depending on the degree of severity of the reading problem, how well the child is coping in the classroom, and the specific eligibility criteria that are used by the education agency (Chalfant, 1984).

Lerner (1985) pointed out that eligibility for special education services, including services for reading disabled children, is and should be a value judgment and should not be made exclusively on the basis of discrepancy formulas. There are many considerations that are not taken into account by statistical formulas and standardized test scores. Eligibility decisions for reading disabilities should be made by a multidisciplinary team and be based on observation of school performance and behavior, informal assessment, and responsiveness to instruction, as well as standardized test scores (Council for Learning

Disabilities, 1986; Lerner, 1985). Discrepancy formulas are one small part of the process and should be kept in perspective.

ASSESSMENT METHODS

Education agencies may adopt regulations specifying the assessment methods that must be used to classify a child as reading disabled in order to qualify for services. Many education agencies require that norm-referenced tests be used to qualify a child for special education services. In some cases, norm-referenced tests from a state or district "approved list" must be used by the diagnostician. Regulations such as these may partially account for the fact that, in practice, most eligibility decisions for reading disabilities are made using norm-referenced measures (Salvia & Ysseldyke, 1988).

Regulations that mandate the exclusive use of norm-referenced tests do not take into account the fact that many tests used in the assessment of students with reading disabilities reflect problems in validity and reliability (Salvia & Ysseldyke, 1988). The results obtained from these instruments are not always properly interpreted in light of the limitations of these instruments. This may result in the overinclusion or exclusion of students with reading disabilities. For example, a student might achieve a satisfactory score on a norm-referenced test of reading that focuses almost exclusively on decoding skills. Yet the same student might not be able to exploit the syntactic and semantic redundancies of language necessary for text comprehension. In this case, the exclusive use of a norm-referenced test with limited focus and validity might result in the exclusion of the student from services for true difficulties with reading. The problems with norm-referenced tests of reading and oral language have been well documented. In a comprehensive discussion of diagnostic assessment in reading, Salvia and Ysseldyke (1988) have noted that there are few technically adequate tests of reading. For many norm-referenced reading tests, there is no description of the standardization sample. Others are inadequately standardized. There is no evidence of reliability and/or validity of many diagnostic reading tests.

The same problems are evident in norm-referenced tests of oral language that a speech-language pathologist might administer to a child with reading disabilities. Many norm-referenced tests of language meet only minimal requirements for reliability, validity, and standardization (McCauley & Swisher, 1984). In cases where language tests may be reliable, there is seldom evidence of construct or ecological validity (Muma, Lubinski, & Pierce, 1982). That is, few tests are based on a theoretical model of language (construct validity), and many tests do not sample language abilities as they are needed in real-life situations (ecological validity). In addition, the majority of norm-referenced language tests focus almost exclusively on structural aspects of language and give little or no consideration to pragmatic, discourse, and metalinguistic aspects. This is problematic given the relationship between these aspects of language and reading problems in some individuals with reading disabilities (Catts & Kamhi, 1986, 1987).

When appropriately administered, scored, and interpreted, norm-referenced tests of reading and oral language can provide some useful information in making screening or placement decisions for children with reading disabilities (Salvia & Ysseldyke, 1988). However, education-agency regulations that specify the exclusive use of norm-referenced tests are inconsistent with current approaches to the assessment of reading (Salvia & Ysseldyke, 1988) and the assessment of oral language (Carrow-Woolfolk & Lynch, 1982; Lahey, 1988; Lund & Duchan, 1988; Muma, 1986). Among other things, current approaches to reading and language assessment stress criterion-referenced assessment, descriptive assessment based on observation of behavior in naturally occurring contexts, and curriculum-based assessment. These assessments are more likely to lead to appropriate educational interventions for individual students with reading problems than exclusive use of norm-referenced tests.

Determining eligibility of reading disabled students for reading and/or language intervention can be difficult when professional practices are constrained by assessment regulations. Most professionals hold the view that the determination of program eligibility is the prerogative of a qualified/certified service provider in their area of expertise. Eligibility decisions should be based on the individual needs of the child.

Professionals involved with reading disabled students, in concert with other specialists and parents, should determine eligibility based on at least four factors: (1) current knowledge of the strengths and limitations of the assessment procedures used, (2) the nature of children's reading disabilities and their relationship to language, (3) prognosis for change, and (4) state and local eligibility policies and practices. Professionals working with reading problems must be familiar with the actual regulations that apply to them. In those cases where education agency regulations conflict with optimal service delivery (professional practices), professionals should become politically active and play a role in changing existing standards and in formulating new ones.

Current perspectives on reading and multidisciplinary approaches to intervention require a cooperative effort across disciplines. In practice, this can be difficult to achieve given that professional associations with common interests in reading disabilities typically have little or no communication with each other. However, at the national and state levels, professional associations may assist individual practitioners in informing parents, educators, administrators, and legislators about appropriate professional roles and practices. In addition, professional associations may be able to provide suggestions for monitoring legislation concerning special education regulations and lobbying those responsible for making decisions about special education. Although political activism is important, professionals also need to find ways to work within the existent policies and regulations and make sure that professional considerations in determining eligibility for services are not overshadowed by political or bureaucratic considerations.

CATEGORICAL LABELS FOR FUNDING

The question of who should serve a poor reader is often based on a ''diagnostic label'' given to a child to determine the appropriate ''funding category.'' Because separate or additional funding is needed in order to serve exceptional children, it is the policy of virtually all education agencies to categorize or label children with various exceptionalities as defined by state and federal law. Most special education regulations explicitly state that such labels should be used for funding purposes only, and not used for programming or instructional purposes. In practice, however, this is not always the case (Lieberman, 1980; Snyder, 1984). Poor readers who have been labeled as learning disabled tend to be served by a learning disabilities specialist or resource-room teacher certified in special education. Children with reading problems without a special education label usually receive remedial instruction from the classroom teacher. Occasionally, a reading specialist may consult with the classroom teacher or even see certain children with reading problems on an itinerant basis. Many children labeled as language impaired also have reading problems and will therefore receive services from the speech-language pathologist. Lieberman (1980) has noted that in many cases, the administrative category in which a child is placed relates to school politics. When this occurs there is little or no opportunity for multidisciplinary efforts on behalf of the reading disabled child. For example, there are school systems where learning disabilities teachers are not allowed to use reading books lest they encroach on the reading specialist's territory. In some schools, learning disabilities teachers may teach spelling and mathematics but not reading. In addition, it is not uncommon for speech-language pathologists to be discouraged or prohibited from working with reading disabled students, even if language problems are present (Cornett & Chabon, 1986).

CHILD-STUDY TEAMS

Decisions about who is eligible for special education services are usually made by a team of personnel, sometimes called a child study team. While the specific structure of teams varies across schools, the decision-making process used by many child study teams is often flawed because of the difficulties in group decision making (Ysseldyke & Thurlow, 1983). Ysseldyke (1983) reported on several studies in which child study teams made eligibility and placement decisions for learning disabled and reading disabled students. At virtually all team meetings, four members were present: a school administrator, a school psychologist, a special education teacher, and a regular education teacher. Speech-language pathologists and reading specialists were not routinely included in team meetings. Ysseldyke also reported that less than five minutes were devoted to intervention planning, even though meetings typically lasted between 30 and 45 minutes. In general, team members tended to merely present the data represented by their discipline rather than integrate information across disciplines for treatment planning. Under these conditions, the amount of cooperative planning necessary to develop a multidisciplinary program for a student with a reading disability would be extremely limited, unless this was done by individual professionals outside of the team structure.

Ysseldyke (1983) suggested training teams for effective decision making, including organized procedures, a clearly stated agenda, participation by all members, and use of all data relevant to the decision. In addition, he suggested that inservice training for all team members in each discipline's assessment and intervention methods is critical for efficient team functioning, and would help ensure appropriate placement and intervention decisions. In addition, some education agencies are beginning to implement more flexible policies on the composition of child study teams based on the problems of the individual student. For students with reading disabilities, the child-study team should consist of an administrator, the classroom teacher, the school psychologist, the learning disabilities specialist, the reading specialist, and the speech-language pathologist.

The provision of optimal services to reading disabled students requires that those professionals who can provide appropriate services be routinely included on child study teams for individuals with reading problems. Team membership is sometimes related to political factors operating within a particular school system. An initial strategy for the professional who desires to be included on teams for reading disabled children would be to contact a direct supervisor following established administrative guidelines. A written outline of the professional's rationale, a statement of specific assessment or programming contributions, and other information is often desirable when making the case for a position on a child study team. In addition, some professionals have found it helpful to share relevant professional association position papers with administrators when proposing changes in their existing roles. Position papers regularly appear in *The Journal of Learning Disabilities* and *ASHA* magazine.

PROFESSIONAL TERRITORIALITY

Professional territoriality exists when professionals from different disciplines do not agree on ''who does what to whom.'' Territoriality may result, in part, from different role perceptions of special education personnel. Role perceptions will be influenced by the philosophy of training received, understanding of the professional literature, and personal values and expectations (Cook & Leffingwell, 1982). This composite of expectations may differ from expectations of colleagues and from other professionals involved in special education services. The issue of territoriality is especially problematic as it pertains to reading disabilities. Not only is everyone involved because of the multidisciplinary nature of the disorder, everyone claims to be able to perform teaching functions that everyone else can (Lieberman, 1980). Questions of primary responsibility for a specific reading disabled child may arise (Lerner, 1985). Several specialists may lay claim to a child with reading problems; The learning disabilities specialist, the reading specialist, and the speech-language pathologist may all perceive their expertise as encompassing a broad realm (if not the entire realm) of reading problems, including language problems that may underlie the reading disorder (Lerner, 1985).

Relationships among different professionals may be the most delicate and demanding aspects of providing optimal services to children with reading disabilities. The role responsibilities of one discipline may not mesh with the perceptions of other specialists on the staff. Coping with such differences in role perception requires sensitivity to both personal and political factors. This section will review causes of jurisdictional problems and the way educational and theoretical biases influence service delivery. In addition, suggestions for cooperative planning will be presented as a way to minimize territoriality.

JURISDICTIONAL PROBLEMS WITHIN THE SCHOOL

The duties performed by the learning disabilities specialist as they relate to reading often are similar to those that have been traditionally performed by other school personnel. Jurisdictional problems, when they occur, involve the learning disabilities specialist, the classroom teacher, the reading specialist, and the speech-language pathologist (Myers & Hammill, 1976).

Historically, it has been the learning disabilities teacher who has had primary responsibility for teaching reading disabled children to read. This division of responsibility was generally accepted by the regular education establishment, even though in some areas, remedial reading teachers (sometimes called reading specialists) retained this responsibility. It is only in recent years that interest in children's reading has broadened to include other disciplines (Lerner, 1985). For example, speech-language pathologists have assumed a larger role in the assessment and treatment of some reading disordered individuals (ASHA Committee on Language Learning Disorders, 1982; Rees, 1974) because a growing body of research now demonstrates that language deficits underlie many reading disabilities (Stanovich, 1986; Thomson, 1984; Vellutino, 1979). However, the historical role that learning disabilities teachers have taken in the treatment of reading problems, as well as the overlapping areas of interest, have caused some territorial conflicts.

EDUCATIONAL AND THEORETICAL BIASES

One factor that has contributed to territoriality is that the professionals involved with reading disabilities hold different theoretical views and come from different educational backgrounds. These differences pertain to each discipline's theoretical orientation to reading, theoretical orientation to oral language, approaches to assessment, approaches to intervention, and formal training in reading and language.

Taking reading first, formal training in reading, reading disabilities, reading assessment, and reading intervention make up the major curricular emphasis for reading specialists and many learning disabilities specialists. These professionals are specifically trained in the assessment and remediation of children's reading problems. It should be recognized, however, that even within these disciplines, the theoretical and clinical orientations toward reading and reading disabilities may differ widely. Several authors have suggested that until recently, reading has been viewed from a "skill mastery" perspective rather than as a process based on a linguistic foundation (Hasenstab, 1985; Salvia & Ysseldyke, 1988; Smith, 1982, 1985). Typical "reading skills" that children are thought to master and that may be assessed and taught include oral reading, word analysis, word attack, word recognition, word meaning, reading rate, and sentence comprehension. In practice, this is probably the most common view of reading held by reading specialists. Another view held by some professionals in reading, learning disabilities, and speech-language pathology is that reading is a linguistic process governed by components of text cohesion, pragmatics, and semantics (Hasenstab, 1985). These differences in theoretical orientation carry through to views on targets and procedures for the assessment and remediation of reading.

A similar point can be made in relation to theoretical orientation and formal training in oral language. Training in linguistics, language acquisition, language disorders, language assessment, and language intervention is a major curricular emphasis for speech-language pathologists and other professionals with an interest in language-based disorders (Muma, Pierce, & Muma, 1983). Children's oral language problems have been, and will continue to be, the province of the speech-language pathologist with regard to training and utilization of services (Myers & Hammill, 1976). However, because "language" cannot be separated from "learning" and "reading," and because of the relationship between children's reading and language problems, common boundaries of interest in language exist for many disciplines.

As with reading, there are different theoretical orientations to language, and different views may be held within and across professional boundaries. According to Reid and Hresko (1981), the predominant view of language in the field of learning disabilities comes from behavioral psychology. An example of a language program that defines both its goals and procedures in accordance with behavioral principles is DISTAR. Reid and Hresko (1981) have noted that DISTAR and other similar language programs are frequently used by learning disabilities teachers for reading disabled children with oral language deficits.

Although some special education teachers assess several aspects of language, such as phonology, morphology, syntax, and semantics, they rely almost exclusively on the use of norm-referenced tests to assess these language areas (Salvia & Ysseldyke, 1988). In contrast, many speech-language pathologists hold a theoretical view of language that is less behavioristic and focuses on the acquisition and use of cognitive-linguistic-communicative systems and the processes of language content, language form, and language use (Bloom & Lahey, 1978; Carrow-Woolfolk & Lynch, 1982; Muma, 1986). This orientation emphasizes the integration of language components and includes pragmatics, discourse, and metalinguistics in the theoretical model. As previously mentioned, current approaches to language assessment in speech-language pathology emphasize descriptive methods as much as, or more than, norm-referenced tests.

While there may be honest differences of opinion in a given content area between professionals with different theoretical and clinical orientations, in some cases these differences can lead to territorial disputes. It is possible that as a consensus is reached in the professional literature on theories of reading and language, on preferred assessment approaches, and on effective clinical procedures, territorial disputes over who should serve individuals with reading disabilities may diminish. However, it is likely that both the educational and theoretical biases of individual practitioners will continue to contribute to interprofessional "turf" differences (Butler & Wallach, 1984). In addition, as the trend to serve more children with reading disabilities continues (beyond just the most severe cases), the jurisdictional problems existing between learning disabilities, remedial reading, and speech-language pathology are likely to be aggravated (Myers & Hammill, 1976).

In the long run, jurisdictional problems over children with reading disabilities may be resolved by (1) arbitrary or political agreements between local program directors, (2) specific guidelines established by state education department personnel, (3) serious reductions in state or federal support funds for either remedial reading or learning disability programs, which would encourage school administrators to reclassify defunded programs in order to continue to qualify for money, and (4) possible merging of efforts between programs, thus minimizing or eliminating the problems of jurisdiction (Myers & Hammill, 1976).

Cooperative Planning to Minimize Territoriality

Cooperative planning between disciplines involved in reading disabilities would be a means of minimizing problems of jurisdiction or territoriality *and* ensuring that optimal services are provided to children with reading problems. Alley and Deshler (1979) view cooperative planning as a process involving direction and input from several professionals. All too frequently the interchange between ancillary personnel (learning disabilities specialist, reading specialist, speech-language pathologist) and the regular class teacher consists of the specialist telling the regular class teacher what to do and what to change. To successfully minimize territoriality, all professionals must recognize that each one alone cannot meet all of the needs of the reading disabled student, but that through an interdisciplinary approach their collective efforts have a much greater chance of meeting the child's needs.

It must be recognized that each professional involved has some unique knowledge and expertise that can be brought to bear on the needs of the reading disabled student. In short, to minimize the adverse effects of territoriality on providing an optimal program for a reading disabled student, it is necessary for each professional to maintain and apply an area of expertise, but at the same time gain an awareness and appreciation of what others can do on behalf of the reading disabled student (Alley & Deshler, 1979; Cook & Leffingwell, 1982; Lieberman, 1980).

The following are suggestions for involving various school personnel in different aspects of reading disabilities, and broadening understanding of other professional's expertise and interests.

- Inservice education. Inservice is one of the most common vehicles for information dissemination. Personnel involved with reading problems need to understand normal reading processes, normal language processes that underlie reading, and how to recognize reading and language problems of poor readers. Other critical information includes each discipline's approach to reading problems, as well as referral sources if any professional suspects a child might have a reading or language problem. Inservice provided by each discipline should also include a complete description of how that discipline assesses and remediates those aspects of reading disabilities under its purview. Effective inservice presentations may also be made by outside speakers who can cut across discipline boundaries and help foster multidisciplinary approaches to reading problems. Many school districts have special inservice days each semester for just such a purpose.
- Demonstration of methods and materials. Each discipline can demonstrate materials, methods, techniques, and tests used with reading disabled students.
- Case-study method. An in-depth discussion of a particular case can be used to present certain concepts and principles from several disciplines' points of view. Emphasis may be on assessment, intervention, or other aspects of the case. A cross-discipline discussion of a case can be an effective way to illustrate commonalities and differences in orientations to reading, language, assessment, and intervention. Case studies that illustrate successful multidisciplinary programming attempts can emphasize the utility of this approach.
- Sharing professional literature. Professionals may begin to broaden their knowledge base on reading, language, and clinical issues by sharing "critical" literature from their disciplines. Each professional could contribute several critical literature sources to a "multidisciplinary information packet" to be disseminated among disciplines and discussed at a later time.

If cooperative planning is to be successful in a school setting, the staff, beginning with the top administrator on down, must be committed to the concept. Any service delivery model is less likely to meet with success if the program does not have the backing of the principal and other key administrators. Because a cooperative approach requires the involvement of several professionals and taps several resources within a school, administrative support is essential.

Service Delivery Models

Traditional service delivery models for children with reading problems have tended to limit successful efforts at cooperative planning among professionals. Using such a model, a student might be identified and tested by the speech-language pathologist for a language learning disorder and at the same time be attending remedial reading. In some instances the two specialists involved might not know that they were sharing a pupil. Or a child might be dismissed from language intervention for an oral language problem at the end of the second grade without anyone in the school recognizing that this pupil had been at risk for reading problems throughout his or her entire time in school. In a traditional model, learning disabilities specialists have provided reading instruction through the resource room, while reading specialists and speech-language pathologists have provided services through an itinerant model, with little or no communication between professionals.

There are many factors that influence the choice of service models for reading disabled children or children at risk for reading problems. The age of the child may determine whether direct or indirect services will be provided. It is not likely that a preschool child would receive direct services from a reading specialist even if the child were at risk for future reading problems because of a language disorder. In most education agencies, the diagnostic category that the child is placed in to qualify for funding will tend to limit the available service delivery options. For example, a reading disabled child who meets district criteria for "learning disabilities" is likely to be served primarily through the resource room. The different reading problems that children manifest will influence placement to some extent. A child with mild reading difficulties caused by instructional or motivational factors will probably be served by the classroom teacher with consultation from the reading specialist. The different language abilities that characterize the population of children with reading problems will also influence who does what to whom. For example, most language impaired children on the case load of the speech-language pathologist will also have reading problems. These children will tend to be served on an itinerant basis by the speech-language pathologist with consultation provided by the reading specialist.

One important factor that will affect the choice of service delivery model is the individual professional's familiarity and expertise with a variety of service options. A specialist whose training is limited to an itinerant approach might be reluctant to employ one of the many consultation models available. Comprehensive service delivery of instructional services to a reading disabled child demands a multidisciplinary approach using a continuum of alternative placements. The roles of regular educators, special educators, and speech-language pathologists will overlap in the delivery of services to the reading disabled. Several of the numerous potential service delivery models that can be adopted by combining placement types and staffing patterns are discussed below.

CONSULTANT SERVICES

A collaborative consultation model can be discussed in terms of the consultant's degree of involvement with the child. There are at least three types of consultation that vary in the amount of direct service provided to the child. These three types may be applied either to an individual child or a group of children (Frassinelli, Superior, & Meyers, 1983).

The first type of consultation service involves ongoing direct contact. This type features the combined use of direct therapy and collaborative consultation where the consultation is based on ongoing direct contact with the child or group of children. The teacher and consultant jointly devise activities designed to follow-up on intervention goals. The teacher implements and monitors programs in the classroom. An example would be a child receiving remedial reading instruction who achieves the goals with the remedial reading teacher with minimal carry-over in the classroom. Through consultation, the teacher may design a system to reward target skills that occur during classroom activities. The teacher would then chart the child's performance in the classroom.

A second type of consulting involves one-time or periodic contact by the consultant. This usually involves a consultation regarding a child or group of children following a diagnostic evaluation. Consultation is based on one-time or periodic contact with the child for purposes of assessment. The teacher and consultant would devise a program that is implemented in the classroom by the teacher. An example would be a kindergarten student at risk for reading problems who has difficulties with tasks that require metalinguistic awareness. Through assessment and observation in the classroom, the speech-language pathologist would identify specific metalinguistic problems. The consultant and the teacher would then determine strategies to structure classroom activities that elicit and reinforce various aspects of metalinguistic awareness and print awareness.

A third type of consultation service involves no direct contact with the child. Data collection and observations are done by the teacher or other school personnel, but not by the consultant. An example would be a middle school child who reads poorly because of a lack of motivation. The resource room teacher or reading specialist would discuss the issue with the teacher. The teacher would then gather data regarding factors that affect the child's motivation to read and perhaps modify her curriculum to include facilitating factors. Frassinelli et al. (1983) noted that each approach can be applied to either an individual child or a group of children. In addition, there will be many instances where more than one approach is used, and there will be occasional overlap between categories.

Consultant services may be used in conjunction with several setting types. For example, the regular education setting with special consultant services is particularly appropriate for children with mild reading problems or for children with mild-to-moderate language delays who have long been recognized as high-risk candidates for potential reading difficulties (Gerber & Bryen, 1981). Consultation is based on a three-person chain of service in which the consultant directly serves the teacher for the benefit of the student who is under the teacher's care (Meyers, Martin, & Hyman, 1977). The consultant's service to the child is indirect. The interdisciplinary flow of information is bidirectional; that is, the knowledge possessed by the child's classroom teacher and the reading tasks used in the classroom are as vital to the effectiveness of the consultation process as is the specialized expertise of a specialist/consultant. The consultant model is ultimately time-saving. By helping the teacher with one child, the consultant has the potential of subsequently influencing all children under the teacher's care. Consulting has the advantage of utilizing the teacher's unique position of maximum child influence.

The consultant needs skills in both content and process (Schien, 1978). *Content* involves using the expertise of both the consultant and the consultee in data collection and analysis in order to define a specific problem, develop and implement a highly specific program, and monitor progress. *Process* involves knowing when the consultation strategy is an appropriate form of intervention, establishing an effective interpersonal relationship with the consultee, and defining the roles of both the consultee and consultant in a mutually acceptable agreement or contract. Specific process skills include learning to be an active listener, learning how to ask informed questions, involving the consultee in problem solving, and dealing with resistance on the part of the consultee or consultant (Frassinelli, Superior, & Meyers, 1983).

ITINERANT SERVICES

Itinerant services are the traditional form of specialist service delivery in which a specialist takes a child from a classroom and works with the child directly. Children can be seen individually or in small groups. The specialist using the itinerant model provides direct service to the reading disabled child, including assessment and clinical/educational management. The specialist also provides indirect service to the child by arranging for referrals and by counseling teachers, parents, and other professionals concerning the problems of educational management, including carry-over of learning activities. In this model, the specialist has an opportunity to work directly with the reading disabled child for purposes of comprehensive assessment and educational management. The specialist determines the strategies that seem to work best with the child, implements them, and receives immediate feedback concerning their effectiveness. The supportive one-to-one interaction can be highly effective in ameliorating specific reading or language problems.

Direct service delivery can also be used with small groups of clients. Although the client's individual time is somewhat decreased, benefits include peer modeling, peer reinforcement, a natural or more "classlike" environment, and the ability to see more clients. When combined with the consultant model, the itinerant model can be even more effective, because both the teacher and specialist can provide information, assist in developing critical program decisions, develop instructional recommendations, implement the instructional program, and evaluate progress (Dublinske, 1974). Direct itinerant specialist services and consultant services are most typically utilized in conjunction with the regular education classroom for children with moderate reading disabilities or language impaired children with reading problems.

RESOURCE ROOM SERVICES

A resource room is a part-time class, usually less than half time but no less than one hour every day, in which a specialist or specialists provide individual or small group assessment and clinical/educational management. It is an effective service-delivery model for children with moderate to severe reading problems who require intensive special services but who are typically enrolled in a regular classroom (Garrard,

1979). Consultation and collaborative intervention are frequently combined with the resource room model. The resource room model provides some flexibility of programming that allows the amount of special service support a child receives to be increased or decreased depending on the child's need rather than on complex scheduling issues as is often the case with the itinerant model. A summary of possible professional roles for children with reading disabilities is presented in Table 10-1 (adapted from Catts and Kamhi, 1987).

Table 10-1.
Professional roles and service delivery intervention of reading disabilities

Speech-language pathologist roles

I. Preschool

A. Itinerant services

(Direct) Identification/assessment of language impaired children.
- Traditional language intervention including metalinguistic awareness and print awareness.

B. Consultant services

(Indirect)
- Parent counseling and implementation of home programs.

II. School-age

A. Itinerant services

(Direct)
- Identification/assessment of language impaired children.
- Traditional language intervention including phonological awareness, print awareness, narrative and discourse aspects.

B. Consultant service to classroom

(Direct)
- Follow-up of language impaired children.
- Screening, identification, assessment of children at risk for reading problems.

(Indirect)
- Collaboration with teachers in design and implementation of remedial language programs (including metalinguistics).
- Inservice on relationship between reading/language problems; intervention strategies used in the classroom.

(continued)

C. Consultant to special education
(Direct) • Follow-up of language impaired children.
• Serve as member of interdisciplinary assessment and placement teams.
(Indirect) • Collaboration with special educators in designing and implementing remedial language program (including metalinguistics).
• Inservice on relationship between reading/language problems.

Special education/reading specialist roles

I. Preschool

A. Consultant services to classroom
(Indirect) • Inservice and parent counseling on early reading, facilitating reading schema.

II. School-age

A. Resource room
(Direct) • Traditional reading assessment and remediation.
• Serving as members of interdisciplinary assessment and placement team.
(Indirect) • Parent counseling and implementation of home programs.

B. Consultant services to classroom
(Direct) • Follow-up of reading disabled children.
• Screening, identification, assessment of suspected reading problems.
(Indirect) • Collaboration with teachers in design and implementation of remedial reading programs.
• Inservice on reading disabilities, reading remediation strategies in the classroom.

C. Consultant to speech-language pathology
(Direct) • Follow-up of reading disabled children.
(Indirect) • Collaboration with speech-language pathologist to coordinate remedial reading and language goals, materials, procedures where appropriate.
• Inservice on reading disabilities.

Classroom teacher roles

I. Preschool

A. Classroom
(Direct) • Traditional reading readiness instruction, development of reading schema, and appreciation of reading.
(Indirect) • Parent counseling regarding quality children's literature, importance of reading.

II. School-age

A. Classroom

(Direct) • Traditional reading instruction.

(Indirect) • Parent counseling regarding quality children's literature, importance of reading.

B. Consultant to speech pathology and special education

(Indirect) • Collaboration with speech-language pathologist in designing and implementing methods and materials for language impaired students.

• Collaboration with special educator in designing and implementing methods and materials for reading disabled students.

Adapted from Catts and Kamhi, 1987.

Serving Reading Disabled Students

Several important issues must be considered when professionals use cooperative planning and alternate service delivery models to provide comprehensive services to reading disabled children. One important issue is for all disciplines to consider the need for both direct services (actual contact time with the reading disabled student) and indirect services (services to those who interact with the reading disabled student). Another important issue is that there is a sequential hierarchy to the components of any service delivery model. Larson and McKinley (1987) described six service delivery components. With regard to reading disabilities, people need to know what reading problems are, why they exist, and how each discipline serves the reading disabled child. This is *information dissemination*. They also need to recognize when a child has a suspected reading problem or language problem and how to refer such individuals. This allows *identification* of students needing assessment. The identified students participate in *reading* and/or *language assessment*. Next, those students requiring services from reading specialists, learning disabilities specialists, or speech-language pathologists require *program planning* and then *direct* and/or *indirect intervention*. Finally, the results of intervention are determined by various *follow-up procedures*.

Larson and McKinley (1987) presented detailed information on how one might operationalize each of these service delivery components. One caution that is especially relevant for professionals interested in multidisciplinary programs for reading problems is not to jump to direct intervention too quickly. For example, it may take several years of information dissemination to develop a program to a point where the learning disabilities teacher, the reading specialist, and the speech-language pathologist understand each other's contributions to reading disabilities. It might also take time for the school administration to support a multidisciplinary program with alternate service delivery approaches.

Professionals with interest in developing a multidisciplinary approach to children's reading problems may also be wise to begin with one student and to expand services slowly. As team members become familiar with current approaches to reading and language, territorial boundaries will diminish and the team can increase the number of children with reading problems that receive cooperative planning efforts.

In conclusion, a major theme of this chapter has been how to provide the best possible services to children with reading problems by making the best use of the professionals who have an interest in reading problems. The heterogeneity of children with reading problems and the traditional models of service delivery make this a question that cannot be answered simplistically.

References

Alley, G., and Deshler, P. (1979). *Teaching the Learning Disabled Adolescent*. Denver: Love Publishing Co.

American Speech-Language-Hearing Association Committee on Language Learning Disorders. (1982). Position statement on language learning disorders. *ASHA, 24*, 937–944.

Bloom, L., and Lahey, M. (1978). *Language Development and Language Disorders*. New York: Wiley.

Boyan, C. (1985). California's new eligibility criteria: Legal and program implications. *Exceptional Children, 52*(2), 131–141.

Butler, K., and Wallach, G. (1984). The final word: From theory to intervention. In G. Wallach and K. Butler (Eds.), *Language learning disabilities in school-age children*. Baltimore: Williams and Wilkins.

Carrow-Woolfolk, E., and Lynch, J. (1982). *An integrative approach to language disorders in children*. New York: Grune and Stratton.

Catts, H., and Kamhi, A. (1986). The linguistic basis of reading disorders: Implications for the speech-language pathologist. *Language, Speech, and Hearing Services in Schools, 17*(4), 329–341.

Catts, H., and Kamhi, A. (1987). The relationship between reading and language disorders: Implications for the speech-language pathologist. *Seminars in Speech and Language, 8*, 377–392.

Chalfant, J. (1984). *Identifying learning disabled students: Guidelines for decision making*. Burlington, VT: Northeast Regional Resource Center, Trinity College.

Cook, J., and Leffingwell, R. (1982). Stressors and remediation techniques for special educators. *Exceptional Children, 49*(1), 54–59.

Cornett, B., and Chabon, S. (1986). Speech-language pathologists as language learning disabilities specialists: Rites of passage. *ASHA, 28,* 29–31.

Council for Learning Disabilities (1986). Position statement on the use of discrepancy formulas in the identification of learning disabled individuals. *Learning Disabilities Quarterly, 9,* 245.

Dublinske, S. (1974). Planning for child change in language development remediation programs carried out by teachers and parents. *Language, Speech, and Hearing Services in School, 5,* 225–237.

Frassinelli, L., Superior, K., and Meyers, J. (1983). A consultation model for speech and language intervention. *ASHA, 25*(11), 25–30.

Garrard, K. (1979). The changing role of speech and hearing professionals in public education. *ASHA, 21,* 91–98.

Gerber, A., and Bryen, D. (Eds.) (1981). *Language and learning disabilities.* Baltimore: University Park Press.

Hasenstab, M. (1985). Reading evaluation: A psychosociolinguistic approach. In C. Simon (Ed.), *Communication skills and classroom success: Assessment of language learning disabled students.* San Diego: College-Hill Press.

Lahey, M. (1988). *Language disorders and language development.* New York: Macmillan.

Larson, V., and McKinley, N. (1987). *Communication assessment and intervention strategies for adolescents.* Eau Claire, WI: Thinking Publications.

Lerner, J. (1985). *Learning disabilities: Theories, diagnosis, and teaching strategies,* 4th Ed. Boston: Houghton Mifflin.

Lieberman, L. (1980). Territoriality—Who does what to whom? *Journal of Learning Disabilities, 13*(3), 15–19.

Lund, N., and Duchan, J. (1988). *Assessing children's language in naturalistic contexts,* 2nd Ed. Englewood Cliffs, NJ: Prentice Hall.

McCauley, R., and Swisher, L. (1984). Psychometric review of language and articulation tests for preschool children. *Journal of Speech and Hearing Disorders, 49*(1), 34–42.

Meyers, J., Martin, R., and Hyman, I. (Eds.) (1977). *School Consultation.* Springfield, IL: Charles C. Thomas.

Muma, J. (1986). *Language acquisition: A functionalist perspective.* Austin, TX: ProEd.

Muma, J., Lubinski, R., and Pierce, S. (1982). A new era in language assessment: Data or evidence. In N. Lass (Ed.), *Speech and language: Advances in basic research and practice,* 7. New York: Academic Press.

Muma, J., Pierce, S., and Muma, D. (1983). Language training in speech-language pathology: Substantive domains. *ASHA, 25*(6), 35–40.

Myers, P., and Hammill, D. (1976). *Methods for learning disabilities,* 2nd Ed. New York: Wiley.

Rees, N. (1974). The speech pathologist and the reading process. *ASHA, 16,* 255–258.

Reid, D., and Hresko, W. (1981). *A cognitive approach to learning disabilities.* New York: McGraw-Hill.

Salvia, J., and Ysseldyke, J. (1988). *Assessment in special and remedial education,* 3rd Ed. Boston: Houghton Mifflin.

Schien, E. (1978). The role of the consultant: Content expert or process facilitator? *Personnel and Guidance Journal, 6,* 339–343.

Smith, F. (1982). *Understanding reading,* 3rd Ed. New York: Holt, Rinehart, and Winston.

Smith, F. (1985). *Reading without nonsense,* 2nd Ed. New York: Teachers College Press, Columbia University.

Snyder, L. (1984). Developmental language disorders: Elementary school age. In A. Holland (Ed.), *Language disorders in children: Recent advances.* San Diego: College-Hill Press.

Stanovich, K. (1986). Cognitive processes and the reading problems of learning-disabled children: Evaluating the assumption of specificity. In J. Torgesen and B. Wong (Eds.), *Psychological and educational perspectives on learning disabilities.* New York: Academic Press.

Thomson, M. (1984). *Developmental dyslexia.* Baltimore: Edward Arnold.

Vellutino, F. (1979). *Dyslexia: Theory and research.* Cambridge, MA: MIT Press.

Ysseldyke, J. (1983). Current practices in making psychoeducational decisions about learning disabled students. *Journal of Learning Disabilities, 16*(4), 226–233.

Ysseldyke, J., and Thurlow, M. (1983). *Identification/classification research: An integrative summary of findings.* Minneapolis: University of Minnesota Press.

11

Conclusion

During the last 10 to 15 years, considerable attention has been devoted to the language bases of reading and reading disabilities. It has been the purpose of this book to acquaint readers with this body of literature and the theoretical and clinical implications that can be derived from it. For too many years, reading was viewed largely as a visual perceptual task, and disorders of reading were assumed to be perceptually based. However, it should be clear from the material presented in this book that a visual perceptual view of reading has little descriptive or explanatory adequacy. Reading involves much more than a simple visual perceptual analysis; it requires sophisticated linguistic and metalinguistic knowledge as well as a full range of cognitive and metacognitive processes.

The Developmental Language Perspective

The research reviewed throughout this book is quite conclusive in indicating a strong, positive relationship between spoken and written language deficits. Classification studies discussed in Chapter 2 clearly show that despite individual differences in children with specific reading impairments, the majority of these children have language deficits. As noted throughout the early chapters (particularly Chapters 4 and 5), these language problems often take the form of phonological processing deficits; that is, difficulty in developing and using phonological memory codes to store verbal information. Such a deficit is manifested not only in tasks that tap encoding processes, but also in tasks that tap retrieval processes (e.g., naming tasks) and speech production abilities (see Chapter 4). In addition to deficits in phonological processing, children with reading disabilities often have problems in other aspects of language processing. Roth and Spekman, in Chapter 6, reviewed a large body of research indicating that reading disabled children may have problems in morphologic, syntactic, and discourse level processing. Westby, in Chapter 7, provided numerous examples of how poor readers may lack the schema knowledge or metacognitive strategies necessary for proficient reading comprehension during the later elementary school years and beyond. In Chapter 9, Scott discussed the linguistic aspects of writing disorders.

The strong relationship between oral and written language problems has led us, as well as others (e.g., Chasty, 1985), to view a specific reading disability or dyslexia as a developmental language impairment. According to this view, a reading disability is seen as a more general language impairment that affects the development of spoken as well as written language. This impairment is believed to be constitutional in nature, and its effects on spoken and written language are thought to be present throughout childhood, adolescence, and adulthood. Early in development, the impairment may manifest itself in difficulty learning spoken language. Children may be delayed in producing their first words and phrases or have morphologic and syntactic deficits. Some children may demonstrate ostensibly normal spoken language development during the preschool years, but show early problems in phonological processing abilities. On entering school, the primary manifestation of the impairment is difficulty in learning to read. In the early grades, problems are restricted to the decoding or word recognition component of reading. Although some disabled readers may also have higher-level reading comprehension problems at this time, these problems are difficult to identify until decoding processes become more automatic. During the later school years, problems will be most apparent in oral reading, reading comprehension, spelling, and writing ability. With continued practice and effort, many disabled readers may acquire rudimentary reading and writing skills. However, the automaticity of these skills may never match that of normal individuals. Oral language problems can also persist throughout the school years and into adulthood.

Viewing a specific reading disability/dyslexia as a developmental language impairment is a relatively novel notion. This view, however, is a natural extension of 15 years of research that has documented the language bases of reading disorders and the changes that occur in language and reading skills throughout the developmental period. A large part of the present book has been devoted to reviewing and interpreting this research. Several contributors have also presented clinical data to support the strong correlation between spoken and written language disorders. At the very least, the sheer volume of research and clinical data should overwhelm the few remaining holdouts who still question whether a reading disability is a language-based disorder. The descriptive adequacy of characterizing a reading disability as a language-based disorder seems incontrovertible.

Achieving descriptive adequacy is the easy part, however. We have a long way to go before explanatory adequacy is attained. In order to sufficiently explain the underlying causes of a reading disability, it is necessary to overcome the tendency to assume that more precise and accurate descriptions have explanatory value. Causal issues are inherently more complex than descriptive or taxonomic ones, and we are only first beginning to understand the complex causal interactions that occur between aspects of spoken and written language. Recognizing that the relationship between spoken and written language knowledge is reciprocal is a necessary first step toward this understanding. Too much emphasis on the reciprocal nature of cause-effect relationships, however, can obscure the fact that some initial deficit(s) must be present to set off the subsequent chain of reciprocal interactions. General intellectual, environmental, emotional, and sensory deficits can be ruled out because individuals with deficits in these areas would not be considered to have a specific reading disability.

In Chapter 3, it was suggested that some basic processing limitation underlies (i.e., initially causes) the reading problem. Several possibilities for this basic processing limitation have been suggested throughout the book, including (a) difficulty forming accurate representations of phonological information in long-term memory (Vellutino, Harding, Phillips, & Steger, 1975), (b) slow rate of access to phonological information stored in long-term memory (Miles & Ellis, 1981; Perfetti, 1985), (c) low-level perceptual deficits (Tallal, 1980), (d) inefficient regulation of information in working memory (Shankweiler & Crain, 1987), and (e) difficulty constructing narrative and discourse schemata (see Perfetti, 1985 or Stanovich, 1986). The evidence presented in Chapters 3 and 4 suggests that the first two limitations are more likely sources of the initial reading disability than the latter three.

Whatever the processing limitation(s) turn out to be, this limitation must explain the various manifestations of a developmental language impairment—most notably, difficulties in spoken and written language. This is easier said than done, however, because one must explain not only the extent of the reading/language impairment, but also its nature. For example, why do some children have difficulty learning to talk and read, whereas others seem to have difficulty only in learning to read? Or, why do some children have poor word recognition skills and seemingly adequate higher-level language and conceptual knowledge, whereas other children show the reverse pattern of performance?

One way to account for these differences is to propose that the processing limitation that underlies spoken and written language problems varies in its severity or along a continuum. Children at the extreme low end of the continuum would have difficulties in acquiring spoken language during the preschool years and exhibit spoken and written language disorders during the school years and beyond. A child with severe processing limitations would thus be identified as having a language impairment very early in life. In contrast, children with a moderate processing limitation would not experience difficulties learning most aspects of spoken language. However, on entering school, problems in reading would be apparent. Children with mild processing limitations would represent the group of poor (not clinically identified) readers. These children are at the low end of the normal range of reading ability.

The idea of a continuum is not novel. Several years ago, Perfetti (1985) suggested that the factors that contribute to a reading disability seemed to be the same as those that contribute to reading ability in general. These factors included deficiencies in working memory capacity and general linguistic processing ranging from syntax to phonological processes.

Although the continuum notion has a certain appealing simplicity, both research and clinical data do not support its predictions. For example, it would be predicted that children with severe processing limitations would exhibit more severe reading disabilities than children with moderate processing limitations. Yet some children with preschool language impairments, who presumably have a severe processing limitation, have been found to read no worse than children who demonstrate reading disabilities without a previous history of preschool language impairment (Kamhi & Catts, 1986; Kamhi, Catts, Mauer, Apel, & Gentry, 1988). These latter children are presumed to have a moderate processing limitation because the disability first became evident during the school years in reading. In addition, not all children with preschool spoken language deficits have difficulty learning to read (Aram, Ekelman, & Nation, 1984; Shriberg & Kwiatkowski, 1988).

Perfetti (1985, p. 199) pointed out the related problem of subtypes. If there are in fact distinct subtypes of reading disability/dyslexia, such as a dysphonetic and dyseidetic, dyslexia cannot represent a point on an ability continuum. Perfetti's solution to this problem is to posit discontinuities along the continuum. He suggests that there is a continuum of linguistically based ability that includes the dysphonetic and low-ability readers at one end and good readers at the other. The dyseidetic would be treated as a specialized form of reading disability.

Positing discontinuities is one way to deal with the problems in the continuum notion. But how many discontinuities are there? How should these discontinuities be represented on the continuum? Perhaps a better alternative is to acknowledge that individual differences in oral and written language profiles are motivated by both quantitative and qualitative differences in underlying processing abilities. Quantitative differences in the severity of the processing limitation can account for some of the different manifestations of spoken and written language disorders. But qualitative differences in the type of processing limitation are needed to explain other important individual differences. For example, reading disabled children who demonstrate preschool language learning problems may have a different type of processing limitation than reading disabled children who have no history of early language difficulties. This different type of processing limitation may likely occur in conjunction with the processing limitation that best accounts for the reading disability.

Differences in the nature of the processing limitation can take several forms. For example, some children may have difficulty processing phonological information, some may have difficulty dealing with syntactic and semantic information, and some may have difficulty constructing narrative and discourse schemata. A more specific claim would be that the processing limitation in reading disabled children without a preschool language impairment is restricted to phonological information. In contrast, reading disabled children with preschool language disorders might have a more broad-based language processing problem that affects all aspects of spoken and written language. Another possibility is that children with preschool language problems may have speech motor or planning limitations that contribute to the spoken language impairment. Expressive language problems that characterize children with preschool language impairments could also be attributed to deficiencies in rote, imitative processes. Rote, imitative processes are involved in producing unanalyzed chunks of language. For example, the early use of grammatical morphemes is thought to be unanalyzed. Bates, Bretherton, and Snyder (1988) have recently made a compelling case for the independence and importance of rote-imitative processing abilities in language development and disorders.

It should be clear why we have a long way to go in order to adequately explain reading disabilities. Although we have begun to narrow down the number of possible processing limitations that might underlie a reading disability, the relationship between these processing limitations and spoken language impairments is less clear cut. As suggested above, quantitative differences by themselves do not appear to account for the range of individual differences in spoken and written language abilities demonstrated by reading disabled children. Qualitative differences in the nature of the processing limitation are needed to account for some of these individual differences. Even if we could specify the nature of the processing limitations that initially cause spoken and written language problems, this is only the beginning. We still need to understand the complex reciprocal interactions that occur between basic processing limitations and spoken and written language abilities. These reciprocal interactions are of course not static; they change throughout development, in part due to the influence of environmental and motivational factors. The next few years promise to be exciting ones as researchers and practitioners strive toward better explanatory accounts of reading disabilities.

SPECIFICITY OF THE PROCESSING LIMITATION

Future research will also need to deal with the specificity of the processing limitations that underlie reading disabilities. As suggested in the previous section, some processing abilities may be specific to reading, some specific to spoken language, and some specific to language in general. In Chapter 3, we asked the more general question about whether the processing limitations that underlie spoken and written language disorders are specific to phonological or linguistic information. A related question was whether the processors themselves are language specific.

It seems clear that the processing limitation affects more than just reading. Stated another way, very few children just have a reading problem. The vast amount of research showing that some reading disabled children have rather pervasive language disabilities presents problems for the notion of specificity. The more pervasive the language disability associated with reading disabilities, the more difficult it is to argue that the disorder is specific to reading. Stanovich (1988) has suggested that one way to circumvent this problem is to argue that a specific reading disability is not causally related to a pervasive language impairment (or the processing limitation that underlies this impairment), but rather is the result of a specific cognitive deficit. He has suggested that the best candidate for this specific problem is deficient phonological awareness. Such a deficit is specific enough so that its effects might be isolated to written language. Stanovich (1986) has further suggested that a pervasive language disorder can be viewed as a consequence rather than a cause of the reading disability.

What Stanovich does not consider, however, is the nature of the processing limitation that underlies the phonological awareness deficit. Although phonological awareness per se is causally related to early reading performance, the processing limitation(s) that underlies the problem in phonological awareness (e.g., accessing phonological memory codes, low-level perceptual deficits) may not be specific to reading. This limitation may contribute to delays in learning spoken language as well. Reciprocal causation effects also do not seem sufficient to explain the extent of the language, conceptual, and metacognitive processing difficulties experienced by many reading disabled individuals.

In short, we do not believe that the processing limitation is specific to reading. It might, however, be specific to phonological or linguistic information. The alternative claim is that the processing deficiency is not specific to phonological or linguistic input but to any input that places similar demands on the processing system. Support for this claim would involve showing that disabled readers perform poorly on certain nonlinguistic tasks. The tasks most likely to cause problems are those that involve rapid sequential processing of discrete information. There is currently not much evidence to support this claim (Stanovich, 1986), but we (Kamhi et al., 1988) recently found evidence that children with reading disabilities performed below age level on two mental imagery tasks. Although these tasks did not involve rapid sequential processing, our findings suggest that the processing limitation might not be limited to phonological or linguistic information. Further research is clearly needed to determine the specificity of the processing limitation.

CLINICAL AND EDUCATIONAL IMPLICATIONS

A developmental language perspective of reading disabilities has several significant implications for assessment and remediation procedures, service delivery models, and territoriality issues. These implications have been discussed throughout the book, but particularly in Chapters 5, 7, and 10. To summarize briefly: first, the emphasis on language bases of reading means that the assessment of language abilities must be an integral component of the evaluation process; second, remediation procedures need to target language knowledge and processes; third, professionals with expertise in spoken and written language should be involved in the assessment and remediation process; and finally, alternative or nontraditional service delivery models should be used that take full advantage of the range of professional expertise that exists in a particular setting. Alternative service delivery models were discussed in Chapter 10.

FINAL THOUGHTS

In the preface to their book, Wallach and Butler (1984) wrote: "As professionals in the midst of a new decade of research and practice, we continue our quest by asking new and provocative questions about old and continuing problems" (p. v). It is now the end of the new decade, and the quest still continues. It will probably continue for a long time. Indeed, one might legitimately question what the end of the quest is and whether we would recognize the Holy Grail if we saw it. For some, the quest might be to eliminate all reading disabilities, which is probably as realistic as tilting at windmills. For others, the quest might be to understand the causes of reading disabilities and to develop effective procedures to remediate reading problems. This is probably a more reasonable quest. The problem with this quest, however, is that one person's Holy Grail is another person's coffee cup. The quest for our Holy Grail begins with the recognition that a large group of individuals with reading problems are best characterized as having a developmental language impairment. This characterization focuses the quest toward a search for the processing limitations that underlie the different manifestations of the language impairment throughout development.

REFERENCES

Aram, D., Ekelman, B., and Nation, J. (1984). Preschoolers with language disorders: 10 years later. *Journal of Speech and Hearing Research, 27,* 232–244.

Bates, L., Bretherton, I., and Snyder, L. (1988). *From first words to grammar: Individual differences and dissociable mechanisms.* New York: Cambridge University Press.

Chasty, H. (1985). What is dyslexia? A developmental language perspective. In M. Snowling (Ed.), *Children's written language difficulties: Assessment and management,* 11–28. Windsor Publishers: Nfer-Nelson Publishing Co.

Kamhi, A., and Catts, H. (1986). Toward an understanding of developmental language and reading disorders. *Journal of Speech and Hearing Disorders, 51,* 337–347.

Kamhi, A., Catts, H., Mauer, D., Apel, K., and Gentry, B. (1988). Phonological and spatial processing abilities in language and reading impaired children. *Journal of Hearing and Speech Disorders, 53,* 316–327.

Miles, T., and Ellis, N. (1981). A lexical encoding deficiency I and II: Experimental evidence and classical observations. In G. Pavlidis and T. Miles (Eds.), *Dyslexia research and its application to education,* 53–89. Chichester: Wiley.

Perfetti, C. (1985). *Reading ability.* New York: Oxford University Press.

Shankweiler, D., and Crain, S. (1987). Language mechanisms and reading disorder: A modular approach. In P. Bertelson (Ed.), *The onset of literacy: Cognitive processes in reading acquisition,* 139–169. Amsterdam: Elsevier.

Stanovich, K. (1986). Matthew effects in reading: Some consequences of individual differences in the acquisition of literacy. *Reading Research Quarterly, 21,* 360–406.

Stanovich, K. (1988). Science and learning disabilities. *Journal of Learning Disabilities, 21,* 210–215.

Tallal, P. (1980). Auditory temporal perception, phonic and reading disabilities in children. *Brain and Language, 9,* 182–198.

Vellutino, F., Harding, C., Phillips, F., and Steger, J. (1975). Differential transfer in poor and normal readers. *Journal of Genetic Psychology, 126,* 3–18.

Wallach, G., and Butler, K. (1984). *Language learning disabilities in school-age children.* Baltimore: Williams and Wilkins.

Subject Index

Italic page numbers refer to tables and figures.

Notes

Notes

Notes

Notes

Notes

Notes

Notes

Notes

Notes

Notes

Notes

Notes

Notes

Notes